interactive
SCIENCE

Named the ornate horned frog, this hungry predator can eat prey almost as big as itself!

SAVVAS
LEARNING COMPANY

Authors

You are an author!

You are one of the authors of this book. You can write in this book! You can take notes in this book! You can draw in it too! This book will be yours to keep.

Fill in the information below to tell about yourself. Then write your autobiography. An autobiography tells about you and the kinds of things you like to do.

Name ....

School ....

Town, State ....

Autobiography ....

My Photo

ON THE COVER
Named the ornate horned frog, this hungry predator can eat prey almost as big as itself!

24 2021

ISBN-13: 978-0-328-52100-5
ISBN-10: 0-328-52100-0

Program Authors

DON BUCKLEY, M.Sc.
*Information and Communications Technology Director,
The School at Columbia University, New York, New York*
Mr. Buckley has been at the forefront of K–12 educational technology for nearly two decades. A founder of New York City Independent School Technologists (NYCIST) and long-time chair of New York Association of Independent Schools' annual IT conference, he has taught students on two continents and created multimedia and Internet-based instructional systems for schools worldwide.

ZIPPORAH MILLER, M.A.Ed.
Associate Executive Director for Professional Programs and Conferences, National Science Teachers Association, Arlington, Virginia
Associate executive director for professional programs and conferences at NSTA, Ms. Zipporah Miller is a former K–12 science supervisor and STEM coordinator for the Prince George's County Public School District in Maryland. She is a science education consultant who has overseen curriculum development and staff training for more than 150 district science coordinators.

MICHAEL J. PADILLA, Ph.D.
Associate Dean and Director, Eugene P. Moore School of Education, Clemson University, Clemson, South Carolina
A former middle school teacher and a leader in middle school science education, Dr. Michael Padilla has served as president of the National Science Teachers Association and as a writer of the National Science Education Standards. He is professor of science education at Clemson University. As lead author of the *Science Explorer* series, Dr. Padilla has inspired the team in developing a program that promotes student inquiry and meets the needs of today's students.

KATHRYN THORNTON, Ph.D.
Professor and Associate Dean, School of Engineering and Applied Science, University of Virginia, Charlottesville, Virginia
Selected by NASA in May 1984, Dr. Kathryn Thornton is a veteran of four space flights. She has logged more than 975 hours in space, including more than 21 hours of extravehicular activity. As an author on the *Scott Foresman Science* series, Dr. Thornton's enthusiasm for science has inspired teachers around the globe.

MICHAEL E. WYSESSION, Ph.D.
Associate Professor of Earth and Planetary Science, Washington University, St. Louis, Missouri
An author on more than 50 scientific publications, Dr. Wysession was awarded the prestigious Packard Foundation Fellowship and Presidential Faculty Fellowship for his research in geophysics. Dr. Wysession is an expert on Earth's inner structure and has mapped various regions of Earth using seismic tomography. He is known internationally for his work in geoscience education and outreach.

Instructional Design Author

GRANT WIGGINS, Ed.D.
President, Authentic Education, Hopewell, New Jersey
Dr. Wiggins is a co-author with Jay McTighe of *Understanding by Design, 2nd Edition* (ASCD 2005). His approach to instructional design provides teachers with a disciplined way of thinking about curriculum design, assessment, and instruction that moves teaching from covering content to ensuring understanding.
UNDERSTANDING BY DESIGN® and UbD® are trademarks of ASCD, and are used under license.

Planet Diary Author

JACK HANKIN
Science/Mathematics Teacher, The Hilldale School, Daly City, California Founder, Planet Diary Web site
Mr. Hankin is the creator and writer of Planet Diary, a science current events Web site. Mr. Hankin is passionate about bringing science news and environmental awareness into classrooms.

Activities Author

KAREN L. OSTLUND, Ph.D.
Advisory Council, Texas Natural Science Center, College of Natural Sciences, The University of Texas at Austin
Dr. Ostlund has more than 35 years of experience teaching at elementary, middle school, and university levels. She was Director of WINGS Online (Welcoming Interns and Novices with Guidance and Support) and Director of the UTeach | Dell Center for New Teacher Success at the University of Texas at Austin. She served as Director of the Center for Science Education at the University of Texas at Arlington, President of the Council of Elementary Science International, and on the Board of Directors of the National Science Teachers Association. As an author of *Scott Foresman Science*, Dr. Ostlund was instrumental in developing inquiry activities.

ELL Consultant

JIM CUMMINS, Ph.D.
Professor and Canada Research Chair, Curriculum, Teaching and Learning Department at the University of Toronto
Dr. Cummins focuses on literacy development in multilingual schools and the role of technology in learning. *Interactive Science* incorporates research-based principles for integrating language with the teaching of academic content based on his work.

Program Consultants

William Brozo, Ph.D.
Professor of Literacy, Graduate School of Education, George Mason University, Fairfax, Virginia.
Dr. Brozo is the author of numerous articles and books on literacy development. He co-authors a column in The Reading Teacher and serves on the editorial review board of the Journal of Adolescent & Adult Literacy.

Kristi Zenchak, M.S.
Biology Instructor, Oakton Community College, Des Plaines, Illinois
Kristi Zenchak helps elementary teachers incorporate science, technology, engineering, and math activities into the classroom. STEM activities that produce viable solutions to real-world problems not only motivate students but also prepare students for future STEM careers. Ms. Zenchak helps elementary teachers understand the basic science concepts, and provides STEM activities that are easy to implement in the classroom.

Content Reviewers

Brad Armosky, M.S.
Texas Advanced Computing Center
University of Texas at Austin
Austin, Texas

Alexander Brands, Ph.D.
Department of Biological Sciences
Lehigh University
Bethlehem, Pennsylvania

Paul Beale, Ph.D.
Department of Physics
University of Colorado
Boulder, Colorado

Joy Branlund, Ph.D.
Department of Earth Science
Southwestern Illinois College
Granite City, Illinois

Constance Brown, Ph.D
Atmospheric Science Program
Geography Department
Indiana University
Bloomington, Indiana

Dana Dudle, Ph.D.
Biology Department
DePauw University
Greencastle, Indiana

Rick Duhrkopf, Ph. D.
Department of Biology
Baylor University
Waco, Texas

Mark Henriksen, Ph.D.
Physics Department
University of Maryland
Baltimore, Maryland

Andrew Hirsch, Ph.D.
Department of Physics
Purdue University
W. Lafayette, Indiana

Linda L. Cronin Jones, Ph.D.
School of Teaching & Learning
University of Florida
Gainesville, Florida

T. Griffith Jones, Ph.D.
College of Education
University of Florida
Gainesville, Florida

Candace Lutzow-Felling, Ph.D.
Director of Education
State Arboretum of Virginia & Blandy Experimental Farm
Boyce, Virginia

Cortney V. Martin, Ph.D.
Virginia Polytechnic Institute
Blacksburg, Virginia

Sadredin Moosavi, Ph.D.
University of Massachusetts Dartmouth
Fairhaven, Massachusetts

Klaus Newmann, Ph.D.
Department of Geological Sciences
Ball State University
Muncie, Indiana

Scott M. Rochette, Ph.D.
Department of the Earth Sciences
SUNY College at Brockport
Brockport, New York

Ursula Rosauer Smedly, M.S.
Alcade Science Center
New Mexico State University
Alcade, New Mexico

Frederick W. Taylor, Ph.D.
Jackson School of Geosciences
University of Texas at Austin
Austin, Texas

K-8 National Master Teacher Board

Chapter
1

Unit A
Science, Engineering, and Technology

Unit A
Science, Engineering,
and Technology 1

The Nature of Science

Scientists use different methods to collect information.

myscienceonline.com

Untamed Science
Watch the Ecogeeks as they learn about the nature of science.

Got it? 60-Second Video
Watch and learn about the nature of science.

Envision It!
See what you already know about the nature of science.

Explore It! Animation
Watch a nature of science lab online.

I Will Know...
See how the key concepts of the nature of science come to life.

Chapter 2

Design and Function

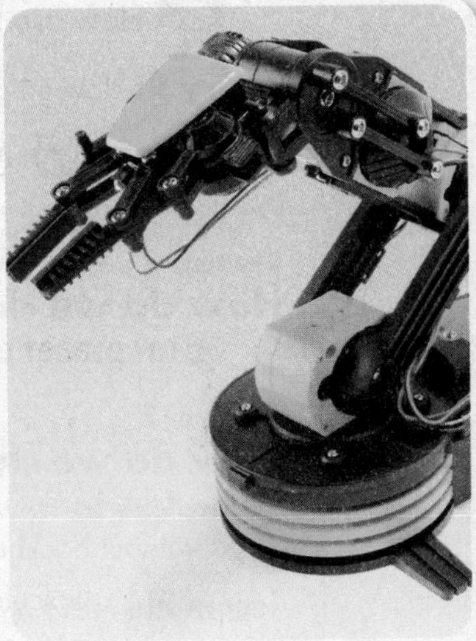

Technology can make work easier and solve problems.

myscienceonline.com

Untamed Science
Ecogeeks answer your questions about design and function.

Got it? 60-Second Video
Review lessons about design and function in 60 seconds!

my planet Diary
Learn some new ways robots are being used in hospitals.

Envision It!
See what you already know about design and function.

Memory Match
Mix and match design and function vocabulary.

Chapter 3

Classifying Organisms

Crawfish belong to the same group as crabs and lobsters.

myscienceonLine.com

UntamedScience
Ecogeeks answer your
questions about classifying
organisms.

Got it? 60-Second Video
See each classifying
organisms lesson reviewed in
one minute!

my planet diary
Learn some fun facts about
classifying living things.

Investigate It! Virtual Lab
Investigate how a key can
help with classification.

I Will Know...
See what you have learned
about classifying organisms.

Chapter 4

Growth and Survival

As a tadpole grows into a frog, its tail becomes smaller.

mYscienceonLine.com

Untamed Science
Watch the Ecogeeks as they learn about growth and survival.

Got it? 60-Second Video
Watch one-minute videos for every growth and survival lesson.

Envision It!
Interact with science to find out what you know about growth and survival.

Explore It! Animation
Explore growth and survival in a new way!

I Will Know...
See what you have learned about growth and survival.

Structure and Function

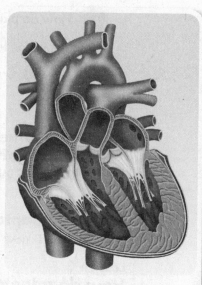

The structure of the heart is ideal for pumping blood.

myscienceonLine.com

Untamed Science™
Ecogeeks answer your questions about structure and function.

Got it? 60-Second Video
Structure and function lessons reviewed in a minute!

I Will Know...
See how the key concepts about structure and function come to life.

Explore It! Animation
Explore structure and function in a new way!

Vocabulary Smart Cards
Hear and see your structure and function vocabulary words online.

Chapter 6

Ecosystems

An organism can play different roles in an ecosystem.

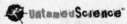

mYscienceonLine.com

Untamed Science
Ecogeeks answer your questions about ecosystems.

Got it? 60-Second Video
See each ecosystems lesson reviewed in one minute!

Explore It! Animation
Explore ecosystems in a new way!

I Will Know...
See how the key concepts about ecosystems come to life.

Vocabulary Smart Cards
Hear and see your ecosystems vocabulary words online.

Unit C
Earth Science

Chapter 7

The Water Cycle and Weather

The water in this river may have been part of the air or the ocean before.

myscienceonline.com

Untamed Science™
Watch the Ecogeeks as they learn about the water cycle and weather.

Got it? 60-Second Video
Watch one-minute videos for every water cycle and weather lesson.

Explore It! Animation
Explore the water cycle and weather in a new way!

I Will Know...
See what you have learned about the water cycle and weather.

MY PLANET DiARY
Connect the fresh water you drink to the salt water in the ocean.

Chapter 8

Earth's Surface

Earth's surface can change fast when a volcano erupts.

myscienceonline.com

Untamed Science
Watch the Ecogeeks as they learn about Earth's surface.

Got it? 🕑 **60-Second Video**
Watch one-minute videos for every Earth's surface lesson.

Explore It! Animation
Explore Earth's surface in a new way!

I Will Know...
See what you have learned about Earth's surface.

Vocabulary Smart Cards
Mix and match Earth's surface vocabulary online.

Earth and Space

*Earth is warmer near the tropics,
where sunlight is direct.*

myscienceonline.com

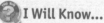 **Untamed Science**
Watch the Ecogeeks learn
about Earth and space.

Got it? 60-Second Video
Take one minute to learn
about Earth and space.

Envision It!
See what you already know
about Earth and space.

Explore It! Animation
Try a quick-and-easy
experiment about Earth and
space.

? **I Will Know...**
See how key concepts of each
lesson about Earth and space
are brought to life!

Properties of Matter

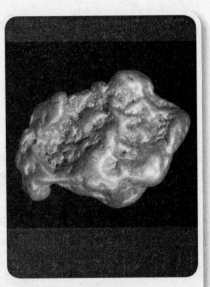

*Gold has properties that
determine how it can be used.*

mYscienceonLine.com

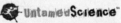 **Untamed Science**
Ecogeeks answer your
questions about properties
of matter.

Got it? 60-Second Video
Review lessons about
properties of matter in
60 seconds!

MY PLANET DIARY
Learn some fun facts about
properties of matter.

Memory Match
Mix and match properties of
matter vocabulary practice.

Investigate It! Virtual Lab
Learn some ways to separate
a mixture.

Chapter 11

Forces and Motion

Forces and motion can be used for recreation.

mys:cienceonLine.com

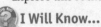 **Untamed Science™**
Ecogeeks answer your
questions about force
and motion.

Got it? ⏱ **60-Second Video**
Watch your force and motion
lessons reviewed in a minute!

🌍 **MY PLANET DIARY**
Fix some misconceptions
about forces and motion.

▶ **Investigate It!** Virtual Lab
Explore this rocket lab online!

I Will Know...
See what you have learned
about forces and motion.

Chapter 12

Changing Forms of Energy

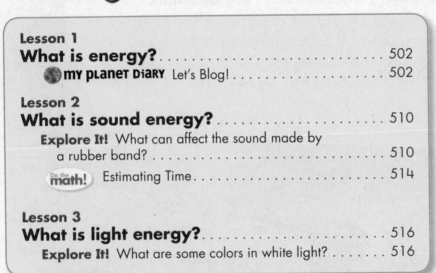
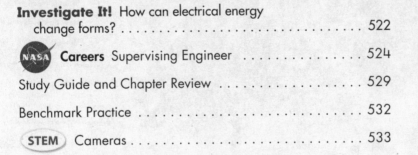

*This athlete can store energy in
the pole and then get it back.*

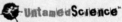

myscienceonline.com

🌿 **Untamed Science**
Ecogeeks answer your
questions about changing
forms of energy.

Got it? ⏱ **60-Second Video**
Review lessons about
changing forms of energy
in 60 seconds!

I Will Know...
See how the key concepts
about changing forms of
energy come to life.

Envision It!
See what you already
know about changing
forms of energy.

Explore It! Animation
Try a quick-and-easy
experiment about changing
forms of energy.

interactive SCIENCE

Big Question

At the start of each chapter you will see two questions—an **Engaging Question** and a **Big Question.** Just like a scientist, you will predict an answer to the Engaging Question. Each Big Question will help you start thinking about the Big Ideas of science. Look for the symbol throughout the chapter!

The Water Cycle and Weather

Chapter **7**

Try It! How can water move in the water cycle?

Lesson 1 What is the water cycle?

Lesson 2 What is the ocean?

Lesson 3 What is weather?

Lesson 4 How do clouds and precipitation form?

Lesson 5 What is climate?

Investigate It! Where is the hurricane going?

It has not rained, but after spending the night resting, this fly was covered with droplets in the morning.

Predict Where do you think this water came from?

 How does water move through the environment?

WHERE
did these drops
come
from?

254

myscienceonline.com Untamed Science

255

Let's Read Science!

You will see a page like this toward the beginning of each chapter. It will show you how to use a reading skill that will help you understand what you read.

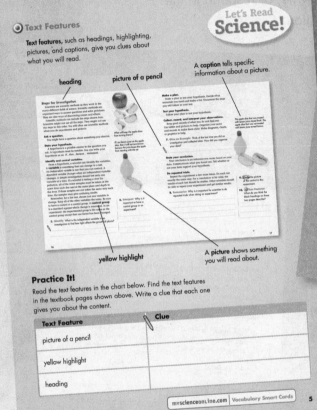

Let's Read Science!

Text Features

Text features, such as headings, highlighting, pictures, and captions, give you clues about what you will read.

heading

picture of a pencil

A **caption** tells specific information about a picture.

yellow highlight

A **picture** shows something you will read about.

Practice It!

Read the text features in the chart below. Find the text features in the textbook pages shown above. Write a clue that each one gives you about the content.

Text Feature	Clue
picture of a pencil	
yellow highlight	
heading	

myscienceonline.com | Vocabulary Smart Cards | 5

Vocabulary Smart Cards

Go to the end of the chapter and cut out your own set of **Vocabulary Smart Cards.** Write a sentence, draw a picture, or use a vocabulary strategy to learn the word. Play a game with a classmate to practice using the word!

Look for **MyScienceOnline.com** technology options.
At MyScienceOnline.com you can immerse yourself in virtual environments, get extra practice, and even blog about current events in science.

"Engage with the page!"

interactive SCIENCE

Envision It!

At the beginning of each lesson, at the top of the page, you will see an **Envision It!** interactivity that gives you the opportunity to circle, draw, write, or respond to the Envision It! question.

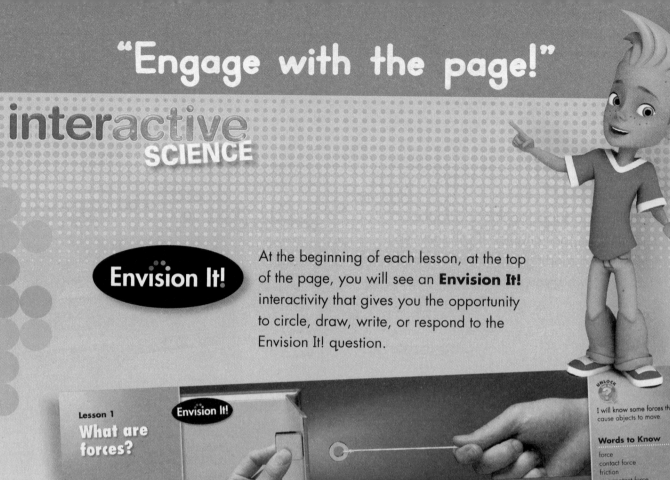

Lesson 1
What are forces?

Envision It!

Tell why the metal ring on the string does not fall.

I will know some forces that cause objects to move.

Words to Know
force
contact force
friction
non-contact force
gravity

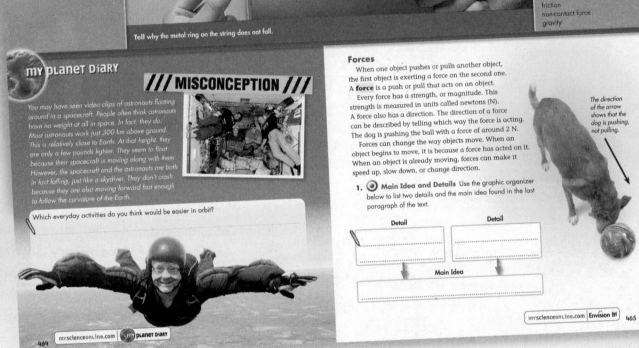

MY PLANET DIARY

/// MISCONCEPTION ///

You may have seen video clips of astronauts floating around in a spacecraft. People often think astronauts have no weight at all in space. In fact, they do. Most astronauts work just 300 km above ground. This is relatively close to Earth. At that height, they are only a few pounds lighter. They seem to float because their spacecraft is moving along with them. However, the spacecraft and the astronauts are both in fact falling, just like a skydiver. They don't crash because they are also moving forward fast enough to follow the curvature of the Earth.

Which everyday activities do you think would be easier in orbit?

myscienceonline.com my planet diary

464

Forces

When one object pushes or pulls another object, the first object is exerting a force on the second one. A **force** is a push or pull that acts on an object.

Every force has a strength, or magnitude. This strength is measured in units called newtons (N). A force also has a direction. The direction of a force can be described by telling which way the force is acting. The dog is pushing the ball with a force of around 2 N.

Forces can change the way objects move. When an object begins to move, it is because a force has acted on it. When an object is already moving, forces can make it speed up, slow down, or change direction.

The direction of the arrow shows that the dog is pushing, not pulling.

1. **Main Idea and Details** Use the graphic organizer below to list two details and the main idea found in the last paragraph of the text.

Detail	Detail

Main Idea

myscienceonline.com Envision It!

465

MY PLANET DIARY

My Planet Diary interactivities will introduce you to amazing scientists, fun facts, and important discoveries in science. They will also help you to overcome common misconceptions about science concepts.

Read See DO!

After reading small chunks of information, stop to check your understanding. The visuals help teach about what you read. Answer questions, underline text, draw pictures, or label models.

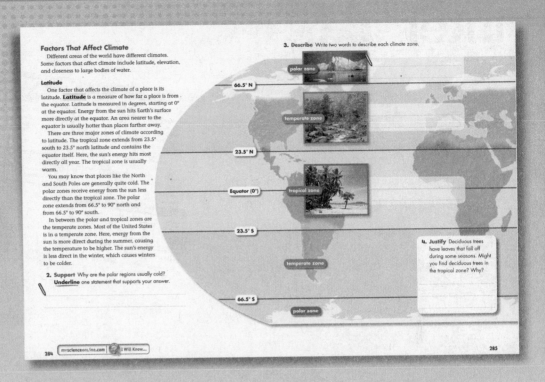

Factors That Affect Climate

Different areas of the world have different climates. Some factors that affect climate include latitude, elevation, and closeness to large bodies of water.

Latitude

One factor that affects the climate of a place is its latitude. **Latitude** is a measure of how far a place is from the equator. Latitude is measured in degrees, starting at 0° at the equator. Energy from the sun hits Earth's surface more directly at the equator. An area nearer to the equator is usually hotter than places farther away.

There are three major zones of climate according to latitude. The tropical zone extends from 23.5° south to 23.5° north latitude and contains the equator itself. Here, the sun's energy hits most directly all year. The tropical zone is usually warm.

You may know that places like the North and South Poles are generally quite cold. The polar zones receive energy from the sun less directly than the tropical zone. The polar zone extends from 66.5° to 90° north and from 66.5° to 90° south.

In between the polar and tropical zones are the temperate zones. Most of the United States is in a temperate zone. Here, energy from the sun is more direct during the summer, causing the temperature to be higher. The sun's energy is less direct in the winter, which causes winters to be colder.

2. Support Why are the polar regions usually cold? **Underline** one statement that supports your answer.

3. Describe Write two words to describe each climate zone.

66.5° N
23.5° N
Equator (0°)
23.5° S
66.5° S

polar zone
temperate zone
tropical zone
temperate zone
polar zone

4. Justify Deciduous trees have leaves that fall off during some seasons. Might you find deciduous trees in the tropical zone? Why?

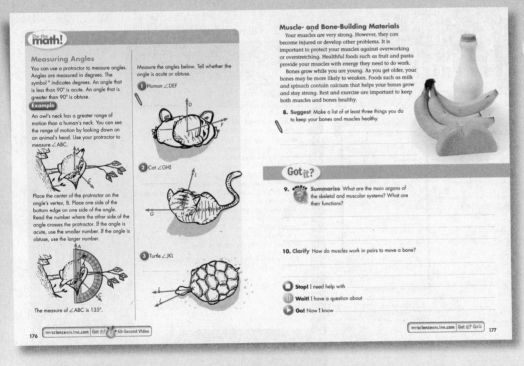

Do the math!

Measuring Angles

You can use a protractor to measure angles. Angles are measured in degrees. The symbol ° indicates degrees. An angle that is less than 90° is acute. An angle that is greater than 90° is obtuse.

Example

An owl's neck has a greater range of motion than a human's neck. You can see the range of motion by looking down on an animal's head. Use your protractor to measure ∠ABC.

Place the center of the protractor on the angle's vertex, B. Place one side of the bottom edge on one side of the angle. Read the number where the other side of the angle crosses the protractor. If the angle is acute, use the smaller number. If the angle is obtuse, use the larger number.

The measure of ∠ABC is 135°.

Measure the angles below. Tell whether the angle is acute or obtuse.

1. Human ∠DEF

2. Cat ∠GHI

3. Turtle ∠JKL

Muscle- and Bone-Building Materials

Your muscles are very strong. However, they can become injured or develop other problems. It is important to protect your muscles against overworking or overstretching. Healthful foods such as fruit and pasta provide your muscles with energy they need to do work.

Bones grow while you are young. As you get older, your bones may be more likely to weaken. Foods such as milk and spinach contain calcium that helps your bones grow and stay strong. Rest and exercise are important to keep both muscles and bones healthy.

8. Suggest Make a list of at least three things you do to keep your bones and muscles healthy.

Got it?

9. Summarize What are the main organs of the skeletal and muscular systems? What are their functions?

10. Clarify How do muscles work in pairs to move a bone?

Stop! I need help with

Wait! I have a question about

Go! Now I know

Got it?

At the end of each lesson you will have a chance to evaluate your own progress! After answering the **Got it?** questions, think about how you are doing. At this point you can stop, wait, or go on to the next lesson.

Do the math!

Scientists commonly use math as a tool to help them answer science questions. You can practice skills that you are learning in math class right in your *Interactive Science* Student Edition!

"Have fun! Be a scientist!"

interactive SCIENCE

Try It!

At the start of every chapter, you will have the chance to do a hands-on inquiry lab. The lab will provide you with experiences that will prepare you for the chapter lessons or may raise a new question in your mind.

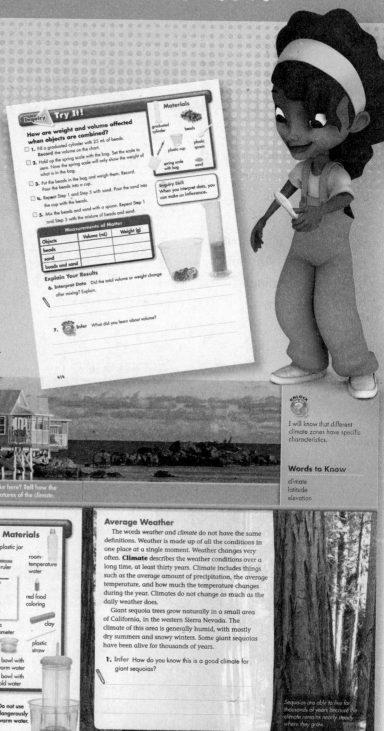

Explore It!

Before you start reading the lesson, **Explore It!** activities provide you with an opportunity to first explore the content!

Design It!

The **Design It!** activity has you use the engineering design process to find solutions to problems. By identifying the problem, doing research, and developing possible solutions, you will design, construct, and test a prototype for a real world problem. Communicate your evidence through graphs, tables, drawings, and prototypes and identify ways to make your solution better.

STEM activities are found throughout core and ancillary materials.

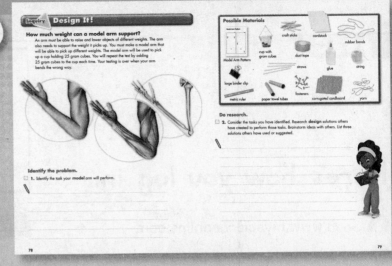

Investigate It!

At the end of every chapter, a Directed Inquiry lab gives you a chance to put together everything you've learned in the chapter. Using the activity card, apply design principles in the Guided version to Modify Your Investigation or the Open version to Develop Your Own Investigation. Whether you need a lot of support from your teacher or you're ready to explore on your own, there are fun hands-on activities that match your interests.

Apply It!

At the end of every unit, an Open Inquiry lab gives you a chance to explore science using scientific methods.

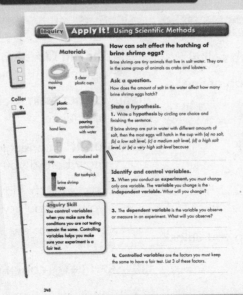

"Go online anytime!"

interactive SCIENCE

Here's how you log in...

1. Go to **www.myscienceonline.com**.
2. Log in with your username and password.

Username: _____

Password: _____

3. Click on your program and select your chapter.

Check it out!

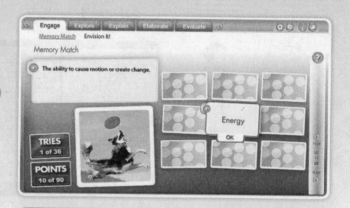

Watch a Video!

Untamed Science Join the Ecogeeks on their video adventure.

Got it? 60-Second Video Review each lesson in 60 seconds.

Go Digital for Inquiry!

Explore It! Simulation Watch the lab online.

Investigate It! Virtual Lab Do the lab online.

Show What You Know!

Got it? Quiz Take a quick quiz and get instant feedback.

Benchmark Practice Prepare for the "big test."

Writing for Science Write to help you unlock the Big Question.

Get Excited About Science!

The Big Question Share what you think about the Big Question.

my planet diary Connect to the world of science.

Envision It! Connect to what you already know before you start each lesson.

Memory Match Play a game to build your vocabulary.

Get Help!

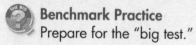 **Get help at your level.**

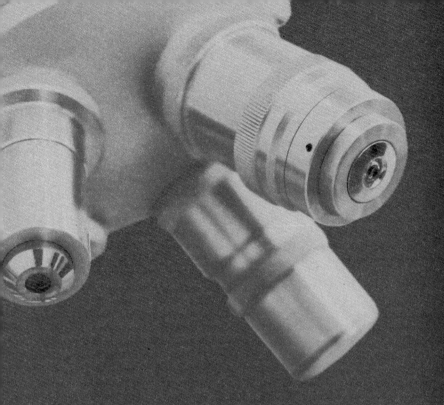

Science, Engineering, and Technology

Science, Engineering, and Technology

Chapter 1
The Nature of Science

What is science?

Chapter 2
Design and Function

How does technology affect our lives?

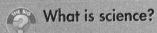

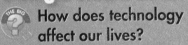

What is she trying to DISCOVER?

The Nature of
Science

Try It!   What questions do
scientists ask?

Investigate It! How does a banana slice
change over time?

Scientists use a variety of skills and tools to discover new
things about the world around them.

Predict How is this young scientist using tools to
learn more about her world?

....

....

What is science?

What questions do scientists ask?

Scientists ask questions about objects, organisms, and events. Good scientific questions can be answered by making observations and measurements.

☐ **1.** Work in a group. Cut apart the questions.
   Classify the questions into 2 piles.
   Pile 1 Good Scientific Questions

   Pile 2 Not Good Scientific Questions

☐ **2.** Discuss how you made each sorting decision.

Explain Your Results

3. Draw a Conclusion
   Pick one question from Pile 1. Letter of question: _____
   Explain why is it a good scientific question.

   ....

   ....

4. Pick one question from Pile 2. Letter of question: _____
   Explain why it is not a good scientific question.

   ....

   ....

5. **UNLOCK THE BIG ?** Pick another question from Pile 2. Letter of question: _____
   Rewrite it to make it into a good scientific question.
   Then explain why it is a good scientific question.

   ....

   ....

Materials

Scientific or Not?

scissors

Inquiry Skill
You **classify** when you sort things into groups.

Text Features

Text features, such as headings, highlighting, pictures, and captions, give you clues about what you will read.

heading   picture of a pencil

A **caption** tells specific information about a picture.

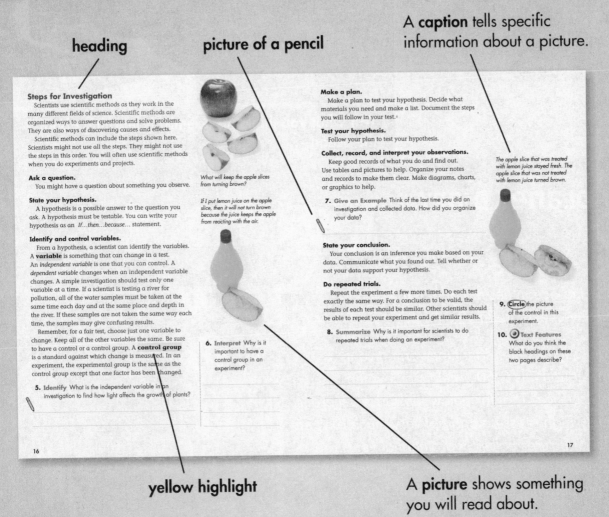

yellow highlight

A **picture** shows something you will read about.

Practice It!

Read the text features in the chart below. Find the text features in the textbook pages shown above. Write a clue that each one gives you about the content.

Text Feature	Clue
picture of a pencil	
yellow highlight	
heading	

Lesson 1

What do scientists do?

Tell what you think this scientist is learning about the ocean.

my planet diary

giant tubeworms

Deep in the ocean lies a world that is almost completely unexplored by humans.

Animals, such as the giant tubeworm, live in extreme conditions 2,600 meters below the ocean's surface. That far below the surface there is extremely high pressure and not very much oxygen or light. Structures called hydrothermal vents are near volcanoes and release very hot water. The water temperature can be more than 400°C!

Giant tubeworms can grow to be up to 2.5 meters long and 10 centimeters wide. They do not have mouths. Instead, giant tubeworms absorb nutrients made by tiny bacteria that live inside of them!

Describe What might a scientist do to find out how giant tubeworms interact with their environment?

....

....

....

I will know how scientists use inquiry to learn about the world around them.

Words to Know

hypothesis
observation

Problems, Decisions, and New Ideas

How deep is the ocean? What creatures live in its depths? The world around us is filled with things that are still unknown. To better understand the world, scientists first define a problem and then try to find answers.

Scientific investigation begins with a testable question. Almost every part of your life has been improved in some way by science or by something science made possible. Science can help you get the information you need to make good decisions too. Should you snack on a banana or a soda? What can you do to avoid catching a cold? Scientists can help people answer questions, solve problems, and form new ideas through the use of scientific processes.

1. ◉ **Text Features** Complete the chart to explain the text features on this page.

This instrument shows water temperature and depth. It is used in fishing.

2. **Predict** Tell what problem you think the tool above might help solve.

Text Feature	Clue
photograph	shows an example of a tool used to find depth
blue heading	

Scientific Research and Knowledge

After scientists define a problem, they begin their investigation with research. Scientists need to use a variety of appropriate reference materials to do research. The reference materials they use need to be sources of information that scientists have agreed upon. Scientists cannot draw valid conclusions from information that cannot be verified by other scientists. For example, a scientist researching ocean water cannot simply find information from a random Internet source and use it in an investigation. The source must be reliable, and the information must have been reviewed and verified by other scientists.

Examples of appropriate reference materials may include books and scientific journals. Scientists may use articles in the scientific journals to do their research. These articles are written by scientists and reviewed by other scientists before they are published. Many of these journals can be found in libraries and on the Internet. Sometimes, information even from reliable sources can change. New findings might cause scientists to rethink old ideas.

3. **Analyze** The scientists below found information on the Internet in a blog. Could they use this piece of information to answer a scientific problem they have defined?

Predict and Make Hypotheses

Scientists use a problem they have defined and research from appropriate sources to form a prediction, or a hypothesis. A **hypothesis** is a statement of what you think will happen during an investigation. It is often written in the form of an *if… then… because* statement. Scientists use experience and what they have found in their research to predict what they think will be a solution to the problem.

Look at the picture above. One example of a hypothesis that scientist might have made is, *If the level of water pollution increases, then the population of manatees will decrease because the plants they eat cannot live in highly polluted water.*

4. **Compose** You have read one possible hypothesis about manatees. Write an example of a different hypothesis the scientist could have formed.

....

....

....

....

Go Green

A Bright Invention
Through research and careful observation, scientists often find solutions to everyday problems. Think about your community. Define a pollution problem that affects it. What are some ideas you can think of to solve this problem? Share your ideas with others.

Make Observations

Scientists use many skills and processes to find answers to problems. One of these is making observations. An **observation** is something you find out about objects, events, or living things by using your senses. Scientists make observations very carefully. In this way, they can be sure that the information they gather is reliable. Scientists often use tools, such as thermometers, to extend their senses. Scientists are also good at organizing their observations. When scientists have collected their information, they analyze and evaluate it to draw conclusions. They also share their findings with other scientists, who can then see if their own results are similar.

For example, scientists may have observed that a group of sea turtles returns to the same beach every year to lay eggs. The scientists want to find out what causes the turtles to return and where they go between the yearly beach visits. Scientists used identification tags and radio transmitters to observe that a sea turtle might travel thousands of kilometers in one year and return to the same beach.

5. **Analyze** The scientist below is observing a sea turtle. What problem might the scientist define, and how might she find answers to the problem?

....

....

....

....

....

myscienceonline.com | Got it? | 60-Second Video

Draw Conclusions

Scientists use their observations to draw conclusions. When they draw a conclusion, they summarize what they have learned by analyzing their observations. For example, a scientist may observe that some populations of birds that eat certain fish are decreasing. The scientist may then observe that the fish have been dying. By testing the properties of soil samples from the riverbed, the scientist may be able to observe qualities of the soil, such as the presence of pollution. Using this observation, the scientist might conclude that pollution in the river is causing the living things there to be unhealthy and to die or move away.

These scientists are testing for pollution.

6. **Describe** Tell how scientific testing helps scientists draw conclusions.

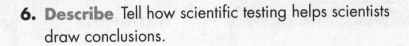

Got it?

7. **Explain** What are four things that scientists do?

....

....

8. **Explain** How can people solve problems?

....

....

9. **Draw Conclusions** Why should you use a variety of sources when you do research for an investigation?

....

◻ **Stop!** I need help with ....

❚❚ **Wait!** I have a question about ....

▶ **Go!** Now I know ....

How do scientists investigate?

Envision It!

Tell how you think scientists use this wind tunnel to build better cars.

Inquiry Explore It!

Which method keeps bread freshest?

☐ **1.** Put 2 slices of bread on a plate. **Observe** with a hand lens. **Record.** Cover 1 slice with waxed paper.

☐ **2.** Put another slice in a paper bag. Close the bag. Put another slice in a plastic bag. Seal the bag.

☐ **3.** Wait 5 days. Observe the slices. Record your observations on the chart.

Materials

4 slices of bread

paper bag

waxed paper

plastic bag

paper plate

hand lens

Bread Observations			
	Waxed Paper	**Plastic Bag**	**Paper Bag**	**Uncovered Slice**
Day 5				

Explain Your Results

4. Interpret Data Compare the freshness of the bread slices after 5 days.

5. Infer How could you combine methods to keep bread fresh longer?

UNLOCK THE BIG ?

I will know how scientists investigate problems in many different ways.

Words to Know

experiment   control group
variable   procedures

Scientific Investigation

Scientific investigation usually begins with an observation. Someone observes that cars with a certain shape are more fuel efficient. Scientists then ask a question about the observation and collect data to answer their question. One important way to find reliable answers is to do an experiment. An **experiment** is the use of scientific methods to test your hypothesis. Remember that a hypothesis is a statement of what you think will happen in an investigation.

There is no single "scientific method" for finding answers. Biologists study living things with different methods than astronomers use to study the stars. For both types of scientists, however, it is important to observe, collect information, test ideas, make predictions, and share their findings with other scientists who can disagree with or confirm the findings.

However, it is not always possible to manipulate variables in a way that can answer scientific questions. Sometimes you have to design an investigation to test a hypothesis without doing a controlled experiment. In addition to controlled experiments, three types of investigations that scientists use are models, surveys, and sampling. These often help scientists test hypotheses.

1. Predict Write a possible hypothesis that this scientist is thinking about as he does his experiment.

....

....

....

....

....

Falling Water

Carefully make a hole 2 cm from the top of a cup. Make an identical hole 5 cm below the first one. Hold your fingers over the holes. Fill the cup with water. Predict what will happen when you let go. Try it. Hold the cup high over a sink or tub. Observe. Try it again. State your conclusion.

Models

Scientists often use models to learn more about the world or to test designs and materials. Models are objects or ideas that represent other things. They show how something is constructed or how it works. Models are often used to study things that are very large, have many parts, or are difficult to observe directly.

The car model in the picture below is a computer-generated model. Testing a computer model of a car has some advantages over testing real cars. For example, it is easier to control parts of the experiment, such as driving conditions, in a computer model. Once a computer-generated model car has been tested virtually, a machine is used to carve the car out of clay. The physical model can be used to help scientists learn more about how an actual car will work.

Models are helpful tools. However, they are not the actual objects. Testing different models or the real car, for example, may give different results. Scientists may have to do more research and testing to find more information about the cars. Even so, models are valuable tools that help scientists understand the world around them.

2. **Give an Example** What is another advantage of using a computer-generated model of a car?

....

....

....

These models help scientists study cars.

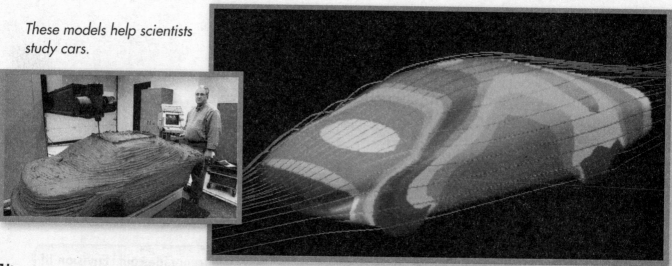

Surveys and Sampling

Scientists do investigations in many different fields of science. Sometimes the best way for a scientist to investigate is by using a survey. Surveys can be questionnaires that are given to a number of people whose answers are recorded and then analyzed. Sometimes people are interviewed in person or on the phone. For example, if a number of people became ill at a picnic, doctors would want to know what each person ate and drank. They would also want to know who got sick and who did not. The answers will help them find the source of the illness.

Scientists also use sampling to collect data. Scientists examine random individuals from a population. For example, doctors may examine a few people from the picnic and see how healthy they are. Doctors can then generalize their results to all the people at the picnic. This may also help the doctors find the source of the illness.

3. **Evaluate** Write one question that the doctor could be asking the patients in the picture below in his survey.

....

....

4. CHALLENGE How could a scientist use sampling to investigate the health of the deer population in a forest preserve?

....

....

....

....

....

....

....

Steps for Investigation

Scientists use scientific methods as they work in the many different fields of science. Scientific methods are organized ways to answer questions and solve problems. They are also ways of discovering causes and effects.

Scientific methods can include the steps shown here. Scientists might not use all the steps. They might not use the steps in this order. You will often use scientific methods when you do experiments and projects.

Ask a question.

You might have a question about something you observe.

State your hypothesis.

A hypothesis is a possible answer to the question you ask. A hypothesis must be testable. You can write your hypothesis as an *If...then...because...* statement.

What will keep the apple slices from turning brown?

If I put lemon juice on the apple slice, then it will not turn brown because the juice keeps the apple from reacting with the air.

Identify and control variables.

From a hypothesis, a scientist can identify the variables. A **variable** is something that can change in a test. An *independent variable* is one that you can control. A *dependent variable* changes when an independent variable changes. A simple investigation should test only one variable at a time. If a scientist is testing a river for pollution, all of the water samples must be taken at the same time each day and at the same place and depth in the river. If these samples are not taken the same way each time, the samples may give confusing results.

Remember, for a fair test, choose just one variable to change. Keep all of the other variables the same. Be sure to have a control or a control group. A **control group** is a standard against which change is measured. In an experiment, the experimental group is the same as the control group except that one factor has been changed.

6. Interpret Why is it important to have a control group in an experiment?

....

....

....

....

5. Identify What is the independent variable in an investigation to find how light affects the growth of plants?

....

....

Make a plan.

Make a plan to test your hypothesis. Decide what materials you need and make a list. Document the steps you will follow in your test.

Test your hypothesis.

Follow your plan to test your hypothesis.

Collect, record, and interpret your observations.

Keep good records of what you do and find out. Use tables and pictures to help. Organize your notes and records to make them clear. Make diagrams, charts, or graphics to help.

7. **Give an Example** Think of the last time you did an investigation and collected data. How did you organize your data?

....

State your conclusion.

Your conclusion is an inference you make based on your data. Communicate what you found out. Tell whether or not your data support your hypothesis.

Do repeated trials.

Repeat the experiment a few more times. Do each test exactly the same way. For a conclusion to be valid, the results of each test should be similar. Other scientists should be able to repeat your experiment and get similar results.

8. **Summarize** Why is it important for scientists to do repeated trials when doing an experiment?

....

....

....

The apple slice that was treated with lemon juice stayed fresh. The apple slice that was not treated with lemon juice turned brown.

9. **Circle** the picture of the control in this experiment.

10. **⊙ Text Features** What do you think the black headings on these two pages describe?

....

....

Document Procedures

Meaningful scientific results come from experiments that can be replicated. In order for a scientific experiment to be replicated, the procedures must be thoroughly explained, or documented. **Procedures** are step-by-step instructions for completing a task.

Procedures are important when experimenting but also when doing things such as making certain foods or playing games.

A recipe is a type of procedure.

Apple Freshness

Materials: 3 different varieties of apples, lemon juice, knife, tray

Procedures:

1. Gather materials.

2. Ask an adult to help you cut the apples into slices.

3. ....

   ....

4. Dip 4 slices of each apple in lemon juice. Let the apples sit for 1 hour. Compare the apples with lemon to the apples without. Record any differences.

5. ....

   ....

   ....

11. `CHALLENGE` Read the procedure for apple freshness. Fill in the missing procedures. What might happen if one step was missing?

When you design an experiment, it is important to write your procedures so that someone who reads them can follow them and repeat your experiment. If you leave out details, your procedure may not be followed exactly. The experiment may then give unintended results. This means the original experiment was not repeated and the conclusion may be different.

12. Evaluate Look at the procedures for the Apple Freshness experiment again. What might you change about the procedures to make it easier for others to follow?

....

....

....

Got it?

13. Explain Why would a scientist use a model in an investigation? Write two reasons.

....

....

....

14. Describe What are some ways you can use to investigate different types of questions?

....

....

⬜ **Stop!** I need help with ....

⏸ **Wait!** I have a question about ....

▶ **Go!** Now I know ....

How do scientists collect and interpret data?

Tell how scientists studying strong storms could help people stay safe.

Inquiry Explore It!

Why do scientists use thermometers?

☐ **1. Record** the air temperature of the room.

☐ **2.** Pour room-temperature water into Cup A. Pour warm water into Cup B. Pour slightly warm water into Cup C.

☐ **3.** Feel the water in each. Record *cool, warm,* or *neither*. **Measure** the temperatures in °C and °F. Record.

Materials

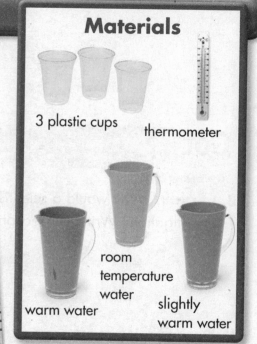

3 plastic cups   thermometer

room temperature water

warm water   slightly warm water

Comparing Temperatures			
	Temperature		
	Feels (warm, cool, neither)	° C	° F
Cup A (room-temperature water)			
Cup B (warm water)			
Cup C (slightly warm water)			

Explain Your Results

4. Interpret Data Compare how warm the water felt with your **measurements**.

5. Draw a Conclusion Discuss why scientists use thermometers to **collect** temperature **data**.

myscienceonline.com | **Explore It!** Animation

I will know that scientists collect and interpret data using many different kinds of tools in a safe way.

Words to Know
....

data   accuracy
precision   inference

Data Collecting

Tornadoes can be very dangerous. In a tornado, winds can gust to more than 100 miles per hour, lift up objects, and cause very serious damage. What makes a tornado form? Scientists have done a great deal of research to try to understand the causes of tornadoes, but there is still a lot to learn in order to predict when tornadoes will happen.

In order for scientists to be able to predict tornadoes more successfully, they need to collect large amounts of data. **Data** are information from which a conclusion can be drawn or a prediction can be made.

For example, scientists can collect data about the air temperature before a tornado forms. These data can be connected to information they already know about other weather patterns during that time. It is important that each type of data is collected consistently and recorded in a useful way. Scientists can find relationships among data and possibly make predictions about how a tornado forms.

1. **Decide** You collect data about the type of weather your town has been experiencing. Can you use the data to draw conclusions about all other areas in the state? Explain.

....

....

....

2. **Circle** what scientists need to do to understand how tornadoes form.

Doppler radar towers track weather patterns and help scientists collect data to predict future storm patterns.

Precision and Accuracy

When collecting data, scientists try to control their experiments. This means they avoid having things happen that might interfere with good data collection. Data from a controlled experiment are consistent and precise.

Precision is the ability to consistently repeat a measurement. **Accuracy** is the ability to make a measurement that is as close to the actual value as possible. Look at the targets in the example below. In science, valid data are data measured with precision and accuracy.

4. ⊙ **Text Features**
What does the yellow highlighting tell you about the words on this page?

This target shows high precision because the marks are very close to one another. It shows low accuracy because the marks are not at the center of the target.

This target shows high accuracy because the marks are close to the center of the target. It shows low precision because the marks are not very close to one another.

3. Demonstrate Draw marks on the target to the right to represent data that are both accurate and precise.

Tools

Scientists use many different kinds of tools to collect data. The tool used depends on the task. You can use tools to help you see things that you normally could not see. If something is very small or very far away, a tool can help you see it in more detail.

Tools also help you measure things and gather information. You can measure volume, temperature, length, distance, mass, time, and more with the proper tools. Tools can help you gather information and analyze your data. Scientists share their findings. Because they do, tools can help you find information collected by others.

5. Describe Underline four things that tools help you do.

6. Infer Why should you look at a graduated cylinder at eye level when reading the scale?

....

....

....

7. Infer Scientists use tools other than the ones on this page. What tool could help you gather information, analyze data, and find information collected by others?

....

A microscope makes objects appear much larger.

You can use a *balance* to measure mass.

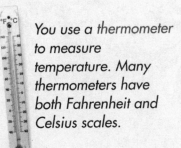

You use a *thermometer* to measure temperature. Many thermometers have both Fahrenheit and Celsius scales.

A *spring scale* is used to measure force.

You can use a *stopwatch* or *timer* to measure elapsed time.

Scientists use a *meterstick* to measure length and distance.

A *calculator* helps you analyze data easier and faster than you could with paper and pencil.

A *graduated cylinder* is used to measure volume.

23

Safety

Scientists know they must work safely when doing experiments. You need to be careful when doing science activities too. It is important to keep yourself and other people safe. Care must be taken to make sure all living organisms, including plants and animals, are handled properly. Follow these safety rules.

8. Explain Why might it be important to ask questions after your teacher gives instructions?

....

....

....

Tie long hair back and avoid wearing loose clothing.

Wear safety goggles when needed.

Never taste or smell any substance unless directed to do so by your teacher.

Listen to the teacher's instructions. Ask questions.

Use chemicals carefully.

Help keep the plants and animals that you use safe.

Read the activity carefully before you start.

Handle sharp items and other equipment carefully.

Organize Data

When scientists use tools to make observations, they collect data. In order to be useful, data must be organized. Organizing data allows a scientist to more easily recognize patterns that may be present. Data can be organized in many ways, including tables, graphs, charts, and graphics.

Tables and Graphs

One way that scientists organize data is by using a table. Look at the table below. It shows that scientists have collected data on the frequency of tornadoes in various states and have organized the information.

Once the information has been organized into a table, it may be displayed in a graph, such as the bar graph below. Graphs can help scientists see mathematical relationships in their data. The information in both the table and the graph is the same, but it is shown in different ways.

9. Compute Use data in the table to complete this bar graph.

10. Infer Based on the table and graph, what might land descriptions tell you about tornadoes and where they are most likely to occur?

....

....

....

....

....

....

....

Number of Tornadoes This Year for Selected States		
State	**Number of Tornadoes**	**Land Description**
Florida	55	flat
Indiana	22	flat
Louisiana	27	flat
New York	7	hilly
Oregon	2	hilly

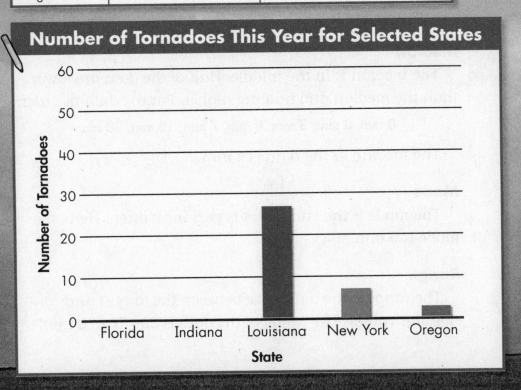

Number of Tornadoes This Year for Selected States

11. **Calculate** Look at the table on the previous page. What is the median number of tornadoes for the five states in the table and graph? What is the mean?

Interpret Data

When scientists interpret data, they look at the information they have collected by using tools safely to observe, measure, and estimate. Then they try to find patterns in that data. Patterns may help them make predictions. Weather forecasts are predictions that may help people better prepare for severe storms.

Scientists use values such as the mean, median, mode, and range when they interpret data. These values can help scientists determine the quality and usefulness of data. This analysis may help scientists decide whether they have enough information or whether they should collect more data.

Mean

The mean is the average. You find the mean by adding the data together and then dividing by the number of data. Rainfall measurements were taken daily for one week and the following data were obtained:

0 mm, 4 mm, 15 mm, 7 mm, 20 mm, 3 mm, 0 mm

mean = sum of data ÷ number of data

Step 1: Find the sum.

$$0 + 4 + 15 + 7 + 20 + 3 + 0 = 49$$

Step 2: Divide the sum by the number of data to find the mean.

$$49 \div 7 = 7$$

The mean of the data is 7 mm.

Median

The median is in the middle. Half of the data are lower than the median and half are higher. Put the data in order:

0 mm, 0 mm, 3 mm, 4 mm, 7 mm, 15 mm, 20 mm

The median of the data is 4 mm.

Mode

The mode is the value that occurs most often. Here, the mode is 0 mm.

Range

The range is the difference between the largest and smallest values. The range of the data is 20 − 0 = 20 mm.

Make Inferences

Science deals with observations and facts. Imagine that you hear a dog barking in the distance. This is a scientific observation because anyone listening to and looking at the dog would agree that the dog is barking. Data and observations are facts. For example, the statement *Dogs bark* is a fact.

Scientific observations are different from opinions. An opinion is a personal belief and is not always based on facts. An example of an opinion in this case would be *The dog is a bad dog*. A scientist uses facts and observations to draw conclusions and make inferences. An **inference** is a conclusion based on observations. An example of an inference is *The dog is barking because it sees a rabbit*. In science, for a conclusion to be valid, it must be based on observations and sound reasoning, not on opinion.

12. Infer Look at this picture of a dog. Write a statement that is an observation. Write a statement that is an inference.

....

....

....

Got it?

13. Describe Why is it important to organize data with consistency and precision?

....

....

....

....

14. UNLOCK THE BIG **?** How are data used in science?

....

....

⬛ **Stop!** I need help with ....

⏸ **Wait!** I have a question about ....

▶ **Go!** Now I know ....

How do scientists support their conclusions?

Envision It!

Tell what you can conclude about these birds' beaks based on your observations.

Inquiry **Explore It!**

Which towel absorbs the most water?

☑ **1.** Pour 100 mL of water into a cup. **Measure** carefully. Wad up one Brand A towel. Dip it completely into the cup and remove it. Measure and **record** the water left in the cup.

☑ **2.** Repeat twice using the same brand of towel.

☑ **3.** Repeat Steps 1 and 2 with each of the other brands.

Explain Your Results

4. Draw a Conclusion
Which towel absorbed the most?

....

5. How did carrying out repeated trials help you trust your conclusions?

....

....

Paper Towel Testing			
Trial	Water Left in Cup (mL)		
	Brand A	Brand B	Brand C
1			
2			
3			
Total			

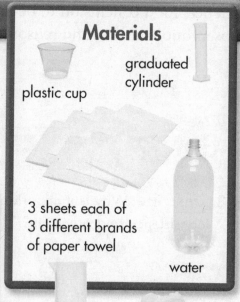

Materials

plastic cup

graduated cylinder

3 sheets each of 3 different brands of paper towel

water

For each trial, dip your towel the same way.

mysCienceonLine.com | **Explore It!** Animation

I will know how scientists draw conclusions and support them using evidence.

Word to Know

evidence

Draw and Defend Conclusions

After analyzing the information that has been collected, scientists draw conclusions about what they have discovered. Scientists defend those conclusions by using the observations they made during their investigations. Sometimes, different conclusions can be drawn from the same set of data. Other scientists may question the methods that the scientists used to draw their conclusions, and the evidence from the investigations must be researched and reviewed.

For example, the behavior of some types of birds is not well known. Scientists must continue to collect and interpret data in order to understand the different behavior of the birds, such as their migration patterns, diet, and shelter preferences. Scientists have drawn conclusions about these bird behaviors, but the scientists' conclusions must be defended with appropriate scientific observations.

1. **Give an Example**
   What is one way a scientist may defend a conclusion? **Underline** a statement in the text to support your answer.

These scientists are collecting data about bird behavior by placing identification bands around the birds' legs.

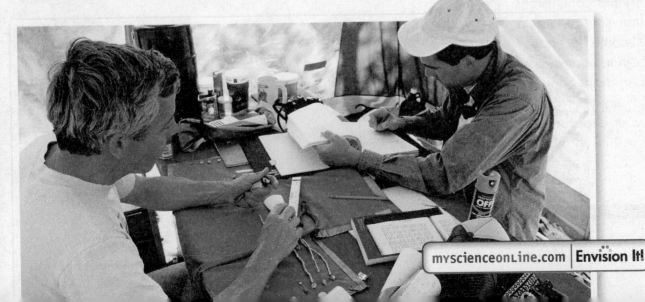

Evidence

One way for scientists to ensure that their work is valid is to share their results with others. Each of their investigations must be replicable, or repeatable, by other scientists. In addition, the conclusions that the scientists drew about their experiments must be based on evidence. **Evidence** is a set of observations that make you believe that something is true. When scientists have testable experiments that are based on evidence, they are able to give their results to other members of the scientific community.

During a scientific investigation, evidence may show results that are unexpected. The evidence may not support a scientist's hypothesis. However, this does not mean the experiment was not useful. The unexpected findings can lead to a new understanding of a scientific concept or cause scientists to experiment further.

Sometimes, scientists may misinterpret evidence from an investigation. They may come to an incorrect conclusion. This is why it is important for scientists to communicate with and accept feedback from one another.

2. **Justify** This scientist is testing a sample of ice from Antarctica. Do you think other scientists will be able to replicate this experiment? Why or why not?

....

....

....

....

....

....

This scientist may be able to use his data as evidence to support his hypothesis.

Lightning Lab

Coin Flip

Scientists gather evidence to make valid conclusions. How often do you think a coin will come up heads? Flip a coin ten times. How often did it come up heads? Have your partner repeat your experiment. Did the results change? Draw a conclusion and explain it.

myscienceonline.com | Got it? ⏱ 60-Second Video

Review and Retest

Scientists must describe exactly what they did in an experiment and how they did it. This allows other scientists working in the same field to replicate the experiment to see if the results are the same. They may also ask questions about the experiment and point out problems.

In science, communication is important. Scientists must describe their procedures and report their findings honestly. They must answer questions. Although some variation in results is acceptable, the results from different scientists should be similar. If results are not consistent, then the experiment must be done again.

3. List two things these scientists may be talking about. **Underline** a statement in the text that supports your answer.

....

....

....

....

Got it?

4. Contrast Explain the difference between an observation and an inference.

....

....

5. UNLOCK THE BIG ? **Evaluate** Why is it important that scientists' conclusions are based on evidence?

....

....

⬜ **Stop!** I need help with ....

⏸ **Wait!** I have a question about ....

▶ **Go!** Now I know ....

How does a banana slice change over time?

As you carry out this investigation, practice the inquiry skills you have learned.

Follow a Procedure

☐ **1.** Place a whole banana slice in a cup.

☑ **2.** Use a spoon to cut another banana slice into 4 pieces. Place the pieces in a second cup.

☑ **3.** Put another banana slice into a third cup. Mash this slice with a spoon.

Materials

3 banana slices

3 plastic cups

plastic spoon

Be careful! Wash your hands when finished.

Inquiry Skill
Scientists begin by asking a question. Then they make careful observations and record data accurately. They use their data to help make **inferences.**

4. Observe the slices when you place them in the cup and each hour for 3 hours.
Record your observations in the chart.

Changes to Banana Slices over Time			
Time	Observations		
	Whole Slice	Cut-Up Slice	Mashed Slice
When placed in cup			
After 1 hour			
After 2 hours			
After 3 hours			

Analyze and Conclude

5. Communicate Examine your data. Identify a simple pattern you **observed.**

....

....

6. Make an **inference** to explain about the pattern you identified:

....

....

7. UNLOCK THE BIG **?** How can investigating cut bananas help scientists learn about other fruits?

....

....

Interpret Graphs

In science, graphs are often used to analyze, interpret, and display data. By looking at a graph, a scientist can visualize any trends, or patterns, that might be present. Scientists are able to support the conclusions they draw from data by using graphs.

Example

The students at Oakview School want to find out what things are most popular to collect among boys and girls. They asked 50 boys and 50 girls to choose their favorite collectible. Look at the double-bar graph.

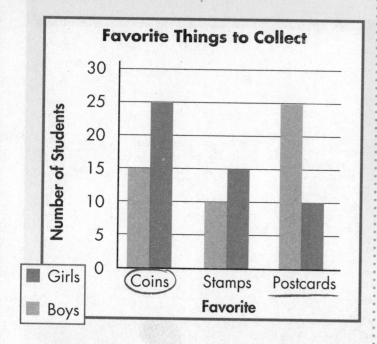

Favorite Things to Collect

1 (Circle) the most popular collectible among girls.

2 **Underline** The most popular collectible among boys.

Practice

Parents at Oakview School want to buy books for the library. They asked 30 fifth-graders to come into the library to choose their favorite type of book to read: science fiction, biography, or nonfiction. Look at the bar graph.

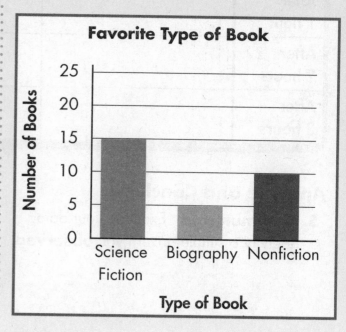

Favorite Type of Book

3 (Circle) the most popular type of book.

4 **Analyze** The parents decide to buy more biography books because they think those are better for the students. Is this decision based on fact or opinion? Explain.

....

....

....

....

Vocabulary Smart Cards

hypothesis
observation
experiment
variable
control group
procedures
data
precision
accuracy
inference
evidence

Play a Game!

Cut out the Vocabulary Smart Cards.

Work with a partner. Choose a card.

Say one word you can think of that is related to that vocabulary word in some way. It might be an example.

Have your partner guess the word. How many clues did it take to guess the correct word?

variable

variable

hypothesis

If... then... because...
hipótesis

control group
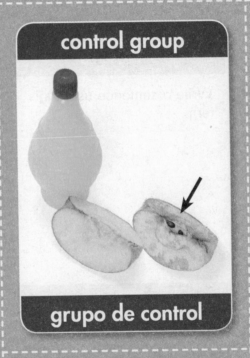
grupo de control

observation

observación

procedures

procedimientos

experiment

experimento

statement of what you think will happen during an investigation

Write three related words.

....

....

....

enunciado de lo que crees que ocurrirá en una investigación

something that can change in a test

Write a sentence using this term.

....

....

algo que puede cambiar durante una prueba

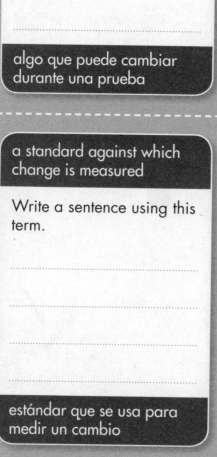

find more information about an observation	test a hypothesis
control the variables	experiment

Make a Word Square!

Choose a vocabulary word and write it in the center of the square. Fill in the squares with related ideas, such as a definition, a characteristic, an example, or something that is not an example.

something you find out about objects, events, or living things using your senses

Write a sentence using this term.

....

....

algo que descubres con tus sentidos sobre los objetos, sucesos o seres vivos

a standard against which change is measured

Write a sentence using this term.

....

....

....

....

estándar que se usa para medir un cambio

the use of scientific methods to test a hypothesis

Write three related words.

....

....

....

uso de métodos científicos para poner a prueba una hipótesis

step-by-step instructions for completing a task

Give an example of a procedure you have followed.

....

....

....

instrucciones paso por paso para realizar una tarea

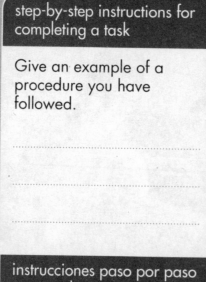

inference

The dog is barking because it sees a rabbit.

inferencia

data

datos

evidence

evidencia

precision

precisión

accuracy

exactitud

information from which a conclusion can be drawn or a prediction can be made

Write the singular form of this word.

....
....
....

información de la cual se puede sacar una conclusión o hacer una predicción

---

a conclusion based on observations

Use any form of this word in a sentence.

....
....
....
....

conclusión basada en observaciones

---

the ability to consistently repeat a measurement

Name the adjective form of this word.

....
....

capacidad de repetir una medición de manera consistente

---

observations that make you believe something is true

Write a sentence using this word.

....
....
....
....

observaciones que te hacen creer que algo es cierto

---

ability to make a measurement that is as close to the actual value as possible

Name the adjective form of this word.

....
....

capacidad de hacer una medición que se aproxime tanto como sea posible al valor verdadero

Lesson 1

What do scientists do?

- Scientists define a problem and try to find answers.
- Scientists make hypotheses and observations.
- Scientists draw conclusions based on their investigations.

Lesson 2

How do scientists investigate?

- Scientists use many different types of scientific investigations.
- Scientists use models, surveys, and sampling to gather data.
- Scientific methods are organized steps for doing an investigation.

Lesson 3

How do scientists collect and interpret data?

- Scientists collect data with tools.
- Scientists organize data using tables and graphs.
- Scientists interpret and draw conclusions from the data they collect.

Lesson 4

How do scientists support their conclusions?

- Scientists use facts, not opinions, when drawing conclusions.
- Scientific investigations should be based on evidence.
- Other scientists must be able to replicate scientific investigations.

Chapter Review

REVIEW THE BIG ? **What is science?**

Lesson 1

What do scientists do?

1. **Vocabulary** What is an observation?
   A. something that helps you measure
   B. something that has been made for the first time
   C. using the senses to gather information
   D. new ideas or new understandings

2. **Demonstrate** Why do scientists make hypotheses before beginning scientific investigations?

Lesson 2

How do scientists investigate?

Do the **math!**

3. The Wright brothers' airplane, *Flyer,* had a wingspan of 12 m. You build a model with a wingspan of 10 cm. How many times larger is *Flyer* than your model?

4. **Communicate** Explain why a control group is important in an experiment.

Lesson 3

How do scientists collect and interpret data?

5. **Analyze** Suppose you are doing a presentation for your class about the daily growth of a bean plant over the course of a month. Would you use a chart, a table, or a graph to help explain your results to your class? Explain your answer.

6. ◉ **Text Features** Use the following paragraph to answer the question.

   In order for scientists to be able to predict tornadoes more successfully, they need to collect large amounts of **data.** Data are information from which a conclusion can be drawn.

Why is the word *data* highlighted in yellow?

Lesson 4

How do scientists support their conclusions?

7. Identify How do scientists use evidence in their investigations?

....

....

....

....

8. Write About It Why is it important that scientists communicate?

....

....

....

9. Identify You watch your neighbors as they leave their apartment building. They have suitcases with them. They all get into the car and drive away. You think they are going on vacation. Is your thought a fact or an inference? Explain.

....

....

....

10. APPLY THE BIG ? What is science?

....

Explain why scientists will do exactly the same experiments that other scientists have done.

....

....

....

....

....

....

....

....

....

....

....

....

41

Chapter 1
Benchmark Practice

Science,
Engineering,
and
Technology

Fill in the bubble next to the answer choice you think is correct for each multiple-choice question.

1 _____ are observations from which a conclusion can be drawn.

Ⓐ Predictions
Ⓑ Inventions
Ⓒ Data
Ⓓ Discoveries

2 Which statement about a hypothesis is NOT true?

Ⓐ A hypothesis is an explanation of what you think will happen.
Ⓑ A hypothesis can be tested.
Ⓒ A hypothesis is written as a question.
Ⓓ A hypothesis may be a true statement.

3 Which statement about opinions is true?

Ⓐ They are beliefs or value judgments.
Ⓑ They are a valuable tool used by scientists.
Ⓒ They are supported by research.
Ⓓ They can be used to help write a hypothesis.

4 You are testing to see if music helps plants grow better. You divide the plants into four groups.

Plant Groups	
Group	**Music Type**
A	jazz
B	classical
C	rock
D	none

What is group D called?
Ⓐ the model group
Ⓑ the control group
Ⓒ the population group
Ⓓ the experimental group

5 Why is it important for scientists to repeat the investigations of other scientists?

_____

_____

_____

_____

There are different types of flight simulators. This flight simulator is a full-cockpit simulator.

STEM

Flight Simulators

How could you learn to fly an airplane without flying? You could use a flight simulator! What is a flight simulator? It is computer technology that simulates, or duplicates, a realistic impression of flying without actually flying. A flight simulator gives a pilot practice in different scenarios. These scenarios include bad weather, crashing, landing, and taking off. Engineers use technology to develop accurate scenarios. Without accurate scenarios, pilots and companies might not know how they or their technology would respond in an emergency.

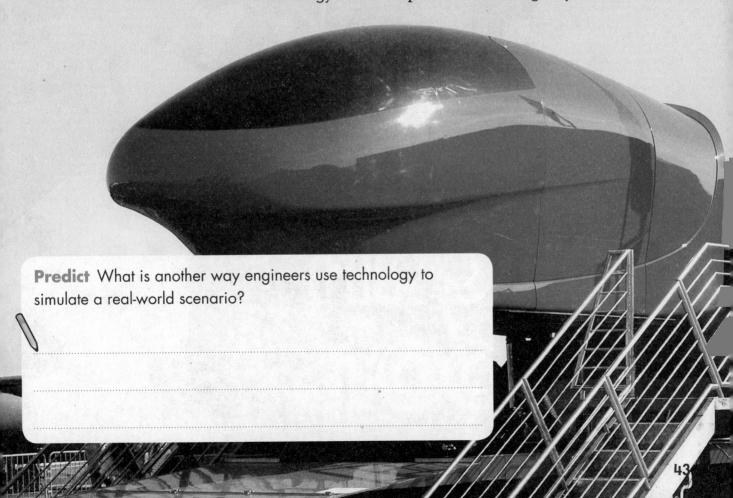

Predict What is another way engineers use technology to simulate a real-world scenario?

....

....

....

what can robots do?

Design and Function

Try It! How can you design a strong glue?

Lesson 1 What is technology?

Lesson 2 How does technology mimic living things?

Lesson 3 What is the design process?

Investigate It! How can you make and redesign a model of a robotic arm?

Robots are designed to do many different tasks. This robot assists shoppers in finding and carrying their groceries. Other robots help people who cannot walk get in and out of their wheelchairs.

Predict What do you think robots will be used for in the future?

....

....

THE BIG ? How does technology affect our lives?

How can you design a strong glue?

□ **1.** List 3 properties of a strong glue.

....

□ **2. Observe** the properties of each mixture. **Record.**

Mixture	Properties
Cornstarch and water	
Flour and water	
Gelatin and water	

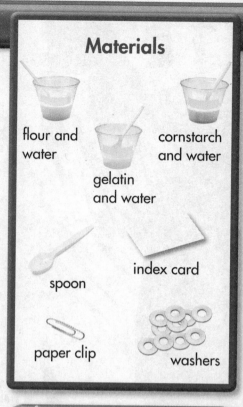

Materials

flour and water

cornstarch and water

gelatin and water

spoon

index card

paper clip

washers

□ **3. Design** a glue that will hold the most weight by combining up to 2 spoonfuls of each mixture.

□ **4. Test** your glue. Spread it at the bottom of an index card. Pull out the large end of a paper clip to make a hook. Press the small end into the glue. Let the glue dry overnight.

□ **5.** Hold the card. Hang washers on the hook until the paper clip pulls off the card. Record your results.

Inquiry Skill
Recording your observations on a chart can help you make **inferences.**

Mixture	Spoonfuls	Number of Washers Held
Cornstarch and water		
Flour and water		
Gelatin and water		

Explain Your Results

6. **UNLOCK THE BIG ?** Compare you results with other groups.
Infer Did different quantities of starting materials result in glue with different properties? Explain.

....

....

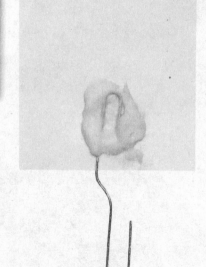

⊙ Main Idea and Details

- Learning to find **main ideas** and **details** can help you understand and remember what you read.
- Details can help you to infer the main idea of the article.

Technology and Our Homes

Technology can be found throughout our homes and is used in many ways. Technology makes it easier to do many things in the home. Thermostats can maintain or change the temperature inside the home. Dishwashers get dishes and eating utensils clean. We use technology for entertainment purposes too. Televisions, video games, and MP3 players are all technology. The way people keep and store food has been improved by technology. Refrigerators and freezers offer a healthy way of keeping food fresh for longer periods of time. Even plastic containers offer airtight storage to keep food fresher.

Practice It!

Use the graphic organizer below to list the main idea and details from the article above.

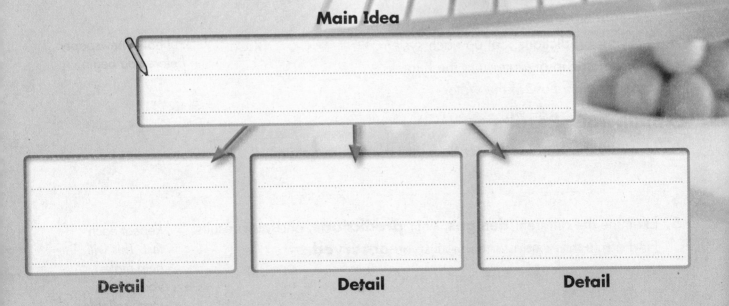

Main Idea

Detail   **Detail**   **Detail**

What is technology?

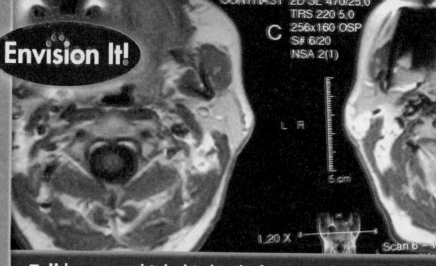

Envision It!

Tell how you think this kind of image can help doctors.

Inquiry **Explore It!**

Which transport system works best?

☐ **1.** Examine *Possible Water Transport Systems.*

☐ **2.** **Predict** which systems will always work, which will never work, and which will trap some water.

☐ **3.** Test your predictions. Set up each system. Pour a half cup of water into the funnel. **Observe** the flow of the water.

Explain Your Results

4. In what direction does water flow best through a system?

5. Examine the different **designs,** your **predictions,** and your results. Find a rule that explains the results you **observed.**

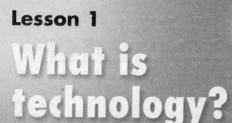

Materials

newspaper

plastic tube

empty cup and cup with water

funnel

Possible Water Transport Systems

Put down newspaper before you begin.

Repeat each test. This will help make your results more reliable.

myscienceonLine.com | **Explore It!** Animation

UNLOCK
THE BIG
?

I will know how technology solves problems and provides solutions.

Words to Know

technology
microchip

Problems and Solutions

People constantly gain knowledge and make new discoveries. These discoveries and knowledge often result in technology that makes tasks easier, faster, or more efficient. **Technology** is the knowledge, processes, and products that solve problems and make work easier. Many years ago, illnesses were treated with few medicines. Over time, people began to learn the causes of some illnesses. This allowed people to develop better ways of treating and preventing disease.

Technology has improved people's lives, but it has also caused problems. Medical products and other technologies help people stay healthy. However, new medicines may cause unanticipated side effects.

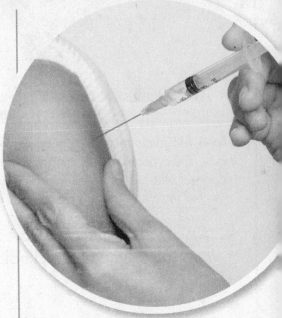

Vaccines were discovered by Edward Jenner in 1796.

1. ◉ **Main Idea and Details** Use the graphic organizer below to list two details and the main idea found in the last paragraph of the text.

2. **Apply** What problem did this technology in the picture above solve?

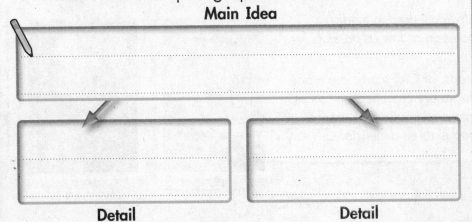

Main Idea

[ ]

Detail   **Detail**

[ ]   [ ]

Tools in Medicine

Technology has contributed to the scientific knowledge of medicine. Since the late 1800s there have been many advances in medical technology.

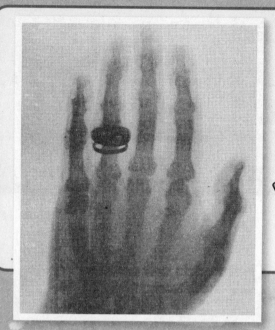

Then *William Röntgen took this X ray of his wife's hand in 1895. It is one of the first X rays used in medicine. X rays allowed doctors and scientists to see things inside a living thing. An X ray is a wave with very high energy. It can go though materials light rays cannot. The harmful effects of exposure to large amounts of X-ray radiation were not known until later.*

3. Infer What features can you recognize? What are the dark oval areas?

....

....

Now *Magnetic resonance imaging (MRI) produces images of the body. The procedure uses magnetic fields and radio wave pulses. Scanned information is fed into a computer. The result is a highly-detailed image. MRI technology does not use harmful radiation.*

4. Analyze What are two advantages of MRI over other imaging technologies?

....

....

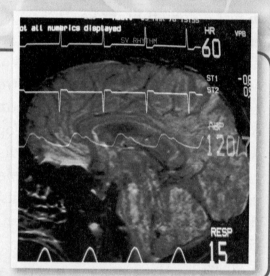

Now *X rays are still very useful and widely used in medicine. Care is taken to keep exposure to radiation as low as possible for both the patient and the technician.*

Now *CT (computed tomography) scans, or CAT scans, are made with a series of X rays. The X-ray images are cross section "slices" of the body. The information is fed into a computer. The process produces an image that can be viewed in three dimensions.*

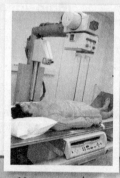

X-ray machine   CT scanner

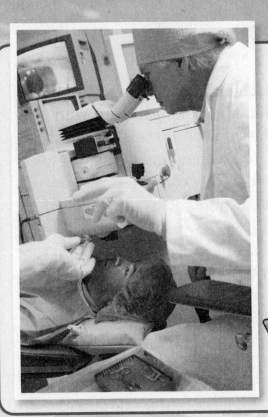

Then This antique scalpel has a wooden handle. Wood cannot be sterilized to remove germs. The idea that germs cause disease was not widely accepted in this country until the 1890s.

Now Surgeons still use scalpels, but they are made of steel and plastic. These scalpels can be sterilized easily to remove germs. However, today there is another option. Lasers produce light waves that are concentrated on a tiny spot. Laser scalpels are able to cut through skin and other soft tissue.

antique scalpel

5. **CHALLENGE** Weaker lasers are found in everyday life. Give an example where a laser might be used.

....

....

Then Doctors used stitches, also called sutures, to hold wounds closed until they healed. Some sutures are made with a material that dissolves into the body and does not need to be removed.

Now Researchers are developing a glue to hold wounds together. The idea for glue came from animals called mussels that live in the ocean and can bond, or stick, to things underwater. Sutures are still preferred for some procedures, but one day doctors may be able to use glue during surgery.

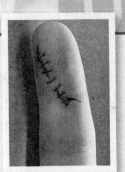

stitches   *glue*

6. **Predict** Do you think surgical glue or sutures are better at keeping water out of wounds?

....

....

....

At-Home Lab

Design Solutions
Cut out pictures from magazines of three different technologies that help people. Write a short paragraph about who would use each technology.

51

UNIVAC (Universal Automatic Computer) was built in the United States in 1951. It was the first electronic computer. UNIVAC took up a space of 943 cubic feet.

Today, microchips are used in computers, cars, mobile phones, and video games. Some microchips are the width of a fingernail and others as wide a strand of hair.

7. Infer How did the invention of the microchip change computers?

Computer Technology

Early Computers

Computer technology began in the 1930s and 1940s. These early computers replaced mechanical parts with electrical parts, but used the same basic steps as today's computers—input, processing, output, and feedback—to solve mathematical problems. Early computers were so large that most of them filled entire rooms and weighed thousands of pounds.

The large size and high cost of early computers made them impractical for most people. Computer manufacturers became aware of the need for smaller, faster, and less expensive computers. One of the most important developments in computer technology was the microchip. A **microchip** is a small piece of a computer that contains microscopic, or tiny, circuits. Microchips make it possible for computers to process information very quickly. They also made the cost of a computer much lower because it became less expensive to manufacture computers.

World Wide Web

In the 1980s, computer technology was used to solve another problem. A British computer scientist wanted to make it easier for physicists to communicate with each other. The result was the World Wide Web. The World Wide Web is a computer-based network of information sources. It was first developed for use by the European Organization for Nuclear Research. The first version of the Web was completed in 1990. Today, a person using a computer can search through the Web to find information about practically anything.

8. Explain How has the World Wide Web improved communication and research?

Computers Today

Before computer technology, people spent months doing work that one of today's computers does in seconds. A computer only takes a few moments to process tasks such as calculating workers' salaries or figuring out how to steer a rocket. However, some tasks take even computers a long time to complete. Powerful supercomputers or computer networks often help out with very complex tasks.

The invention of the computer has led to many other technologies. Computers can be used with many tools and devices. Several kinds of microscopes, telescopes, thermometers, and cameras use computers. They help people find and record accurate information or results. Computer and other technologies can be found in schools. Students can easily find information for research using the Internet. DVD players and interactive whiteboards help present information in new ways.

9. ⊙ **Main Idea and Details**
Underline the main idea in the second paragraph.

Got it?

10. **UNLOCK THE BIG ?** **Identify** What are three additional technologies that you can benefit from?

....

....

11. **Analyze** Name a technology that has changed quickly. Name a technology that has changed more slowly.

....

....

◻ **Stop!** I need help with ....

▯▯ **Wait!** I have a question about ....

▷ **Go!** Now I know ....

Lesson 2

How does technology mimic living things?

How can this device help someone speak?

my PLANET DiaRY

Did You Know?

Robotics is the study, design, construction, and use of robots. New Lutheran Hospital in Fort Wayne, Indiana is using robotics to help save lives. The Sensei X Robotic Catheter System looks like a thin, flexible tube. The design allows it to go into areas of the heart that are hard for doctors to reach. A video camera connects to the robot. This allows doctors to see inside a patient's body. The video camera also helps doctors control the robot's movement.

What is the need for robotics in the medical field?

During surgery, the doctor uses a joystick to control movements of the Sensei X.

 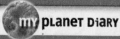

UNLOCK THE BIG ?

I will know how some technology can mimic the muscular and skeletal systems.

Words to Know

prosthetic limb

Technology and the Human Body

The human body is an amazing structure. Engineers sometimes use scientific knowledge of how the body works to develop technologies. Some of the technologies help people whose bodies do not function as they should. Some technologies do tasks that are too dangerous for people.

Technologies that have moving parts can be like the human body. A robot is one of these technologies. Robots can have a body structure and movable joints, which are similar to the human skeletal and muscular systems. Robotic technologies use an electrical energy source to help them move. The human body uses energy from food to help it move. Robots have a sensor system and a computer to control movements. In the human body, the brain and nervous system help to control movement.

1. **Explain** How do you think this robot is like you?

....

....

Nexi is a social robot developed by engineers at Massachusetts Institute of Technology.

Even though these prosthetic legs look different than real legs, they allow this woman the ability to run.

2. Compare How are this runner's prosthetic legs similar to the legs of the other runners?

....

....

....

Prosthetic Limbs

Robotic technology that mimics movements of the human body is also used to make a prosthetic limb move. A **prosthetic limb** is an artificial arm, hand, leg, or foot that replaces a missing one. Modern prosthetic limbs can be controlled by electrical signals from the brain.

Past prosthetic hands had few fingers and could not do many things. Today, they have a thumb and four fingers that are controlled individually. These prosthetic hands can turn a key, pick up small objects, and hold a glass.

Current prosthetic legs and feet allow their users to walk and even run. As technology advances, prosthetic legs and feet work more like real legs and feet. The latest prosthetic limbs also look more like real limbs.

3. Summarize How do prosthetic limbs help people?

....

....

Each finger on this prosthetic hand can be moved separately. This woman can do many everyday things that she could not do without a prosthetic hand.

Animals and Technology

Some technologies mimic the muscular and skeletal systems of animals. These systems help animals to move in different ways. The wings and tails of birds help the birds fly. Fish have muscular and skeletal systems that help them swim.

Airplanes have parts that mimic the wings and tails of birds. Like the wings and tails of birds, airplane wings and tails can be adjusted to control how the airplane moves. Some robots can also fly. The robotic bat flaps its wings and flies like a bat. It can search collapsed buildings and other areas people cannot get to. Some robots used to explore the ocean have parts that mimic the muscular and skeletal systems of fish.

Scientists use robotic animals to study the behavior of real animals. A robotic squirrel makes noise and moves its tail like a real squirrel. It can be placed in an area where real squirrels live. A real squirrel may wiggle its tail and make noises at the robotic squirrel. Scientists can use this information to learn how squirrels communicate with one another.

Robotic bats have movements similar to a real bat. They can access places too small or dangerous for people to access.

4. Predict Why do scientists use robotic squirrels to help study real squirrels?

....

....

....

Robotic squirrels can help scientists study the behavior of real squirrels. This robotic squirrel can make sounds and wiggle its tail like a real squirrel.

Nanobots

How can you build a robot that is only a few billionths of a meter long? Scientists hope to be able to build these tiny robots using nanotechnology. Scientists have found ways to move one atom at a time. They hope to be able to use this technology to build tiny robots, or nanobots, that can perform all kinds of tasks.

One idea is to use nanobots inside the human body. Nanobots may be able to deliver medications better than current methods. Scientists are also researching how to make a nanobot that can remove cholesterol from the walls of arteries.

5. Generate How do you think nanobots might be useful?

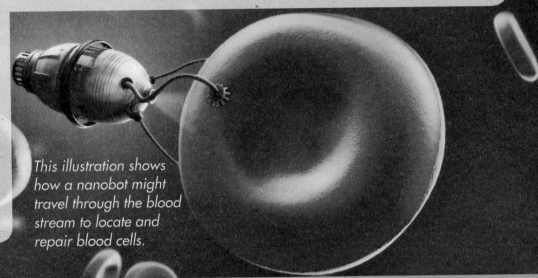

This illustration shows how a nanobot might travel through the blood stream to locate and repair blood cells.

Got it?

6. **UNLOCK THE BIG ?** How does one kind of technology mimic human muscular and skeletal systems?

7. Hypothesize Why do you think engineers build robots that mimic human or animal systems?

⬛ **Stop!** I need help with ....

⏸ **Wait!** I have a question about ....

▶ **Go!** Now I know ....

What is the design process?

Explain how you think people design new technologies.

Inquiry **Explore It!**

How can the design of a model arm help you learn about how your arm works?

☐ **1. Make a model** of an arm as shown.

☐ **2.** Pull on Yarn A. **Observe.** Pull on Yarn B. Observe.

☐ **3.** Bend the arm pieces together. What happens to the yarn?

Materials

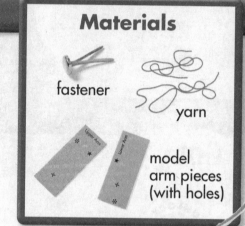

fastener

yarn

model arm pieces (with holes)

Explain Your Results

4. Communicate   In your model, what do the yarn, the cardboard, and the fastener represent?

....

....

5. Draw a Conclusion   How can people use models to help them learn about the human body?

....

....

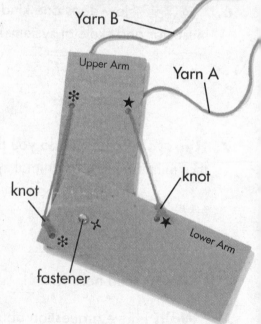

Yarn B

Yarn A

Upper Arm

knot

knot

Lower Arm

fastener

myscienceon**L**ine.com | **Explore It!** Animation

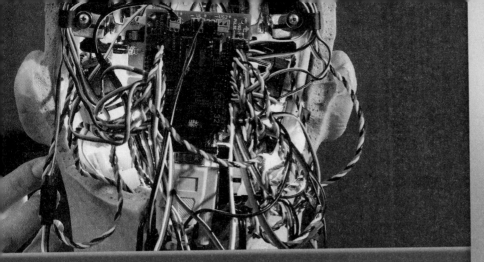

Words to Know

design process
prototype

Design Process

Technology helps to solve many of the problems we have. We use technology in our homes, schools, and offices. There are technologies for constructing buildings, communicating with others, transporting people and products, and so much more.

Who makes all this technology? People all over the world develop technologies. You may be surprised to know that even students your age develop new technologies. An engineer is a person who designs new technologies. People work in many different fields to apply scientific knowledge to everyday life. People use the design process to develop new technologies. The **design process** is a set of steps for developing products and processes that solve problems.

1. (Circle) what a person who designs technology is called.

2. **Predict** Why is it important to use the design process when developing new technologies?

....

....

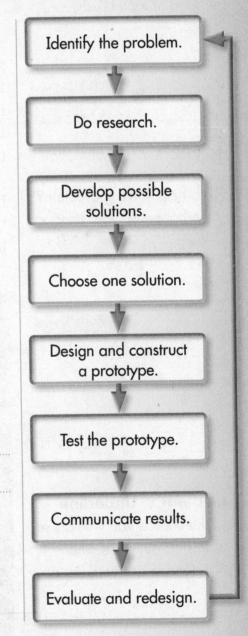

Identify the problem.

Do research.

Develop possible solutions.

Choose one solution.

Design and construct a prototype.

Test the prototype.

Communicate results.

Evaluate and redesign.

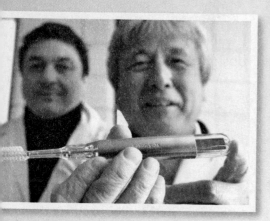

Dr. Kunio Komiyama is an engineer in the field of dentistry. He designed a new kind of toothbrush.

Steps of the Design Process

While some engineers may use different steps or use them in a different order, they all have an end goal of finding a solution to a problem.

Identify the problem.

The first step in the design process is to identify a need or problem. All technology comes from the need for a solution to a problem. It is important in this step to determine who would be helped by the solution. For example, a toothbrush that cleans teeth with less effort could potentially help everyone reduce cavities and gum problems.

Do research.

Research is another important step in the design process. In order to make or improve on existing technology, scientists need to know what technology already exists. Scientific journals, magazines, the Internet, informational books, and encyclopedias can be helpful as you study ways to solve a design problem. Sometimes the best way to find the information you need is to interview an expert.

Engineers designing a new toothbrush might research how the shape of the handle affects how people brush their teeth. Engineers should also know how different bristle materials affect teeth.

3. **Apply** What kind of product would you make to help solve a problem? Who would your product help?

....

....

....

....

....

4. **Identify** **Underline** the source you would use to find out what other scientists are working on.

Develop possible solutions.

Using what they learned in their research, scientists and engineers think of ways to improve an existing technology. Each possible solution should be carefully planned. Charts and diagrams can be used to communicate the design solution to others.

5. **Interpret** Look at the drawing below. What information can you find in the drawing?

....

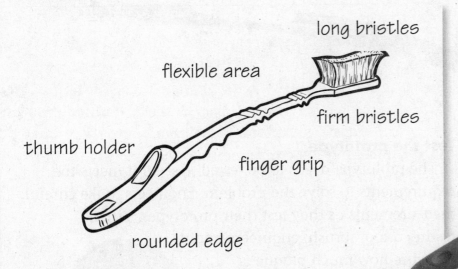

long bristles

flexible area

firm bristles

thumb holder

finger grip

rounded edge

This toothbrush uses advanced technology. It works very well, but it costs more than other toothbrushes.

Choose one solution.

It is important to choose wisely the one solution you will build. Making many solutions may take too much time. The cost of making the solution can also affect your decision. For example, if the toothbrush works very well, but is very expensive, people may not buy it.

6. **Identify** (Circle) two things that may affect which design solution you choose to build.

7. Explain Why do engineers build prototypes of their design solutions?

....

....

....

....

....

8. Infer What do you think this toothbrush is made of? Why do you think the engineers used those materials?

....

....

....

....

....

9. Interpret What do you think is one important thing that must be done when making a test to evaluate a prototype?

....

....

....

....

Design and construct a prototype.

The next step is to build a version of the solution, called a **prototype.** It is used to test the solution. It is important to identify the kinds of materials you use to build your prototype. The properties of the materials you use affect the function of your prototype. You will need a strong, flexible material for parts that bend. If you do not want the part to bend you should use a rigid material. You will also need to identify the tools you use to build your prototype.

toothbrush prototype

Test the prototype.

The prototype needs to be tested to see if it meets the requirements to solve the problem. Engineers make careful measurements as they test their prototypes. When testing a toothbrush, engineers might measure how much plaque is left on the teeth after brushing for one minute. These measurements help the engineers evaluate how well the prototype works.

Testing a toothbrush is important to make sure it works for everyone that will be using it.

Communicate results.

Throughout the design process it is important to document your work. Document means to record what you learn. Documentation helps you communicate with others. If you are working in a company, you will need to communicate your process and design to managers, salespeople, and many others. Often others will need to repeat your tests to verify the results. They will need to know your test procedures and the specifics of your design. The people who you share your design with may be able to offer advice on how to improve your idea.

Your design solution can be communicated in many ways. Labeled diagrams can show the size and shape of the parts of your product. Graphic organizers can be used to show how parts are put together. You will also need a list of materials and tools used to make each part. Tables, charts, and graphs can help you communicate the results of your tests.

Evaluate and redesign.

Using the results of your tests and feedback from others, you can evaluate how well your design solved the problem. This information can help you redesign your product to make it work better. You may need to make minor adjustments or choose a completely new solution.

10. Infer Why do you think an engineer might redesign a prototype?

....

....

11. Predict What might happen if you fail to document your design?

....

....

....

12. Evaluate Look at the redesigned prototype below. It has improvements such as a better handle. Work with a partner. Tell why you think the handle is a better design.

....

....

....

....

....

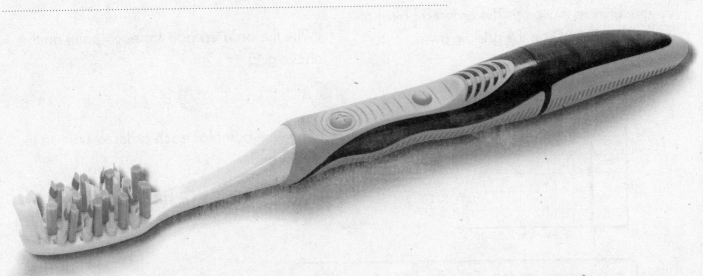

Designing Robotic Arms

Engineers use the design process to develop robotic arms. Robotic arms are designed and built to mimic the movement of human arms.

The first robotic arm used in a factory was developed by George Devol. The robotic arm picked up and stacked metal parts that were too hot for workers to handle. George Devol and his partner, Joseph Engelberger, called the robotic arm, the *Unimate*.

The *Unimate* had a "shoulder" but no "elbow." Devol and Engelberger continued to redesign the robotic arm. They developed a new robotic arm with an "elbow" that allowed it to perform more tasks. Today's robotic arms can move in many different directions.

PUMA, an industrial programmable robot, was introduced in 1980. It had all the characteristics of a human arm.

13. **Compare** How do you think the picture on the right might be better than the PUMA robotic arm?

....

Do the math!

Ordered Pairs

The computer that controls robot movement uses a coordinate grid system. An ordered pair is used to identify a point on a coordinate grid. The x-coordinate, or the first number, tells how many units to move to the right. The y-coordinate, or second number, tells how many units to move up. The ordered pair that identifies Point D on the grid below is (2, 5).

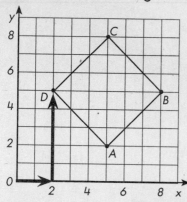

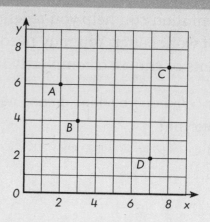

Write the ordered pair for each point on the above grid.

1 A .... **2** B ....

Name the point for each ordered pair on the above grid.

3 (7, 2) .... **4** (8, 7) ....

myscienceonline.com | Got it? 60-Second Video

14. Identify Label the parts of the robotic arm that are like the parts of a human arm.

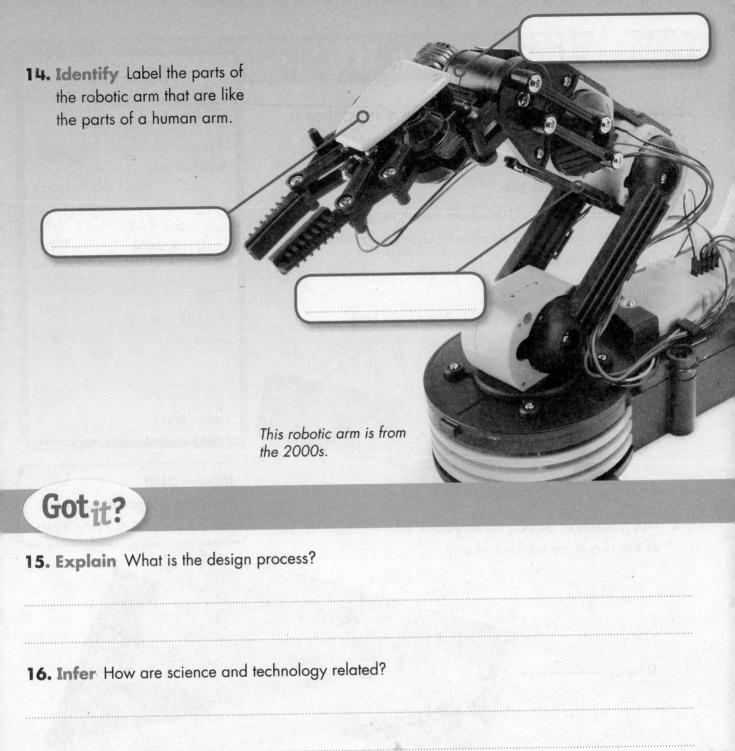

This robotic arm is from the 2000s.

Got it?

15. Explain What is the design process?

....

....

16. Infer How are science and technology related?

....

....

Stop! I need help with ....

Wait! I have a question about ....

Go! Now I know ....

How can you make and redesign a model of a robotic arm?

Follow a Procedure

☑ **1. Make a Model** Use a hole punch to make holes in 3 poster board strips as shown. Use two fasteners to join the strips together.

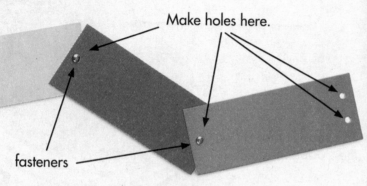

Make holes here.

fasteners

☑ **2.** Use a fastener. Attach the eye hook on the dowel to one of the two holes on the red strip.

Inquiry Skill
Making a model can help you learn about the real thing.

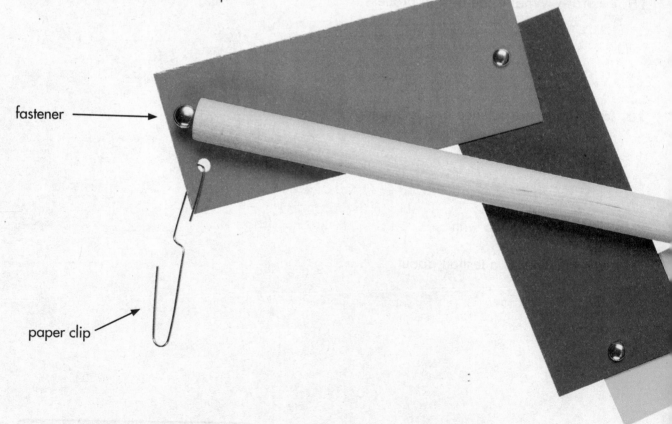

fastener

paper clip

3. Bend a large paper clip into an S shape.
Put the top of the S through the other hole in the red strip.

4. Use the robotic arm. Try to pick up the objects listed in the chart.
Record the number of tries you need. Use up to 5 tries for each object.

5. Redesign your model of a robotic arm. Repeat Step 4.

Objects Chart		
Objects	Number of Tries	
Clay ball with paper clip		
Paper clip		
Rubber band		
String		

Analyze and Conclude

6. Communicate What **design** change did you make to your **model**?

....

....

7. UNLOCK THE BIG ? Describe two ways in which the model is not like a
real robotic arm.

....

....

....

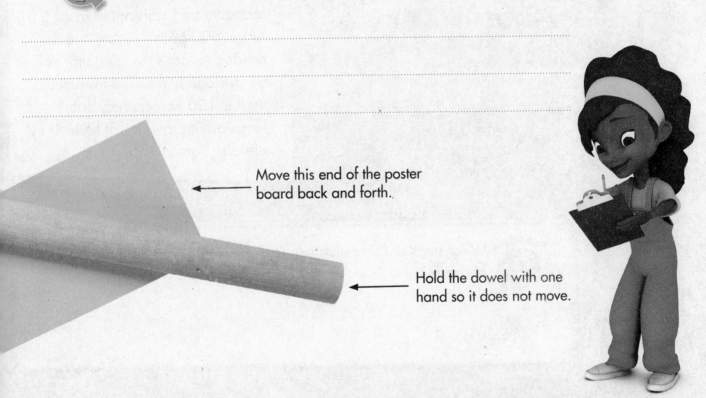

Move this end of the poster
board back and forth.

Hold the dowel with one
hand so it does not move.

Denim Insulation

Are you wearing your favorite pair of jeans right now? When they wear out, they could serve another purpose. The surprise is that they might end up in someone's attic or walls—as insulation.

More than half the energy used in your home goes toward keeping it cool in summer and warm in winter. A good way to save money and use less energy is to insulate. One of the newest technologies is a process that turns denim cloth into fiber insulation.

Denim scraps and old denim jeans are processed into fibers. The fibers are treated with borate, which makes the product fire retardant and resistant to mold. About 500 pairs of jeans are needed to make the insulation for an average home. The insulation itself is 100 percent recyclable. Jeans are no longer just blue. They are also "green"!

APPLY THE BIG ? What steps did scientists use to determine the insulating properties of denim?

Vocabulary Smart Cards

technology
microchip
prosthetic limb
design process
prototype

Play a Game!

Cut out the Vocabulary Smart Cards.

Work with a partner. One person puts the cards picture-side up. The other person puts the cards picture-side down.

Take turns matching each word with its definition.

design process

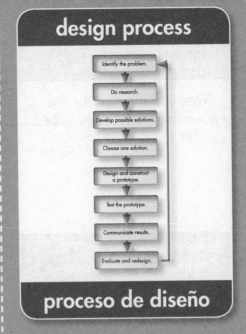

proceso de diseño

technology

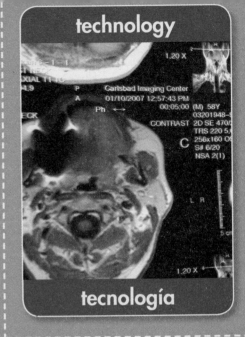

tecnología

prototype

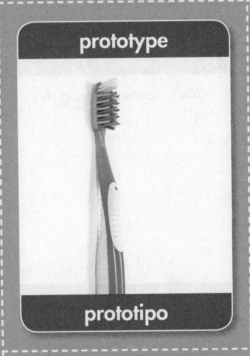

prototipo

microchip

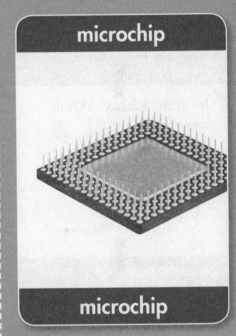

microchip

prosthetic limb

prótesis

the knowledge, processes, and products that solve problems and make work easier

Name three technologies that begin with the same letter of the alphabet.

....

....

conocimiento, procesos y productos que se usan para resolver problemas y facilitar el trabajo

---

a set of steps for developing products and processes that solve problems

Write a definition for the noun form of the first word in this term.

....

....

serie de pasos para desarrollar productos y procesos que resuelven problemas

---

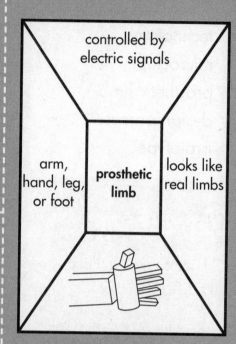

controlled by electric signals

arm, hand, leg, or foot

prosthetic limb

looks like real limbs

---

a small piece of a computer that contains microscopic circuits

Use a dictionary. What does *micro-* mean?

....

....

....

pequeña pieza de computadora que contiene circuitos microscópicos

---

a version of a solution to a problem

Write a sentence using this word.

....

....

....

....

versión de la solución de un problema

Make a Word Frame!

Choose a vocabulary word and write it in the center of the frame. Write or draw details about the vocabulary word in the spaces around it.

---

an artificial arm, hand, leg, or foot that replaces a missing one

Write a sentence using this word.

....

....

brazo, mano, pierna o pie artificial que reemplaza el miembro o la parte que falta

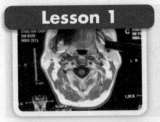

Lesson 1 — What is technology?

- Technology is the knowledge, processes, and products that solve problems and make work easier.
- Medical technologies help us live longer and healthier lives.

Lesson 2 — How does technology mimic living things?

- Many people use prosthetic limbs to help them do everyday tasks.
- Some technologies mimic the way animals move.

Lesson 3 — What is the design process?

- The design process is a set of steps for developing products and processes that solve problems.
- Engineers build and test prototypes of their designs.

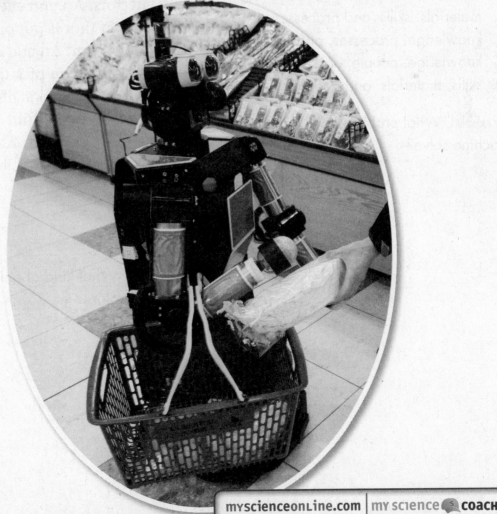

Lesson 1

What is technology?

1. **Write About It** Describe a technology you use every day and the problem it solves.

....

....

....

....

2. **Vocabulary** Technology is the
_____ that solve problems and make work easier.
   A. materials, skills, and processes
   B. knowledge, processes, and skills
   C. knowledge, people, and ideas
   D. skills, materials, and people

3. **Explain** What problem does an X-ray machine solve?

....

....

....

....

Lesson 2

How does technology mimic living things?

4. **Give an Example** What is one technology that mimics the human muscular and skeletal systems?

....

....

5. **Main Idea and Details** Use the following paragraph to answer the question below.

Robotic arms can have different end effectors. An end effector is the attachment that is put on the end of the robotic arm. An end effector may be a claw that can pick things up and place them. Other end effectors include a welding tool and a drill.

What is the main idea of this paragraph?

....

....

6. **Infer** What kind of animal might a robot that explores the ocean mimic?

....

....

....

Lesson 3

What is the design process?

7. Suppose a robot arm can put a toy together five times as fast a person. If a person can make 56 toys in 8 hours, how many toys can the robot make in the same amount of time?

....

....

8. Apply How would an engineer use the design process to build a car that uses less gas?

....

....

....

....

....

....

9. Vocabulary The design process is a set of steps for _____.
  A. developing a product or process
  B. doing an experiment
  C. drawing a diagram
  D. researching a product or process

10. **APPLY THE BIG ?** How does technology affect our lives?

• •

Tell how a technology has affected human life.

....

....

....

....

....

....

....

....

....

....

....

....

....

Chapter 2
Benchmark Practice

Science,
Engineering,
and
Technology

Fill in the bubble next to the answer choice you think is correct for each multiple-choice question.

1 One similarity between a modern computer and an older computer is that _____

Ⓐ they weigh the same.
Ⓑ they both use input and output.
Ⓒ they have the same price.
Ⓓ both use microchips.

2 Before developing possible solutions, an engineer usually _____

Ⓐ communicates his or her results.
Ⓑ makes sure the prototype has been tested.
Ⓒ identifies a problem and does research.
Ⓓ evaluates and chooses a design.

3 Which of these technologies did NOT exist before 1900?

Ⓐ surgical glue
Ⓑ surgical stitches
Ⓒ X-rays
Ⓓ scalpels

4 A prototype is a _____

Ⓐ set of choices for solving a problem.
Ⓑ finished product that can be packaged.
Ⓒ nanobot.
Ⓓ version of the solution to a problem.

5 Suppose you are on a team that is designing a prosthetic eye for a patient with vision loss. What features would be useful in a prosthetic eye?

_____

_____

_____

_____

_____

Infrared Technology

ig World
My World

My World

Big World

u remember the
you got your
ure taken at the
office? Perhaps
r used a
eter that uses
echnology.

ord *infrared*
s a type of light
at people cannot
red energy is often
f as light energy from
urce. You cannot see
energy, but you can use
easure it.

developed technology
a special tool to measure
ed energy that comes
h and outer space.
ls are on satellites that
h and on probes that
ough space. Infrared
gy is useful because
radiation can pass
areas of dust and gas.
mation can give scientists
out clouds on Earth as
lues about the formation
s and stars.

APPLY THE BIG ?

What sort of experiment might you be able to plan that involves using an infrared thermometer?

77

How much weight can a model arm support?

An arm must be able to raise and lower objects of different weights. The arm also needs to support the weight it picks up. You must make a model arm that will be able to pick up different weights. The model arm will be used to pick up a cup holding 25 gram cubes. You will repeat the test by adding 25 gram cubes to the cup each time. Your testing is over when your arm bends the wrong way.

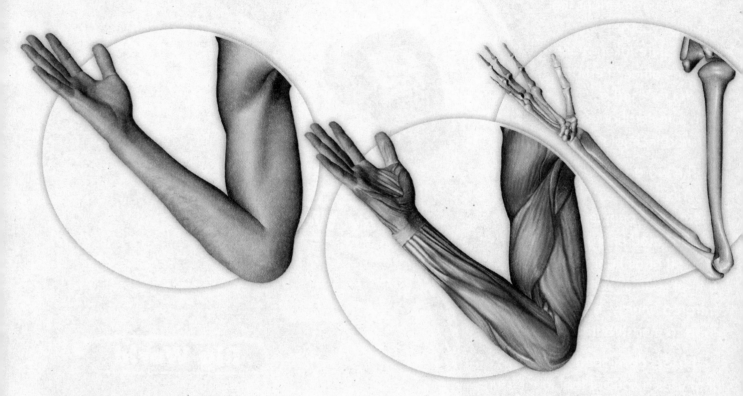

Identify the problem.

☐ **1.** Identify the task your **model** arm will perform.

....

....

....

....

....

....

Possible Materials

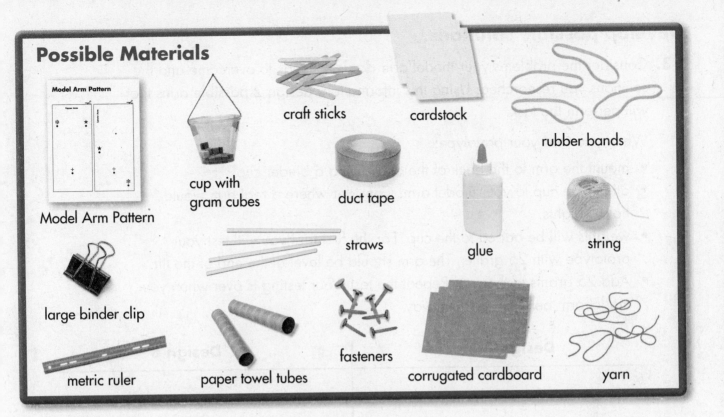

Model Arm Pattern

cup with gram cubes

craft sticks

cardstock

rubber bands

duct tape

glue

string

large binder clip

straws

metric ruler

paper towel tubes

fasteners

corrugated cardboard

yarn

Do research.

2. Consider the tasks you have identified. Research **design** solutions others have created to perform those tasks. Brainstorm ideas with others. List three solutions others have used or suggested.

Develop possible solutions.

☐ **3.** Consider the problems your model arm **design** needs to overcome and the solutions you researched. Using this information, design 2 possible arms that will perform the task.

When you **test** your prototype:

- mount the arm to the back of the chair using a binder clip.
- attach the cup to your model arm. Consider where a real arm would hold weights.
- weights will be added to the cup. For the first trial you will test your prototype with 25 grams. The arm should be level at the end of the lift.
- Add 25 grams to the cup. Repeat the test. Your testing is over when your model arm bends the wrong way.

Design A	Design B

Choose one solution.

☐ **4.** Choose one **design** to build and **test.** Tell which design you chose. Explain why you chose that design.

....

....

....

....

Design and construct a prototype.

☐ **5.** Draw the **design** you will use to make a prototype.

☐ **6.** List the materials you used in your prototype.

....

....

....

Test the prototype.

☐ **7.** Start with 25 grams in the cup. **Record** if the arm passes or fails. A pass is when the arm lifts the cup. A fail is when the arm bends the wrong way.

☐ **8.** Add 25 grams to the cup. Repeat your **test.** Continue testing by adding 25 grams to the cup. Keep repeating your test until the arm fails.

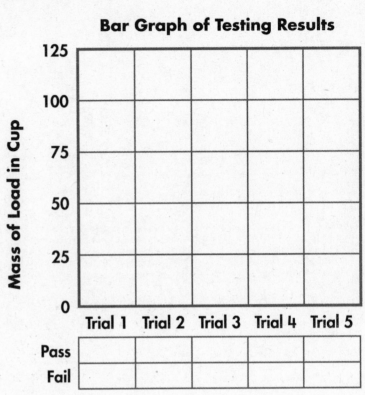

Testing Results

Trial	Load (grams)	Pass or Fail
1	25	
2	50	
3	75	
4	100	
5	125	

Communicate results.

☐ **9.** Which parts of your **design** worked well in your prototype? Use your test results and your **observations** to support your **conclusions.**

....

....

☐ **10.** Which parts of your design could be improved?

....

....

....

Evaluate and redesign.

11. Evaluate what did and did not work in your prototype.
Use what you learned from testing to **redesign** your prototype.

Write or draw your design changes.

....

....

....

....

....

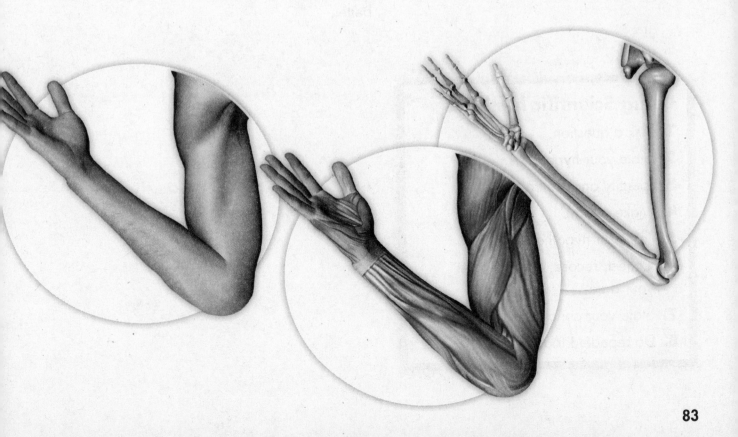

Make a Graph

Test a rubber ball, a table-tennis ball, and a marble to see which bounces the highest. Remember to identify and control all the variables. Measure the height of each bounce. Make a graph of your results. Share your results with your class.

Write a Story

Think of a technology that might be invented in the future. Write a story about how using the technology will affect the lives of people. Describe what the technology will be and what it will do.

Make a Model

Make a model of an animal. Design a way to make the legs, wings, or fins of your model move like the animal you chose. Test how your model works. Redesign your model to make it work better.

Using Scientific Methods

1. Ask a question.
2. State your hypothesis.
3. Identify and control variables.
4. Make a plan.
5. Test your hypothesis.
6. Collect, record, and interpret your data.
7. State your conclusion.
8. Do repeated trials.

Life Science

Is this an INSECT or a FLOWER?

Classifying Organisms

Try It!   How can shells be classified?

Lesson 1   How do we classify living things?

Lesson 2   How do we classify animals?

Lesson 3   How do we classify plants?

Investigate It! How can a key help you identify and classify?

Some kinds of insects, plants, and animals have features that make them look like other living things. These features usually help them.

Predict   What might this be and why might it look the way it does?

....

....

....

THE BIG ?   How are living things organized?

How can shells be classified?

☐ **1. Observe** how the shells are alike and different.

☐ **2. Classify** Sort the shells into groups and label each group.

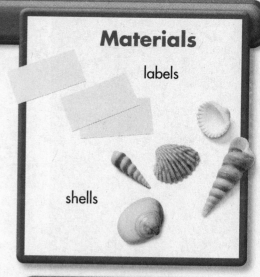

Materials

labels

shells

> **Inquiry Skill** You **classify** objects when you sort them according to properties you observe.

☐ **3. Record** the labels you used.

....

....

....

☐ **4.** Observe how other groups classified their shells. What labels did they use?

....

....

....

Explain Your Results

5. Explain how you approached the task of **classifying** the shells.

....

....

....

....

Main Idea and Details

- The **main idea** is the most important idea in a reading selection.
- Supporting **details** tell more about the main idea.

Citrus Trees

Citrus trees belong to a specific group of plants because they share certain characteristics. They are flowering trees. They produce fruit with thick skin and juicy pulp. They grow well in warm climates. Examples of citrus trees include orange, grapefruit, lemon, and lime.

orange flower

Practice It!

Complete the graphic organizer below to show the main idea and details in the example paragraph.

Main Idea

Detail   **Detail**   **Detail**

How do we classify living things?

Envision It!

Tell another way these fruits could be grouped.

my planet Diary

FunFact

Did you know that there are about 250 types of snakes in the United States? How do scientists keep track of all the different types? They group the snakes by traits that the snakes share. For example, some snakes make venom, a harmful substance. If they bite an animal or person, they can release venom through their fangs that enter the animal or person. Luckily, only about 20 types of snakes in the United States are identified as venomous. The canebrake rattlesnake shown is venomous. The rat snake shown is not.

rat snake

canebrake rattlesnake

Why should snakes be identified as nonvenomous or venomous?

....

....

....

myscienceonLine.com | my planet Diary

UNLOCK THE BIG ?

I will know how to develop
and use a dichotomous
key to classify plants
and animals.

Words to Know

classify   species
kingdom   dichotomous
phylum   key

Reasons to Classify

To **classify** means "to put similar things into groups."
Many types of things can be classified, including
organisms. Scientists use a classification system for
organisms, which makes communicating easier. In this
system, each organism has just one scientific name.
Without this system, scientists might have different names
for the same organism. A classification system also helps
scientists organize information about organisms. This
system helps scientists know a lot about the organism from
its category.

1. ⊙ **Main Idea and Details** Complete the graphic
organizer below. Write details about reasons to classify.

Main Idea

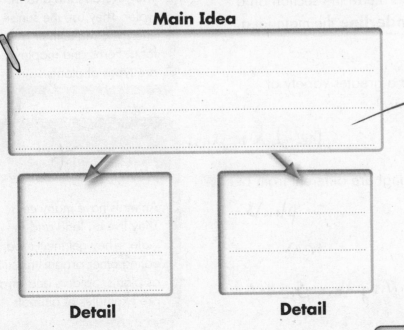

Detail   Detail

2. **Explain** Look at the
animal below. Which name
would you use in a letter
to a scientist? Explain.

....

....

....

....

....

*This animal goes by the
names crayfish, crawfish, or
crawdad. Its scientific name
is Procambarus clarkii.*

A Classification System

A classification system lists organisms in a series of groups. Today's organism classification system has been developed by many people over many years. In fact, it is still changing. The most general group is called a domain. The three domains are Archaea, Bacteria, and Eukarya.

Members of the domain Archaea are single-celled organisms without a nucleus. Some make their own food and live in extreme places. Members of the domain Bacteria are also single-celled organisms without a nucleus. They have materials not found in Archaea. Some bacteria must get their own food. Others make their own food. The cells of organisms in the domain Eukarya all have a nucleus. All multicellular organisms are members of the domain Eukarya. Traditionally, Eukarya are classified into four groups. Each group is called a **kingdom.** The four kingdoms are protists, fungi, plants, and animals.

Within each kingdom, similar organisms are placed into groups. Each group is called a phylum (plural *phyla*). A **phylum** is the next level of classification below kingdom. Each phylum is divided into smaller groups called classes. Classes are divided into smaller and smaller groups, or levels. Below class, the levels are called order, family, genus, and species. A **species** is a group of similar organisms that can mate and produce offspring that can also produce offspring.

3. ◉ **Main Idea and Details** Read the section on a classification system again. **Underline** the main idea. Circle the details.

4. **Interpret** Which would have a greater variety of organisms—a phylum or a family? why?

   phylum, because phylum is the 2nd highest level.

5. **Contrast** What is one way fungi are different from plants?

   Fungi is different from other plants because they absorb food from other living and non living things.

Protists

Protists can be either single-celled or multicellular. They live in water and in moist places on the land. Some must get their food. Others make their own food. Algae are a type of protist.

Fungi

Most fungi are made of many cells. They live on land and absorb food from other living and nonliving things. Mushrooms and yeast are two different types of fungi.

Plants

Plants have tissues and organs made of many cells. They live on land and in water. They use the sun's energy to make their own food. Ferns and maple trees are types of plants.

Animals

Animals have many cells. They live on land and in water. They get their food by eating other organisms such as plants. Spiders and giraffes are examples of animals.

Domain

All these organisms have cells with nuclei. Here you see how the gray wolf is classified at different levels of the classification system. As you go down the levels, the groups get smaller and have less variety of animals.

Animal Kingdom
All these organisms are animals.

Phylum Chordata
All these animals have spinal cords.

Class Mammalia
All these animals give milk to their young.

Order Carnivora
All these animals eat meat.

Family Canidae
All these animals have doglike features.

Genus *Canis*
This level includes all dogs, coyotes, and wolves.

Species *lupus*
This level names a particular kind of wolf, the gray wolf.

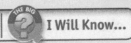

Lightning Lab

Develop a Dichotomous Key

Choose five or six objects from the classroom. Make a dichotomous key that you can use to identify them. How did you decide on different categories in your dichotomous key?

Dichotomous Keys

Scientists use dichotomous keys to help them classify organisms. A **dichotomous key** is a tool used to identify an unknown organism. When you use a dichotomous key, you answer a series of questions about the organism. Each question has two choices. By following the arrow with the correct answer to each question, you can identify the unknown organism.

Use the key to identify the first organism shown. The first question asks if the animal has jointed legs. The animal does. So, follow the arrow with the answer "Yes." The box states that the animal is an arthropod. The next question is about the number of legs the animal has. The animal has eight legs. The arrow with "8 Legs" leads to the box that says that the animal is classified as an arachnid. The final question about the animal appearing furry has the answer "Yes." This path leads to the identity of the animal. It is a ladybird spider.

6. Classify Use the key to classify the other animals. Write the name of each animal below its picture.

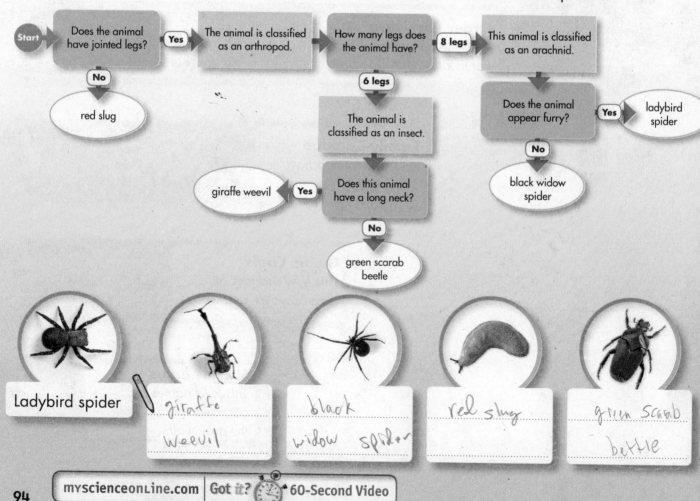

Start → Does the animal have jointed legs? — Yes → The animal is classified as an arthropod. → How many legs does the animal have? — 8 legs → This animal is classified as an arachnid.

No → red slug

6 legs → The animal is classified as an insect.

Does the animal appear furry? — Yes → ladybird spider

No → black widow spider

giraffe weevil ← Yes — Does this animal have a long neck?

No → green scarab beetle

Ladybird spider | *giraffe weevil* | *black widow spider* | *red slug* | *green scarab beetle*

Every key is made to help identify only organisms in a certain area or a certain classification level. Some keys are only for trees. Other keys are only for birds. Dichotomous keys can tell you the scientific names of the organism you identify.

7. [CHALLENGE] The species name for the California sea lion is *Zalophus californianus*. What might this tell you about how some animals get their scientific names?

California sea lion

Got it?

8. **Hypothesize** Why might people long ago have tried classifying living things?

....

....

9. **Infer** What might scientists conclude about an organism that has different characteristics than other organisms?

....

....

☐ **Stop!** I need help with ....

❚❚ **Wait!** I have a question about ....

▶ **Go!** Now I know ....

How do we classify animals?

Describe three characteristics of this animal.

Inquiry **Explore It!**

How can you classify animals without backbones?

☐ **1.** Look at the Animals Without Backbones sheet.

☐ **2.** Compare the characteristics of each animal to the characteristics in the chart.

☐ **3.** **Classify** each animal by its characteristics. Write the name of the animal in the correct row.

Explain Your Results

4. **Communicate** Compare your final chart with the charts of your classmates. Discuss how the charts are alike and different.

....

....

....

....

Materials

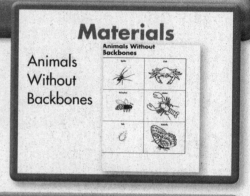

Animals Without Backbones

Characteristics Chart

Number of Legs	Number of Body Sections	Other Features	Names of Animals
6	3	shell to protect its body; jointed legs; may have wings	
8	2	shell to protect its body; jointed legs; no claws	
10	2	shell to protect its body; jointed legs; claws	

UNLOCK
THE BIG
?

I will know that animals can be classified based on their characteristics.

Words to Know

vertebrate
invertebrate

Characteristics of Animals

Animals have certain features that together make them different from other organisms. First, animals are multicellular, or made of more than one cell. Animals are made of trillions of cells. Second, animals cannot make their own food. They must eat other organisms in order to get energy. Third, animals move about during part or all of their lives.

1. **Underline** the features that together identify an organism as an animal.

2. ◎ **Compare and Contrast** How are the animals shown alike? How are they different?

   Similar- animals, multicellular, can't make their own food, Different — One walks, one flys to get around.

At-Home Lab

Classify Animals

With an adult, take a walk in the park or in your yard. Find four or five animals. Then classify the animals by class: fish, amphibian, reptile, bird, or mammal.

Vertebrates

Today, the animal kingdom is divided into more than 30 phyla. Only one phylum, the Chordata, contains organisms with backbones surrounding their spinal cords. An animal that has a backbone is called a **vertebrate.** Backbones protect the spinal cord. The spinal cord carries messages between the brain and the animal's body.

A few animals in the phylum Chordata do not have backbones. Most animals in the phylum are vertebrates. The vertebrate group is divided into five classes. The classes are fish, amphibians, birds, mammals, and reptiles.

3. ◉ **Main Idea and Details** (Circle) the main group of animals in the phylum Chordata. **Underline** the five classes in this group.

Classes of Vertebrates

Fish

Most fish have scales. They live only in water and get oxygen through gills. They are cold-blooded, which means their body temperature changes as the temperature of the water changes. Most fish lay eggs without shells.

Mexican Fire Mouth

Amphibians

Amphibians are covered with soft, moist skin. Like fish, they are cold-blooded. As young, they are like fish. They live in water and get oxygen through gills. As adults, they usually live on land and breathe with lungs. Amphibians usually lay eggs in water.

Spotted Salamander

myscienceonline.com | I Will Know...

Birds

Birds are covered with feathers. They live on land and use lungs to breathe. Birds are warm-blooded, which means their body temperature is nearly the same all the time. All birds have beaks and lay hard-shelled eggs.

brown pelican

Mammals

All mammals have hair or fur. Most live on land, but some live in water. They use lungs to breathe and are warm-blooded. Mammals feed their young with milk produced by the female mammals. Almost all mammals have live births and do not lay eggs.

beaver

Reptiles

Like fish, reptiles have scales. Unlike fish, most reptiles live on land, but some can live in water. They all use lungs to breathe. Reptiles are cold-blooded. The young of most reptiles hatch from leathery-shelled eggs.

box turtle

4. **CHALLENGE** Flying is not a special characteristic of birds. Name two kinds of birds that cannot fly.

    Penguin and chicken

5. **Describe** Why is a turtle not an amphibian?

    They don't lay eggs in water

Invertebrates

Most animals on Earth do not have backbones. An animal without a backbone is called an **invertebrate.** Some invertebrates are too small to be seen without a microscope. The largest invertebrates, giant squids, can easily stretch across the width of a basketball court. Some other kinds of invertebrates are mollusks, worms, and arthropods.

A mollusk has a soft body without bones. This phylum (Mollusca) includes animals such as snails, slugs, clams, and squids. Worms belong in three different phyla. Flatworms are flat and thin. They live in wet or damp places. Roundworms can live in water or on land. Segmented worms include the earthworm. Arthropods is the largest phylum of animals. Arthropods are animals with jointed legs. The word *arthropod* means "jointed feet." Arthropods include insects, lobsters, and spiders. Their bodies are covered in a tough outer skeleton that is divided into separate parts.

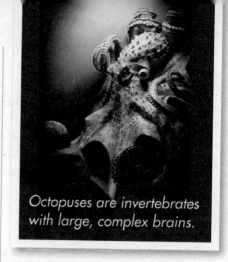

Octopuses are invertebrates with large, complex brains.

6. **Identify** Name an invertebrate that lives on land, one that lives in water, and one that can fly.

worms

octopus

mascito

Do the math!

Calculating Speeds

Some invertebrates are famous for moving slowly. Other invertebrates can move amazingly fast.

1. Some snails move at an average speed of 8 centimeters per hour. At this rate, about how long would the snail take to travel 2 centimeters?

20min

2. Sphinx moths are invertebrates that can fly about 50 kilometers per hour. About how long would it take a sphinx moth to fly 75 kilometers?

75min

sphinx moth

myscienceonline.com | Got it? 60-Second Video

7. Apply Fill in the dichotomous key with the names of the invertebrates shown on the right.

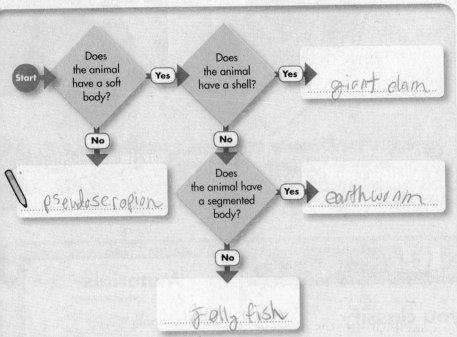

Start → Does the animal have a soft body?
- Yes → Does the animal have a shell?
  - Yes → *giant clam*
  - No → Does the animal have a segmented body?
    - Yes → *earthworm*
    - No → *jellyfish*
- No → *pseudoscorpion*

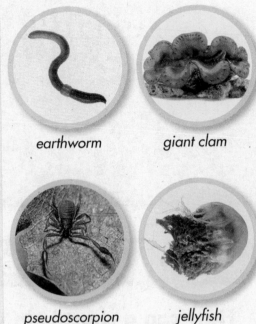

earthworm

giant clam

pseudoscorpion

jellyfish

Got it?

8. Identify An animal has scales and is cold-blooded. It lives in the water. What other information do you need to know before you can classify it?

If it is an invertebrate or a vertebrate.

9. UNLOCK THE BIG ? Think about what you learned in this lesson. How are living things, such as animals, organized?

◻ **Stop!** I need help with

❚❚ **Wait!** I have a question about

▶ **Go!** Now I know

How do we classify plants?

One of these pictures shows a plant. **Circle** the plant. Tell how you decided.

Inquiry Explore It!

How can a chart help you classify living things?

☐ **1. Observe** the six leaves.

Materials

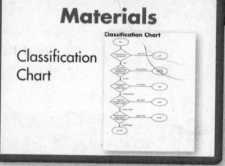

Classification Chart

Leaf A

Leaf B

Leaf C

Leaf D

Leaf E
(This is a single leaf.)

Leaf F

☐ **2. Classify** Pick one leaf. Begin at the top of the Classification Chart. Follow the arrows and answer the questions as you move down the chart until you have identified the leaf. **Record** in the Identification Chart.

☐ **3.** Repeat Step 2 with each leaf.

Explain Your Results

4. Infer Why might a classification chart be useful?

Identification Chart	
Leaf	**Name of Leaf**
A	Maple
B	burroak
C	aspen
D	pine
E	Kentucky coffee tree
F	beech

myscienceonline.com | **Explore It!** Animation

I will know that plants can be classified based on their characteristics.

Word to Know

vascular

Characteristics of Plants

Unlike animals, plants make their own food. Plants use sunlight, water, and carbon dioxide to make sugar for food, and oxygen. Plants have different features too, such as stems, roots, and leaves. Organisms in the plant kingdom are multicellular, just like animals.

Scientists use two main characteristics to classify plants. First, plants are classified as either vascular or not vascular. A **vascular** plant has special tubes for carrying food and water to all its parts. The tubes also strengthen and support the plant. Second, plants are classified according to how they reproduce. Some plants use seeds to reproduce and others do not. Some seed plants use flowers to reproduce.

1. ◉ **Main Idea and Details** Read the second paragraph again. **Underline** the main idea. Circle the supporting details.

2. **Interpret** Is celery a vascular plant? Explain.

yes, because vascular plants have tubes for food and water

This is a magnified slice of the celery stalk.

Vascular and Nonvascular

There are four main groups of plants. They are mosses, ferns, conifers, and flowering plants. They are classified as vascular or nonvascular and by how they reproduce.

3. **CHALLENGE** What advantage does a vascular plant have over a nonvascular plant?

Vascular plants get water without being in it by its tube.

Characteristics of Mosses	
Vascular	no
Seeds	no
Flowers	no

cushion moss

Mosses

Mosses are not vascular plants. They reproduce by forming tiny cells called spores. Mosses do not have seeds or flowers.

Characteristics of Ferns	
Vascular	yes
Seeds	no
Flowers	no

fern fiddlehead

Ferns

Ferns are vascular plants. Like mosses, they reproduce by forming spores. Like mosses, ferns do not have seeds or flowers.

Characteristics of Conifers	
Vascular	yes
Seeds	yes
Flowers	no

California redwood

Conifers

Conifers are vascular plants that do not have flowers. They produce seeds in cones. Seeds may grow into new plants. Most conifers keep their special leaves or needles year-round.

myscienceonLine.com | Got it? 60-Second Video

Characteristics of Flowering Plants	
Vascular	yes
Seeds	yes
Flowers	yes

tulip

Flowering Plants

Flowers are vascular plants. Flowering plants make seeds inside their fruits. The seeds may grow into new plants. Most of the plants you see every day are flowering plants.

4. ⦿ **Compare and Contrast** How are conifers and flowering plants alike? How are they different?

They are both Vascular and have seeds. But Flowering plants have flowers and conifers don't.

Got it?

5. **Classify** How would you classify a plant that is vascular, has leaves, but does not have seeds?

a fERN: Classifing it by a dichotomous Key.

6. **UNLOCK THE BIG ?** Think about what you learned in this lesson. How are plants classified?

By how they look, seena, feel, and smell.

◻ **Stop!** I need help with

⏸ **Wait!** I have a question about

▷ **Go!** Now I know

How can a key help you identify and classify?

Follow a Procedure

☐ 1. **Observe** the shape, color, and skin of several kinds of fruit on the next page. Use the information to complete the chart.

 Be careful! **Do not taste the fruit. Wash your hands when finished.**

☐ 2. Study the steps in the first part of How to Read and Construct Keys. Then follow the steps to identify the fruits.

Materials

watermelon

banana

orange

lemon

apple

How to Read and Construct Keys

Inquiry Skill
Observing objects carefully can help you **classify** them.

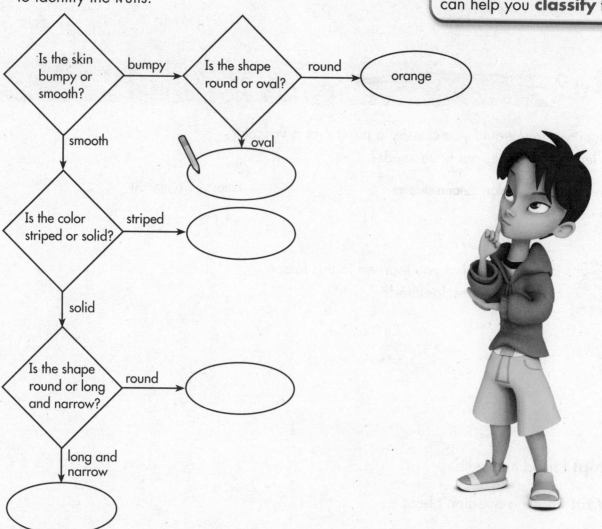

Is the skin bumpy or smooth? → bumpy → Is the shape round or oval? → round → orange

↓ oval → ( )

smooth ↓

Is the color striped or solid? → striped → ( )

solid ↓

Is the shape round or long and narrow? → round → ( )

↓ long and narrow

( )

3. Complete the Fruit Classification Chart. **Classify** the fruits based on your observations.

Apple
shape: round
skin: smooth
color: solid, red

Banana
shape: long, narrow
skin: smooth
color: solid, yellow

Orange
shape: round
skin: bumpy
color: orange

Watermelon
shape: oval
skin: smooth
color: 2-tone striped

Lemon
shape: oval
skin: bumpy
color: solid, yellow

Analyze and Conclude

4. Infer What other characteristics of fruits could be used in a classification chart?

....

....

....

5. How does a classification chart help you identify and organize living things?

....

....

Louisiana Museum of Natural Science

What if you could visit animals from your state and around the world all in one place? The Louisiana Museum of Natural Science in Baton Rouge has a large collection of animals from around the world. In the George H. Lowery Hall of Birds, you will see preserved birds that are found in countries such as Mexico, Belize, and Costa Rica. Birds are classified according to their traits. All birds have wings, feathers, and beaks. Owls are grouped together because they have similar body shapes, short beaks, and sharp talons. Owls, such as the eastern screech owl, barn owl, and short-eared owl, share these traits. They also have traits that are different from each other.

barn owl

short-eared owl

eastern screech owl

Describe What are some advantages of classifying owls?

Vocabulary Smart Cards

classify
kingdom
phylum
species
dichotomous key
vertebrate
invertebrate
vascular

Play a Game!

Cut out the Vocabulary Smart Cards.

Work with a partner. Choose a Vocabulary Smart Card.

Say as many words as you can think of that describe that vocabulary word.

Have your partner guess the word.

species

especie

classify

clasificar

dichotomous key
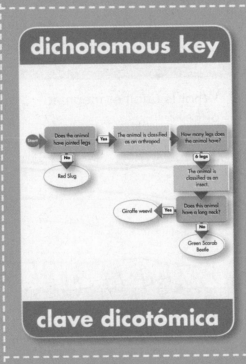
clave dicotómica

kingdom

reino

vertebrate

vertebrado

phylum

filo

put similar things into a group

Write a sentence using this word.

....

....

....

agrupar cosas similares

---

a group of similar organisms that can mate and produce offspring that can also produce offspring

Write an example of this word.

....

....

grupo de organismos parecidos que pueden aparearse y tener crías que a su vez pueden tener crías

---

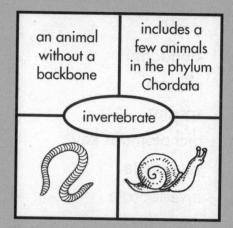

an animal without a backbone

includes a few animals in the phylum Chordata

invertebrate

Make a Word Square!

Choose a vocabulary term and write it in the center of the square. Fill in the squares with descriptions or drawings that relate to the term.

---

the level of classification of living things below domain

Write an example of this word.

....

....

....

nivel de clasificación de los seres vivos que queda por debajo del dominio

---

a tool used to identify organisms

What is another meaning of *key*?

....

....

....

....

método que se usa para identificar organismos

---

the level of classification of living things below kingdom

Write a sentence using the plural form of this word.

....

....

....

nivel de clasificación de los seres vivos que queda por debajo del reino

---

an animal with a backbone

Write three examples of animals with backbones.

....

....

....

....

animal que tiene columna vertebral

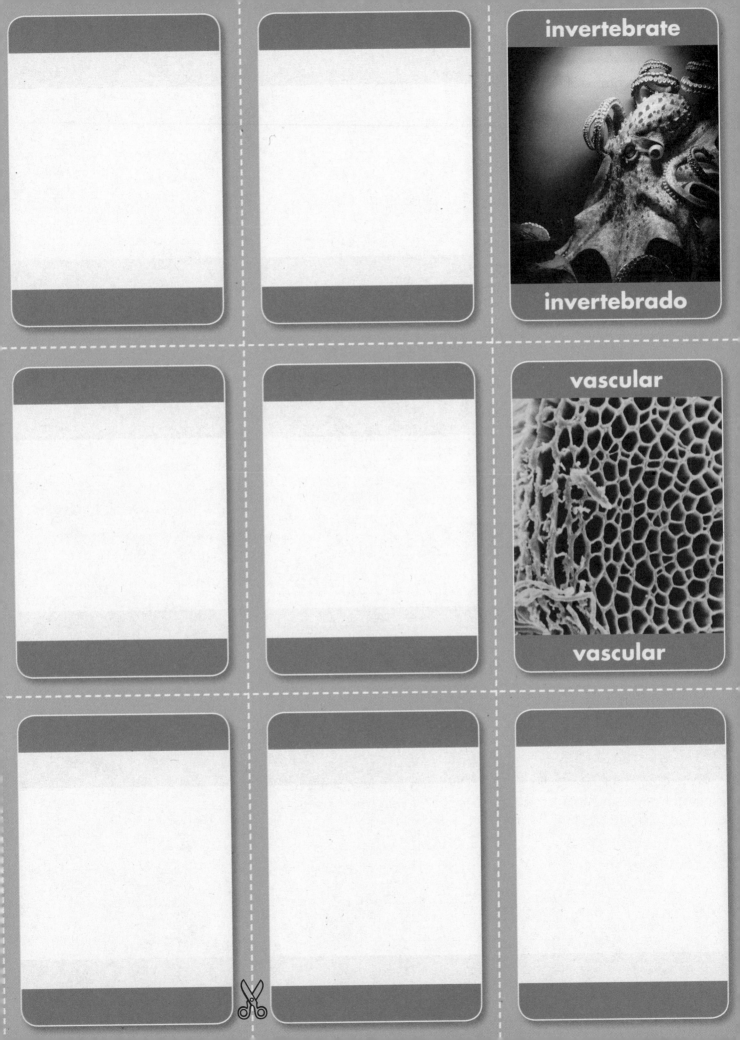

invertebrate

invertebrado

vascular

vascular

an animal without a
backbone

What is the prefix of this
word?

....

....

....

....

animal que no tiene
columna vertebral

---

a type of plant with tubes
that carry food and water
to all parts of the plant

Write a sentence using this
word.

....

....

tipo de planta que tiene
tubos para llevar alimento y
agua a todas las partes de
la planta

Study Guide

REVIEW THE BIG ?

How are living things organized?

Life Science

Lesson 1

How do we classify living things?

- Scientists classify living things into a series of groups: domain, kingdom, phylum, class, order, family, genus, and species.
- Scientists use a dichotomous key to identify organisms.

Lesson 2

How do we classify animals?

- Animals are multicellular organisms that cannot make their own food and move about during part or all of their lives.
- Animals are either vertebrates or invertebrates.

Lesson 3

How do we classify plants?

- Plants are multicellular organisms that make their own food.
- The four main groups of plants are mosses, ferns, conifers, and flowering plants.

Chapter Review

How are living things organized?

Lesson 1

How do we classify living things?

1. **Vocabulary** The smallest level of classification is a _____.
   A. domain
   B. species
   C. kingdom
   D. phylum

2. **Compare** Why are plants and fungi classified in different kingdoms when they have some similar characteristics?

   ....

   ....

   ....

   ....

   ....

3. **Analyze** Explain why scientists use a classification system to organize living things.

   ....

   ....

   ....

   ....

   ....

Lesson 2

How do we classify animals?

4. A horsefly can fly about 24 kilometers per hour. A horse can gallop about 64 kilometers per hour. About how many times slower does a horsefly fly in an hour than a horse gallops in an hour?

5. **Classify** Classify the following animals. Place each animal in its correct class in the chart.

   paddlefish
   Gulf Coast toad
   red wolf
   brown pelican
   leatherback sea turtle

Class	Animal
Mammal	
Reptile	
Bird	
Amphibian	
Fish	

Lesson 3

How do we classify plants?

6. ⊙ **Main Idea and Details**
Underline the main idea and circle the
details in the following paragraph.

Plants and animals are both
multicellular organisms. But plants
have special features that make them
very different from animals. They make
their own food. Plants use sunlight,
water, and carbon dioxide to make
their food. They may also have special
parts, such as stems, roots, and leaves.

7. **Identify** What are the different ways
that plants reproduce?

....

....

8. **Infer** How is being vascular an
advantage to a plant?

....

....

....

....

9. **APPLY THE BIG ?** **How are living things
organized?**

You find a living thing that you have
never seen before in a field. You
know it is not an animal. Write three
questions that you might ask about
the living thing to help you classify
it. Then tell what kingdom you
would put the living thing in. Explain
your choice.

....

....

....

....

....

....

....

....

....

....

Fill in the bubble next to the answer choice you think is correct
for each multiple-choice question.

1 Which of the following animals is
an invertebrate?

Ⓐ rattlesnake
Ⓑ woodpecker
Ⓒ worm
Ⓓ bear

2 What are the levels of classification
from largest to smallest?

Ⓐ kingdom, phylum, class, species
Ⓑ kingdom, class, phylum, species
Ⓒ species, kingdom, phylum, class
Ⓓ species, kingdom, class, phylum

3 Which plant is vascular and produces
both seeds and flowers?

Ⓐ moss
Ⓑ fern
Ⓒ conifer
Ⓓ flowering plant

4 Which best describes an amphibian?

Ⓐ It is cold-blooded and usually lays
its eggs in water.
Ⓑ It is cold-blooded and covered with
scales.
Ⓒ It is warm-blooded and covered
with soft, moist skin.
Ⓓ It is warm-blooded and can live on
land and in the water.

5 Which of the following
is **not** a kingdom?

Ⓐ plants
Ⓑ fungi
Ⓒ mammals
Ⓓ protists

6 How does a dichotomous key help to
identify a plant?

Taxonomist

Imagine you are deep in the rain forest searching for new kinds of plants and animals. You stop when you hear it—a strange peeping sound. You carefully turn over a log, and there it is! You have just discovered a new species of frog! Now, what do you name it?

Taxonomists are scientists who identify and classify organisms. When a new species is found, the taxonomist who found it is allowed to name it. Taxonomists must follow a system of scientific naming that uses two words: the first word is the organism's genus, and the second word is its species. For example, *Acer saccharum* is the scientific name for the sugar maple tree.

To be a taxonomist, a person needs a college degree in biology or a related field. A person must also observe carefully and keep good records. The differences among species are often very slight, so careful records are needed to tell them apart.

Classify Match each animal with its scientific name.

Gopherus polyphemus
Falco peregrinus
Trichechus manatus latirostris

gopher tortoise

peregrine falcon

Florida manatee

WHAT
is this?

Growth and Survival

 Try It!   How can temperature affect seed growth?

Lesson 1   What are some physical structures in living things?

Lesson 2   How do adaptations help plants?

Lesson 3   How do adaptations help animals?

Lesson 4   What are the life cycles of some animals?

Investigate It!   How do seeds grow?

This scaly creature and other species in its family live in warm areas of Asia and Africa.

 Predict   What do you think are some advantages of having scales?

....

....

....

THE BIG ?   How do plants and animals grow and change?

How can temperature affect seed growth?

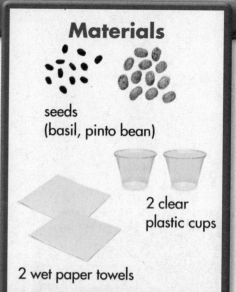

Materials

seeds
(basil, pinto bean)

2 clear
plastic cups

2 wet paper towels

☐ **1.** Choose one type of seed to test.
Use the cups and towels to grow the seeds.

☐ **2.** Put one cup in a refrigerator. Put the other cup in a dark place in your classroom.

☐ **3.** **Predict** how temperature will affect the seeds.

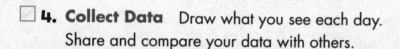

> **Inquiry Skill** You can **collect data** by drawing what you observe.

☐ **4.** **Collect Data** Draw what you see each day.
Share and compare your data with others.

Seed Observations					
Type of Seed					
Temperature	**Day 1**	**Day 2**	**Day 3**	**Day 4**	**Day 5**
Cold					
Room temperature					

Explain Your Results

5. Compare your results with those of other groups.
How did the seeds respond to temperature?
Infer how this response might help a pinto-bean plant respond to changing seasons.

Cause and Effect

- A **cause** is why something happens. An **effect** is what happens.
- When you read, sometimes clue words such as *because* and *since* signal a cause-and-effect relationship.

Jellyfish Blooms

Jellyfish are often found in large groups called "blooms." Since jellyfish are poisonous, jellyfish blooms can be a serious problem. In ocean water near Hawaii and Australia and in the Mediterranean Sea, jellyfish blooms can make the water unsafe for swimmers. Some beaches need to be closed to swimmers until the jellyfish are gone. In other places, such as Ireland, fish farms have been wiped out by jellyfish blooms. Fishing nets can be clogged and damaged by the excessive weight of hundreds of jellyfish.

Practice It!

Use the graphic organizer below to list some causes and effects found in the example paragraph.

Cause

Effect

jellyfish bloom

Lesson 1

What are some physical structures in living things?

Envision It!

The skin of the glass frog is very translucent. **Circle** the parts of the frog's body that you can see through its skin.

MY PLANET DIARY

Connections

When you admire a work of art, what are some of the things you notice? If it is a sculpture, you may notice its shape or form. You may observe the texture of the art. Brightly-colored paintings can catch your attention.

Color and patterns are two properties we use to distinguish items by sight. Birds and other animals use these properties too. Male painted buntings are some of the most vividly colored birds we see in North America. Their colorful patterned feathers are attractive to birdwatchers, and more importantly, to female painted buntings!

A male painted bunting is much brighter than a female.

Explain Why do you think it is important that male painted buntings are brightly colored?

....

....

mYscienceonLine.com | **mY PLANET DiARY**

UNLOCK
THE BIG
?

I will know similarities and differences in the structures and functions of parts of plants and animals.

Word to Know

exoskeleton

Physical Structures

Some trees shed their bark as a normal part of their growth. The tough outer covering of bark peels away so that new tree growth can expand outward. In a similar way, snakes shed their skins as they grow. All living organisms have structures that help them grow, get energy, and stay healthy. Sometimes structures can be very similar even though the organisms are different.

Other times, physical structures can be very different even if they do similar jobs. For example, an animal egg may be very delicate and may need to be hidden from predators. By contrast, many plant seeds have tough coverings and easily survive being swallowed by an animal. The seeds develop inside tasty fruits that animals like to eat. The seeds benefit because an animal can carry them to places where they may grow better.

paperbark maple tree

garter snake

1. ◉ **Cause and Effect** Use the graphic organizer below to list one cause and one effect from the second paragraph of the section above.

Cause

Effect

2. Justify Many stems hold leaves high. Higher leaves are more likely to get sunlight. How is this helpful to a plant?

....

....

The skull is like a strong cage that protects the brain.

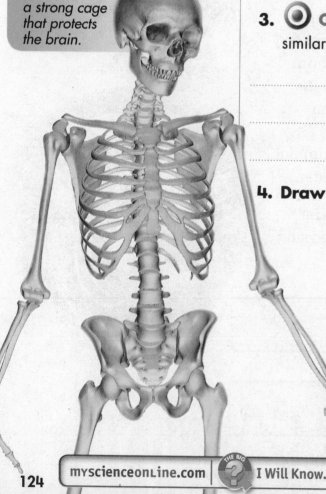

Structures for Support

Some animals, such as fish and humans, have internal skeletons. An internal skeleton supports the body. It also protects organs such as the brain and the heart.

Other animals have **exoskeletons,** which are hard skeletons on the outside of their bodies. Exoskeletons give structure and protection.

Plants have stems that stretch toward the sunlight and can hold the weight of leaves and fruit. Some plants, such as trees, have wood in their stems and branches for additional support.

Insects, such as the cicada, have a hard exoskeleton. In order to grow, insects usually need to shed their old exoskeleton and grow a new one.

3. ◉ Compare and Contrast How is an exoskeleton similar to an internal skeleton? How is it different?

....

....

4. Draw some organs that are protected by the rib cage.

Structures for Reproduction

Living things can make other living things similar to themselves. This process is called reproduction.

Many plants reproduce using flowers. For example, when pollen from a cherry flower is carried to another cherry flower, the receiving flower becomes fertilized. It grows into a cherry with a seed inside. The seed has a source of nutrition and a protective covering. If this seed lands on good soil, a new cherry plant may grow.

Animals reproduce in different ways. For example, some female fish lay eggs on underwater rocks. Then the male fertilizes the eggs. The organism grows inside of the egg, which has a source of nutrition and a protective cover. In other animals, such as mammals, males have structures to fertilize eggs within the body of the female.

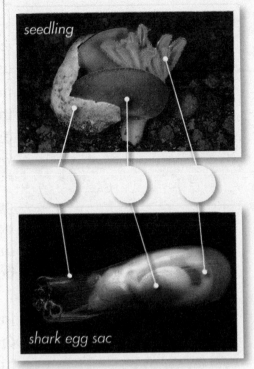

seedling

shark egg sac

5. Diagram Read the steps of Flower Fertilization below. Then, on the flower illustration, (circle) where a seed will develop.

6. Label Write the correct letter in each circle above.

   A organism

   B protective cover

   C nutrition source

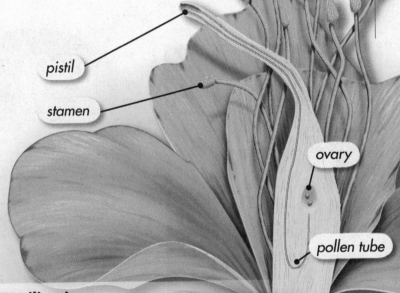

pistil

stamen

ovary

pollen tube

Flower Fertilization

1. Pollen leaves the stamen of a flower.
2. Pollen lands on the pistil of another flower.
3. A pollen tube grows from the pollen grain, and a sperm cell travels down the tube.
4. The sperm cell reaches an egg cell contained in the ovary. Fertilization occurs.
5. The fertilized egg goes on to become a seed.

At-Home Lab

Parts and the Whole
The bones in a skeleton make up a system. A system is a collection of parts that work together. Look at a bicycle. Is it a system? Explain. Think of three other systems that you can find in your home.

7. Draw a picture of one other animal that breathes using lungs and a picture of an animal that breathes with gills. Explain your choices.

Structures for Respiration and Circulation

In order for plants and animals to live, they need to exchange gases with their environments. Animals such as turtles and humans take in air through the mouth or nose and breathe using lungs. Some other animals, such as insects, take air in through structures called spiracles. These are holes in the insect's body. Most fish take in oxygen from water through their gills.

Lungs, spiracles, and gills are three ways animals can get oxygen. A spiracle often allows oxygen to go directly to body tissue. But with lungs and gills, oxygen entering the animal is transported through a circulatory system to the body's cells.

Plants have structures that are similar to spiracles on insects. These microscopic holes are called stomata and are located on the leaves of the plant. The carbon dioxide from the air enters the plant through the stomata. During photosynthesis, a plant uses energy from the sun and carbon dioxide to make sugar, or food. Oxygen is also produced and exits through the stomata.

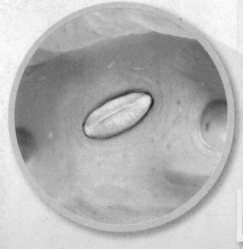

Spiracles on the skin of a caterpillar open up to let gases in or out.

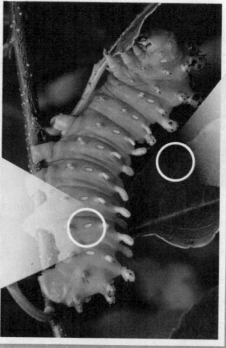

Like the spiracles of insects, stomata on the surface of a leaf open up to let gases in or out.

myscienceonline.com | Got it? 60-Second Video

Some plants also have a circulatory system. These plants are called vascular plants. The tissues in the vascular system act similar to your blood vessels. The plant uses the vascular tissue to transport sugar made in the leaves to the roots for storage.

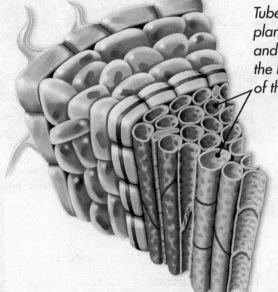

Tube structures within a plant stem transport water and nutrients to and from the leaves, roots, and rest of the plant.

8. Compare Blood travels through your body inside arteries and veins. Compare the function of a plant's vascular system to the function of your arteries and veins.

Got it?

9. Contrast List two structures that have similar functions in plants and animals. How are they different?

10. UNLOCK THE BIG ? What are some structures in plants and animals that serve a similar purpose?

☐ **Stop!** I need help with

⏸ **Wait!** I have a question about

▶ **Go!** Now I know

Lesson 2

How do adaptations help plants?

Envision It!

Write three things you think these plants are getting from their environment.

Inquiry **Explore It!**

How can plants survive in the desert?

☑ **1.** Wet and squeeze out 2 paper towels. Roll up 1 towel. Put the towels on the foil as shown.

☑ **2.** After 1 day unroll the rolled-up towel. **Observe** both towels. Compare. **Record.**

Materials

2 paper towels

plastic container with water

foil

Explain Your Results

3. Infer How does the amount of surface exposed to air affect how fast a leaf loses water?

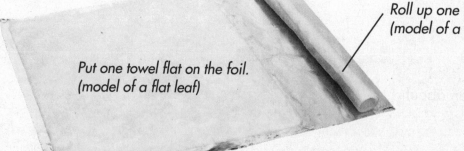

Roll up one towel. (model of a needle-like leaf)

Put one towel flat on the foil. (model of a flat leaf)

myscienceonline.com | **Explore It!** Animation

UNLOCK THE BIG ?

I will know plants can survive in different environments because of adaptations.

Word to Know

adaptation

Plant Adaptations

When an environment changes, plants compete to use the same limited resources, such as sunlight. Plants with the best adaptations are more likely to survive. An **adaptation** is a characteristic that increases an organism's ability to survive and reproduce in its environment. Adaptations do not happen quickly. They develop over many generations.

Plants receive genes from their parents. Genes are instructions that determine how the plant grows. Because of these genes, most characteristics of a plant are the same as in its parents. For example, a plant will have the same type of flowers and leaves as its parents.

However, different combinations of genes may cause a plant to be a bit different. Some plants may be a bit taller than their parents or may have different-colored flowers. A plant may also have a mutation, which is a random change in a gene. A mutated gene may cause a plant to grow roots that are a bit longer than average or to become unable to make wax to protect its leaves.

1. **Infer** How do you think the shape of mangrove roots might help the tree during a storm?

....

....

....

....

This mangrove tree can take in gases through its exposed roots. This adaptation helps it survive in its environment.

Natural Selection

If a mutation helps a plant survive in its environment, that plant will have a better chance to live and reproduce. The plant will pass on its genes to its offspring. If the mutation is harmful to the plant, the plant will be less likely to survive or have offspring.

Over many generations, small mutations can add up to surprising adaptations, such as strong roots or bright flowers. This process is called natural selection. It favors useful mutations and reduces harmful mutations. Natural selection helps species develop adaptations to survive in different environments.

Life-Cycle Variations

The life cycles of plants are adapted to their environments. For example, the seeds of a Venus's-flytrap are programmed to germinate, or sprout, after winter. They will not germinate in an indoor pot unless they have been kept in the refrigerator for several weeks. Some plants, like morning glory vines, take advantage of the warm weather and grow very fast, produce flowers and seeds, and then die before the cold arrives again. Other plants live through the winter but do not produce flowers or seeds until spring.

2. ◉ **Compare and Contrast** Look at the pictures and read the captions on the right. How are the life cycles of the papaya tree and the cherry tree alike and different?

....

....

....

Papaya trees grow in the tropics where the temperature stays more or less the same. They can produce fruit year-round. Each fruit has hundreds of seeds.

Cherry trees grow in regions with cold winters. They produce flowers only in the spring, and the cherries can be harvested in the summer. Each cherry has a single seed.

Physical Characteristics

Changes in the parts of a plant can help it survive in its environment. For example, coconuts are large seeds. If the coconuts from a particular palm tree can float a little better than the average, these coconuts will be more likely to stay afloat when they fall in the water. The floating husk, or outer covering, is a structural adaptation that is helpful when a plant has seeds that are dispersed by water. This type of husk might allow the coconut to travel farther in the ocean than a more dense husk. If the seed travels farther than other seeds, it may have less competition for resources. The seed may then survive and grow into a mature palm tree.

3. **Suggest** Look at the leaves on the plants below. Each leaf is adapted to perform a function. What might be the function of each leaf?

Venus's-flytrap: ....

Prickly pear cactus: ....

Water lily: ....

Coconuts have a lightweight husk that allows them to float for months until they reach a beach where the seed can germinate.

4. ◉ **Cause and Effect** Coconut trees grow in tropical regions. What would be an effect of an ocean current that carried coconuts to colder areas?

....

....

....

....

prickly pear cactus

water lily

Venus's-flytrap

Succession

When an environment changes, communities of organisms in the environment also change. *Succession* is the predictable order of changes in communities after a change occurs. As communities change, conditions might also change. New conditions allow different communities to move into the environment and grow.

In most cases, succession occurs in stages. If conditions are right, bare land might become grassland. Grassland will give way to shrubs. Shrub land will become a forest. Communities grow and replace one another until there is a stable community with few changes.

5. **Sequence** The pictures below show the same lake at different times. Write the numbers 1 through 4 on the pictures to show the sequence of succession at the lake.

This house has been abandoned for several years. Native plants have started to grow in the area around the house.

6. Describe What is an example of succession shown here?

....

....

....

....

Got it?

7. Apply Describe three adaptations that might help a plant survive in a very windy environment.

....

....

8. UNLOCK THE BIG ? Think about what you learned in this lesson. Describe how adaptations can help plants survive.

....

....

Stop! I need help with ....

Wait! I have a question about ....

Go! Now I know ....

How do adaptations help animals?

Envision It!

flying squid

Tell what part of each animal's body you think is adapted for gliding. Explain your answers.

Inquiry Explore It!

Which bird beak can crush seeds?

Materials

4 pieces of straw

2 clothespins

craft sticks

glue

☐ **1. Make a model** of a heron's beak. Glue 2 craft sticks to a clothespin. Use the other clothespin as a model of a cardinal's beak. Use pieces of a straw as models of seeds.

☐ **2.** Use the heron's beak. Pick up a seed. Does the beak crush the seed? Try 5 times. **Record.**

——— ——— ——— ——— ———

☐ **3.** Repeat with the cardinal's beak. Record.

——— ——— ——— ——— ———

Explain Your Results

4. Draw a Conclusion
Which bird crushes seeds?

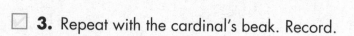

5. There are many seeds in a cardinal's environment. **Infer** how a cardinal's beak helps the cardinal survive.

myscienceonline.com | **Explore It!** Animation

sugar glider

flying dragon

I will know that animals can survive in different environments because of adaptations.

Words to Know

extinct species

Animal Adaptations

When there is a sudden threat, such as an attack by a predator, an animal such as the blue-ringed octopus may respond by changing color. Animals have physical and behavioral adaptations that help them survive by responding to sudden threats. The blue-ringed octopus is usually pale, but when a predator approaches, it turns a bright yellow color with blue rings. Other animals might respond by running, flying, or using poison.

Changes in an environment, such as an increase in the salt content of the oceans over long periods of time, are too slow to affect individual animals. Animal species, like plant species, change over time to adapt to such slow changes in their environment.

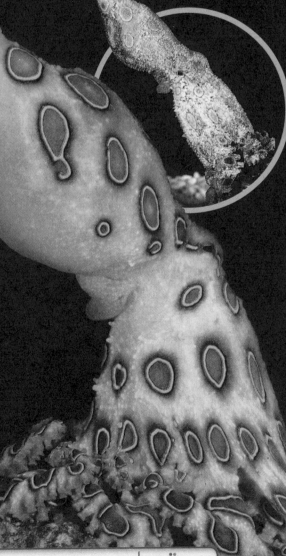

blue-ringed octopus before and after a color change

1. **Infer** Read the adaptations listed in the left column of the chart and write a possible function of the adaptation.

Adaptation	Function
fur	
large eyes	
long legs	

Swimming Birds

With your fingers spread apart, move your hand through a tub full of water. With your fingers still spread apart, wrap plastic around your hand. Move it through the water again. Ducks have webbing on their feet. Infer how this adaptation helps a duck.

2. **Infer** The pictures below show three structural adaptations. Write what you think the purpose of each one is.

Life-Cycle Variations

Different animals have different life cycles that help them survive in their environment. For example, many birds lay their eggs in the spring, when the weather warms up. The young hatchlings then have several months of good weather when food is available. This makes it easier for them to complete their growth.

Physical Characteristics

The body parts of animals have useful physical characteristics that help the animal survive. Useful changes in the body parts of an animal are called structural adaptations. For example, animals that hunt tend to have eyes on the front of their heads. This makes them better at telling how far away their prey is, and they can pounce or swoop with precision. Animals that are hunted often have eyes on the sides of their heads because that helps them see where a predator might be coming from.

Individual animals do not develop structural adaptations. Instead, animal species develop their physical characteristics through the process of natural selection, just as plant species do. Natural selection affects all species of living things.

gecko foot

sea urchin spines

okapi tongue

The process works in animals as it does in plants. If the genes of a bear give the bear thicker fur, the bear is more likely to survive a cold winter. The bear will pass its genes to its offspring, and the offspring will be likely to inherit the useful structural adaptations of their parent.

3. ◉ **Compare and Contrast** What is alike and what is different about the way the two birds below use structural adaptations to find their food?

....

....

....

central shaft ⟶

4. CHALLENGE The large central shaft in a bird's feather is hollow. What advantage might this give to the bird?

....

....

....

....

finch

owl

Extinction

A species cannot survive if it does not adapt to changes or move to a new environment. Some species cannot move to a new environment. For example, plants cannot pull themselves up by the roots and walk to another place. Also, the changes may be so widespread that there is nowhere left to move. If a species does not adapt to harmful changes or move away from them, its population will decrease. When a species has no members left that are alive, it becomes an **extinct species.**

The dodo was a flightless bird that survived well on an island until sailors brought other animals into its environment. The birds could not defend themselves or fly to safety. They became extinct around 1680.

Behavioral Adaptations

Were you born knowing how to build a house? That is impossible! Atlantic ghost crabs, though, are born knowing how to dig deep holes in the sandy beaches where they live. This behavior is due to genes passed from parent to offspring.

Behavioral adaptations are inherited behaviors that help animals survive. Behavioral adaptations are sometimes called instincts. They affect how an animal behaves around other animals. Some animals, like the ghost crab, have an instinct to burrow into the ground to hide from predators, such as shore birds.

Not all behaviors are instincts. Some behaviors are learned by trial and error or as a result of training. For example, lion cubs learn to hunt by watching their parents and other animals. A lion cub learns to pounce on its prey by pouncing on its mother's twitching tail. When a zebra is separated from the herd, the adult lions will chase it toward a group of lions that are hiding. The lions will then pounce on their prey. The cub learns these behaviors over time.

5. **Infer** Why might lion cubs not need to be born knowing how to hunt?

Atlantic ghost crab

Atlantic ghost crab digging a hole

6. ◉ **Compare and Contrast** Write two differences between the digging done by an Atlantic ghost crab and the digging done by a farmer.

lion cubs playing

mYSCIENCEONLINE.com | Got *it?* ⏱ 60-Second Video

Seasonal Changes

In places with cold winters, there is little food for part of the year. Some animals deal with this food shortage by migrating, or moving. In spring and summer, Canada geese live in Canada and the northern United States. They migrate south to escape cold winter weather and to find food.

Another type of seasonal behavior is hibernation. Hibernation is a state of inactivity that occurs in some animals when it gets cold. These animals slow down or become inactive to conserve energy. Some mammals, reptiles, and amphibians hibernate.

7. **Cause and Effect** What effect could less winter snow have on the fur of snowshoe hares over many generations?

The snowshoe hare is brown in the summer and white in the winter. This makes it harder for predators to see it.

Got it?

8. **Hypothesize** Do you think that the speed of a change in the environment might affect whether or not a species becomes extinct? Explain.

9. **UNLOCK THE BIG ?** A hedgehog is a small mammal that is covered with sharp spines for protection. How do the offspring of a hedgehog benefit from this adaptation?

Stop! I need help with

Wait! I have a question about

Go! Now I know

What are the life cycles of some animals?

Envision It!

This butterfly is coming out of its chrysalis. **Tell** why you think a butterfly needs a chrysalis.

Inquiry ▶ **Explore It!**

How do butterflies grow and change?

Over several weeks you will observe the life cycle of a butterfly.

☐ **1. Observe.** Use a hand lens.
Draw what you see.
Use the Butterfly Life Cycle sheet.

☐ **2. Record** your observations when you see a change.
Draw the changes you see on the Butterfly Life Cycle sheet.

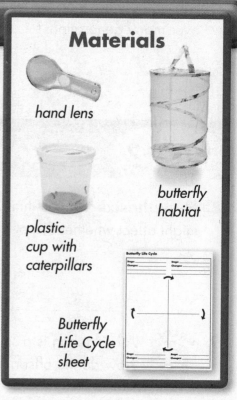

Materials

hand lens

plastic cup with caterpillars

butterfly habitat

Butterfly Life Cycle sheet

Explain Your Results

3. Interpret Data Which stages of the butterfly life cycle did you **observe**? Did you see the complete cycle? Explain.

....

....

....

myscienceonline.com | ▶ **Explore It!** Animation

GLE 4 Design, predict outcomes, and conduct experiments to answer guiding questions (SI-M-A2) (Also **GLE 19** (LA SI-M-A7))

Word to Know

metamorphosis

Metamorphosis

All animals have a life cycle that is a pattern of birth, growth, and death. When many animals are born, they look similar to their parents. Kittens look like small cats. Turtle hatchlings look like tiny turtles. As they grow, they get bigger. But some animals are born looking different from their parents. They develop in a series of stages. They have different forms in each stage. The process of an animal changing form during its life cycle is called **metamorphosis.** Amphibians and insects grow and develop through metamorphosis.

1. ⦿ **Compare and Contrast** Use the graphic organizer to describe how a cat's growth and an insect's growth are alike and different.

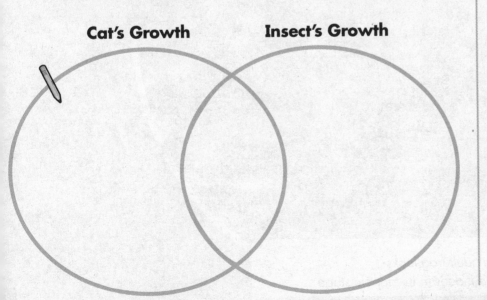

Cat's Growth   Insect's Growth

2. **Identify** Do the young bees shown go through metamorphosis? Explain.

....

....

....

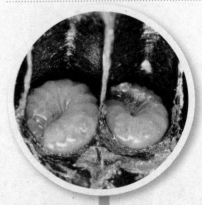

Amphibian Metamorphosis

Frogs, toads, and salamanders develop through metamorphosis. You might be familiar with the stages of the life cycle of a frog. Frogs hatch as tadpoles from eggs laid in water. Tadpoles have gills and a tail. Slowly, the tadpoles grow legs, and their tail shortens. Soon they develop lungs and stop getting oxygen through gills. Then they begin to live on land. As adults, frogs look nothing like they did when they were young.

3. **Describe** How does a frog go through metamorphosis?

....

....

....

5 adult

bullfrog

The adult frog looks .... than it does in its tadpole stage.

142

4. Diagram The diagram numbers stages in a frog's metamorphosis. Fill in the captions to describe each stage.

1 egg

Eggs are laid in

....

2 tadpole

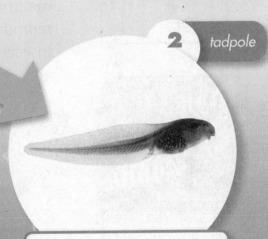

The tadpole has ....
and a tail.

3

The young tadpole grows legs and

its .... shortens.

4

The young tadpole develops
lungs and stops getting oxygen

through its ....

The diagram shows the four stages in a tiger swallowtail butterfly's metamorphosis.

egg

adult

Complete Metamorphosis

Some insects develop in four stages. This type of development is called complete metamorphosis because there is a complete change from one stage to the next stage. An insect begins its development as an egg. The egg develops into a larva. The larva spends its time feeding and growing. It molts, or sheds, its outer covering a few times and then grows into a pupa. The pupa is inactive while many changes happen in its body. Once these changes are finished, the insect breaks out as an adult. It can now reproduce. Butterflies, ants, bees, flies, and beetles are some insects that go through complete metamorphosis.

5. ◉ **Compare and Contrast** How are a larva and a pupa similar? How are they different?

....

....

....

6. **Identify** Label the larva and the pupa in the diagram.

7. **Infer** During its development, a growing butterfly forms a cocoon called a chrysalis. A chrysalis is another name for the pupa of a butterfly. What does the chrysalis provide the growing butterfly?

....

....

mYscienceonLine.com | Got it? ⏱ 60-Second Video

Incomplete Metamorphosis

Insects that have three stages of development go through incomplete metamorphosis. The stages are egg, larva, and adult. In incomplete metamorphosis, the larva is called a nymph. The nymph looks similar to the adult but has no wings. Dragonflies, grasshoppers, and cockroaches go through incomplete metamorphosis.

egg   larva   adult

The diagram shows the three stages in a broad-bodied chaser dragonfly's metamorphosis.

8. Explain Why is a dragonfly's metamorphosis considered incomplete?

....

....

....

....

9. Identify (Circle) a difference you see in the body of a nymph dragonfly and an adult dragonfly.

Got it?

10. Describe How does a frog change during the stages in its metamorphosis?

....

....

11. UNLOCK THE BIG ? How do insects such as butterflies grow and change?

....

....

◻ **Stop!** I need help with ....

❚❚ **Wait!** I have a question about ....

▶ **Go!** Now I know ....

Inquiry Investigate It!

How do seeds grow?

Follow a Procedure

☐ **1.** Fold one paper towel. Place it in a cup. Crumple and push a second towel into the cup. Wet both towels.

Inquiry Skill
Observing a process in the classroom can help you understand what happens when the process occurs in nature.

☐ **2.** Place some bean seeds between the paper towels and the cup.

☐ **3. Observe** the seeds for 5 days.

☐ **4. Record Data** Draw how the seeds look on each day.
Use the chart to record your drawings.

Seed Changes				
Day 1	Day 2	Day 3	Day 4	Day 5

Analyze and Conclude

5. Draw Conclusions How did the seeds change as they grew?

....

....

....

UNLOCK THE BIG ?

6. What made it possible for the seeds to grow?

....

....

....

Zoologist

As a zoologist, your job would be to study animals. Zoologists might study different animal characteristics, such as the behaviors or the needs of animals. Often a zoologist picks a specific type of animal to study. For example, an ichthyologist is a zoologist who studies fish, and an ornithologist is a zoologist who studies birds.

Some zoologists work as zookeepers to help keep animals healthy. Other zoologists might work in museums. Still others work at universities where they might teach or do research in labs.

Among other things, zoologists study animal adaptations to specific environments. A zoologist usually has a degree from a university. If you would like to study animals, the field of zoology might be for you!

If you were a zoologist, what animal behavior would you like to learn about?

_____

_____

_____

_____

An ichthyologist might study the habits of flying fish.

An ornithologist might study the habits of doves.

Vocabulary Smart Cards

exoskeleton
adaptation
extinct species
metamorphosis

Play a Game!

Cut out the Vocabulary Smart Cards.

Work with a partner. Choose a Vocabulary Smart Card. Do not show the word to your partner.

Say clues to help your partner guess what your word is.

Have your partner repeat with another Vocabulary Smart Card.

metamorphosis

metamorfosis

exoskeleton

exoesqueleto

adaptation

adaptación

extinct species

especie extinta

149

a hard skeleton on the outside of the body of some animals

Write the prefix of this word.

....

Write what the prefix means.

....

....

esqueleto duro en el exterior del cuerpo de algunos animales

---

the process of an animal changing form during its life cycle

What is the word root of this word?

....

....

....

proceso en el cual cambia la forma de un animal durante su ciclo de vida

---

a characteristic that increases an organism's ability to survive and reproduce in its environment

Write an example.

....

....

característica que aumenta la capacidad de un organismo de sobrevivir y reproducirse en su medio ambiente

---

....

....

....

....

---

a species that has no more members of its kind alive

Write an example.

....

....

....

....

especie de la que ya no queda vivo ningún miembro

....

....

....

....

Interactive Vocabulary

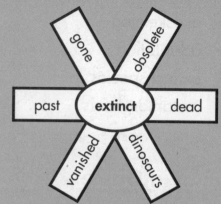

gone obsolete
past **extinct** dead
vanished dinosaurs

Make a Word Wheel!

Choose a vocabulary word and write it in the center of the Word Wheel graphic organizer. Write synonyms or related words on the wheel spokes.

Chapter 4
Study Guide

REVIEW THE BIG ? How do plants and animals grow and change?

Life Science

Lesson 1

What are some physical structures in living things?

- Sometimes the structures of organisms can be similar even though the organisms are different.
- Structures can be different even if they do similar jobs.

Lesson 2

How do adaptations help plants?

- Plants have adaptations to survive in different environments.
- Physical characteristics, such as leaf shape, help plants survive.
- Life cycle variations help plants survive.

Lesson 3

How do adaptations help animals?

- Physical and behavioral adaptations help animals survive.
- A species may become extinct if it cannot adapt to changes.
- Some behavioral characteristics are learned, and others are inherited.

Lesson 4

What are the life cycles of some animals?

- Metamorphosis is the process of an animal changing form during its life cycle.
- The stages of a frog's metamorphosis are egg, tadpole, and adult.

Lesson 1

What are some physical structures in living things?

1. **Vocabulary** A(n) _____ is a hard skeleton on the outside of some animals that gives structure and protection.
   A. internal skeleton
   B. exoskeleton
   C. vascular tissue
   D. system

2. **Compare** How are fish gills similar to plant stomata?

Lesson 2

How do adaptations help plants?

3. **Infer** The apricot tree produces fruit for two to three months out of the year. What can you tell about the climate where apricot trees grow?

Lesson 3

How do adaptations help animals?

4. **Predict** An individual animal may respond to a sudden storm by
   A. developing waterproof feathers.
   B. developing fins.
   C. hiding under a tree.
   D. building a nest.

5. **Justify** Are all behavioral adaptations learned? Explain.

6. Name one physical characteristic of the elephant in the picture below. List three purposes you think it might serve.

Lesson 4

What are the life cycles of some animals?

7. Identify Which stage in a frog's metamorphosis does the picture show?

8. ◉ **Compare and Contrast** How are the stages of complete and incomplete metamorphosis alike and different?

> Insects develop through metamorphosis. Some insects, such as butterflies, grow in four stages: egg, larva, pupa, and adult. Other insects, such as dragonflies, grow in three stages: egg, nymph, and adult.

....
....
....
....

9. **APPLY THE BIG ?** **How do plants and animals grow and change?**

....

A moth is growing inside this cocoon. How does a moth grow and change from egg to adult?

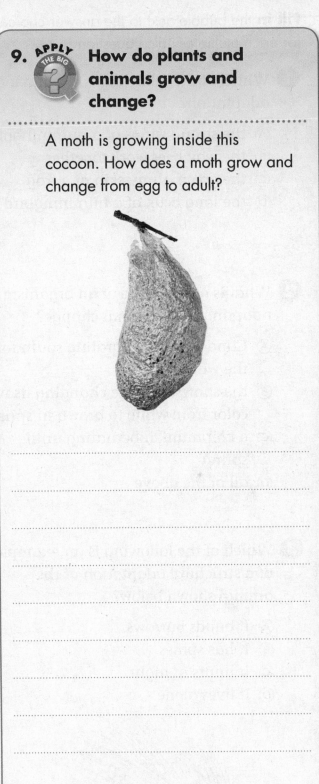

....
....
....
....
....
....
....
....
....

Fill in the bubble next to the answer choice you think is correct for each multiple-choice question.

1 Which of the following is a behavioral adaptation?

Ⓐ the strong wings of a hummingbird
Ⓑ the way bees work together
Ⓒ the green, slimy skin of a frog
Ⓓ the long beak of a hummingbird

2 What is an example of an organism adapting to a seasonal change?

Ⓐ Canada geese migrating south for the winter
Ⓑ the snowshoe hare changing its fur color from white to brown in spring
Ⓒ a chipmunk hibernating until spring
Ⓓ all of the above

3 Which of the following is an example of a structural adaptation of the animal shown below?

Ⓐ It builds burrows.
Ⓑ It has spines.
Ⓒ It hunts at night.
Ⓓ It lives alone.

4 What are the stages in the metamorphosis of a frog?

Ⓐ egg, larva, adult
Ⓑ egg, tadpole, adult
Ⓒ egg, larva, pupa, adult
Ⓓ egg, tadpole, pupa, adult

5 Choose an animal and describe its appearance and behavior. In your description, distinguish between traits that this animal inherited and those that the animal learned.

Charles Darwin

Charles Darwin was born in England in 1809. As a boy, Charles wanted to become a naturalist and study animals, plants, and rocks. When he was 22 years old, he was invited on a long expedition on a ship called the *Beagle*. The *Beagle* took five years to travel around the world, stopping in places such as the Galápagos Islands.

Darwin worked hard collecting animals and plants and trying to understand why there were so many kinds. Twenty years after his trip, Darwin published his most famous work, *On the Origin of Species by Means of Natural Selection*. In this book, he proposed that species can change and adapt to their changing environments over a long time.

Since Darwin's time, many fossil and genetic discoveries have supported his theory. Today, biologists use this theory to answer questions such as how species are related and how germs become resistant to antibiotics.

UNLOCK THE BIG ? We know that climate can change over millions of years. How might Darwin's theory help explain the white fur of polar bears?

These finches have different beaks for eating different kinds of food.

How are these HAIRS like a fence?

Structure and Function

 Try It!   How do parts of the body work together like a system?

Investigate It!   How much air can you exhale?

Some animals, such as cats, have sensitive hairs called whiskers that help them respond to change. The human hairs in this picture are magnified many times. These hairs act like whiskers and can cause a protective reflex.

 Predict   What structure do you think these hairs protect?

....

....

THE BIG ?   How are living things organized?

How do parts of the body work together like a system?

☐ **1.** Follow the directions on each activity card.

☐ **2. Communicate** your results.

Observations of Body Systems

Card	Result
A	
B	
C	
D	

Materials

Card A—Balancing Act
1. Stand with your feet 30 cm apart and your arms down next to your sides.
2. Bend your left knee. Lift your left foot about 10 cm abo
3. Stand next to a w and right shoulde
4. Bend your left kn foot about 10 cm
5. Communicate body worked tog bala

Card B—The Dominant Eye
1. Point to a corner of the room with both eyes open.
2. Keep pointing. Close your right eye. Open it.
3. Did your finger seem to shift away from pointing at the corner? If it did, your right

Card C—Wiggling Fingers
1. Place your hand flat on the table palm up.
2. Lift each finger one at a time and wiggle it.
3. Put wig
4. Ob mo
5. Co ha wig

inger and
n you

Card D—Standing in the Dark
1. Stand on one foot for 1 minute.
2. Close your eyes and stand on one foot for 1 minute.
3. **Communicate** Tell how your eyes worked with your body to help you balance.

Cards A–D

Inquiry Skill
When you communicate your findings, you and others can make sound **inferences.**

Explain Your Results

3. **Infer** Describe how body parts work together like a system.

....

....

....

....

....

◉ Text Features

Text features, such as headings, pictures, and captions, give you clues about what you will read.

A **heading** tells what the page is about.

highlight

A **picture** shows what the reading is about.

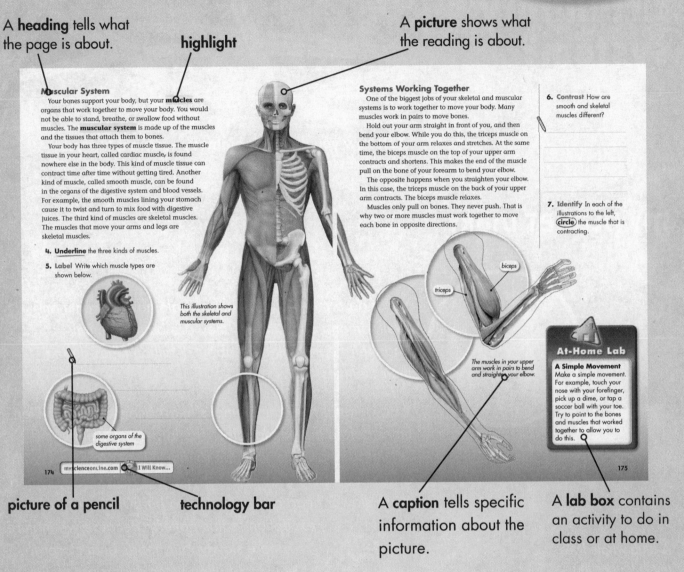

Muscular System

Your bones support your body, but your **muscles** are organs that work together to move your body. You would not be able to stand, breathe, or swallow food without muscles. The **muscular system** is made up of the muscles and the tissues that attach them to bones.

Your body has three types of muscle tissue. The muscle tissue in your heart, called cardiac muscle, is found nowhere else in the body. This kind of muscle tissue can contract time after time without getting tired. Another kind of muscle, called smooth muscle, can be found in the organs of the digestive system and blood vessels. For example, the smooth muscles lining your stomach cause it to twist and turn to mix food with digestive juices. The third kind of muscles are skeletal muscles. The muscles that move your arms and legs are skeletal muscles.

4. Underline the three kinds of muscles.

5. Label Write which muscle types are shown below.

This illustration shows both the skeletal and muscular systems.

some organs of the digestive system

174   myscienceonLine.com   I Will Know...

Systems Working Together

One of the biggest jobs of your skeletal and muscular systems is to work together to move your body. Many muscles work in pairs to move bones.

Hold out your arm straight in front of you, and then bend your elbow. While you do this, the triceps muscle on the bottom of your arm relaxes and stretches. At the same time, the biceps muscle on the top of your upper arm contracts and shortens. This makes the end of the muscle pull on the bone of your forearm to bend your elbow.

The opposite happens when you straighten your elbow. In this case, the triceps muscle on the back of your upper arm contracts. The biceps muscle relaxes.

Muscles only pull on bones. They never push. That is why two or more muscles must work together to move each bone in opposite directions.

biceps

triceps

The muscles in your upper arm work in pairs to bend and straighten your elbow.

6. Contrast How are smooth and skeletal muscles different?

7. Identify In each of the illustrations to the left, (circle) the muscle that is contracting.

At-Home Lab

A Simple Movement
Make a simple movement. For example, touch your nose with your forefinger, pick up a dime, or tap a soccer ball with your toe. Try to point to the bones and muscles that worked together to allow you to do this.

175

picture of a pencil

technology bar

A **caption** tells specific information about the picture.

A **lab box** contains an activity to do in class or at home.

Practice It!

Read the text features in the chart below. Find the text features in the textbook pages shown above. Write a clue each one gives you about the content.

Text feature	What it tells me
yellow highlight	
picture of a pencil	
technology bar	

What is the circulatory system?

Tell how you think this highway system is like your blood vessels.

my PLANET DiARY

Science Stats

What do a mouse and a blue whale have in common? Well, among other things, they are both mammals, and their hearts will beat about 1 billion times during their lifetimes.

As a general rule, a mammal's heart beats about 1 billion times before the animal dies. The larger the animal, the slower its heart rate, and the longer it lives. A mouse, with a fast heart rate, lives about 2 years. A blue whale, with a much slower heart rate, may live to be 80. Humans are an exception to this pattern. Because we mature more slowly, our hearts beat closer to 3 billion times during our lifetimes.

A blue whale lives much longer than a mouse.

Give an Example Name three mammals. Which do you think is more likely to live the longest? Explain.

....

....

....

I will know that the circulatory system moves blood through the body.

Words to Know

tissue	circulatory
organ	system
system	heart

Cells to Organs

The smallest part of your body that is alive is a cell. Cells are the basic units of all living things. The tiniest organisms are made of only single cells. Larger organisms are made of many cells, maybe trillions of them.

Have you ever noticed that teamwork is a great way to get work done? Cells in larger organisms often work together in tissues. A **tissue** is a group of the same kind of cells that work together to do the same job.

Tissues join with other types of tissues to form organs. An **organ** is a group of different tissues that join together into one structure. These tissues work together to do a main job in the body. Your heart, eyes, ears, and stomach are all organs. Organs that work together are called an organ system. A **system** is a set of things that work together as a whole.

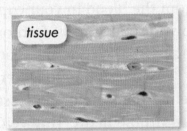

tissue

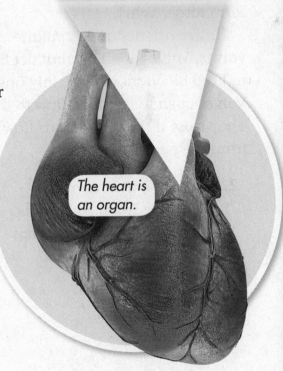

The heart is an organ.

1. ◉ **Text Features** Fill in the chart below. Use the first row as an example.

Text feature	What it tells me
Heading	This section tells how a group of cells form organs.
Highlight	

Circulatory System

The **circulatory system** moves blood through the body. It includes the heart, blood, and blood vessels. Blood vessels are like highways for blood cells. The three kinds of blood vessels are arteries, capillaries, and veins.

Most arteries carry blood with lots of oxygen. Arteries are blood vessels that carry blood away from the heart to other parts of the body. Arteries have thick, muscular walls. These walls stretch as the heart pushes blood through them. Arteries branch many times into smaller and smaller tubes.

The smallest arteries branch to become capillaries. A *capillary* is the smallest kind of blood vessel. Capillary walls are only one-cell thick. Oxygen and nutrients move from the blood in your capillaries through the thin walls to your body's cells. Carbon dioxide and other wastes move from cells to the blood in the capillaries.

Capillaries join together to form your smallest veins. Veins are blood vessels that transport blood toward the heart. Tiny veins join many times to form larger veins.

Unlike arteries and capillaries, veins have valves. Valves are flaps that act like doors to keep blood moving in only one direction. Valves open to let blood flow to the heart. They close if the blood starts flowing away from the heart.

2. Look at the diagram of the circulatory system to the right. (Circle) the organ that pumps blood through your body.

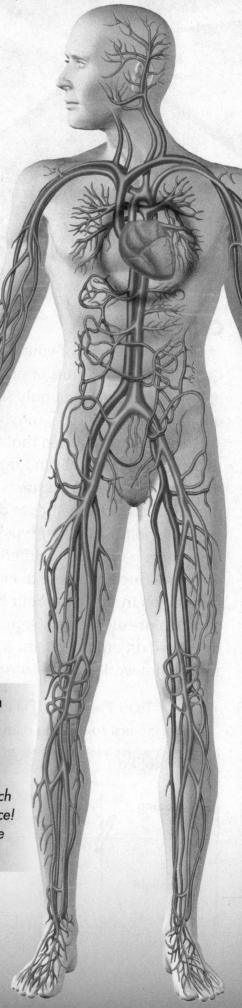

The Circulatory System
Huge numbers of blood vessels form a network throughout your body. If all the blood vessels were laid end to end, they would stretch around Earth more than twice! This picture shows only some of the larger blood vessels.

Veins and Arteries
Veins have thinner walls than arteries but thicker walls than capillaries.

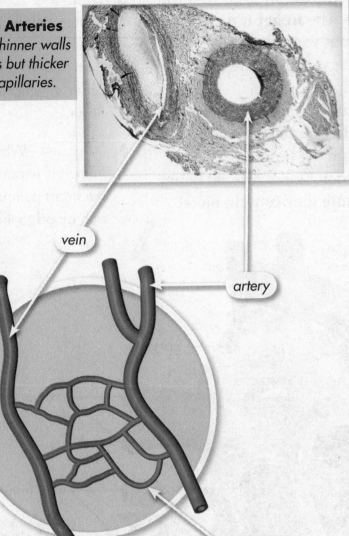

vein

artery

capillary

Capillaries
Side by side, ten capillaries would be barely as thick as one hair! Some capillaries are so narrow that red blood cells must flow through them in a single-file line.

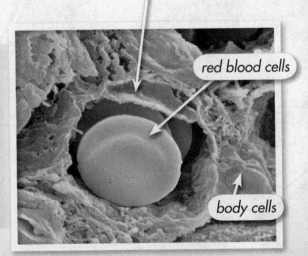

red blood cells

body cells

3. **Compare and Contrast** How are the jobs of a vein and an artery the same? How are they different?

....

....

....

....

....

4. **Interpret** Your body has about ten billion capillaries. Write this number in standard form.

....

At-Home Lab

Read the Label
Read the food labels on a variety of foods. Foods contain fats. Too much fat may clog your arteries. Record the fat content of each food. Compare. What surprised you? How could you reduce the amount of fat in your diet?

Parts of the Heart

Your heart began pumping before your were born. It will keep pumping as long as you live. The **heart** is a muscular organ that pumps blood throughout your body. The right and left atria and the right and left ventricles are the four chambers of the heart.

Usually, illustrations of the circulatory system show most veins colored blue and most arteries colored red. In this drawing of the heart, the veins from the lungs are colored red because they contain oxygen-rich blood. Arteries going to the lungs are colored blue because they contain blood with less oxygen.

5. **Describe** Look at the picture below. Label the chambers of the heart from 1 to 4 to show the order in which blood flows.

6. [CHALLENGE] Why do you think it is important that the heart pumps oxygen-rich blood to the body?

Right Atrium

The right atrium relaxes and fills with blood carrying wastes and carbon dioxide from body cells. Then it contracts, squeezing blood into the right ventricle.

aorta

arteries to lungs

veins from lungs

veins from lungs

Left Atrium

Blood flows from the lungs into the left atrium. The left atrium squeezes blood into the left ventricle.

Right Ventricle

The right ventricle contracts, pumping blood into an artery leading to the lungs, where it can exchange carbon dioxide for oxygen.

Left Ventricle

The left ventricle pumps oxygen-rich blood away from the heart into your body's largest artery, called the aorta. From there, smaller arteries branch off as blood rushes to the body's cells.

aorta to the body

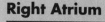

Blood Flow Through the Heart

Your heart is divided into right and left sides. Each side of the heart works as a separate pump and sends blood along different paths. Blood enters the heart in the right atrium. Next, it flows to the right ventricle. The right ventricle pumps blood to the lungs. In the lungs, the blood gets oxygen and gets rid of carbon dioxide. Then, blood returns from the lungs and flows into the left atrium. Finally, blood flows to the left ventricle. The left ventricle pumps the oxygen-rich blood through arteries to the entire body.

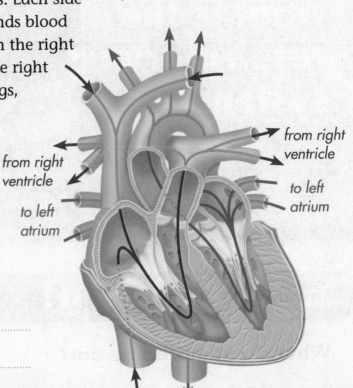

from right ventricle

to left atrium

from right ventricle

to left atrium

7. ● **Text Features** Write a caption to tell about the picture of the heart.

_____

_____

_____

Got it?

8. **Summarize** What is the main organ of the circulatory system? What is its function?

....

9. **UNLOCK THE BIG ?** Tell the order of vessels a blood cell travels through starting from the heart.

....

....

⬛ **Stop!** I need help with ....

❚❚ **Wait!** I have a question about ....

▶ **Go!** Now I know ....

Lesson 2

What is the respiratory system?

Envision It!

Tell how this man is using his respiratory system.

Inquiry **Explore It!**

What do you breathe out?

Water with BTB will change from blue to pale yellow if carbon dioxide is added.

☐ **1.** Fill a cup $\frac{1}{3}$ full of water with BTB. Cover it with plastic. Push a straw through the plastic.

☐ **2.** Gently breathe OUT through the straw into the water. **Observe.**

Materials

safety goggles

2 plastic cups

straw

plastic wrap

water with BTB

Be careful! Wear safety goggles.
Do not drink the BTB water.
Use the straws to breathe OUT only.
Do not share straws.

Explain Your Results

3. Infer Was there carbon dioxide in the air you breathed out? Explain using your **observations.**

....

....

....

....

I will know that the respiratory system is made up of the lungs and other structures. Blood moves oxygen through the body.

Words to Know

respiratory   lungs
  system   trachea
diaphragm

The Respiratory System

Take a long, slow breath. Can you feel your respiratory system at work? The **respiratory system** is the system of the body that helps you breathe. You take in air through your nose and mouth. Several muscles work together when you breathe. When you inhale, a dome-shaped muscle called the **diaphragm** moves down, making more space in your chest for air. Your rib muscles may also pull your rib cage up and out, making still more space. Air quickly rushes into your lungs and fills the space. The **lungs** are organs that help the body exchange oxygen and carbon dioxide with the air outside the body. When you exhale, your diaphragm and rib muscles relax, move up, and push air out of the lungs.

1. **Identify Underline** two ways that your chest makes room for the air you breathe.

2. **Label** Complete the captions on the diagrams to the right.

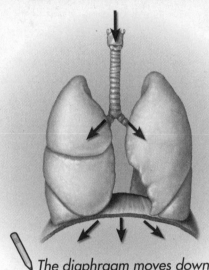

The diaphragm moves down when you ....

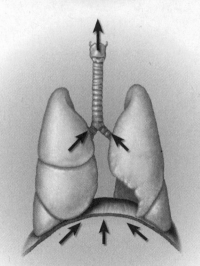

The diaphragm moves up when you ....

Breathe It In
Slouch forward in your chair. Take a deep breath and then exhale. Now sit up straight. Take a deep breath and then exhale. In which position could you take a deeper breath? Explain.

Parts of the Respiratory System

When you breathe, air comes in through your nose or mouth. Hairs and a layer of mucus in the nose trap dust, germs, and other things that may be in the air. Mucus is a sticky, thick fluid. Many parts of the respiratory system are coated with mucus.

From the nose, air passes through the nasal cavities. The nasal cavities warm and moisten the air. Then, the air moves to the back of the throat and into the larynx. The larynx contains the vocal cords, where the voice is produced. The sound of your voice is the result of your breath making the vocal cords vibrate. When muscles stretch the vocal cords tighter, your voice gets a higher pitch.

From the larynx, a tube called the **trachea** carries air to the lungs. The trachea leads to two branches called bronchi that go into the lungs. In the lungs, the bronchi branch into smaller and smaller tubes called bronchioles. Asthma is a disease in which these tubes may become swollen. This keeps air from moving easily through the lungs.

The bronchioles end in clusters of tiny, thin-walled air sacs in the lungs. The air sacs are where oxygen enters the blood and carbon dioxide leaves the blood.

3. ◉ **Sequence** List the parts of the respiratory system the air passes through.

....

....

4. CHALLENGE Your left lung is smaller than your right lung. Why do you think this is so?

....

....

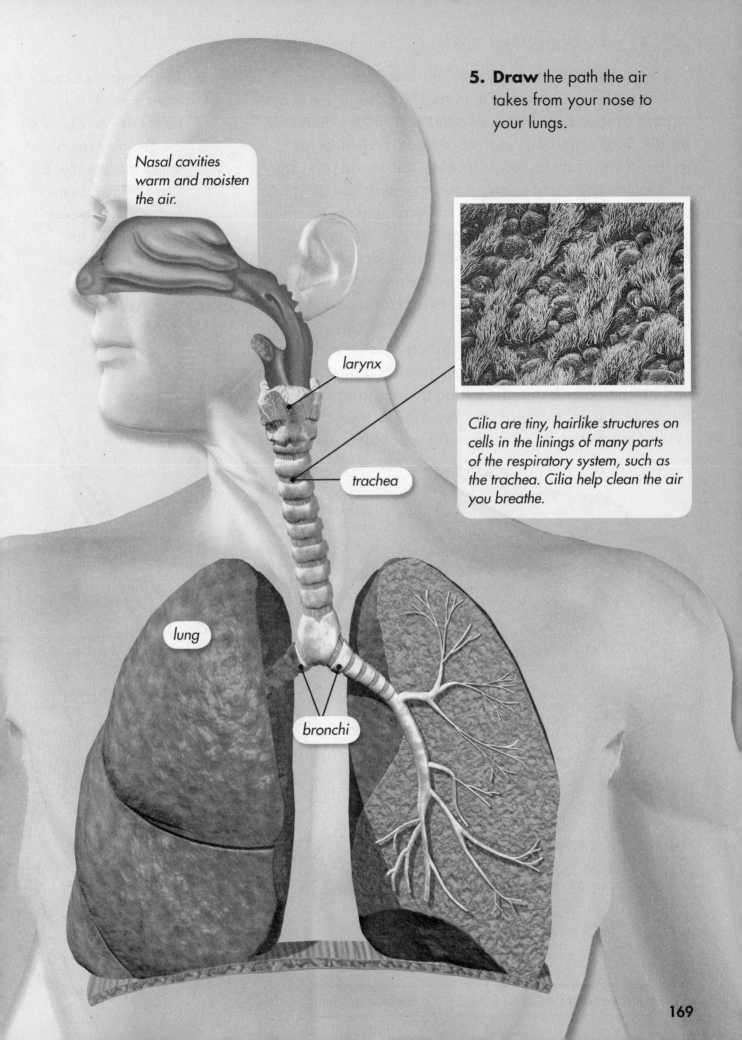

5. Draw the path the air takes from your nose to your lungs.

Nasal cavities warm and moisten the air.

larynx

trachea

Cilia are tiny, hairlike structures on cells in the linings of many parts of the respiratory system, such as the trachea. Cilia help clean the air you breathe.

lung

bronchi

169

Getting Oxygen to Cells

All of your cells need oxygen. You have a respiratory system and a circulatory system that work together to get oxygen to your cells. Oxygen enters your body when you inhale. Your respiratory system gets the oxygen as far as the tiny air sacs inside your chest. The blood picks up the oxygen there and carries it to your heart, where it is pumped to all of your cells—all the way down to your toes!

Two things happen at the same time in the air sacs. Oxygen leaves the lungs and enters the blood. Carbon dioxide moves the other way. It leaves the blood and enters the lungs. When you exhale, the extra carbon dioxide leaves your body.

When you hold your breath, carbon dioxide builds up in your blood. Your brain senses this. It sends a message to the diaphragm and rib muscles telling them to contract. As a result, your chest expands and you inhale. Several systems of your body work together to make sure your cells get oxygen.

6. **Diagram** As blood flows through the capillaries on air sacs, oxygen from the air enters into the blood. Draw arrows on the red and blue blood vessels below to show the direction of blood flow.

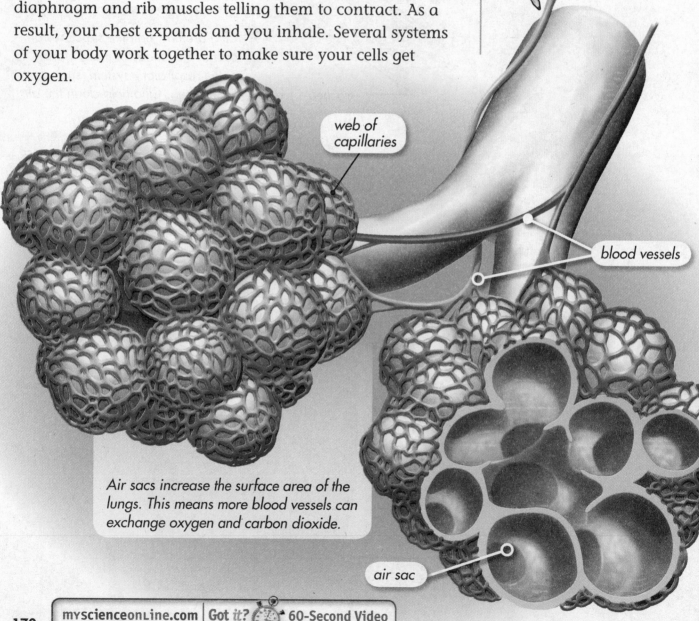

web of capillaries

blood vessels

Air sacs increase the surface area of the lungs. This means more blood vessels can exchange oxygen and carbon dioxide.

air sac

myscienceonline.com | Got it? | 60-Second Video

Surface Area

The air sacs in your lungs have a large surface area. Surface area is the measure of the area on the outside of a shape. Look at the pictures of the blocks. The first picture shows the blocks placed together in a cube. The second shows the blocks separately.

At first glance, it may seem like the surface area would be the same whether the blocks were placed together or they were separated. Let's find out if that is true.

1cm

1cm

 1 Find the surface area of the cube.

Find the surface area of all the blocks after they have been separated.

2 Was there a difference in the surface areas? Explain why you think that is true.

Got it?

7. **Summarize** What is the main organ of the respiratory system? What is its function?

8. **UNLOCK THE BIG ?** What is the order of structures that oxygen passes through between your nose and your bloodstream?

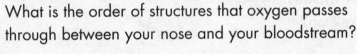

Stop! I need help with

Wait! I have a question about

Go! Now I know

What are the skeletal and muscular systems?

Envision It!

Tell how this structure works.

Inquiry Explore It!

How do the parts of the skeletal system fit together?

- ☐ 1. **Make a Model** Cut out each part from the Human Skeletal System. Put each part in the correct position.

- ☑ 2. Glue each part in place. Label the parts you know.

Materials

Human Skeletal System

Human Skeletal System

glue

paper

scissors

Explain Your Results

3. **Communicate** How is your **model** alike and different from a real human skeleton?

....

....

....

....

4. How do you think your skeletal system helps you?

....

....

myscienceonline.com | Explore It! Animation

Words to Know

skeletal system
skeleton
muscles
muscular system

Skeletal System

Think about what your body would be like without any
bones. How would you move? What would you look like?
Each of your bones is an organ. Your **skeletal system** is
made up of bones that support your body and help you
move. Different kinds of bones perform different functions.

Bones have several functions. Your **skeleton** is made
up of all the bones in your body. It supports your body
and gives you height. Bones of the skull, rib cage, and
back protect important organs. Some bones form new
blood cells. Bones also store minerals, such as calcium
and phosphorus. Small amounts of stored minerals
are released when the body needs them. These
same minerals make bones hard and strong.

1. **Underline** three functions of bones.

2. CHALLENGE Why do you think it is important that
   you have so many bones in your skeleton?

   ....

   ....

   ....

3. **Identify** Look at the skeleton. Circle some bones
   that protect organs such as the heart and lungs.

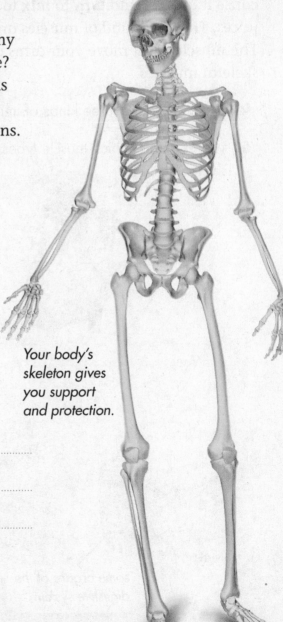

*Your body's
skeleton gives
you support
and protection.*

Muscular System

Your bones support your body, but your **muscles** are organs that work together to move your body. You would not be able to stand, breathe, or swallow food without muscles. The **muscular system** is made up of the muscles and the tissues that attach them to bones.

Your body has three types of muscle tissue. The muscle tissue in your heart, called cardiac muscle, is found nowhere else in the body. This kind of muscle tissue can contract time after time without getting tired. Another kind of muscle, called smooth muscle, can be found in the organs of the digestive system and blood vessels. For example, the smooth muscles lining your stomach cause it to twist and turn to mix food with digestive juices. The third kind of muscles are skeletal muscles. The muscles that move your arms and legs are skeletal muscles.

4. **Underline** the three kinds of muscles.

5. **Label** Write which muscle types are shown below.

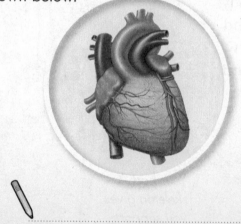

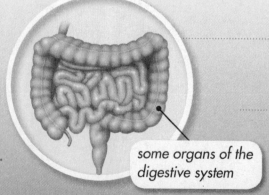

some organs of the digestive system

This illustration shows both the skeletal and muscular systems.

mYscienceonLine.com THE BIG ? | I Will Know...

Systems Working Together

One of the biggest jobs of your skeletal and muscular systems is to work together to move your body. Many muscles work in pairs to move bones.

Hold out your arm straight in front of you, and then bend your elbow. While you do this, the triceps muscle on the bottom of your arm relaxes and stretches. At the same time, the biceps muscle on the top of your upper arm contracts and shortens. This makes the end of the muscle pull on the bone of your forearm to bend your elbow.

The opposite happens when you straighten your elbow. In this case, the triceps muscle on the back of your upper arm contracts. The biceps muscle relaxes.

Muscles only pull on bones. They never push. That is why two or more muscles must work together to move each bone in opposite directions.

6. Contrast How are smooth and skeletal muscles different?

....

....

....

....

7. Identify In each of the illustrations to the left, (circle) the muscle that is contracting.

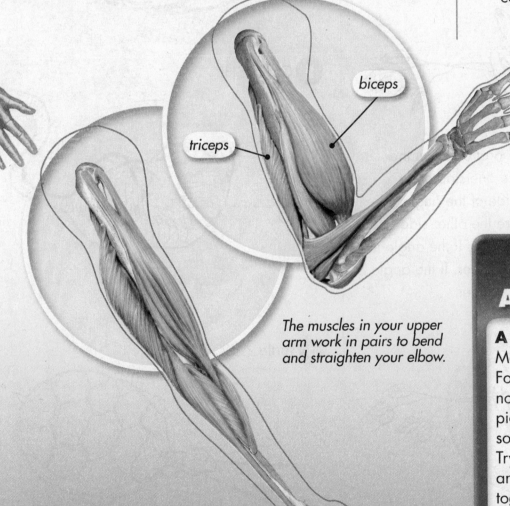

biceps

triceps

The muscles in your upper arm work in pairs to bend and straighten your elbow.

At-Home Lab

A Simple Movement
Make a simple movement. For example, touch your nose with your forefinger, pick up a dime, or tap a soccer ball with your toe. Try to point to the bones and muscles that worked together to allow you to do this.

175

Measuring Angles

You can use a protractor to measure angles. Angles are measured in degrees. The symbol ° indicates degrees. An angle that is less than 90° is acute. An angle that is greater than 90° is obtuse.

Example

An owl's neck has a greater range of motion than a human's neck. You can see the range of motion by looking down on an animal's head. Use your protractor to measure ∠ABC.

Place the center of the protractor on the angle's vertex, B. Place one side of the bottom edge on one side of the angle. Read the number where the other side of the angle crosses the protractor. If the angle is acute, use the smaller number. If the angle is obtuse, use the larger number.

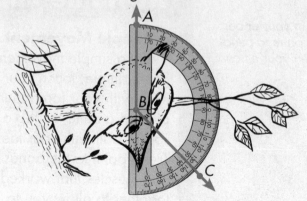

The measure of ∠ABC is 135°.

Measure the angles below. Tell whether the angle is acute or obtuse.

1 Human ∠DEF

....

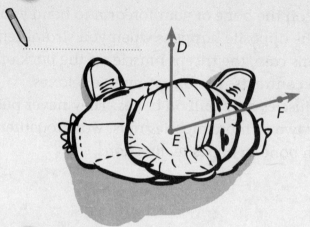

2 Cat ∠GHI

....

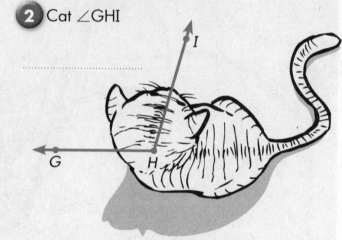

3 Turtle ∠JKL

....

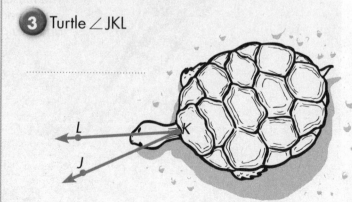

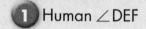

myscienceonline.com | Got it? | 60-Second Video

Muscle- and Bone-Building Materials

Your muscles are very strong. However, they can become injured or develop other problems. It is important to protect your muscles against overworking or overstretching. Healthful foods such as fruit and pasta provide your muscles with energy they need to do work.

Bones grow while you are young. As you get older, your bones may be more likely to weaken. Foods such as milk and spinach contain calcium that helps your bones grow and stay strong. Rest and exercise are important to keep both muscles and bones healthy.

8. **Suggest** Make a list of at least three things you do to keep your bones and muscles healthy.

....

....

....

Got it?

9. **UNLOCK THE BIG ?** **Summarize** What are the main organs of the skeletal and muscular systems? What are their functions?

....

....

....

10. **Clarify** How do muscles work in pairs to move a bone?

....

....

....

⬛ **Stop!** I need help with ....

⏸ **Wait!** I have a question about ....

▶ **Go!** Now I know ....

Lesson 4

What is the nervous system?

Circle the square that you think is darker. Then cover all the other squares with paper. Is your answer the same?

Inquiry **Explore It!**

What is your reaction time?

☐ **1.** Hold out your hand, slightly open. Have a partner hold a meterstick so that the end is even with your thumb.

☑ **2.** Watch the meterstick.
As soon as your partner lets go of it, catch it.

☑ **3.** Read the number closest to the top of your thumb. On the Reaction Time Bar Graph, color in the bar for Trial 1 to **record** your data.

☑ **4.** Repeat 9 more times.

Explain Your Results

5. Compare your results to other groups' results.

....

....

6. Infer Based on your data, how does practice affect reaction time?

....

Materials

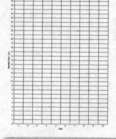

meterstick

Reaction Time Bar Graph

Reaction Time Bar Graph

You use the number of centimeters as a simple way to measure reaction time.

UNLOCK THE BIG ?

I will know that the nervous system includes the brain, spinal cord, nerves, and sense organs. It tells your body how to react to its environment.

Words to Know

nervous system
brain

Nervous System

In order to stay healthy, comfortable, and safe, your body needs information about your environment. It needs to know whether it is too cold or too hot, whether you are sitting down or standing up, and whether or not something hurts. Your body also needs to react appropriately, based on this information. Maybe you need to walk faster because you saw a bicycle heading your way. Or maybe you decide to eat because you are feeling hungry.

The system that receives information from your environment and controls how you react to it is the nervous system. The **nervous system** tells you what is going on in the world around you. It also tells your muscles how to contract to move the bones of your body. The nervous system includes nerves, the spinal cord, the brain, and sense organs.

1. **List** What are some different ways the juggler is using his body systems?

....

....

....

....

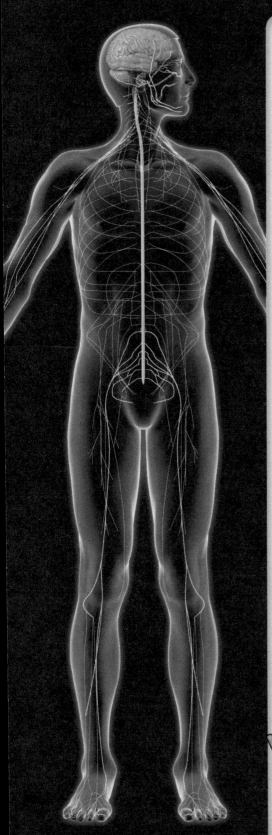

The nervous system is a system of structures that send information throughout the body.

Nerves

Nerve cells are also called neurons. Neurons pass messages throughout your body. Neurons are made of three parts: a cell body, an axon, and one or more dendrites. The cell body is the main part of the neuron. Dendrites receive messages from other neurons. The axon sends messages from the cell body to other neurons.

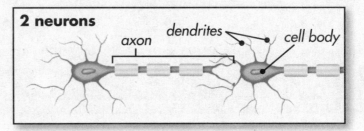

Messages can only travel in one direction between neurons. Most messages travel along neurons to the brain, which controls almost everything you experience and do. The brain interprets the message and responds by sending messages through neurons to different parts of the body telling them to act.

2. **Analyze** Draw an arrow on the neuron showing the direction a message travels through the axon.

Spinal Cord

Another important part of your nervous system is your spinal cord. Messages received and sent by the brain pass through your spinal cord. This long bundle of nerves runs down your back and is protected by your backbone. Parts of the spinal cord carry messages to the brain. Others carry messages from the brain.

3. **Describe** What is the function of the spinal cord?

....

....

....

Brain Functions

Performing tasks, such as remembering, pretending, and feeling, are functions of the brain. So are running, playing games, and listening to music. The **brain** is the main organ, or control center, of the nervous system.

Your brain is made up of three major parts. The largest part of your brain is the cerebrum. This part of your brain learns, reasons, decides, stores memories, and feels fear and joy. Another part of your brain is the cerebellum. The cerebellum controls balance and posture. A third part of your brain is the brain stem. Your brain stem controls your blood pressure, heartbeat, breathing, and digestion.

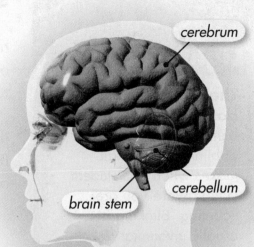

cerebrum

cerebellum

brain stem

4. **Analyze** If a person has a head injury and the cerebellum is damaged, what might the consequences be?

....

....

Voluntary Actions

A major function of your nervous system is to control voluntary actions. Voluntary actions are actions you decide to do, such as chewing, walking, or talking. The part of your brain that controls voluntary actions is the cerebrum.

Involuntary Actions

Another major function of your nervous system is to control involuntary actions. You do not need to think about starting and stopping involuntary actions. Your brain stem controls some involuntary actions, such as the beating of your heart.

Some messages that the body receives do not pass to the brain at all. One example is the response of your body when you touch your hand to a hot surface. The response to that action is a reflex, a response that happens automatically without the brain "thinking" about it.

5. **Hypothesize** Why are reflexes important?

....

....

6. **Fill in** the captions with the correct type of action.

Kicking a ball is a(n)

.... *action.*

Sneezing is a(n)

.... *action.*

Senses and Sense Organs

You walk outside. The smell of freshly cut grass fills the air. A cool breeze blows against your forehead. The sound of birds singing echoes through the air. You use your senses to know what is happening around you.

The nervous system is constantly collecting information both inside and outside your body. It allows you to speak, think, taste, hear, and see. It helps the body stay balanced by processing and responding to the information it receives.

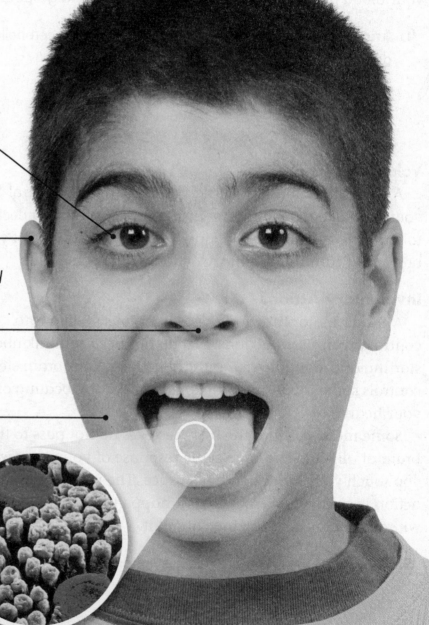

Sight *The eyes have parts that sense light and send signals to the brain.*

Hearing and Balance *Ears have sensors that detect vibrations in sound waves. They also have sensors that help you control your balance.*

Smell *Sense organs in the nose respond to chemicals in odors. Impulses from these organs are read by the brain.*

Touch *Special sensors in the skin help you feel texture, changes in temperature, and sometimes pain.*

Taste *Taste buds are small sense organs located on the tongue.*

myscienceonline.com | Got it? | 60-Second Video

7. Describe Your alarm clock rings. Name the senses that are used while turning your alarm off. Tell how each of these senses helps you turn the alarm off.

....

....

....

8. CHALLENGE Why is it that sometimes it takes longer to go through the steps of turning off your alarm?

....

....

....

Got it?

9. UNLOCK THE BIG ? **Group** What three main parts make up the nervous system? What are their functions?

....

....

10. Contrast How are the three parts of the brain different?

....

....

....

....

⬜ **Stop!** I need help with ....

⏸ **Wait!** I have a question about ....

▶ **Go!** Now I know ....

What are some other systems?

Tell how this kitchen tool is similar to your digestive system.

Inquiry Explore It!

What can speed digestion?

☐ **1.** Place a sugar cube in a bag. Gently crush it with your foot.

☐ **2.** Fill two cups about ½ full with water.

☐ **3.** Drop a whole sugar cube in one cup. Stir it with a spoon until dissolved. **Record** how long it takes to dissolve. ....

☐ **4.** Repeat Step 3 with the crushed cube in the other cup. Record how long it takes to dissolve. ....

Explain Your Results

5. Compare the dissolving times of both cups.

....

....

6. **Infer** how the size of pieces of food might affect digestion time.

....

....

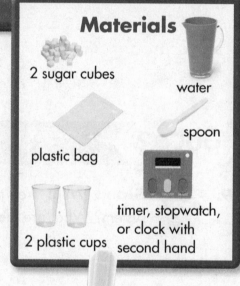

Materials

2 sugar cubes

water

spoon

plastic bag

2 plastic cups

timer, stopwatch, or clock with second hand

myscienceonline.com | **Explore It!** Animation

UNLOCK THE BIG ?

I will know the parts and the functions of several other body systems.

Words to Know

digestive system	excretory system
stomach	kidneys
intestines	bladder
	skin

Digestive System

Food must be changed before your body can use it for energy. The **digestive system** breaks down food into very small parts that the body can use. Food can then be carried in the blood to your cells. Many organs work together to digest food. This process is called digestion.

Digestion starts in the mouth. When you chew, your teeth, tongue, and salivary glands work together to make the food easy to swallow. Chewing grinds the food down, and saliva helps to make a soft paste. Saliva also begins to break down starches in the food. These changes begin the process of digestion.

The esophagus is a tube that carries food to the stomach. Gravity alone does not move food to the stomach. The esophagus moves the food by squeezing rings of muscles in a pattern. Muscles behind the food contract as the lump of food passes each ring of muscle. This pushes the food through the esophagus to the stomach.

1. **Visualize** When food "goes down the wrong pipe," people can choke. Look at the picture. **Circle** what you think is the "wrong pipe." Tell what the tube is and where it leads.

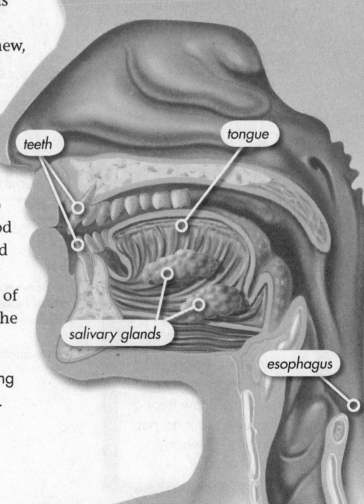

teeth

tongue

salivary glands

esophagus

Stomach

The lower end of your esophagus is kept closed by a tight ring of muscle. When you swallow, this muscle relaxes and opens to let food into your stomach. The muscle then closes to keep the food from moving back into your esophagus.

The **stomach** is the organ where food begins to break down after swallowing. Your stomach is under your ribs on the lower left. The walls of the stomach can stretch to store all of the food from a meal. The stomach releases acids that help break down food. As strong muscles in the stomach wall squeeze, the food and acids mix. The mixture becomes a soupy paste and is now ready to leave the stomach.

2. **Describe** What role does the stomach play in digestion?

....

....

....

One function of the liver is filtering blood.

stomach

The pancreas helps to control blood sugar levels.

large intestine

small intestine

At-Home Lab

Chew Your Food
Put a saltine cracker in your mouth. Chew it for 5 minutes or so, but do not swallow it. Tell what you observe.

Intestines, Liver, and Pancreas

Partly digested food is squeezed from the stomach into the small intestine. The **intestines** are tube-shaped organs through which most nutrients and water are absorbed from food. The small intestine is about 7 meters long. In the small intestine, food is made less acidic and broken down into small particles that the blood can absorb. Muscles of the small intestine move food in one direction. Your liver and pancreas are organs that send chemicals to the small intestine to help you digest food.

During digestion, most nutrients move into blood vessels in the walls of the small intestine. Tiny finger-shaped structures called *villi* cover the inside walls of the small intestine. Villi give the small intestine more surface area to absorb food.

Food that cannot be digested in the small intestine moves into a wider tube called the large intestine, often called the colon. Sections of the large intestine perform different jobs. One part recovers some water from the indigestible parts of food. Another part stores this waste until the waste is ready to leave the body.

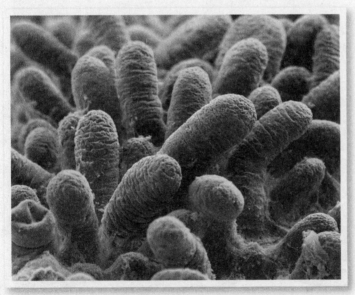

Villi help your body get more nutrients from your food.

3. **Summarize** How do the villi help the small intestine digest food?

4. **Calculate** There are about 3.3 feet in 1 meter. About how long is the small intestine in feet?

5. **Hypothesize** Look at the picture to the left. Beneath these villi's thin walls is a web of capillaries. Why is it helpful to have capillaries here?

Excretory System

Your body cells make wastes that enter your blood. Wastes can become toxic. For this reason, organisms have structures that remove waste from the blood. In your body, this job is done mostly by the **excretory system.**

Your **kidneys** are a pair of organs that remove waste from your blood. Kidneys have the shape and dark red color of kidney beans. The kidneys take out some water with the wastes. This mix of wastes and water is urine. A tube carries urine away from each kidney to the urinary bladder. The **bladder** is a hollow organ that collects and stores urine formed by the kidneys. At the bottom of the bladder is a tight round muscle that keeps urine inside until it is removed from the body by urination.

In addition to the kidneys and bladder, your **skin** also helps you get rid of wastes from the blood. The wastes are released through sweat glands along with water and salt. Skin also covers and protects the outside of your body.

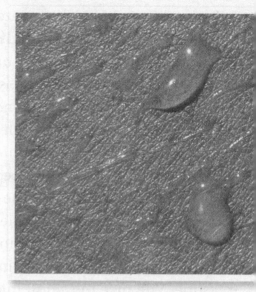

When you sweat, wastes are removed through the skin and the body is cooled.

6. ◉ **Compare and Contrast** Tell how kidneys, lungs, and sweat glands are alike. Tell how they are different.

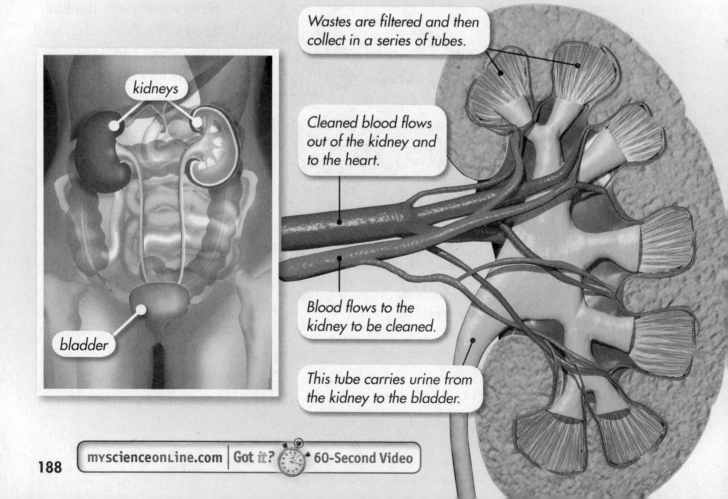

kidneys

bladder

Wastes are filtered and then collect in a series of tubes.

Cleaned blood flows out of the kidney and to the heart.

Blood flows to the kidney to be cleaned.

This tube carries urine from the kidney to the bladder.

mYscienceonLine.com | Got it? 🕐 60-Second Video

Reproductive System

Humans, like other organisms, have body structures that make it possible to reproduce and have offspring. Different types of sex cells are made by organs in males and females. Sex cells from a male and a female join to form an offspring. The body structures that make it possible for an organism to reproduce make up the reproductive system.

7. Describe What is the function of the reproductive system?

....

....

....

8. Fill in the crossword puzzle below.

Across
2. Organ involved in digestion
4. Organ that filters waste from blood

Down
1. A hollow organ
3. Organ with glands that get rid of waste

Got it?

9. ◉ **Sequence** List, in order, the body structures food passes through as it moves from the mouth to the end of the large intestine. Choose one and tell its function.

....

....

....

10. **UNLOCK THE BIG ?** What system removes waste from the body?

....

⬛ **Stop!** I need help with ....

⏸ **Wait!** I have a question about ....

▶ **Go!** Now I know ....

How much air can you exhale?

Follow a Procedure

☐ **1.** Lay a trash bag over the top of a desk or table. Remove as many wrinkles as possible. Tape down the edges.

☐ **2.** Pour about 50 mL of bubble solution onto the bag.

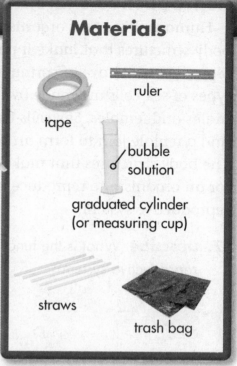

Materials

tape

ruler

bubble solution

graduated cylinder (or measuring cup)

straws

trash bag

Be careful! Do not inhale through the straw. Do not share straws.

Inquiry Skill
Scientists make careful observations and **measurements.** They record data accurately and use it to help make inferences.

☐ **3.** Spread the solution around on the bag with the ruler. Dip a straw in the jar of bubble solution. Touch the straw to the wet bag. Take a deep breath and slowly blow as much breath as you can into the straw. **Observe** a bubble forming.

4. Pop the bubble. **Measure** and **record** the diameter of the ring left on the bag. Use the Volume Chart to estimate the volume of air you exhaled.

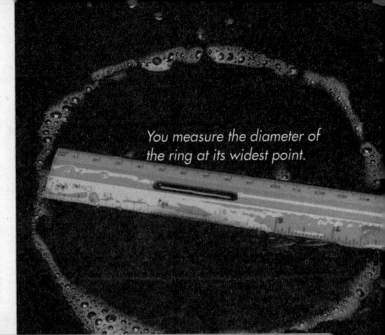

You measure the diameter of the ring at its widest point.

5. Record data for each student in your group.

Data Table					
Name of Student	Diameter of Ring (cm)	Volume of Air (L)	Name of Student	Diameter of Ring (cm)	Volume of Air (L)

Analyze and Conclude

6. When you blew into the straw, what happened to the air you breathed out?

....

....

7. **Infer** Why did different students have rings of different diameters?

....

....

....

....

....

Volume Chart	
Diameter of Ring (cm)	Volume of Air (L)
14	0.7
15	0.9
16	1.1
17	1.3
18	1.5
19	1.8
20	2.1
21	2.4
22	2.8
23	3.2

Charles Drew

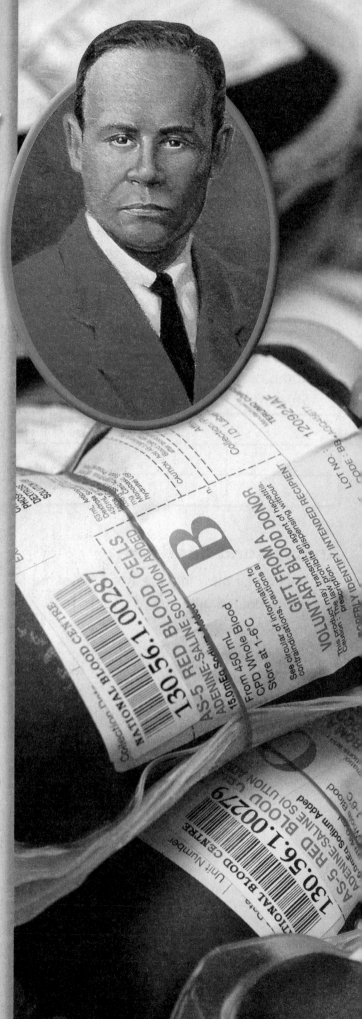

Around the world, people owe their lives to the work of Dr. Charles Drew. He found ways of preserving blood in blood banks.

After graduating from medical school, Dr. Drew became interested in studying blood. In particular, he studied the problem of storing blood. Healthy people gave their blood to be stored until a patient needed it. The problem was that blood spoiled in a matter of days. Dr. Drew learned that plasma could be stored longer than whole blood and could sometimes be given to a patient instead of whole blood.

During World War II, Dr. Drew headed a program that sent blood and plasma to Great Britain. It was his idea to have "bloodmobiles," which were refrigerated trucks that went to locations where blood was donated. Later, Dr. Drew directed the first American Red Cross Blood Bank.

REVIEW THE BIG ? How did Charles Drew's knowledge of the characteristics of blood help him find ways of helping people?

Vocabulary Smart Cards

tissue
organ
system
circulatory system
heart
respiratory system
diaphragm
lungs
trachea
skeletal system
skeleton
muscles
muscular system
nervous system
brain
digestive system
stomach
intestines
excretory system
kidneys
bladder
skin

Play a Game!

Cut out the Vocabulary Smart Cards. Choose a word. Draw a picture of the word. Have a partner guess which word your picture shows. Take turns.

circulatory system

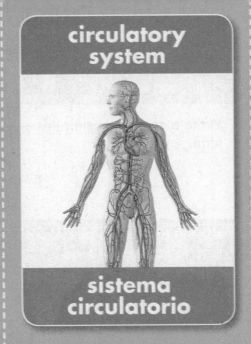

sistema circulatorio

tissue

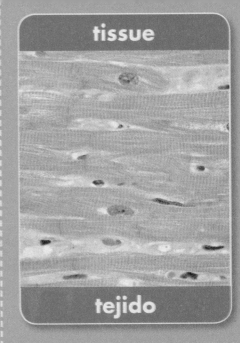

tejido

heart

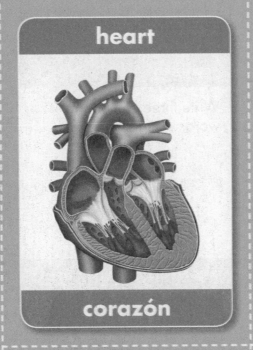

corazón

organ

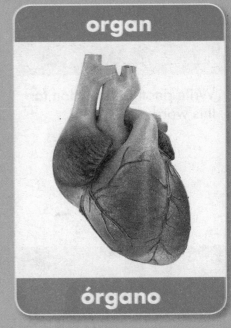

órgano

respiratory system

sistema respiratorio

system

sistema

a group of the same kind of cells that work together to do the same job

Write another definition for this word.

grupo de células del mismo tipo que trabajan en conjunto para realizar una misma función

---

a body system that moves blood through the body and includes the heart, blood, and blood vessels

Write a sentence using this term.

sistema del cuerpo que lleva la sangre por todo el cuerpo e incluye el corazón, la sangre y los vasos sanguíneos

---

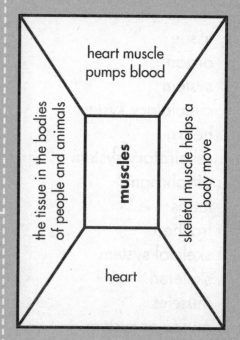

the tissue in the bodies of people and animals

heart muscle pumps blood

muscles

skeletal muscle helps a body move

heart

Make a Word Frame!

Choose a vocabulary term and write it in the center of the frame. Write details about the vocabulary term.

---

a group of different tissues that join together into one structure

Write another definition for this word.

grupo de diferentes tejidos que se unen en una estructura

---

a muscular organ that pumps blood throughout your body

Write three compound words using this word.

órgano muscular que bombea sangre por todo el cuerpo

---

a set of things that work together as a whole

Write three related words.

conjunto de objetos que funcionan como una unidad

---

the system of the body that helps you breathe

Draw a picture.

sistema del cuerpo que te ayuda a respirar

muscular system	skeletal system	diaphragm
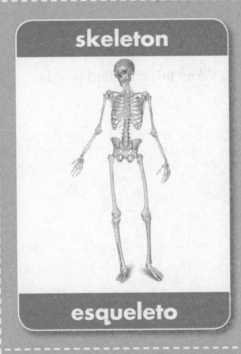	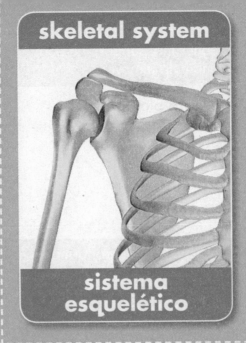	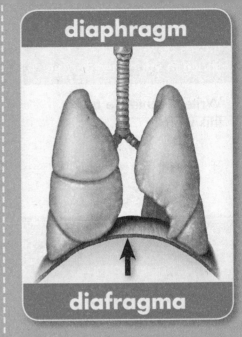
sistema muscular	sistema esquelético	diafragma

nervous system	skeleton	lungs
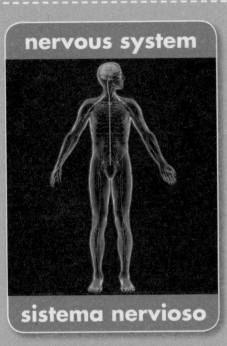	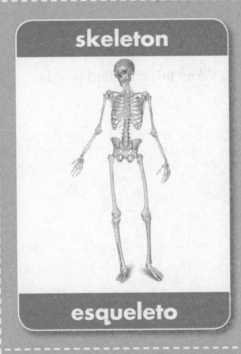	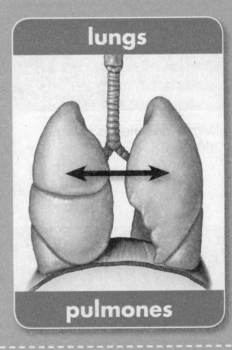
sistema nervioso	esqueleto	pulmones

brain	muscles	trachea
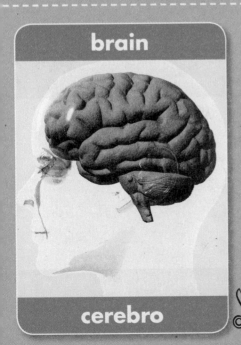	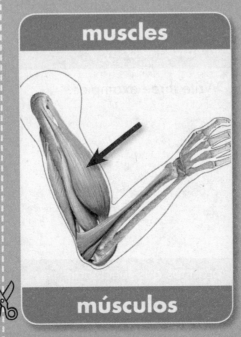	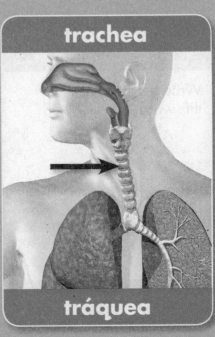
cerebro	músculos	tráquea

a dome-shaped muscle that moves down to make more space in your chest for air

Write a sentence using this word.

....
....

músculo en forma de cúpula que se mueve hacia abajo, haciendo más espacio en tu pecho para que entre el aire

---

a body system made up of bones that support the body and help it move

Draw a picture.

sistema del cuerpo formado por huesos que sostienen el cuerpo y lo ayudan a moverse

---

a system of the body that is made up of muscles and the tissues that attach them to bones

Write a sentence using this term.

....
....

sistema del cuerpo formado por músculos y los tejidos que unen los músculos a los huesos

---

organs that help the body exchange oxygen and carbon dioxide with the air outside the body

Write a sentence using this word.

....

órganos que ayudan a que el cuerpo intercambie oxígeno y dióxido de carbono con el aire fuera del cuerpo

---

all the bones in the body

Write three related words.

....
....
....
....
....

todos los huesos del cuerpo

---

a system of the body that tells you what is going on in the world around you

Draw a picture.

sistema del cuerpo que te dice qué está ocurriendo a tu alrededor

---

a tube that carries air to the lungs

Write a synonym of this word.

....
....
....
....

tubo que lleva aire hacia los pulmones

---

organs that work together to move the body

Write three examples.

....
....
....
....

órganos que funcionan como una unidad para mover el cuerpo

---

the main organ, or control center, of the nervous system

Write three compound words using this word.

....
....
....
....

órgano principal, o centro de control, del sistema nervioso

skin	excretory system	digestive system
	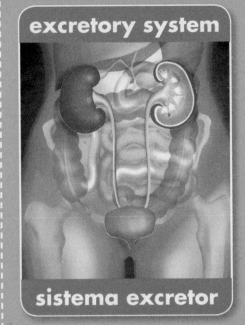	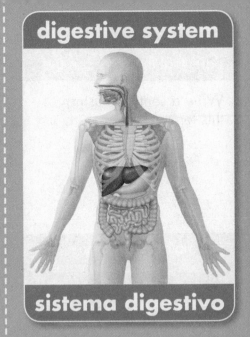
piel	sistema excretor	sistema digestivo

	kidneys	stomach
	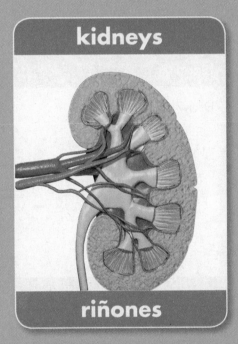	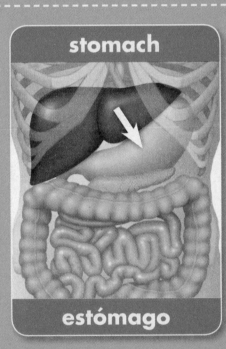
	riñones	estómago

	bladder	intestines
	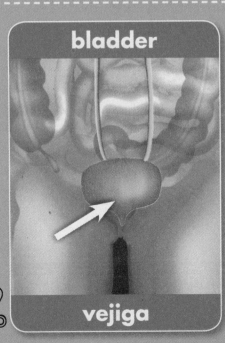	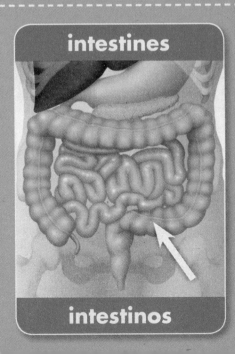
	vejiga	intestinos

the body system that breaks down food into very small parts that the body can use

Write a sentence using this term.

....

....

sistema del cuerpo que descompone los alimentos en trozos pequeñitos que el cuerpo puede usar

---

a system of the body that removes waste from the blood

Write a sentence using this term.

....

....

....

sistema del cuerpo que elimina los desechos de la sangre

---

an organ that covers and protects the body and releases wastes from the blood through sweat glands

Write a sentence using this word.

....

órgano que cubre y protege el cuerpo y elimina los desechos de la sangre a través de las glándulas sudoríparas

---

organ where food begins to break down after swallowing

Draw a picture.

órgano donde los alimentos comienzan a descomponerse después de que los tragamos

---

a pair of organs that remove waste from the blood

Draw a picture.

par de órganos que elimina desechos de la sangre

....

....

....

---

tube-shaped organs through which most nutrients and water are absorbed from food

Write a sentence using this word.

....

órganos de forma tubular a través de los cuales se absorbe la mayoría de los nutrientes y el agua de los alimentos

---

a hollow organ that collects and stores urine formed by the kidneys

Write another meaning for this word.

....

....

órgano hueco que acumula y almacena la orina que se forma en los riñones

---

....

....

Chapter 5
Study Guide

REVIEW THE BIG ?

How are living things organized?

Life
Science

Lesson 1

What is the circulatory system?

- The circulatory system moves blood through the body.
- The circulatory system includes the heart, blood, and blood vessels.

Lesson 2
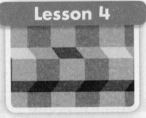

What is the respiratory system?

- The respiratory system exchanges gases between air and the blood.
- The respiratory system includes the nose, mouth, trachea, bronchi, bronchioles, and air sacs in the lungs.

Lesson 3

What are the skeletal and muscular systems?

- The skeletal and muscular systems support your body and help it move.
- These systems include the bones and muscles.

Lesson 4

What is the nervous system?

- The nervous system gathers information about the environment and tells the different parts of the body what to do.
- The nervous system includes the brain, sense organs, and nerves.

Lesson 5

What are some other systems?

- The digestive system changes food into forms the body can use.
- The excretory system removes wastes from the body.
- The reproductive system makes it possible to form offspring.

Chapter Review

REVIEW THE BIG ?

How are living things organized?

Lesson 1

What is the circulatory system?

1. **Analyze** Blood entering the heart is pumped to the lungs before being pumped back out to the body. Why is this important?

2. ◉ **Text Features** Use the following paragraph to answer the question.

> Tissues join with other types of tissues to form organs. An **organ** is a group of different tissues that join together into one structure. These tissues work together to do a main job in the body.

Why is the word *organ* in a yellow highlight?

Lesson 2

What is the respiratory system?

3. **Describe** What might happen if the cilia in the trachea were damaged?

Lesson 3

What are the skeletal and muscular systems?

4. **Explain** Why are two or three muscles needed to move each bone?

Lesson 4

What is the nervous system?

5. Infer How do reflexes keep your body safe?

....

....

....

....

....

Lesson 5

What are some other systems?

6. Compare What different jobs do the small and large intestines do?

....

....

....

....

....

7. ANSWER THE BIG **How are living things organized?**

Choose two systems of the human body. How do they work together?

....

....

....

....

....

....

....

....

....

....

....

....

....

....

....

....

....

....

Fill in the bubble next to the answer choice you think is correct for each multiple-choice question.

1 Which body systems help to exchange oxygen and carbon dioxide?

- Ⓐ respiratory and digestive
- Ⓑ circulatory and digestive
- Ⓒ respiratory and circulatory
- Ⓓ digestive and excretory

2 To what human body system do the organs shown belong?

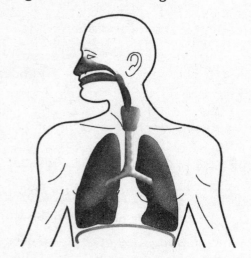

- Ⓐ digestive system
- Ⓑ respiratory system
- Ⓒ excretory system
- Ⓓ circulatory system

3 Which body system transports needed materials to cells and carries cell wastes away from cells?

- Ⓐ circulatory system
- Ⓑ digestive system
- Ⓒ excretory system
- Ⓓ nervous system

4 What are the parts of the nervous system?

- Ⓐ kidneys, the bladder, skin
- Ⓑ the mouth, the esophagus, the stomach
- Ⓒ nerves, the spinal cord, the brain, and sense organs
- Ⓓ the heart, blood, and blood vessels

5 Which organ removes waste from the blood?

- Ⓐ heart
- Ⓑ stomach
- Ⓒ large intestine
- Ⓓ kidney

6 Cells are the building blocks of life. Explain how your body is organized from cells to organ systems.

....

....

....

....

....

....

Occupational therapists can reteach basic tasks.

Occupational therapists help patients relearn how to perform daily tasks.

Occupational therapists can help refine motor skills.

Occupational Therapist

Occupational therapists help people do the things they need to do each day. The goal of an occupational therapist is to help his or her patients lead productive and independent lives.

Patients' muscular, skeletal, and nervous systems may have suffered damage during an accident or a stroke. The occupational therapist determines the needs of a patient. Then, the therapist makes a list of exercises or tasks that will best help the patient.

A person who wants to become an occupational therapist will need four years of college. States may require therapists to pass certain tests before they are licensed to work. Occupational therapists need more than just medical knowledge. They need to be friendly and able to work with people.

APPLY THE BIG ?

How does knowledge of the way different body systems work together help occupational therapists do their jobs?

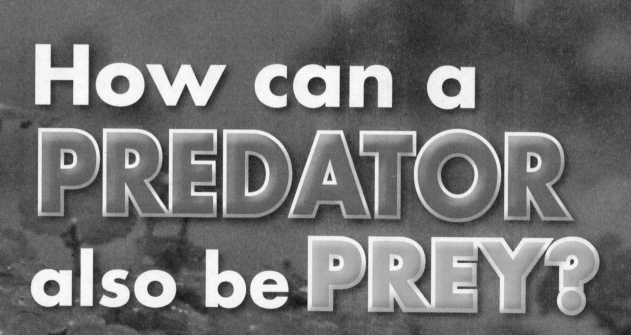

How can a PREDATOR also be PREY?

Ecosystems

Try It!   What is in a local ecosystem?

Lesson 1   What are the parts of an ecosystem?

Lesson 2   How do organisms interact in ecosystems?

Lesson 3   How do ecosystems change?

Lesson 4   How do humans impact ecosystems?

Investigate It!   What heats up air?

The little blue heron, the frog, and the plants all live in the same swamp. Many different living things interact with one another in this ecosystem.

Predict   If the little blue heron left this swamp, what would happen to the frogs there?

....

....

THE BIG ?   How do living things interact with their environments?

What is in a local ecosystem?

An ecosystem has living and nonliving parts.
Even the area around your school is an ecosystem.

☐ **1.** Choose an area at your school. Make an Ecosystem Map.

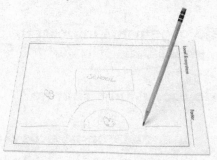

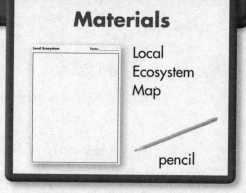

Materials

Local
Ecosystem
Map

pencil

Inquiry Skill You use
what you observe to **infer**.

☐ **2.** Choose an environmental factor. Circle the factor you will study.

sunlight temperature sound level air movement

moisture leaf litter plant cover human activity

☐ **3.** Make a + on your map to show 3 areas where the environmental factor is high.
Make a – to show 3 areas where the environmental factor is low.

☐ **4.** **Observe** and describe a plant or animal you observe in one area.

Local Ecosystem Observations	
Draw	**Describe**

Explain Your Results

5. **UNLOCK THE BIG ?** **Infer** Think about the environmental factor you chose.
Describe how it affects your plant or animal.

....

....

◉ Main Idea and Details

- The **main idea** is the most important idea in a reading selection.
- Supporting **details** tell more about the main idea.

Wetlands

A wetland is partly covered with water or is flooded at least part of the year. There are many kinds of wetlands, including swamps, marshes, and bogs. A swamp has many trees and bushes. Plants such as water lilies, vines, and cypress trees grow in some swamps. Animals such as alligators, turtles, frogs, and insects may live there too.

Another kind of wetland is a marsh, which is grassy with no trees. Muskrats and wading birds often live in this kind of wetland. Bogs are another kind of wetland. Bogs contain peat, a material formed by decomposing plants that floats on the water. Evergreen trees, shrubs, and moss are some plants that grow in bogs. Moose, deer, and lynx are some animals that live near bogs.

muskrat in wetlands

Practice It!

Complete the graphic organizer below to show the main idea and details in the example paragraph.

Main Idea

> [ ]

Detail

> [ ]

Detail

> [ ]

Detail

> [ ]

What are the parts of an ecosystem?

Envision It!

Tell how you think the living things in this picture interact with the nonliving things.

My Planet Diary

VOICES FROM History

Can you name an animal that lives in the lowland rain forests of Africa? Chimpanzees! African rain forests provide all the things these animals need to live. These things include water, shelter, fruits, nuts, seeds, and insects to eat. Scientist Jane Goodall made a career of studying chimpanzees in their natural surroundings. She once said, "It can be exhausting climbing high, far and fast, around 3 P.M. you feel very weary because of spending a lot of the day on your stomach, crawling, with vines catching your hair."

Why might Jane Goodall have continued her research despite the hard work it took?

She continued her work because she wanted to learn more about chimpanzees

Jane Goodall began her chimpanzee research in 1960.

mYscienceonLine.com | mY PLANET DiARY

UNLOCK THE BIG ?

I will know some ecosystems in which organisms live and interact.

Words to Know

ecosystem   population
habitat   community

Ecosystems

There are many parts to an ecosystem. An **ecosystem** is all the living and nonliving things in an area and their interactions. Ecosystems can be large, like a desert, or small, like a puddle. What kind of ecosystem are you in right now? Your classroom is an ecosystem. The organisms in an ecosystem live in a habitat. A **habitat** is a place that provides all the things an organism needs to live. These things include food, water, and shelter.

Ecosystems contain biotic and abiotic factors. Biotic factors are all the living organisms in an ecosystem. Abiotic factors are the nonliving parts in an ecosystem. Air, water, soil, temperature, and sunlight are some abiotic factors.

The fish are biotic factors in this ocean habitat. Water is an abiotic factor.

1. ◉ **Main Idea and Details** Complete the graphic organizer below. Write the details about ecosystems.

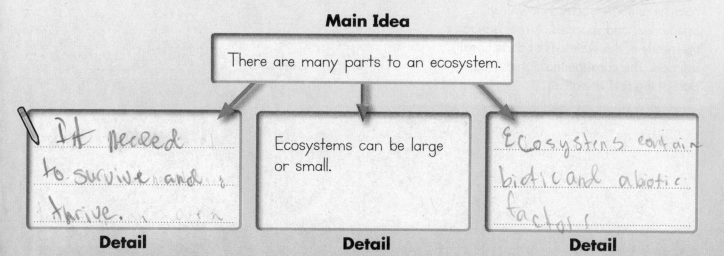

Main Idea

There are many parts to an ecosystem.

Detail

It needed to survive and thrive.

Detail

Ecosystems can be large or small.

Detail

Ecosystems contain biotic and abiotic factors.

2. Identify Read the description of the ecosystems on these pages. Underline the details in each description that tell how some organisms survive in their environment.

3. Classify What is an example of a population in the picture below of the coral reef?

all the fish in the
Coral Reef.

Types of Ecosystems

There are many different types of ecosystems. The abiotic factors in an ecosystem often determine what kinds of organisms live in it. For example, only organisms that can withstand the extreme heat and dryness of a desert can live there. Organisms living in an ecosystem often have similar traits, or characteristics. These traits help them survive in their ecosystem. Frogs, turtles, and alligators have webbed feet that help them swim in a water ecosystem, such as a swamp.

All types of ecosystems contain populations and communities. A **population** is a group of organisms of one species that live in an area at the same time. A population may be all the oak trees in an area. Different populations in an area make up a **community.** A community may have populations of oak trees, maple trees, and pine trees. Members of a community depend on one another to fill needs, such as food and shelter.

Coral Reef

Organisms that live in a coral reef have traits that help them live in warm, clear, shallow water. For example, some algae carry on photosynthesis. As a result, they grow only in shallow water where sunlight can reach them. The coral reef can support the algae, which produce food for consumers, including the coral animals. A coral reef may have many colorful animals, such as clown fish, anemones, and sponges. A reef is made up mostly of the skeletons of dead coral animals. The coral animals on the top part of the reef are alive.

panda butterflyfish

toucan

Tropical Rain Forest

The traits of organisms that live in a tropical rain forest help them survive in a warm, rainy climate all year long. The shape of the leaves of some plants cause rain drops to fall off the plants quickly. The high amount of moisture in the air allows other plants, such as orchids, to grow on trees, not in soil. Butterflies, tree frogs, monkeys, and parrots are some animals that live in this ecosystem.

Desert

Deserts have little rain. Most have hot days and cool nights. Some deserts have sand dunes. Some are rocky. Others are covered by a layer of salt. Organisms living in the desert have traits that help them survive the hot, dry conditions. Plants, such as cactuses, can store water in their stems when it rains. To deal with high temperatures, many animals rest during the day. Animals such as coyotes, desert tortoises, lizards, and rattlesnakes live in deserts in the United States.

desert tortoise

arctic fox

Tundra

The traits of organisms that live in a tundra help them survive cold weather with little rain. Thick fur coats cover many of the animals that live there. Most tundras are found in the most northern areas of Earth or high up in mountains. Rodents, rabbits, and caribou feed on small plants and grasses. Weasels, polar bears, and foxes also live on the tundra.

4. **Compare** How are the traits of organisms living in a desert similar to the traits of organisms living in a tundra?

They both have little rain.

Other Types of Ecosystems

In addition to the coral reef, tropical rainforest, tundra, and desert ecosystems you have read about, there are also many more. The United States has a variety of different ecosystems. Four more examples are the taiga, wetland, prairie, and mixed-forest ecosystems.

5. Identify Find and color your state with a pencil or crayon. Then identify the ecosystem that your state is in or near. Describe the ecosystem to a partner.

Lake Michigan

red-tailed hawk

Taiga

Trees such as fir, spruce, and hemlock are some of the plants that are able to live in the taiga. The taiga has harsh, long, cold winters, and most land has soil that is low in nutrients. Some small animals, such as squirrels, birds, and insects, eat berries and the seeds of trees. Larger animals, such as elk and moose, eat tree bark and young plants. Predators, such as hawks and grizzly bears, eat other animals.

raccoon

Mixed Forest

The mixed forests are home to many types of trees and animals. Trees, such as oak, maple, and beech, lose their leaves in the winter. As the leaves decompose, they return nutrients to the soil below. Shrubs and small plants grow in the mixed forest. Songbirds, deer, bears, and raccoons are some common animals. In the cold winter of the mixed forest, many animals hibernate. Many birds migrate to warmer areas for the winter.

6. Describe Draw or write about the type of land, weather, and organisms in an ecosystem near you or one you would like to visit.

[handwritten] Lake Michigan or Sea water ecosystem

Prairie

Prairie ecosystems are found throughout the Midwest and Great Plains. Prairies do not receive enough rain to support many large trees, but they have nutrient-rich soil that is excellent for farming. Every year, millions of tons of wheat, corn, and soybeans are produced in the prairies of the United States. Tall grasses and other small plants cover the land. Some of the largest animals on Earth, including bison, live in prairie ecosystems. Also common are coyotes, prairie dogs, and grasshoppers.

prairie dog

7. **Compare and Contrast** How are the tropical rainforest and mixed-forest ecosystems alike? How are they different?

[handwritten] There both forests. Differ The animals migrate in winter. Mixed forest is cold. Tropical Rainforest Is very Humid

Coastal Wetland

In a wetland, water partly covers the land during at least part of the year. Trees, such as the mangrove, and some grasses are able to grow in the salty water of a coastal wetland. Some animals that live here may include many types of birds, snakes, and a variety of insects. Coastal wetlands are found along all of the coasts in the United States. The characteristics of coastal wetlands may vary depending on their geographic locations.

Balance in Ecosystems

Every organism in an ecosystem has a niche and a habitat. A *niche* is the role that an organism has in an ecosystem. The niche of a northern pygmy owl in the mixed forest is that of a hunter. It eats small animals, such as mice and chipmunks. A habitat is the place where an organism lives. A habitat is made up of the soil, air, and water, as well as the plants of the area. The habitat of northern pygmy owls is the trees and the land on which they live. The trees' habitat is the land.

All the relationships among parts of an ecosystem keep it balanced. For example, in a forest owls eat small animals, such as mice. If the number of mice in the forest decreases, the owls have less food. So, the number of owls will decrease. But with fewer owls hunting, fewer mice will be eaten. As a result, the population of mice will grow. Then, with more mice to hunt, the number of owls will increase again. In this way, the populations of owls and mice balance.

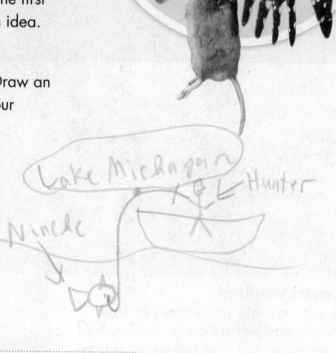

northern pygmy owl
hunting a mouse

8. ⦿ **Main Idea and Details** Read the first paragraph again. **Underline** the main idea. **Circle** the details.

9. [CHALLENGE] Think of a local ecosystem. Draw an organism you might find there. Label your organism and describe its niche.

a fish

Lake Michigan
Hunter
Niche

It is a prey for the Hunter.

myscienceonline.com | Got *it?* 🕐 60-Second Video

Limiting Factors

The number of organisms that can live in a habitat is called the carrying capacity. Factors that limit the carrying capacity of a habitat are the amount of food, water, space, and shelter. With the right conditions, such as plenty of food, few diseases, and few predators, a population in a habitat will grow larger. But a population may grow only to a certain size and still have all its needs met. Overcrowding may happen if a population grows larger than the carrying capacity. When overcrowding occurs, food supplies can run out. Organisms must move to another area or they will not survive.

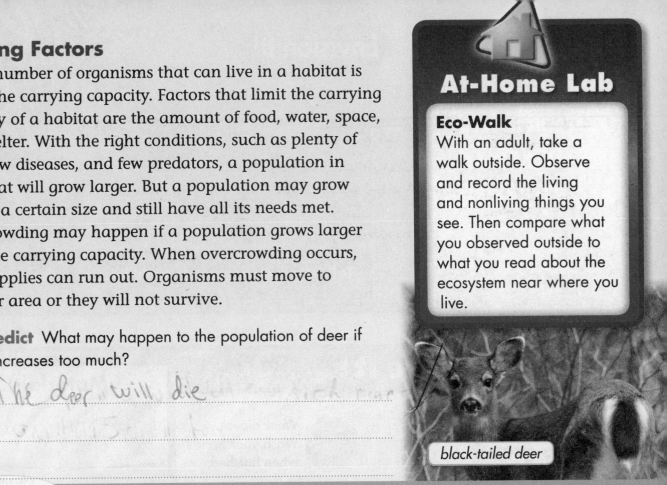

At-Home Lab

Eco-Walk
With an adult, take a walk outside. Observe and record the living and nonliving things you see. Then compare what you observed outside to what you read about the ecosystem near where you live.

black-tailed deer

10. **Predict** What may happen to the population of deer if it increases too much?

The deer will die

Got it?

11. **Describe** Identify an ecosystem near where you live. Describe the living and nonliving things in that ecosystem.

Lake Michagon has fish, shark, and octupus are living. Coral, water, and sand are non-living.

12. **Compare** How are the traits of some plants living in a tropical rain forest similar?

Most won't live on the ground because of all the water on the Gound and the plants could have the same trut.

⬛ **Stop!** I need help with _coolything_

⏸ **Wait!** I have a question about _everything_

▶ **Go!** Now I know _nothing_

How do organisms interact in ecosystems?

Tell how these organisms might interact in this ecosystem.

Inquiry **Explore It!**

What do some molds need to grow?

Be careful! **Wear gloves. Wash your hands when finished.**

1. Rub some mold from a strawberry onto a piece of bread and onto a piece of foil.

2. Put the bread in a bag. Put the foil in the other bag. Place 10 drops of water onto the 2 places you rubbed the mold.

3. Place the sealed bags in a warm, dark place for 4 days.

4. **Communicate** What did you **observe** in each bag?

_____

_____

Explain Your Results

5. **Draw a Conclusion** Why did the mold grow only in one bag?

_____

_____

_____

Materials

moldy strawberry

plastic cup with water

2 plastic bags

dropper   latex-free gloves

hand lens

foil square

bread slice (without preservatives)

I will know the different ways that organisms interact in an ecosystem.

Words to Know

predator	consumer
prey	decomposer
producer	food chain
	food web

Interactions in Ecosystems

Ecosystems are made up of living and nonliving things. The living things in ecosystems interact with each other in a variety of ways. Some organisms help one another meet their needs. Some organisms may eat other organisms and get energy or nutrients from them. Some organisms compete with one another for space or food.

In some ecosystems, birds may flock near larger animals. The animals may disturb insects in high grasses. As the insects fly or jump away, the birds are able to catch them for food. The birds are helped by this relationship, but the larger animal is not affected.

Some animals in an ecosystem must hunt other organisms to fill their energy needs. In this type of interaction, only one organism is helped. An animal that hunts and eats another animal is called a **predator.** Any animal that is hunted by others for food is called **prey.** The predator gets energy from the prey when the predator eats the prey.

1. **Classify** Use the picture below to classify the animals as predator or prey. Explain their roles.

The predator is a aligat fish a prey. The aligator gets energy by eating the fish

These plants make their own food. They are producers.

The moose eats the plants. Moose are herbivores.

Bears are omnivores. They eat plants and animals.

Energy Roles in Ecosystems

Perhaps the most common interaction in an ecosystem occurs when organisms get energy. All organisms need energy to live. How an organism gets its energy determines its energy role. An organism's energy role makes up part of its niche in an ecosystem. Each organism in an ecosystem fills the energy role of producer, consumer, or decomposer.

Producers

Plants and some other organisms are producers. **Producers** make their own food for energy. Most producers use energy from the sun to make food. Some producers use chemicals from their environment for energy. Producers either use the energy to grow or store it for later. The food they make is often a source of energy for other organisms.

Consumers

Many organisms depend on producers to get energy. **Consumers** are organisms that cannot make their own food. They get energy from producers or other consumers. All animals and some microorganisms are consumers.

There are several kinds of consumers. They are classified by what they eat. Herbivores, such as moose, eat only plants. Carnivores eat only other animals. One example of a carnivore is a lion. Omnivores eat both plants and animals. Black bears are omnivores.

Some carnivores feed on dead animals. These consumers are called *scavengers*. Vultures and hyenas are two examples of scavengers.

2. **Give an Example** Write two examples of consumers. Tell whether they are herbivores, omnivores, carnivores, or scavengers.

Tiger and lions are consumers and carnivores

Decomposers

Producers and consumers take in nutrients from the environment as they use energy and grow. **Decomposers** are organisms that get their energy by breaking down wastes and dead organisms. During this process, decomposers return materials to an ecosystem. In turn, other organisms reuse these materials for their own needs. Most decomposers are too small to see without a microscope.

3. **Classify** Read the caption to the right about the organisms shown. Use the key to label the organisms.

> **Key**
> **C** = consumer   **P** = producer   **D** = decomposer

The plant gets its energy from sunlight. The hummingbird sips nectar from the plant's flower for food. The mushrooms get energy from the dead tree.

These decomposers are too small to be seen without a microscope. They are breaking down the dead leaf.

Lightning Lab

You in the Food Chain
Think about a fresh food you ate or drank yesterday, such as an apple or a glass of milk. Make a food chain to show the path of energy from sunlight to you.

Food Chains

Energy passes through an ecosystem when food is eaten. This energy often begins as the sunlight that plants use to make food. The energy can take many different paths in an ecosystem. This movement of energy through an ecosystem can be shown in food chains. A **food chain** is a series of steps by which energy moves from one type of living thing to another. The shortest food chains involve only a plant and a decomposer. Other food chains involve a carnivore or an omnivore too. Arrows on a food chain show the path in which energy moves.

4. **Fill in the Blanks** Write a word that best describes each part of the Prairie Food Chain diagram below.

Prairie Food Chain

Grass is an example of a
producer

Deer eat grass. They are
Consumer

Coyotes eat deer. They are
Consumer

5. **Sequence** Water oak trees are a source of food for termites. Black bears often look in rotting logs for insects such as termites to eat. Make a food chain for these organisms.

| oak trees | → | termites | → | Black bare |

Food Webs

Relationships among organisms in an ecosystem can be complicated. There are many food chains in an ecosystem, but a food chain can only describe one way energy flows in an ecosystem. To see how these food chains are all connected in an ecosystem, you can use a food web. A **food web** is a diagram that combines many food chains into one picture. Like a food chain, a food web uses arrows to show the energy relationships among organisms.

6. ⦿ **Main Idea and Details** **Underline** the main idea in the paragraph about food chains. **Circle** the supporting details.

7. **Circle** Use different-colored crayons to show two food chains in this food web.

This food web shows the complex flow of energy in a salt marsh ecosystem.

Roles in Ecosystems

Every organism in an ecosystem has a niche, or role in that ecosystem. A niche includes the type of food the organism takes in, how it gets its food, and which other species use the organism as food. An organism may compete for the things it needs. Plants may compete for sunlight, soil, or water. Animals may compete for territory, water, light, food, or mates. For example, male black bears will compete with each other for territory and mates. Rabbits, mice, and other animals of a desert community compete with one another for plants to eat. An animal that cannot compete may die or be forced to move away.

8. **Infer** Kudzu is a vine that quickly grows and covers other plants. What is one resource for which kudzu competes with other plants?

kudzu

Do the math!

Read a Graph

The graph shows how the population sizes of a hunter, such as an owl, and the animal it hunts might change over time. Use the graph to answer these questions.

1 Which is a reasonable estimate for the difference between the greatest and the least number of hunters?

A. 5   **B.** 16   **C.** 22   **D.** 40

2 What happens after the hunter's population becomes greater than the hunted animal's population?

A. This never happens.

B. The hunter's population decreases to zero.

C. The hunter's population decreases.

D. The hunted animal's population increases.

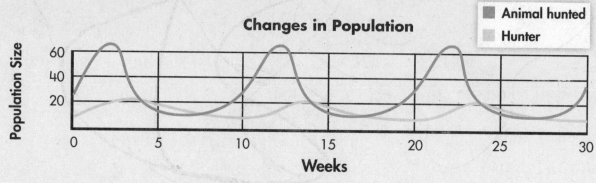

Changes in Population

Legend: ■ Animal hunted ■ Hunter

Y-axis: Population Size (20, 40, 60)
X-axis: Weeks (0, 5, 10, 15, 20, 25, 30)

mysCienceonLine.com | Got it? | 60-Second Video

Symbiosis

A long-term relationship between two different organisms is called symbiosis. One organism is always helped. The other organism might be harmed, helped, or not affected. A *parasite* is an organism that lives on or inside of another organism. Parasites take nutrients away from the organisms where they live, which harms organisms.

In other relationships, both organisms are helped. For example, the cleaner shrimp eats parasites from the eel's mouth. The shrimp gets food and the eel keeps its teeth clean and free of parasites.

9. [CHALLENGE] Think about the interaction between bees and apple trees. How is this an example of symbiosis?

....

....

moray eel with cleaner shrimp

Got it?

10. ● **Compare and Contrast** How are food chains and food webs alike and different?

....

....

11. **Describe** What are the roles of producers, consumers, and decomposers in a food chain?

....

....

....

■ **Stop!** I need help with ....

❚❚ **Wait!** I have a question about ....

▶ **Go!** Now I know ....

Lesson 3

How do ecosystems change?

Tell what benefit this fallen tree might have for other organisms in the forest.

my planeт diaRy

The first sign the fisherman saw was smoke rising from the ocean along the southern coast of Iceland. Was it a ship on fire? No, it was Surtsey, a volcanic island, being born on November 15, 1963.

At first, Surtsey was bare. But soon, life began to colonize the new land. Insects arrived early. Mosses, lichens, and then more complex plants established themselves. Birds nested on the island, and migrating birds stopped there. Seals basked on its shores. The island is now a nature reserve and has been named a World Heritage site.

Surtsey covers an area of about 3 square kilometers.

How might plants have arrived on Surtsey?

_____

_____

I will know how environments change and that some animals and plants survive those changes.

Words to Know

environment
competition

Environmental Changes

All organisms live in particular environments where their needs are met. An **environment** is all of the conditions surrounding an organism. Environments may be hot or cold and on land or in water.

Environments change naturally as resources change. For example, a population of millipedes lives in an environment with dead plant matter. As the population grows, it needs more food, water, and living space. As these resources decrease, each millipede will have less food, water, and space. Some millipedes will die or move away. More resources will be available for the remaining millipedes. The population will grow, and the cycle will start again. Organisms must change to take advantage of new opportunities and protect themselves from new dangers in a changed environment.

1. **Explain** Puddles like this may be home to frogs, fish, worms, or shrimp. Which of these animals might be able to survive after the puddle is dry? Why?

   frogs
   Worms and frogs because they can breathe
   in and out of water, Worms because they live
   In soil.

This puddle has been drying up for some time, and the mud around it is cracking as it dries.

2. **Cause and Effect** Use the graphic organizer to list one cause and one effect from the text.

Cause

As a millipede ✓
population grows

Effect   Resources

they need ✓
more food, water,
and living space

Very slowly, the orange lichens growing on this rock are helping break down the rock to form new soil.

Slow Changes

Sometimes environments change very slowly. For example, the climate in a region may become drier and drier over thousands of years. This has happened in the Sahara, which has had both wet and dry periods in the past.

Seasons change slowly every year. This gives animals time to grow winter fur. Plants have time to grow new leaves for the summer.

The continents also change their position over millions of years. For example, Antarctica used to be much closer to the equator, and much warmer.

Rocks are slowly broken down by the weather and by plants and animals. They become part of the soil.

Fast Changes

Hurricanes, floods, and fires, along with volcanic eruptions and earthquakes, are natural events that can quickly change the environment. A hurricane's strong winds can rip up trees and flatten plants. Heavy rains and huge waves can flood a coastal community. When lightning strikes a tree, it can start a forest fire that burns almost everything in its path.

These rapid changes may force species to leave the area because the resources they need are no longer available.

3. **Underline** two examples of slow environmental changes. **Circle** two examples of fast changes.

4. **Give an Example** What is another type of fast environmental change?

   a tornado breaking everything.

A volcano can quickly destroy or bury many organisms, but it can also cover the soil with nutrients that other organisms can use.

Changes Caused by Organisms

Organisms themselves may alter their environment as they feed, grow, and build their homes. For example, locusts are insects that travel in large groups called swarms. The members of these large swarms can quickly eat all the plants in large fields and destroy farm crops. After locusts pass through, an area that was green and full of plants will look dead and bare.

Plants also cause changes. In fact, plants affect the quality of the air for the entire planet. They absorb carbon dioxide from the air and release oxygen back into the atmosphere.

A swarm of locusts can be many kilometers long and eat tons of plant matter.

5. **Suggest** What kind of animal might benefit from a locust swarm?

a frog would. A bird would.

Changes Caused by Humans

Humans are one of the most important causes of environmental change. We change the land to plant crops, build dams to get energy, fish to get food, and clear forests to get construction materials. We change the environment when we build buildings and roads, and when we burn fuel.

There are many ways in which we can reduce the impact of human activity on the environment. For example, tunnels have been built in some places with busy traffic so that animals can cross from one side of the road to the other without getting hit by cars.

6. **Classify** Look at the picture of a farm on this page. What parts of this environment probably were not there before people arrived?

Barn, Tractor, and animals.

Farming often requires flat land with no trees or rocks.

227

Adapting to Changes

Changes that are harmful for some organisms may be beneficial for others. A forest fire destroys trees and bushes that help protect the soil from being washed away by rainwater. In addition, a forest fire adds smoke and carbon dioxide to the atmosphere and destroys the habitats of many animals. However, a forest fire may also help organisms in a forest. A forest fire clears away dead and dying plant matter, making room for new plants to grow. It also returns nutrients to the soil in the form of ashes.

In any environment, resources are limited. The struggle of organisms for the same limited resources is called **competition.** Organisms are more likely to survive if they are adapted to compete for resources.

Birds and other fast animals can easily escape the flames.

7. **Explain** How can competition affect a group of organisms in an environment? *Keep them from getting fat*

   It would effect them because they couldn't survive with limited resources and they would fight.

8. **Fill in the Blank** Look at this forest scene. Write the missing words in the captions that are incomplete.

Some seeds only start to grow when there is smoke.

The growing parts of grasses are underground. They can quickly grow back after a fire. This helps them in the _Search_ *for nutrients.*

Some plants store food in tuber roots. The food is used to regrow burned stems and leaves.

Some trees, such as the Table Mountain pine, have sealed cones that only open with the heat of a fire.

The thick bark of the sequoia tree protects it from the fire. This bark is an adaptation that helps the tree survive in its _enviorment_.

9. **Infer** Some trees lose their lower branches before there is a fire. How might this help the tree survive during a fire?

It would spread to the higher branches.

Slow animals, such as the mole, can survive a fire if they live underground.

Resurrection plants can survive very dry seasons because they can dry up without dying. The plant below is the same plant as above, only one day after being watered.

Survival

In any species of plant or animal there are differences between individuals. A plant that has deeper roots than other plants may be able to reach deeper into the soil to get water. An animal that runs a little faster than others of its kind has a better chance of surviving an attack by a predator. Even a small advantage can help a plant or animal survive. Only the individuals that survive will be able to reproduce and pass along their beneficial characteristics to their offspring.

10. Infer How do you think the environment of a resurrection plant might change over time?

Dry to Wet in time

Do the math!

Subtracting Fractions

When subtracting fractions from a whole, use equivalent fractions.

Example

A forest fire destroys $\frac{1}{3}$ of a forest. If another $\frac{1}{4}$ of the forest area burns, what fraction of the forest is left unburned?

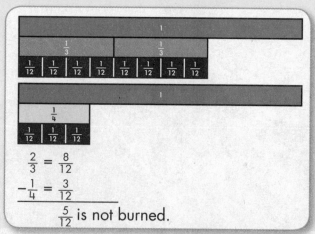

$$\frac{2}{3} = \frac{8}{12}$$
$$-\frac{1}{4} = \frac{3}{12}$$
$$\frac{5}{12} \text{ is not burned.}$$

1 One year, $\frac{1}{2}$ of a sea turtle population could not find nest space on a beach. The next year, another $\frac{1}{3}$ of the population relocated. What fraction of the turtle population is left?

Work area

myscienceonline.com | Got it? | 60-Second Video

The wood frog can survive the winter because its body can be frozen without killing the frog.

11. CHALLENGE What do you think might help the wood frog stay alive when it is frozen?

The exel skeleton Keeps internal organsims from being damadged

Got it?

12. **Decide** Do you think plants and animals can adapt more easily to slow changes or fast changes? Explain.

13. UNLOCK THE BIG ? Think about what you learned in this lesson. Give an example of how a change in the environment can affect the way living things interact.

⬜ **Stop!** I need help with ....

⏸ **Wait!** I have a question about ....

▶ **Go!** Now I know ....

Lesson 4

How do humans impact ecosystems?

Tell how you think this factory might affect the environment.

Which materials break down fastest in soil?

☑ **1.** Put a cup of soil into each of 4 plastic bags. Add water to dampen the soil.

☑ **2.** Place a piece of tissue into one bag. Insert a straw at one edge and seal. Repeat with the plastic wrap, newspaper, and foam.

☑ **3.** Label each bag. Place bags in a warm, dark place for 1 week.

Be careful! **Wear gloves. Wash your hands when finished.**

Materials

water

4 plastic straws

plastic cup

newspaper

soil

4 plastic bags

facial tissue

foam square

plastic wrap

Explain Your Results

4. Record how each material changed after 1 week.

....

....

5. Infer Why is it important to recycle materials? Explain how one of these materials can be recycled.

....

....

....

UNLOCK THE BIG ?

I will know how people can affect the environment and change ecosystems.

Words to Know

pollution
conservation

People Change Ecosystems

Organisms interact and can change their environments. Unlike most other organisms, people can change large parts of the environment. Changing the environment can upset the balance in ecosystems. People may cause pollution. People also change their environments by bringing new plants or animals into an ecosystem. They may also hunt and fish too much.

Pollution

Any substance that damages the environment is called **pollution.** Pollution can affect the air, water, and land. Cars and factories put gases that cause harm into the air. Chemicals that people use may end up in rivers and in the ocean. People also make trash. Some of it is dumped in landfills and then covered with soil. If the trash does not break down, it can cause pollution.

1. **Infer** Describe how chemicals dumped in a river might affect the organisms living in it.

   Some chemicals are toxic and can kill living organisms there.

2. **Hypothesize** What are three other items that should not be placed in trash and dumped in landfills?

   plastic, glass, and Alluminum.

Batteries contain metals that can harm the environment if the batteries are not disposed of properly.

Go Green

Make a Brochure

Research a nonnative species in your state. Use the information to make a brochure that describes the nonnative species and gives ideas on how to control its population. Distribute your brochure to your community.

3. Infer Describe how these zebra mussels might affect the clam they are growing on.

Zebra mussels will make it hard for the clam to move so he will die.

4. Hypothesize Why do you think the population of a species brought into a new area might grow quickly?

A new species could grow quick because animals wouldn't eat it if they didn't know what it is.

Nonnative Species

People may bring new plants and animals into ecosystems. New species often harm some populations in ecosystems. A nonnative species is a plant or animal that does not grow naturally in an ecosystem.

Zebra mussels are animals that people accidentally brought to the United States around 1988. They entered the Great Lakes attached to a ship that traveled from Russia. Once here, they spread throughout the lakes and then moved into rivers. They ate the food and took the space that other species needed. These events changed some ecosystems permanently.

Zebra-mussel populations grow quickly. These animals can cover almost any surface.

The garlic-mustard plant grew only in Europe and parts of Asia many years ago. People brought the plant to the United States to use as food and medicine. Since animals did not eat the plant, it spread quickly. Less space was left for other plants to grow. As a result, some animals had less to eat.

Garlic-mustard plants can spread over a forest floor.

Regulation and Conservation

Too much hunting or fishing can also harm the environment. Regulation puts limits on how many animals a person can hunt and fish. Regulation is one way governments practice conservation. **Conservation** is an attempt to preserve or protect an environment from harmful changes. Towns, cities, states, and the government put aside large areas for conservation. People can go to these areas to enjoy nature.

5. CHALLENGE Describe how fishing licenses might help regulate overfishing.

A fishing license might help regulate overfishing because some people might not have their fishing license so they can't fish.

Got it?

6. **Summarize** What are the ways that people can protect the environment?

People can protect their enviorment by putting a fence up.

7. **Describe** What is the consequence of bringing a nonnative species into an ecosystem?

It can kill other animals.

⬜ **Stop!** I need help with ....

❚❚ **Wait!** I have a question about ....

▶ **Go!** Now I know ....

What heats up air?

Living things interact with the environment. Carbon dioxide is a gas given off by organisms into the environment. In this activity, you will use fizzy antacid tablets to make carbon dioxide and to find out how it affects the atmosphere.

Follow a Procedure

☐ **1.** Label one Bag A. Label the other Bag B. Tape a thermometer inside each bag. Make sure to tape the thermometer so you can read the numbers.

☐ **2.** Add 50 ml of water to Bag A. Remove as much of the air as possible from the bag. Add 4 fizzy antacid tablets and seal the bag.

☐ **3.** The fizzy antacid in Bag A will help inflate the bag. When Bag A is done inflating, seal up Bag B with only air inside it. Make sure both bags have similar volumes.

☐ **4.** **Record** the temperature in each bag. Place them in sunlight. Check and record the temperature every 10 minutes.

Materials

water

2 resealable plastic bags

clock

graduated cylinder

masking tape

4 fizzy antacid tablets

Inquiry Skill You can **draw conclusions** based on what you learn in an experiment.

Temperature in the Bags		
Time (minutes)	Bag A (temperature)	Bag B (temperature)
0		
10		
20		
30		
40		
50		
60		

5. Plot your data on the graph. Use one color for Bag A.
Use another color for Bag B.

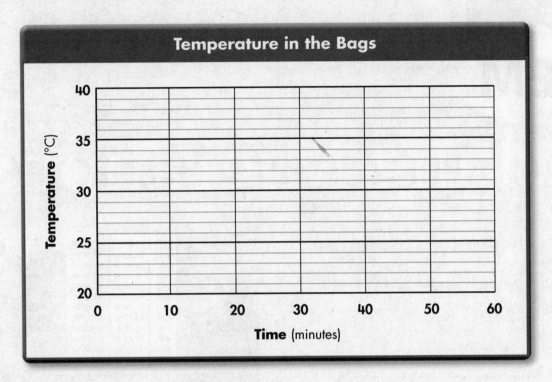

Temperature in the Bags

Analyze and Conclude

6. Interpret Data Look at the two lines of your graph.
How are they the same? How are they different?

....

....

....

7. **Draw Conclusions** What does your model
show you about how carbon dioxide from living
things might affect the atmosphere?

....

....

....

....

....

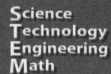

STEM

Tracking Migrations

Each year, spring signals change for many living things. These signals include longer days and warmer temperatures. During spring, many species migrate. They migrate from their winter homes in the warmer southern areas to areas farther north.

The sandhill crane is one species of migrating birds. Scientists use NASA satellites to track different sandhill crane populations. They combine this information with data about plant growth along the migratory path. The green in the image shows areas where food is available. This information shows the health of the species, the route they take, and how long migration lasts. Scientists use this information to learn about sandhill cranes. This information may help scientists protect the sandhill cranes from extinction.

Date	Latitude	Longitude
1/29	24.98°N	99.34°W
2/01	32.67°N	99.56°W
2/06	37.52°N	98.55°W
2/19	37.18°N	98.48°W
2/22	40.73°N	98.45°W
4/01	40.76°N	98.40°W
4/04	44.57°N	99.12°W
4/07	48.28°N	99.89°W
4/20	49.72°N	95.86°W
4/23	53.72°N	83.64°W
4/29	53.83°N	82.71°W

In April, sandhill cranes migrate from their southern feeding grounds to their northern breeding grounds.

Solve Look at the map and table showing the migration of a group of sandhill cranes. How far in degrees of latitude did this group of sandhill cranes travel? Show your work.

Vocabulary Smart Cards

ecosystem
habitat
population
community
predator
prey
producer
consumer
decomposer
food chain
food web
environment
competition
pollution
conservation

Play a Game!

Cut out the Vocabulary Smart Cards.

Work with a partner. Choose a Vocabulary Smart Card. Do not show the word to your partner.

Say clues to help your partner guess what your word is.

Have your partner repeat with another Vocabulary Smart Card.

community

comunidad

ecosystem

ecosistema

predator

predador

habitat

hábitat

prey

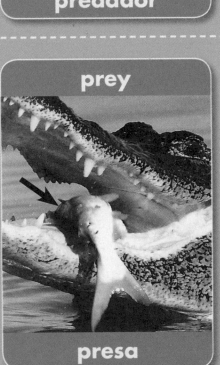

presa

population

población

all the living and nonliving things in an area and their interactions

Write a sentence using this word.

....

....

....

todos los seres vivos y las cosas sin vida que hay en un área y sus interacciones

---

the group of all populations in an area

Write a word that is not an example.

....

....

....

....

grupo de todas las poblaciones de un área

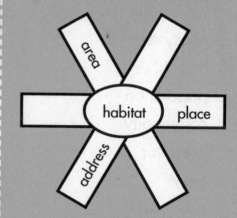

Make a Word Wheel!

Choose a vocabulary word and write it in the center of the Word Wheel graphic organizer. Write synonyms or related words on the wheel spokes.

---

a place that provides all the things an organism needs to live

Draw an example.

lugar que proporciona todas las cosas que necesita un organismo para vivir

---

a consumer that hunts and eats another animal

Write a sentence using the plural form of this word.

....

....

....

consumidor que atrapa a otro animal y se lo come

---

a group of organisms of one species that live in an area at the same time

What is another meaning of this word?

....

....

....

grupo de organismos de la misma especie que viven en un área al mismo tiempo

---

any animal that is hunted by others for food

Write an example of this word.

....

....

....

....

cualquier animal que es cazado por otros para alimentación

240

competition

competencia

food chain

cadena alimentaria

producer

productor

pollution

contaminación

food web

red alimentaria

consumer

consumidor

conservation

FISHING LICENSE REQUIRED

conservación

environment

medio ambiente

decomposer

descomponedor

organism that makes its own food for energy

Draw an example.

organismo que hace su propio alimento para obtener energía

---

a series of steps by which energy moves from one type of living thing to another

Draw an example.

serie de pasos mediante los cuales la energía pasa de un ser vivo a otro

---

the struggle among organisms for the same limited resources

Use a dictionary. Find another definition for this word.

....

....

lucha entre organismos por los mismos recursos limitados

---

organism that cannot make its own food

Use this term in a sentence.

....

....

....

organismo que no puede hacer su propio alimento

---

a diagram that combines many food chains into one picture

Use this term in a sentence.

....

....

....

diagrama que combina varias cadenas alimentarias en una sola imagen

---

any substance that damages the environment

Draw an example.

cualquier sustancia que le hace daño al medio ambiente

---

organism that gets its energy by breaking down wastes and dead organisms

Draw an example.

organismo que obtiene su energía descomponiendo desechos y organismos muertos

---

all of the conditions surrounding an organism

Write a sentence using this word.

....

....

....

....

todas las condiciones que rodean a un ser vivo

---

an attempt to preserve or protect an environment from harmful changes

Write a sentence using the verb form of this word.

....

....

....

intento de conservar o de proteger el medio ambiente de cambios dañinos

Chapter 6
Study Guide

REVIEW THE BIG ? How do living things interact with their environments?

Life Science

Lesson 1

What are the parts of an ecosystem?

- An ecosystem is made up of living and nonliving things.
- There are many different types of ecosystems.
- All the relationships among parts of an ecosystem keep it balanced.

Lesson 2

How do organisms interact in ecosystems?

- Food chains and food webs show the movement of energy.
- Organisms interact in ecosystems through competition, symbiosis, and predator-and-prey relationships.

Lesson 3

How do ecosystems change?

- Environments can change slowly over time or very quickly.
- Natural processes, animals, and people can change environments.
- Organisms must adapt or move to survive an environmental change.

Lesson 4

How do humans impact ecosystems?

- People may cause pollution that affects the air, water, and land.
- People may bring new species into an ecosystem that harm it.
- Too much hunting and fishing can negatively affect the environment.

Chapter Review

How do living things interact with their environments?

Lesson 1

What are the parts of an ecosystem?

1. Identify Which of the following is an example of a community?
A. squirrels, blue jays, and oak trees
B. a group of twenty sandhill cranes
C. a school of tuna
D. rocks, soil, and air

2. Write About It How are an organism's niche and habitat related?

....

....

....

Lesson 2

How do organisms interact in ecosystems?

3. ◉ **Main Idea and Details**
Underline the main idea and (circle) the details in the following paragraph.

An organism may compete for the things it needs. Plants may compete for sunlight, soil, or water. Animals may compete for territory, water, light, food, or mates.

Lesson 3

How do ecosystems change?

4. Vocabulary When organisms share limited resources, there is
A. an extra resource.
B. competition.
C. extinction.
D. mutation.

5. Analyze How can a forest fire have both beneficial and harmful changes?

....

....

....

6. Write About It Describe an organism that has an adaptation that allows it to survive.

....

....

....

Do the math!

7. In a forest, $\frac{1}{4}$ of birds' nests are blown away by high winds and $\frac{2}{5}$ are destroyed by a flood. What fraction of the birds' nests are left?

....

Lesson 4

How do humans impact ecosystems?

8. **Explain** Why must pollution be regulated?

....

....

9. **Predict** How might hunting too many rabbits affect the balance of an ecosystem?

....

....

....

....

10. **Apply** Purple loosestrife is a plant that people brought from Europe. It grows thickly in wetlands. How might this plant harm the wetlands ecosystem?

....

....

....

11. **APPLY THE BIG ?** **How do living things interact with their environments?**

. . . .

Describe an ecosystem near you. Discuss how the living things interact. Use the terms *food chain, producer,* and *consumer.*

....

....

....

....

....

....

....

....

....

....

....

....

....

....

Benchmark Practice

Fill in the bubble next to the answer choice you think is correct for each multiple-choice question.

1 Which of the following is an environmental change caused by humans?

Ⓐ farm
Ⓑ lichen on rocks
Ⓒ heavy rain
Ⓓ beaver dam

2 Which **most likely** limits a desert's ability to support plant life?

Ⓐ too much sunlight
Ⓑ not enough space
Ⓒ not enough shelter
Ⓓ not enough rain

3 A nonnative plant in an ecosystem spreads quickly. This will **most directly** affect the native plants by

Ⓐ leaving them less space.
Ⓑ giving them more food.
Ⓒ helping them grow.
Ⓓ leaving them more sun.

4 In one ecosystem, snakes eat birds, plants make fruit, and birds eat fruit. Which is the correct food chain?

Ⓐ snake → plant → bird
Ⓑ bird → plant → snake
Ⓒ plant → bird → snake
Ⓓ snake → bird → plant

5 What is the role of this organism in a food chain?

Ⓐ It breaks down wastes and dead organisms.
Ⓑ It uses the sun's energy to make food.
Ⓒ It eats other organisms.
Ⓓ It cannot make its own food.

6 What are some benefits of a natural forest fire in an environment?

....

....

....

Create a Compost Pile

Food waste and yard clippings make up 24 percent of solid waste in the United States. You can help reduce this waste by putting food waste such as apple cores, stale bread, and eggshells into a compost pile.

A compost pile is a mixture of food scraps, wood products, yard trimmings, soil, and worms. The worms, which are decomposers, eat the food scraps and break them down into "worm castings," or rich, fertile soil.

Composting can be simple and fun. It can be done indoors or outdoors. To make a compost pile, start with a wood, plastic, or brick bin. Fill it with shredded cardboard or clean paper. Add water and soil. Then add some worms. Bury food scraps, tea bags, dry leaves, and grass under the paper. Avoid composting meat and dairy products. Keep the compost pile moist and turn it over every week or so. The worms and natural processes will do the rest. Soon you will have nutrient-rich soil that can be used to fertilize a garden. So the next time you finish an apple, don't put it in the trash. Compost it!

APPLY THE BIG ?

How do worms interact with a compost pile?

Materials

masking tape

5 clear plastic cups

plastic spoon

hand lens

pouring container with water

measuring cup

noniodized salt

flat toothpick

brine shrimp eggs

Inquiry Skill

You **control variables** when you make sure the conditions you are not testing remain the same. Controlling variables helps you make sure your experiment is a fair test.

How can salt affect the hatching of brine shrimp eggs?

Brine shrimp are tiny animals that live in salt water. They are in the same group of animals as crabs and lobsters.

Ask a question.

How does the amount of salt in the water affect how many brine shrimp eggs hatch?

State a hypothesis.

1. Write a **hypothesis** by circling one choice and finishing the sentence.

If brine shrimp are put in water with different amounts of salt, then the most eggs will hatch in the cup with (a) *no salt,* (b) *a low salt level,* (c) *a medium salt level,* (d) *a high salt level,* or (e) *a very high salt level* because

....

Identify and control variables.

2. When you conduct an **experiment,** you must change only one variable. The **variable** you change is the **independent variable.** What will you change?

....

3. The **dependent variable** is the variable you observe or measure in an experiment. What will you observe?

....

....

....

4. Controlled variables are the factors you must keep the same to have a fair test. List 3 of these factors.

....

Design your test.

☐ **5.** Draw how you will set up your test.

☐ **6.** List your steps in the order you will do them.

Do your test.

☑ **7.** Follow the steps you wrote.

☑ **8.** Make sure to **record** your results in the table.

Collect and record your data.

☑ **9.** Fill in the chart.

Interpret your data.

☐ **10.** Analyze your data. Think about the level of salt.
Think how many brine shrimp were moving after
4 days.

In which level of salt did you observe the most brine shrimp
moving after 4 days?

....

....

....

State your conclusion.

11. Communicate your conclusion.
Compare your **hypothesis** with your results.
Compare your results with those of other groups.

....

....

....

....

....

Soil Survival

Find a large clump of dry soil. If it is not dry, let it dry for a few days. Put it in a jar and add enough water to moisten it. Close the jar to keep the moisture in. After a few days, look at the soil closely. Are there any signs of life? Are there plants germinating? Are there small worms or insects? Record your observations.

Your New Job in the Circulatory System

Imagine that you are an experienced red blood cell. You travel the circulatory system many times each day, and you know all the points of interest. Millions of fresh red blood cells enter the bloodstream every day. Write a training brochure for these new red blood cells. Explain to them what they will find as they are carried around the body. Tell them about the important things they will be doing at each major organ they visit.

Animals Keeping Warm

Animals have body coverings that keep them warm in cold weather. Write a hypothesis and plan a test to see what kinds of materials best protect against cold. Wrap jars of warm water with different materials. Record how fast the water cools.

Using Scientific Methods

1. Ask a question.
2. State a hypothesis.
3. Identify and control variables.
4. Test your hypothesis.
5. Collect and record your data.
6. Explain your data.
7. State your conclusion.
8. Go further.

Unit
C

Earth
Science

WHERE did these drops come from?

The Water Cycle and Weather

It has not rained, but after spending the night resting, this fly was covered with droplets in the morning.

Predict Where do you think this water came from?

_____

_____

_____

THE BIG ? How does water move through the environment?

How can water move in the water cycle?

ice cube

plastic cup

resealable plastic bag

tape

☐ **1.** Put an ice cube in the cup.

☐ **2.** Place the cup into the bag. Seal the bag.

☐ **3.** Tape the bag to a sunny window. **Predict** what will happen.

☐ **4.** **Observe** the bag. **Record** what happens.

Predictions and Observations of Changes Over Time		
Time	**Prediction**	**Observations**
After 2 hours		
After 2 days		
After 3 days		

Inquiry Skill
You can **communicate** by using drawings and labels.

Explain Your Results

5. **UNLOCK THE BIG ?** **Communicate** using a diagram of your **model.** Use arrows to show how water moved from the ice cube through the bag. Label the arrows *melting, evaporation,* and *condensation.*

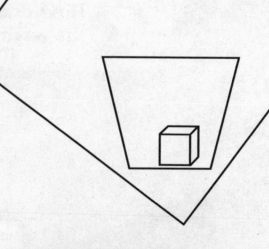

Draw Conclusions

- A good reader can put together facts to build a new idea, or a conclusion.
- Learning to **draw conclusions** can help you evaluate what you read and observe.

Fulgurite

Lightning strikes the ground about 25 million times per year in the United States alone! When lightning hits ground covered in sand, fulgurites can form. A fulgurite is a glassy formation of sand that has been melted by the heat of lightning. They are commonly found on the shores of the Atlantic Ocean and Lake Michigan.

Practice It!

Use the graphic organizer. List facts from the example paragraph and draw a conclusion.

Fact

Fact

Conclusion

fulgurite

What is the water cycle?

Envision It!

Why do you think it is possible to see the lion's breath?

my planet diary

Connections

One liter of sea water contains around 35 g of salt.

There's nothing like a tall glass of cool water on a hot day. Much of our planet is covered in water, but the water in the ocean is salt water. People in all parts of the world need fresh water to drink and to grow crops.

Geographically, there are places that do not have much fresh water, such as the Middle East. However, people can use water from the sea after the salt has been removed from it. Desalination removes salt from seawater to get fresh water. Seawater can be distilled. This involves boiling seawater to make water vapor, which condenses into fresh water and leaves the salt behind. Desalination takes a lot of energy and is expensive, but costs are decreasing as technology improves.

What do you think might happen to the salt that comes out of seawater during desalination?

....

....

....

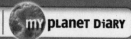

Words to Know

water cycle   condensation
evaporation   precipitation

Water in the Air

Look around you. Can you see any water? Even if you do not see it, water surrounds you all the time. This water is not in a liquid form as in rivers or a solid form as in glaciers. This water is an invisible gas called water vapor. Air always has some water vapor in it, even in the driest deserts. This water vapor was liquid water at some time in the past. A water particle from a plant, a tropical river, or the Arctic Ocean could become water vapor, and eventually it could return to Earth's surface in the form of rain.

Water vapor makes up a small percentage of the gases in the air. Particles of water vapor, like particles of other gases, are constantly moving.

2. **Synthesize** Moisture has frozen on this man's beard. Where might the moisture have come from?

The moisture could have come from the man's breath or water vapor

1. ◎ **Sequence** Use the graphic organizer to sequence the events described above.

First

A water particle starts from a plant, tropical river or Ocean

↓

Next

The water particle becomes vapor

↓

Finally

The water returns to the earth in rain

The Water Cycle

Water is always moving on, through, and above Earth as it changes from one form to another in the water cycle. The **water cycle** is the repeated movement of water through the environment in different forms. The water cycle is continuous, but we can talk about the different processes as steps. The steps of the water cycle include evaporation, condensation, precipitation, and runoff. These steps can be affected by temperature, pressure, wind, and the elevation of the land. A diagram of the water cycle is shown here.

Evaporation is the changing of a liquid, such as water, to a gas. Water evaporates from the ocean or other water bodies into the atmosphere. Water vapor is water in the form of a gas in the air. In **condensation**, a gas, such as water vapor, turns into liquid. Clouds form when water vapor condenses into water droplets and ice crystals. In **precipitation**, the water falls from clouds as rain, snow, sleet, or hail. The water cycle can follow different paths. For example, condensation forms clouds, but it can also form dew.

Sublimation and frost formation are other possible paths in the water cycle. Sublimation is ice changing into water vapor without first melting. Water vapor can turn into ice without first becoming liquid water. The ice crystals that form on surfaces are called frost.

3. Fill in the Blank In the diagram to the right, complete the sentences to finish the labels.

4. CHALLENGE Look at the diagram below. Where do you think the water cycle begins?

I thing the water cycle begins anywhere; water changes form

Some water vapor rises and _Condenses_ to form clouds. Some water vapor turns into frost or dew. Frost and dew often form in the morning and evaporate soon after sunrise.

Water _evaporates_ from the ocean, lakes, and puddles.

5. Apply How might pesticides and fertilizers on land become a problem in an ocean ecosystem?

Chemicals poston lan ecosystem which leads to death among the animals living there

Very slowly, snow and ice turn into water vapor by sublimation.

Raindrops and snowflakes fall to Earth. Most ___participrant___ falls on the ocean.

Some rain or melted snow soaks into the ground and becomes groundwater.

Runoff is water that flows off the land into streams, rivers, lakes, and the ocean.

Groundwater slowly moves into rivers, lakes, and the ocean.

261

Water condenses as it loses energy.

Water evaporates as it absorbs energy from the sun.

Frozen water (absorbs/loses) energy from the sun as it melts.

absorbs

At-Home Lab

Watering Can

Fill a can with ice and water. Add a drop of food coloring to the can and stir until the color is even. Observe. When droplets form on the outside of the can, wipe them with a white paper towel. What are the droplets and where did they come from? How do you know?

Energy in the Water Cycle

The sun has a major effect on the water cycle. The energy of sunlight causes most evaporation, sublimation, and melting. Energy is needed to evaporate the water and to move the water vapor by winds. This energy originally comes from the sun.

When water vapor condenses into liquid water, it releases energy and cools. This energy warms the air or water in the immediate area.

6. **Main Idea and Details** Circle the main idea and **underline** two details in the first paragraph above.

7. **Determine** Read and complete the captions in the diagram above. Circle the part of the diagram that shows water vapor turning into liquid water.

Do the math!

Estimating Area

One way to estimate the area of a shape is to use a grid that divides the shape into square units. On the map below, each square unit represents 1 square kilometer. The lake completely covers six squares. Eight squares are about half covered, making 4 more whole squares. A good estimate for the area of the lake is 10 square kilometers.

1km

unit is half covered

On the map below, each square unit represents one square kilometer. Estimate the area of the lake below.

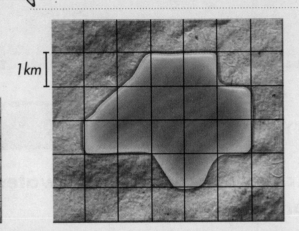

1km

Got it?

8. Infer There is usually more water vapor in the air in summer than in winter. What could be a reason?

There is more water vapor in the summer because it is more moisture in the summer.

9. UNLOCK THE BIG ? Think about what you learned in this lesson. How does water move through the environment?

Water moves through the environment by going through the water cycle.

⬜ **Stop!** I need help with ....

⏸ **Wait!** I have a question about ....

▶ **Go!** Now I know ....

Lesson 2

What is the ocean?

Envision It!

Look at the picture of the Northern Hemisphere shown above. **Tell** how land looks different than the ocean.

Inquiry **Explore It!**

What can happen when salt water evaporates?

☐ **1.** Put 5 spoonfuls of salt water into a bowl.
   Put a cup in the middle. Cover with plastic wrap.
   Put a metal marble on the plastic wrap.

☐ **2.** Set the bowl in sunlight for several hours. **Observe.**

☐ **3.** Remove the marble, plastic wrap, and cup.
   Put the bowl and cup in a warm place for 3 days.

Explain Your Results

4. Communicate What did you find in the bottom of the bowl and the bottom of the cup? Explain.

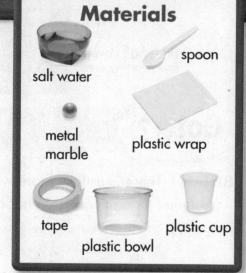

Materials

salt water

spoon

metal marble

plastic wrap

tape

plastic bowl

plastic cup

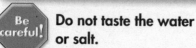 **Be careful!** **Do not taste the water or salt.**

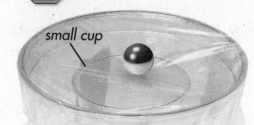

small cup

Tape plastic wrap to the bowl. Plastic wrap should not touch the small cup.

myscienceonline.com | **Explore It!** Animation

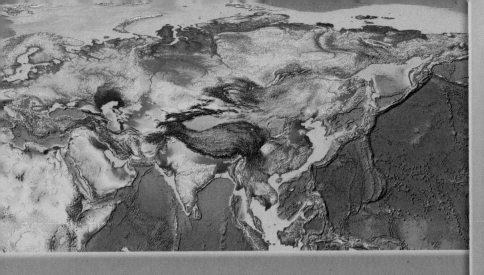

UNLOCK
THE BIG
?

I will know that the ocean is a major reservoir in Earth's water cycle.

Words to Know

hydrosphere
reservoir

The Hydrosphere

All the waters of Earth make up the **hydrosphere**. The ocean makes up almost all of the hydrosphere. The ocean covers a little less than $\frac{3}{4}$ of Earth's surface. Only $\frac{3}{100}$, or 3 percent, of the hydrosphere is in other places. The ocean is divided into five regions. The Pacific Ocean is the largest, followed by the Atlantic Ocean, the Indian Ocean, the Southern Ocean, and the Arctic Ocean. On a map or globe, you can see that these oceans are all connected.

The ocean serves as the major reservoir for water on Earth. A **reservoir** is a storage area, usually for water. Evaporation, condensation, and precipitation connect the ocean with all other water bodies on Earth.

Ocean water is more salty in some places than in other places. Parts of the ocean where rivers bring in fresh water have low salinity. Salinity is a measure of how salty the water is. In warm areas, ocean water evaporates fairly quickly. Salt is left behind, and the ocean water has higher salinity.

1. **Underline** the sentence above that best describes the word *salinity*.

2. **Diagram** About how much of Earth's total surface is covered by the ocean? Make a pie chart in the circle to the right.

The Pacific Ocean is Earth's largest ocean. Its average depth is about 4,500 meters, but in its deepest place, it is more than 11,000 meters deep!

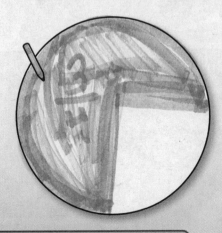

Ocean Temperature and Circulation

The temperature of ocean water varies from place to place. Ocean water near the equator is about 30°C. Near the poles, ocean water can be as cold as –2°C.

The water is not always colder just because it is farther north. Some currents carry warm water toward the poles. The Gulf Stream is such a current. It moves warm water from the Caribbean Sea to the North Atlantic Ocean. Other currents carry cold water toward the equator. The California Current carries cold water southward along the west coast of the United States.

4. CHALLENGE Fresh water freezes at 0°C. What is different about ocean water that might let it get colder than 0°C without freezing?

If it is near the poles

3. Choose In the map below, (circle) the current you think is the California Current. Explain your choice.

I think that because it is pointing up to down from California

5. Generalize Most evaporation and precipitation occur over the ocean. Why do you think this is so?

This is because there is the most water in the Oceans

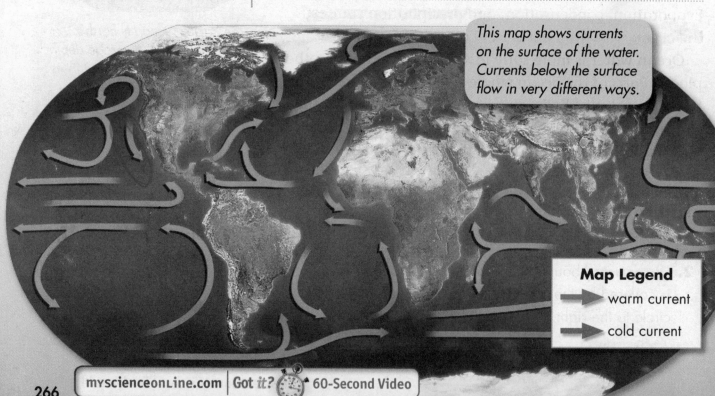

This map shows currents on the surface of the water. Currents below the surface flow in very different ways.

Map Legend
→ warm current
→ cold current

Ocean Resources

The ocean is the source of many useful products. Many materials we use every day, such as table salt, can come from the ocean. One way that we get salt is by evaporating ocean water. Other materials, such as magnesium and drinking water, also come from ocean water. Ocean water can be made drinkable by removing the salt.

6. Give an Example Pearls can be cultured, or produced, in an oyster farm in the ocean. What might be some other resources that come from the ocean?

Food, water, gold, pearls, wood, and rocks

7. Fill in the crossword puzzle below.

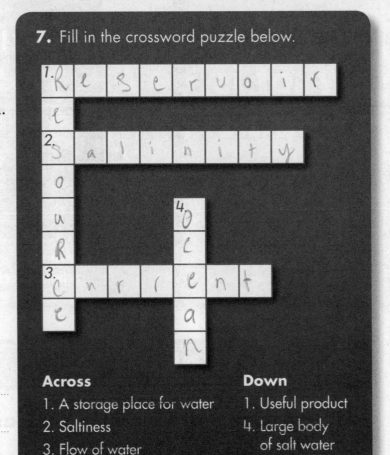

Across
1. A storage place for water
2. Saltiness
3. Flow of water

Down
1. Useful product
4. Large body of salt water

Got it?

8. Interpret What processes connect Earth's ocean to other water reservoirs?

All the waters of the Earth are connected by evaporation, condensation and precipitation.

9. UNLOCK THE BIG ? Think about what you learned in this lesson. Write three characteristics of Earth's ocean.

Three charastics of the Earth's ocean are salinity, reservoir, and currents

⬛ **Stop!** I need help with ....

⏸ **Wait!** I have a question about ....

▶ **Go!** Now I know ....

Lesson 3

What is weather?

This map shows different weather conditions in a particular region. **Circle** the areas where you might find clear skies.

Inquiry **Explore It!**

How accurate are weather forecasts?

☐ **1.** Look at the current 5-day weather forecast. **Record** the forecasted high temperatures.

☐ **2.** Check the weather report each day for the next 5 days. Record the actual high for the previous day.

☐ **3.** Compare the forecasted data with the actual data.

Explain Your Results

4. What was the largest difference between the forecast and actual temperatures?

....

5. Draw a Conclusion Do you see a pattern in the accuracy of the forecasts? Explain.

....

....

....

....

Materials

SATURDAY, OCT. 3	SUNDAY, OCT. 4	MONDAY, OCT. 5	TUESDAY, OCT. 6	WEDNESDAY, OCT. 7
HIGH **LOW**	**HIGH** **LOW**	**HIGH** **LOW**	**HIGH** **LOW**	**HIGH** **LOW**
54 45	58 47	63 54	66 47	60 46

local 5-day weather forecast

Weather Report Predictions

Day	Forecast High (°C)	Actual High (°C)	Difference Between Forecast and Actual (°C)
1			
2			
3			
4			
5			

I will know the factors that determine weather.

Words to Know

weather
barometric pressure
humidity
circulation

Weather

You probably know that a thermometer can be used to measure air temperature. But it takes more than a temperature reading to describe the weather. **Weather** is the state of the atmosphere, including its temperature, wind speed and direction, air pressure, moisture, amount of rain or snow, and other factors.

Scientists called meteorologists study and predict weather. Meteorologists collect data from many tools to tell about the weather today and to predict future weather. Almost all of the data they use are collected automatically at weather observation stations. Knowing and predicting the weather is very important for planning all sorts of activities, including farming, fishing, and outdoor concerts.

1. ◎ **Draw Conclusions** Use the graphic organizer below to draw a conclusion from the text above.

2. **Suggest** Where might be a good place to set up this measuring tool? Explain.

In the ground, because you can see how much of the rain was in the ground, where theres no obstruction to the sky

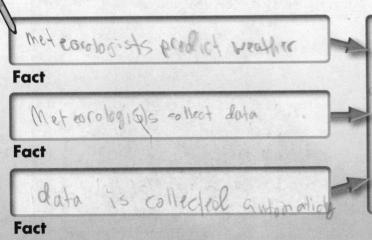

Meteorologists predict weather
Fact

Meteorologists collect data
Fact

data is collected automatically
Fact

Collecting data is key for predicting the weather
Conclusion

Barometric Pressure

When you look up on a clear day, you see a high, blue sky. You are really looking through 9,600 km (about 6,000 mi) of air. The blanket of air that surrounds Earth is its atmosphere. Like other matter, air has mass and takes up space.

Air is made up of a mixture of invisible gases. Over $\frac{3}{4}$ of Earth's atmosphere is nitrogen. Most of the rest is oxygen, but small amounts of carbon dioxide gas are also present. The part of the atmosphere closest to Earth's surface contains water vapor. The amount of water vapor depends on time and place. For example, air over the ocean or a forest has more water vapor than air over a desert.

Gravity pulls the mass of air in the atmosphere toward Earth's surface. The pushing force of the atmosphere is called **barometric pressure.** Air pushes with equal force in all directions. Many kilograms of gas are pressing down on your school building. They do not crush it because the air inside the building exerts pressure too. Air pushing down is balanced by air pushing up and sideways. Air pressure decreases as you go higher in the atmosphere.

A barometer is an instrument that shows air pressure.

Air particles are represented here by small, blue spheres. As you move upward through the atmosphere, air particles are farther apart. This means that higher in the atmosphere, the pressure is lower.

3. CHALLENGE Suppose you take two readings from a barometer. One reading is taken at the top of a tall building and the other at ground level. Which reading is likely to be higher? Why?

on the ground because as you move upward through the atmosphere, air particles are decreasing. This means that higher in the atmosphere, the pressure is lower.

- 12 k
- 11 k
- 10 k
- 9 km
- 8 km
- 7 km
- 6 km
- 5 km
- 4 km
- 3 km
- 2 km
- 1 km
- 0 km

Temperature

Air temperature also affects weather. As the sun warms Earth's surface, air that is in contact with the surface becomes warmer. As the air particles move farther apart, the air pushes down with less pressure. The warm air rises, causing an area of low pressure to form, and air from areas with higher pressure rushes in. If the air near Earth's surface cools, the particles in the air become more closely packed. This denser, cooler air pushes down with more pressure. An area of high pressure forms. Air from this area flows into lower-pressure areas. The temperature of the air also affects the type of precipitation—rain, snow, or sleet.

4. **Predict** What would happen if the air outside the hot air balloon were as hot as the air inside?

The balloon wouldn't leave the ground. The air will be the same weight in and out of the balloon.

Do the math!

Line Graphs

Look at the graph of average monthly high temperatures for Fort Lauderdale, Florida.

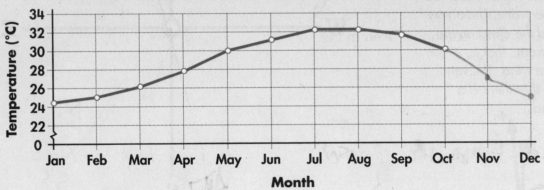

Average High Temperatures in Fort Lauderdale, Florida

1. In November, the average high temperature was about 27°C. In December, it was about 25°C. Plot the missing data points and complete the graph above.

2. Between which two months did Fort Lauderdale have the greatest decrease in average temperature? About how many degrees did the temperature decrease?

Oct. – Nov.   3°C

271

Meteorologists measure wind speed using an instrument called an anemometer.

Winds

Wind is air movement caused by differences in pressure. In general, air moves from areas of high pressure to areas of low pressure. Think about a balloon. When you let air out of a balloon, air rushes from inside the balloon where pressure is higher to where pressure is lower outside the balloon. You can feel wind.

Wind speed and direction affect weather. Local weather can be affected by special winds called jet streams. A jet stream is a narrow band of high-speed wind. A polar jet stream blows from west to east high in the atmosphere over North America. The jet stream affects day-to-day weather and seasons. In the winter, the jet stream can bring cold air from the north to states as far south as Kentucky. In the summer, the jet stream brings warmer air north into Canada.

The name of a wind is the direction from which it blows. A north wind comes from the north and moves toward the south. Winds near the ocean are sometimes named differently.

Wind direction can be observed with a weather vane. The arrow points toward the direction the wind comes from. That is, it points into the wind. The vane below shows that there is a northerly wind.

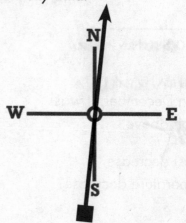

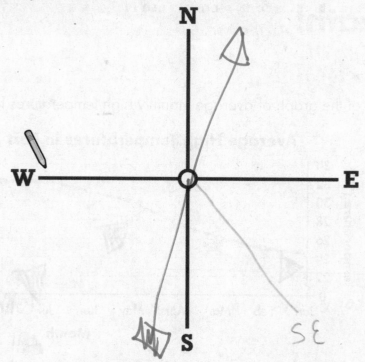

5. Draw On the blank weather vane diagram above, draw an arrow to represent a southeasterly wind.

mysScienceonLine.com | THE BIG ? | I Will Know...

Water in the Atmosphere

Three other factors for determining weather are humidity, clouds, and precipitation. **Humidity** is the amount of water vapor in the air. The particles of water vapor are too small to be visible, but when conditions are right, they can come together to form small water droplets and ice crystals. These droplets and crystals are bigger than water vapor particles and can reflect light from the sun. At this point, we can see the water as a cloud. If the droplets or crystals get large enough, they can fall to the ground as precipitation, such as rain or snow.

6. **Summarize** What do the factors humidity, clouds, and precipitation have in common? List two things.

• They all cause rain

• Are formed by rain

7. **Describe** Write two or more sentences that tell what is going on in the picture below. Use the words *humidity*, *clouds*, and *precipitation*.

Humidity has caused this awesome snowstorm. The Humidity formed into clouds made it snow. The percicipitation effected that is was snow instead of rain.

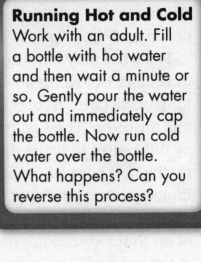

Meteorologists use an instrument called a hygrometer to measure humidity. Zoos use hygrometers to monitor the air for animals that need high humidity.

Circulation

Have you ever used an electric fan to cool a room in the summer? You can also use a fan to make a heater more efficient in the winter. The fan moves air around the room.

The wind may blow from different directions, but winds do follow some large-scale patterns over continents and the ocean. These patterns are determined by differences in temperature and pressure in different parts of the atmosphere. The large-scale movement of air is called circulation. **Circulation** is the movement of air that redistributes heat on Earth.

For example, the trade winds are a persistent pattern of winds that blow near the equator. The warmest parts of our planet are near the equator. The air above this region becomes warm and rises, creating a low pressure zone. High in the atmosphere, this warm air travels away from the equator, cools down, and sinks. It then blows back toward the equator along the surface, causing the trade winds.

In summer, a ceiling fan should blow the air downward. This makes sweat evaporate faster and people feel cooler.

8. **Demonstrate** Below is an example of a route from Europe to the Americas. Draw arrows on the route showing the direction a ship might take to save the most fuel. Explain your answer.

The wind is pushing that way which pushes the boat if you go that way.

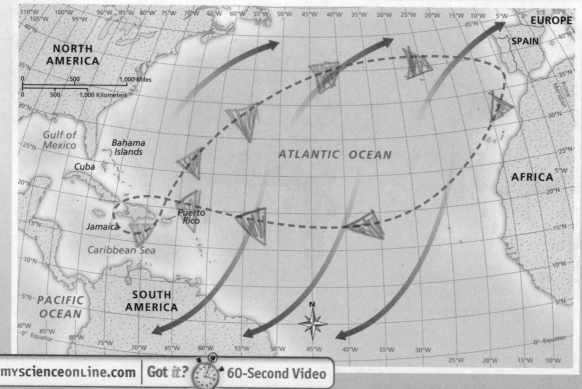

In winter, a ceiling fan should draw the air upward. In a heated room, the hot air rises to the ceiling. The cold air blowing up pushes the hot air toward the walls and then down, where people can be warmed by it.

9. Draw arrows showing the motion of air in this room.

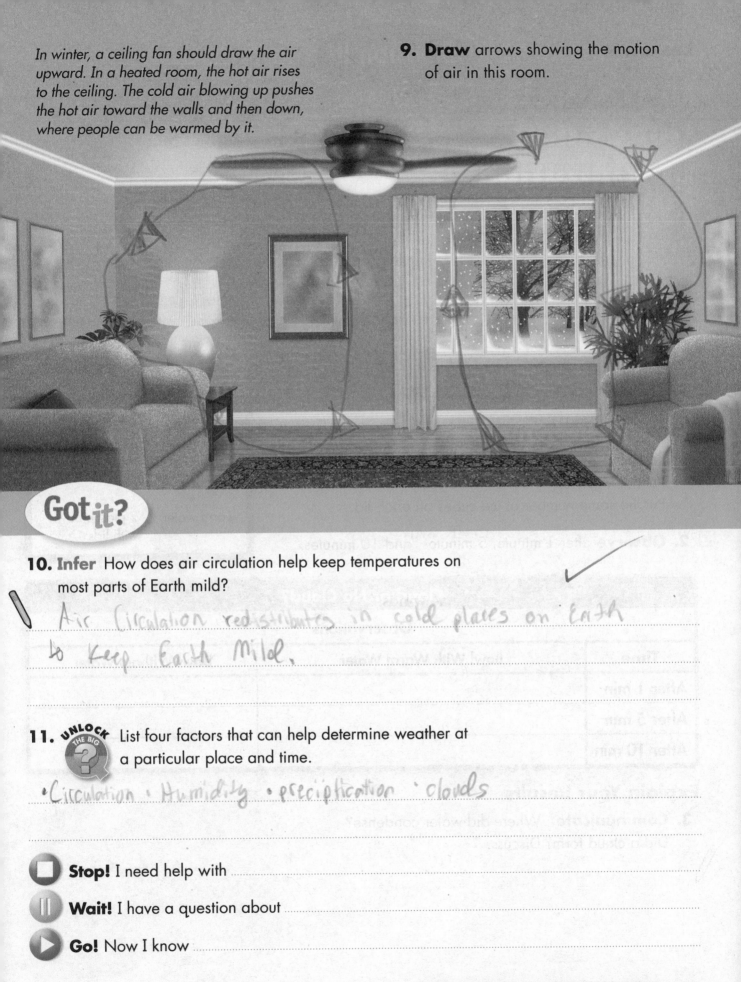

Got it?

10. Infer How does air circulation help keep temperatures on most parts of Earth mild?

Air Circulation redistributes in cold places on Earth to keep Earth mild.

11. UNLOCK THE BIG ? List four factors that can help determine weather at a particular place and time.

• Circulation • Humidity • precipitation • clouds

Stop! I need help with ....

Wait! I have a question about ....

Go! Now I know ....

How do clouds and precipitation form?

Envision It!

A typical snowflake has six points. **Shade in** the spaces that contain six-pointed snowflakes.

Inquiry Explore It!

Does a cloud form?

☐ **1.** Fill one bowl about $\frac{1}{3}$ full with warm water.
Put nothing in the other bowl. Close both lids.
Put the same number of ice cubes on each lid.

☐ **2. Observe** after 1 minute, 5 minutes, and 10 minutes.

Materials

ice cubes

warm water

2 plastic bowls with lids

Cloud or No Cloud?		
Observations		
Time	**Bowl With Warm Water**	**Bowl Without Water**
After 1 min		
After 5 min		
After 10 min		

Explain Your Results

3. Communicate Where did water condense?
Did a cloud form? Discuss.

....

....

....

I will know that there are different types of precipitation and each is connected with other weather conditions.

Words to Know

sleet
hail

Water in the Air

Have you ever watched a cloud get larger? Have you tried to see shapes in the clouds? Clouds come in many shapes and sizes. Remember that clouds form when water vapor changes into tiny water droplets or ice crystals.

Whether a cloud is made of water droplets or ice crystals depends partly on air temperature. The temperature of air high in the clouds is often much lower than the temperature of the air close to the ground. Even on summer days, many clouds are made of ice crystals.

The ice crystals and water droplets in clouds can join together to make larger particles. The particles can get so large that the gravitational force due to the mass of the particles can cause them to fall out of the cloud. This is how precipitation forms.

1. **Identify** What are clouds made of? **Underline** a statement or statements to support your answer.

....

2. **Write About It** Use what you know about water on Earth. Tell why clouds are important.

....

....

Heavy rain storms can happen when there is a large amount of water in the air.

Precipitation

You may be surprised to learn that most rain in the United States starts as snow. The temperature of the air high above the ground is often below 0°C. Clouds of ice crystals form in the cold air. The ice crystals grow larger until they start to fall as snowflakes. As they fall, the crystals sometimes stick to other crystals and become larger snowflakes. If the temperature of all the air between the cloud and the ground is less than 0°C, the ice crystals will fall to the ground as snowflakes.

The ice crystals from a cloud may change as they fall through different layers of air. If the ice crystals fall into air that is warmer than 0°C, they will melt and fall as rain. If the air near the ground is very cold, the rain sometimes freezes before it hits the ground. The frozen raindrops are **sleet.**

Hail Formation

Sometimes, strong winds can blow upward through a thunderstorm cloud. These winds blow raindrops back up into the freezing air at the top of the cloud. This creates a small piece of ice. As the ice is blown through the cloud many times, many layers of water freeze on it. Finally, it gets too heavy for the winds to carry it back up. This frozen precipitation that forms in layers is called **hail.** The hailstone falls to the ground. Most hailstones are about the size of a pea. Some can get bigger than a baseball.

examples of large hailstones

3. ⊙ **Draw Conclusions** Suppose you know the air temperature from the ground all the way to a cloud is cold enough for water to freeze. The cloud forms precipitation. What conclusion could you draw about the type of precipitation that falls? **Underline** the facts that helped you draw your conclusion.

....

....

4. Summarize What causes layers to form in hail?

....

....

....

....

....

....

Rain, Sleet, and Snow Formation

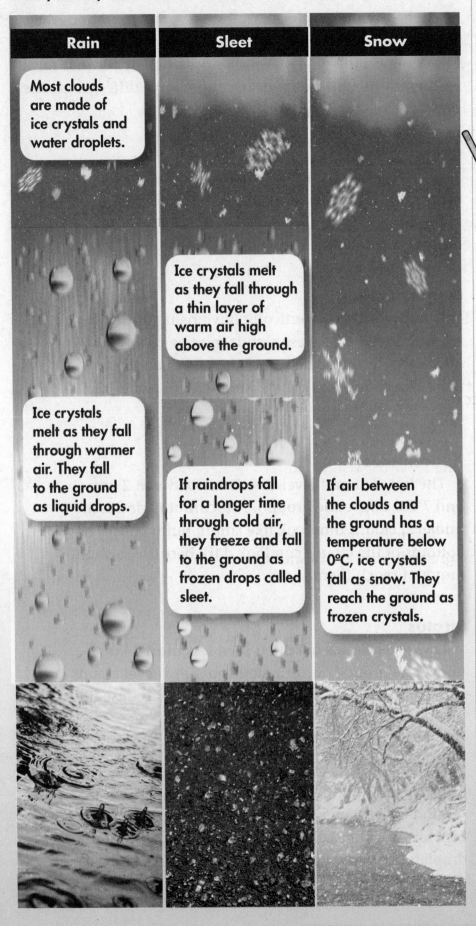

Rain	Sleet	Snow

Most clouds are made of ice crystals and water droplets.

Ice crystals melt as they fall through a thin layer of warm air high above the ground.

Ice crystals melt as they fall through warmer air. They fall to the ground as liquid drops.

If raindrops fall for a longer time through cold air, they freeze and fall to the ground as frozen drops called sleet.

If air between the clouds and the ground has a temperature below 0°C, ice crystals fall as snow. They reach the ground as frozen crystals.

5. Give an Example
Three types of precipitation are rain, sleet, and snow. Do you know two other types? List them here.

....

....

....

6. Compare Look at the chart. (Circle) one way rain and sleet are alike. **Underline** one way sleet and snow are alike.

At-Home Lab

Rainmaker
Spray the inside of a pot lid with water. Keep spraying until droplets form. Use a toothpick to push the smaller drops together to form larger drops. Continue until the droplets run in a stream.

7. Identify Look outside. Do you see any clouds? If so, (circle) the names of the cloud or clouds on this page.

Types of Clouds

When you look at clouds in the sky, you may notice they can look different from day to day. Different cloud types form depending on the type of weather present. Clouds that form at different heights in the atmosphere have different names. Here are five common types of clouds.

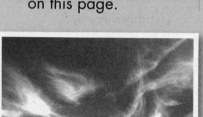

Cirrus

High-level clouds form more than 6 km above the ground. This region overlaps the region for midaltitude clouds. Cirrus clouds are high-altitude clouds that are often thin, wispy, and white.

Cumulonimbus

Clouds that grow vertically have rising air inside them. The bases of these clouds may be as low as 1 km above the ground. The rising air may push the tops of these clouds higher than 12 km. Vertical clouds can cause thunderstorms.

Altocumulus

The bases of mid-level clouds are between 2 km and 7 km above the ground. Altocumulus clouds are midlevel clouds that look like small, puffy balls. The bottoms of the clouds can look dark because sunlight may not reach them.

Stratus

Low-level clouds are often seen less than 2 km above the ground. Stratus clouds are low-level clouds that cover the whole sky. They look dark because little sunlight gets through the layer of clouds.

Fog

Fog is a cloud at ground level. As air near the ground cools, water vapor condenses into tiny droplets and forms a cloud at or near the ground. As more droplets form and get larger, the fog appears thicker.

Sometimes many types of clouds may appear at the same time. Combinations of clouds can help determine the weather at a given place and time.

8. **Classify** Using the information on the left, label the types of clouds in this picture.

8 km
7 km
6 km
5 km
4 km
3 km
2 km
1 km
0 km

Got it?

9. **Sequence** Write the steps taken from water vapor to sleet.

....

....

....

10. **UNLOCK THE BIG ?** How are clouds and weather related?

....

....

....

Stop! I need help with ....

Wait! I have a question about ....

Go! Now I know ....

Lesson 5

What is climate?

Envision It!

What do you think the climate is like here? **Tell** how the house is protected against some features of the climate.

Inquiry **Explore It!**

How does a thermometer work?

☐ **1.** Use the Make a Thermometer sheet. Make a thermometer. Will it work like a regular thermometer? Discuss.

☐ **2.** Place your thermometer in warm water. **Observe.**

☐ **3.** **Predict** what will happen if you place your thermometer in cold water. Tell how you made your prediction. Test your prediction.

....

....

....

Explain Your Results

4. Communicate Explain how you think your thermometer might work.

....

....

....

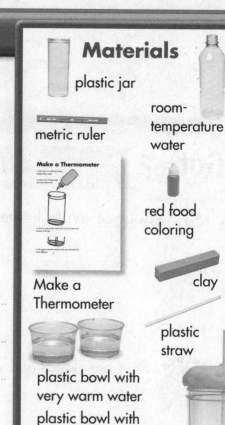

Materials

plastic jar

metric ruler

Make a Thermometer

room-temperature water

red food coloring

clay

plastic straw

plastic bowl with very warm water

plastic bowl with very cold water

Be careful! Do not use dangerously warm water.

I will know that different climate zones have specific characteristics.

Words to Know

climate
latitude
elevation

Average Weather

The words *weather* and *climate* do not have the same definitions. Weather is made up of all the conditions in one place at a single moment. Weather changes very often. **Climate** describes the weather conditions over a long time, at least thirty years. Climate includes things such as the average amount of precipitation, the average temperature, and how much the temperature changes during the year. Climates do not change as much as the daily weather does.

Giant sequoia trees grow naturally in a small area of California, in the western Sierra Nevada. The climate of this area is generally humid, with mostly dry summers and snowy winters. Some giant sequoias have been alive for thousands of years.

1. **Infer** How do you know this is a good climate for giant sequoias?

   The climate is good for giant sequoias because it remains nearly steady where they grow. They have been around 1000 years

Sequoias are able to live for thousands of years because the climate remains nearly steady where they grow.

Factors That Affect Climate

Different areas of the world have different climates. Some factors that affect climate include latitude, elevation, and closeness to large bodies of water.

Latitude

One factor that affects the climate of a place is its latitude. **Latitude** is a measure of how far a place is from the equator. Latitude is measured in degrees, starting at 0° at the equator. Energy from the sun hits Earth's surface more directly at the equator. An area nearer to the equator is usually hotter than places farther away.

There are three major zones of climate according to latitude. The tropical zone extends from 23.5° south to 23.5° north latitude and contains the equator itself. Here, the sun's energy hits most directly all year. The tropical zone is usually warm.

You may know that places like the North and South Poles are generally quite cold. The polar zones receive energy from the sun less directly than the tropical zone. The polar zone extends from 66.5° to 90° north and from 66.5° to 90° south.

In between the polar and tropical zones are the temperate zones. Most of the United States is in a temperate zone. Here, energy from the sun is more direct during the summer, causing the temperature to be higher. The sun's energy is less direct in the winter, which causes winters to be colder.

2. **Support** Why are the polar regions usually cold? **Underline** one statement that supports your answer.

The polar regions are cold because they are the farthest away from the equator

Less energy from sun

66.5° N

23.5° N

Equator (0°)

23.5° S

66.5° S

myscienceonLine.com | I Will Know...

3. Describe Write two words to describe each climate zone.

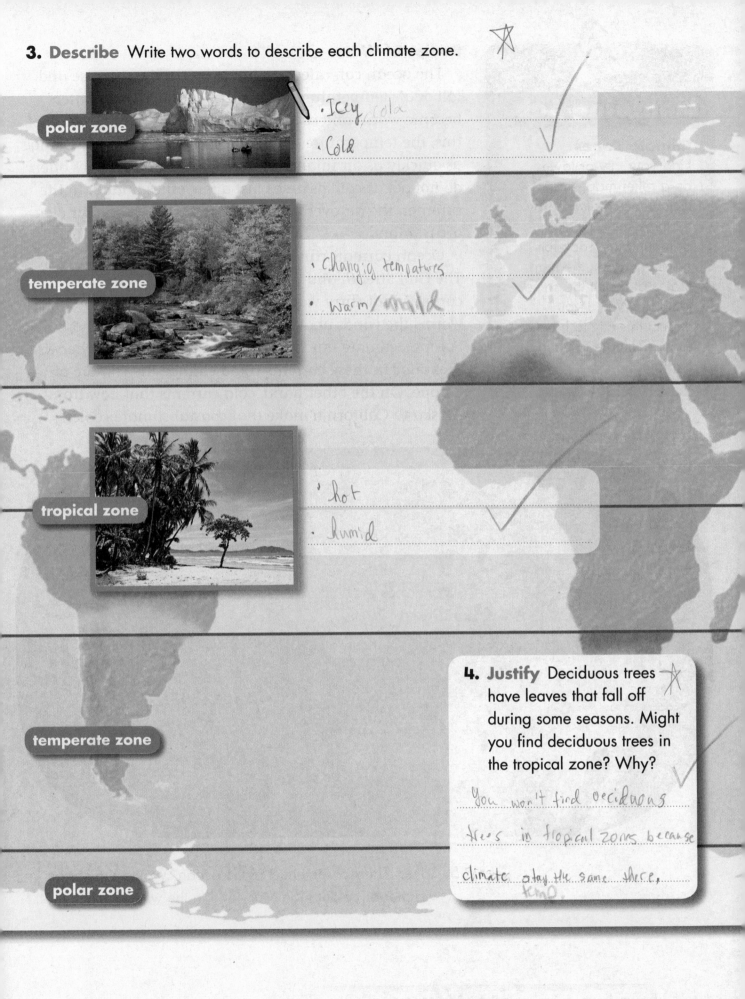

polar zone
- Icey cold
- Cold

temperate zone
- changing tempatures
- warm/mild

tropical zone
- hot
- humid

temperate zone

polar zone

4. Justify Deciduous trees have leaves that fall off during some seasons. Might you find deciduous trees in the tropical zone? Why?

You won't find deciduous trees in tropical zones because climate stay the same there, temp.

Bodies of Water

The ocean can affect a climate by slowing the rise and fall of air temperature. Remember that bodies of water become warm and cool more slowly than land. Because of this, the temperature of the air near water does not change as quickly as air inland. In the winter, large beaches often do not get as cold as areas just a few miles inland. In the summer, the air over beaches is often cooler than air over areas inland.

Ocean currents can make a climate warmer or cooler. The Gulf Stream and the North Atlantic Drift are large currents that carry warm water northward. The water warms the winds above it. These winds make northern Europe's climate much warmer than it would be otherwise. A change in these currents could change the climate of Europe. On the other hand, cold currents that flow from Alaska to California make that coastal climate cooler.

Kansas

Maryland

5. **Infer** Think of the effect of the ocean. Would Kansas be warmer or colder than Maryland in the winter? Explain.

Kansas would be warmer because it is closer to the equator and not near a body of water.

Elevation

Mountain ranges may have different climates than areas around them. Higher land is cooler because in the lower part of the atmosphere temperature decreases with increased elevation. **Elevation** is the height above sea level.

Areas on opposite sides of a mountain range can have very different climates. This happens because the air does not have much moisture in it by the time it reaches the other side.

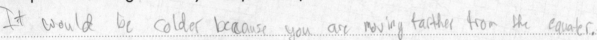

Plaza Huincul, Argentina, average yearly precipitation: 132 mm

This image shows the southern portion of South America.

Valdivia, Chile, average yearly precipitation: 2,593 mm

6. Show Draw an arrow to show how wind flows between the cities shown on the map. Explain your answer.

Because the Precipitation is higher Right/East.

Got it?

7. ⊙ Draw Conclusions You take a bus trip along the Florida coast, from Miami north to Jacksonville. What temperature change would you expect? Explain.

It would be colder because you are moving farther from the equator.

8. UNLOCK THE BIG ? Name three factors that can influence climate.

Rain/water, Wind, and Latitude.

⏹ Stop! I need help with ....

⏸ Wait! I have a question about ....

▶ Go! Now I know ....

Investigate It!

Where is the hurricane going?

Weather forecasters record where a hurricane was and where it is. They find the direction it was going. They look at other things too. Then they predict its path. They warn people in the path that a hurricane might be coming.

Materials

Storm Map

Storm Map

Follow a Procedure

☐ **1.** Look at the Storm Map.
Find where the hurricane was on Day 1 and Day 2. Think about its direction. **Predict** where it will go. What places would you warn that a hurricane might come? Record your first prediction in the Prediction Chart.

Inquiry Skill To help **predict** where a hurricane might go, you make inferences based on what you already know (where the hurricane has been and where it is currently).

Day	Latitude	Longitude
1	22°N	62°W
2	24°N	65°W

Your teacher will give you the rest of the information as you work through the activity

Day	Latitude	Longitude
3		
4		
5		

Map Scale 1 cm = 160 km
0   160 Kilometers

Prediction Chart		
	Prediction What places would you warn that a hurricane might be approaching?	**Accuracy** How accurate was your prediction?
1st prediction (from Step 1)		
2nd prediction (from Step 2)		

☑ **2.** Your teacher will tell you the hurricane's location on Day 3.
Mark this position on the Storm Map.
Predict where the hurricane will go next.
What places would you warn? Record your second prediction.

☑ **3.** Your teacher will tell you the hurricane's locations on Day 4 and Day 5.
Mark these locations on the Storm Map.
Complete the Prediction Chart.

Analyze and Conclude

4. Communicate How did you **predict** where the hurricane might go?

....

....

5. **UNLOCK ESSENTIAL ?** How might people be affected by an accurate prediction? How might they be affected by one that is not accurate?

....

....

....

....

....

....

STEM

Predicting Tsunamis

Engineers use math and technology to warn people of tsunamis, or large waves of water that affect coastlines. One system they have developed consists of technology, such as buoys, sensors, satellites, and computers. The system is called Deep-ocean Assessment and Reporting of Tsunamis (DART®). Each DART station has a buoy on the surface. There is a pressure sensor anchored on the ocean floor. A radio system sends information between the sensor and buoy. The buoy then sends information to a satellite, which sends information to computers for analysis.

The United States government has 32 stations located throughout the Pacific Ocean. Each station has internal detection software. This software converts pressure and temperature data from the sensor to predict and measure tsunamis. The DART system is one example of how science, technology, engineering, and math can work together.

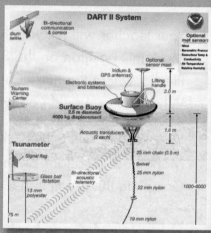

This illustration shows how the DART system uses information to detect tsunamis.

A DART station warns people of tsunamis. DART calculates the height and speed of a tsunami. This early warning can help save lives and property from damage.

Infer How do you think engineers warned people about possible tsunamis before DART?

Vocabulary Smart Cards

water cycle
evaporation
condensation
precipitation
hydrosphere
reservoir
weather
barometric pressure
humidity
circulation
sleet
hail
climate
latitude
elevation

Play a Game!

Cut out the Vocabulary Smart Cards.

Work with a partner. One person puts the cards picture-side up. The other person puts the cards picture-side down.

Take turns matching each word with its definition.

precipitation

precipitación

water cycle

ciclo del agua

hydrosphere

hidrosfera

evaporation

evaporación

reservoir

depósito

condensation

condensación

repeated movement of water through the environment in different forms

Draw a picture that represents the term.

movimiento repetido del agua en formas distintas a través del medio ambiente

---

water that falls from clouds as rain, snow, sleet, or hail

Use a dictionary. Find another definition for this word.

....

....

....

agua que cae de las nubes en forma de lluvia, nieve, aguanieve o granizo

---

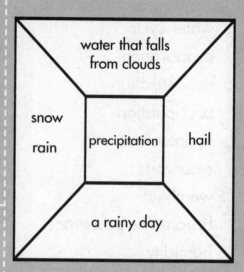

water that falls from clouds

snow
rain
precipitation
hail

a rainy day

Make a Word Frame!

Choose a vocabulary term and write it in the center of the frame. Write details about the vocabulary term.

---

the changing of a liquid to a gas

Write a sentence using verb form of this word.

....

....

....

cambio de líquido a gas

---

all the waters of Earth

Write a sentence using this word.

....

....

....

....

toda el agua de la Tierra

---

the process in which a gas turns into a liquid

Write a sentence using this word.

....

....

....

proceso en el que un gas se convierte en líquido

---

a storage area, usually for water

Write a sentence using this word.

....

....

....

lugar donde se almacena algo, como por ejemplo agua

climate	circulation	weather

clima	circulación	tiempo atmosférico

latitude	sleet	barometric pressure
		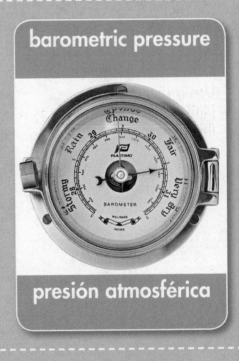
latitud	aguanieve	presión atmosférica

elevation	hail	humidity
		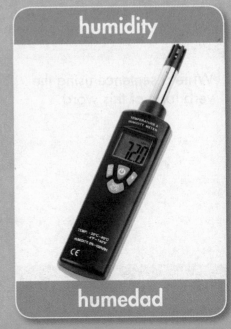
elevación	granizo	humedad

the state of the atmosphere

Write three examples.

....

....

....

....

estado de la atmósfera

movement of air that redistributes heat on Earth

Write a sentence using the verb form for this word.

....

....

....

movimiento del aire que redistribuye el calor en la Tierra

the average of weather conditions over a long time

Write another definition for this word.

....

....

....

promedio de las condiciones del tiempo durante un período largo

the pushing force of the atmosphere

Use a dictionary. Find another term for this phrase.

....

....

....

fuerza que ejerce la atmósfera

frozen raindrops

Write a sentence using this word.

....

....

....

gotas de lluvia congeladas

a measure of how far a place is from the equator

Write another definition for this word.

....

....

....

medida de la distancia entre un objeto y el ecuador

the amount of water vapor in the air

Write a sentence using the verb form of this word.

....

....

....

cantidad de vapor de agua en el aire

frozen precipitation that forms in layers

Write a sentence using this word.

....

....

....

precipitación congelada que se forma en capas

height above sea level

What is the suffix of this word?

....

....

....

....

altura sobre el nivel del mar

Study Guide

How does water move through the environment?

Earth Science

Lesson 1

What is the water cycle?

- Water can be a solid, liquid, or gas and can change state.
- Evaporation, condensation, precipitation, and runoff are parts of the water cycle.

Lesson 2

What is the ocean?

- The ocean covers nearly $\frac{3}{4}$ of Earth's surface.
- The ocean is connected to the rest of the hydrosphere.
- The ocean is the major reservoir in the water cycle.

Lesson 3

What is weather?

- Air temperature, pressure, humidity, wind speed and direction, and precipitation determine the weather in a given place and time.
- Air circulates throughout the planet in predictable patterns.

Lesson 4

How do clouds and precipitation form?

- Precipitation is made up of particles of water that fall from clouds.
- Some forms of precipitation are rain, snow, sleet, and hail.
- Different clouds form from different types of weather.

Lesson 5

What is climate?

- Climate is the average weather conditions over a long period of time.
- Climate is affected by latitude, elevation, and distance from water.
- The climate in a region may change over time.

Chapter Review

REVIEW THE BIG ? **How does water move through the environment?**

Lesson 1

What is the water cycle?

1. The particles of water vapor
   A. are always moving.
   B. are as small as a drop.
   C. form a liquid.

2. A certain cloud contains 220 water droplets per cubic centimeter. If 1 cubic meter = 1,000,000 cubic centimeters, how many drops are in one cubic meter of the cloud?

Lesson 2

What is the ocean?

3. The hydrosphere covers about
   A.   50 percent of the surface of Earth.
   B. 100 percent of the surface of Earth.
   C.   70 percent of the surface of Earth.
   D.   20 percent of the surface of Earth.

4. A coconut is the fruit of a palm tree. Palm trees are found on islands all over the world. How can a coconut reach a distant island?

Lesson 3

What is weather?

5. **Vocabulary** The state of the atmosphere at a given time and place is called _____.
   A. climate
   B. weather
   C. circulation
   D. altitude

6. **Write About It** How does a difference in barometric pressures cause wind?

7. **List** Write three factors that determine the weather shown below.

Lesson 4

How do clouds and precipitation form?

8. **Draw Conclusions** Read the paragraph and fill in the graphic organizer.

> Hail forms when falling ice crystals get blown up through a thunderstorm cloud by a strong wind. After they begin to fall again, the upward wind blows them up through the cloud again. Hail happens during thunderstorms.

Fact

Fact

Conclusion

Lesson 5

What is climate?

9. **Predict** St. Louis, Missouri, experiences large differences in temperature between summer and winter. Predict how the temperature difference might change if St. Louis were next to the ocean.

10. **Identify** *Tropical*, *temperate*, and *polar* describe climate zones due to
   A. latitude.
   B. rainfall amount.
   C. temperature.

11. **ANSWER THE BIG ?** How does water move through the environment?

Describe the movement of water near where you live. Is there a large body of water, such as the ocean? Does it rain a lot? Does the water come from wells in the ground?

Benchmark Practice

Fill in the bubble next to the answer choice you think is correct for each multiple-choice question.

1 In the water cycle on Earth, water is in which form?

Ⓐ solid
Ⓑ liquid
Ⓒ gas
Ⓓ all of the above

2 The hydrosphere covers about how much of Earth's surface?

Ⓐ $\frac{4}{5}$
Ⓑ $\frac{1}{2}$
Ⓒ $\frac{3}{4}$
Ⓓ $\frac{2}{3}$

3 An area's latitude helps determine its

Ⓐ climate zones.
Ⓑ elevation.
Ⓒ precipitation.
Ⓓ time zone.

4 Which of the following land features affects weather?

Ⓐ mountains
Ⓑ swamps
Ⓒ deserts
Ⓓ all of the above

5 Precipitation includes

Ⓐ rain, snow, and air.
Ⓑ rain, wind, and snow.
Ⓒ snow, sleet, and hail.
Ⓓ all of the above

6 How does the water cycle affect the salinity of the ocean?

....

....

....

....

....

....

....

Keep a Weather Journal

The date is July 4, 1776. The business at hand is the Declaration of Independence. The weather this day in Philadelphia is mild—in the mid-70s. How do we know? We know because a young Thomas Jefferson kept a weather journal.

You can keep a weather journal too. Start by looking at the sky each day. Is the sun shining brightly? Is the sky cloudy or hazy? Make a note. Record the high and low temperatures for the day. Now add more detail. This might include the wind speed and direction and the relative humidity. Note rainfall or snowfall amounts. Use your own observations whenever you can. You can also watch the weather reports or check online for information. Organize your findings in a chart.

If you like, add a sentence or two about how the weather affected you or your plans each day.

Sunday:
warm and sunny

Monday:
warm and sunny

Tuesday:
hot and overcast

Wednesday:
thunderstorms

Does the weather change quickly where you live?
Tell about it.

....

....

What makes this ROCK look like a WAVE?

Earth's Surface

Chapter 8

Wave Rock is a formation in Australia. It is about ten meters high and 100 meters long and is made of solid granite. Wave Rock's curved shape has taken millions of years to form.

Predict What forces might have shaped this formation?

....

....

THE BIG ? What kinds of processes change Earth's surface?

How are minerals alike and different?

☐ **1. Observe** the minerals with a hand lens.

☐ **2.** Place all the minerals in the top rectangle on the Classifying Minerals sheet.

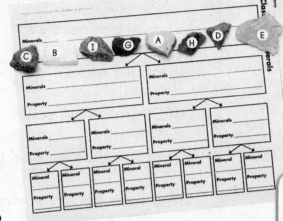

☐ **3. Classify** Divide the minerals into 2 equal groups. List the property used to sort the minerals.

☐ **4.** Divide each group equally into 2 groups again.

☐ **5.** Finally, divide the groups so each mineral is in a separate box.

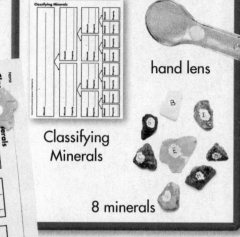

Materials

Classifying Minerals

hand lens

8 minerals

Inquiry Skill
Observing minerals carefully can help you **classify** them.

Explain Your Results

6. UNLOCK THE BIG ? **Classify** Think about the properties you used to classify each mineral. In the chart below, identify those properties.

How Are Minerals Alike and Different?

A	B	C	D
E	G	H	I

◎ Sequence

- The order in which events happen is the **sequence** of those events.
- Signal words such as *first*, *next*, *then*, and *last* tell the order of events.

Fossils

A fossil is the preserved remains or traces of living things. Fossils such as this fish took many years to form. Millions of years ago this fish died and sank into shallow water. Next, stones and sand, or sediment, covered the fish. Last, the sediment became rock, preserving parts of the fish. Weather and the wearing away of land eventually exposed a fossil at the surface. Fossils are clues to how Earth's surface has changed.

Practice It!

Use the graphic organizer below to list
a sequence of events found in the example paragraph.

First

Next

Last

Lesson 1

What are minerals?

One of these pictures shows a real diamond. **Tell** how you might know which one is the diamond.

Inquiry · Explore It!

What do mineral crystals look like?

☐ **1.** Place a few crystals of Mineral A on a slide. Use a microscope to **observe.**

☐ **2.** Repeat Step 1 using Mineral B.

☐ **3.** Compare these pictures with the minerals.

salt

alum

Materials

Mineral A   Mineral B

microscope

2 microscope slides

2 toothpicks

Be careful! Wash your hands after handling the minerals.

Explain Your Results

4. Communicate Compare and contrast the crystals.

....

....

....

5. Draw a Conclusion Identify the minerals.

....

mysscienceonLine.com | **Explore It!** Animation

UNLOCK THE BIG ?

I will know how to identify common minerals. I will know the uses of some minerals.

Word to Know

mineral

Minerals

Mineral is a word that is used in different ways. There are minerals in your breakfast cereal that you need for good health. But to a scientist who studies Earth's layers, a mineral is something different. A **mineral** is a nonliving, naturally occurring solid that has its own regular arrangement of particles in it. Minerals are found in soil and rocks. Although many different minerals exist, only a few dozen make up most of the rocks on Earth.

People use minerals for different purposes. For example, people add salt to foods to make them taste better. Jewelry is often made from minerals such as gold and gemstones. A mineral in your pencil is what leaves marks as you write.

1. ◉ **Main Idea and Details** (Circle) the main idea in the second paragraph. **Underline** the details that support the main idea.

2. **Identify** List three objects that you use every day that contain minerals.

....

....

Metals, such as the silver present in this rock sample, are minerals. They are used in many objects, such as coins, tools, and electronic devices.

Mohs Scale for Hardness

Hard

10 Diamond

9 Corundum

8 Topaz

7 Quartz

6 Feldspar

5 Apatite

4 Fluorite

3 Calcite

2 Gypsum

1 Talc

Soft

Properties of Minerals

There are more than 4,000 kinds of minerals. How do scientists tell them apart? Minerals have certain properties that scientists can use to identify them. These properties are hardness, luster, color, streak, shape, and magnetism. Some minerals can be identified by the way they smell. A mineral may give off a sour, sweet, earthy, or rotten-egg smell.

Hardness

Scientists test a mineral's hardness by finding out how easily it can be scratched. They use a special chart called the Mohs scale. The scale rates the hardness of minerals from 1 to 10. A mineral with a greater number can scratch all minerals with lesser numbers. For example, if a piece of topaz (8) is rubbed against a piece of quartz (7), the topaz will scratch the quartz.

3. **Hypothesize** Suppose you want to test the hardness of fluorite and feldspar. Which mineral will scratch the other?

....

Luster

Luster describes how a mineral's surface reflects light. A glassy luster is shiny like glass. An earthy luster is chalky and dull. A metallic luster can look like polished metal. A soft shine has a waxy, silky, or pearly luster.

4. **Describe** Write a word to describe the luster of the two minerals.

This hematite has a

.... luster.

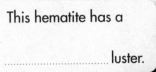

Amethyst quartz has a

.... luster.

Color

Color describes a mineral's outside appearance. Elements that make up a mineral may affect its color. The element copper gives malachite a green color. The mineral beryl is green from the element chromium. Amethyst quartz gets its purple color from iron.

5. **Explain** Tell why color is the least useful property to use for mineral identification.

Streak

Streak is the color of a mineral in its powdered form. To see a mineral's streak, you rub it on a hard, rough, white surface. This rubbing produces a line of fine powder. The powder can be the same as or very different from the mineral's outside appearance.

6. **Compare** How do the streaks of these minerals compare with their colors?

Cinnabar has a bright red streak.

Pyrite has a green-black streak.

Shape

The shape of a mineral's crystals is not always easy to see. But some minerals have a definite shape that is helpful for identification. Mineral crystals are often in the shape of familiar solid figures.

7. **Identify** What shape do you see in this pyrite?

Magnetism

A few minerals have magnetic properties. They can attract other metals. Pyrrhotite and magnetite are strongly magnetic.

This magnetite has attracted iron filings to its surface.

At-Home Lab

Mineral Search
Work with an adult to find objects that may contain minerals in your home. List the objects. Then identify the minerals they contain.

Identifying Minerals

In order to identify an unknown mineral, scientists first make many observations. Then, they compare their observations with charts of known minerals. The chart gives the names and properties of several minerals.

Mineral Properties				
Mineral	**Color**	**Hardness**	**Luster**	**Streak**
Halite	colorless	$2\frac{1}{2}$	glassy	white
Pyrite	gold	6 to 7 (for crystals)	metallic	greenish black
Sulfur	pale to bright yellow	$1\frac{1}{2}$ to $2\frac{1}{2}$	dull to glassy	white to pale yellow
Arsenopyrite	brassy white or gray	$5\frac{1}{2}$ to 6	metallic	black

8. **Identify** Read the description of each mineral shown. Use the chart to identify the minerals pictured below. Then write the name of each mineral.

This mineral has a hardness of $2\frac{1}{2}$. It leaves a white streak. Its luster is glassy.

This mineral has a metallic luster. It has a hardness of $5\frac{1}{2}$ to 6 and a black streak.

This mineral has a dull to glassy luster. It has a white streak and a hardness of $1\frac{1}{2}$ to $2\frac{1}{2}$.

myscienceonline.com | Got it? 60-Second Video

308

Economic Significance

Many common products contain minerals. Jewelry often contains gemstones such as rubies and sapphires. Gemstones are hard, colorful minerals. People also use gemstones for mechanical parts and for grinding and polishing. Minerals are the source of metals such as iron, copper, and silver. Metal tools, aluminum foil, and the steel used to make cars all began as minerals. Many other minerals are used in foods, medicines, fertilizers, and building materials. Quartz is used in making glass. Gypsum, a soft, white mineral, is used to make wallboard and cement.

9. **Infer** Powerful drills often contain very small pieces of diamonds on their surface. Why do you think people use diamonds to help them drill?

....

....

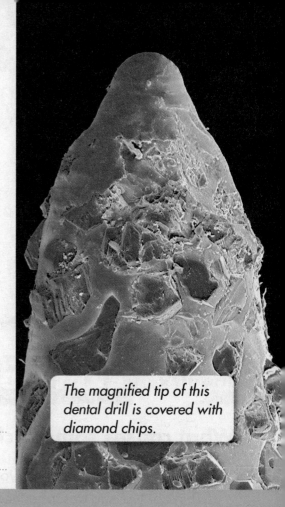

The magnified tip of this dental drill is covered with diamond chips.

Got it?

10. **Recognize** You want to identify two minerals. They both have a hardness of 3 and a white streak. What other properties must you compare to identify each mineral?

....

....

11. **Explain** What are some uses of minerals?

....

....

....

⬛ **Stop!** I need help with ....

⏸ **Wait!** I have a question about ....

▶ **Go!** Now I know ....

Lesson 2

What are rocks?

Describe the rocks you see in this photo.

Inquiry **Explore It!**

What causes some rocks to float?

☐ **1.** Hold and feel 3 rocks with your hands. Think of ways to describe them.

☐ **2.** Examine the rocks with a hand lens. List differences and similarities between the rocks.

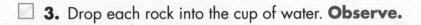

☑ **3.** Drop each rock into the cup of water. **Observe.**

Explain Your Results

4. Communicate within your group and with other groups. Which of the rock samples floated? Explain.

Materials

3 rocks

hand lens

plastic cup of water

---

myscienceonline.com | **Explore It!** Animation

I will know how to identify rocks. I will know the uses of some rocks.

Words to Know

igneous · · · · · · · metamorphic
sedimentary · · · rock cycle

Kinds of Rocks

There are three kinds of rocks. Each kind of rock is formed in a different way. By looking at how the minerals in the rock are arranged, it is often possible to determine how the rock was formed.

Igneous Rocks

Rocks that form when melted rock cools and hardens are called **igneous** rocks. Igneous rocks can form deep inside Earth or from lava that hardens on Earth's surface. As hot, liquid rock cools, crystals of minerals form. Melted rock that cools slowly results in igneous rocks with large crystals of minerals. Melted rock that cools quickly results in igneous rocks with small crystals.

Granite and basalt are examples of igneous rock. Granite forms when magma slowly cools underground. Basalt forms when lava cools quickly.

Pumice is a rock formed when lava is quickly cooled by air at the surface. It often has many tiny holes where gases were trapped in the lava as it cooled.

1. Apply Does basalt have large or small crystals? Explain.

granite

basalt

Basalt is one of the most common rocks on Earth.

Sedimentary Rocks

Most **sedimentary** rocks form when layers of materials and rock particles settle on top of each other and then harden. Minerals from water may act like cement. They hold the particles together.

Sandstone and conglomerate are examples of sedimentary rock. Sandstone can form when layers of sand are buried and put under pressure. Large, rounded particles that have been pressed together form conglomerate.

2. **Identify** Identify each sedimentary rock below. Complete the captions.

_____ is formed from particles.

_____ is formed from sand.

Metamorphic Rocks

When solid rock is squeezed and heated to very high temperatures, the particles inside the rock can take on different arrangements. New minerals may also be formed. These rocks are metamorphic rocks. **Metamorphic** rock is rock formed inside Earth from other rocks under heat and pressure. Under very high temperature and pressure, solid rock particles form rough layers, as seen in gneiss. At lower pressure, fine, thin layers are formed, as seen in slate.

3. **Sequence** What can happen to rock particles after they are squeezed and heated to high temperatures?

_____

_____

gneiss

slate

myscienceonline.com | THE BIG ? | I Will Know...

The Rock Cycle

Rocks are constantly being formed and destroyed in a process called the **rock cycle.** Rocks may be changed from one kind to another in any order or stay the same for millions of years. The remains of organisms can be part of the rock cycle. The diagram shows the different ways that one type of rock can become another type of rock.

4. **Interpret** Use the rock-cycle diagram to determine the type of rock that igneous rock can become.

....

....

Igneous rocks

Melting

Cooling

Wearing away

Soil

Heat and Pressure

Melting

Magma

Melting

Melting

Wearing away

Wearing away

Cementation

Heat and Pressure

Metamorphic rocks

Sedimentary rocks

Identifying Rocks

You can find rocks almost anywhere. When you do find a rock, how do you identify it? Scientists identify rocks by looking at how they formed. Scientists also consider their mineral content, their color, and their texture.

Minerals in Rock

Rocks are made of mixtures of minerals and other materials. Some rocks contain only one type of mineral. Others contain many minerals. For example, granite is made up of the minerals quartz, feldspar, hornblende, and mica.

Color

A rock's color helps scientists determine the type of minerals in the rock. Granite that has a high amount of reddish feldspar is a speckled pink. Quartz crystals in granite add light gray or smoky specks.

Texture

A rock's texture is the look and feel of the rock's surface. Most rocks are made up of particles of minerals or other rocks. These particles are called grains. Grains give the rock its texture. Some rocks are smooth and glassy. Others are rough and chalky.

The color in this granite comes from the mineral feldspar.

5. **Identify** Read the information given for each common rock below. Then use the information to identify each rock as igneous, sedimentary, or metamorphic.

Coal is a soft rock that forms when layers of dead plant materials pile up over a very long time.

Pure marble is white and is made up of the mineral calcite. Marble is formed from limestone that is heated to a high temperature and is under intense pressure.

Obsidian has a glassy texture. It is formed when lava cools quickly.

myscienceonline.com | Got it? | 60-Second Video

Economic Significance

People use rocks for different purposes. Many rocks are used in building materials. Thin, polished sheets of granite make up curbstones, floors, and kitchen counters. People use sandstone and limestone on the outside walls of buildings. Limestone is also used to make cement and steel.

Rocks have other uses too. Marble is a soft rock that comes in different colors. It can be carved and polished to make many shapes. These characteristics make marble a good material for buildings and statues. The rough surface of pumice makes it good for cleaning and polishing.

The United States Supreme Court building is made mostly of marble.

6. **Infer** Slate splits easily into flat pieces. Which rock might be more useful for carving chess pieces, slate or marble? Explain.

....

....

Got it?

7. **Summarize** What characteristics do you use to identify rocks?

....

....

....

8. **Explain** What are some uses of rocks?

....

....

....

⬛ **Stop!** I need help with ....

⏸ **Wait!** I have a question about ....

▶ **Go!** Now I know ....

Lesson 3

What makes up soil?

Envision It!

Tell how you think this soil formed.

Inquiry **Explore It!**

What are the parts of soil?

☐ **1.** Use a hand lens. **Observe** the soil.

☐ **2.** Identify some organic and inorganic parts.

☐ **3.** Add 10 spoonfuls of water. Squeeze the wet soil in your hand. Write your observations.

Explain Your Results

4. What kinds of organic parts could you identify in the soil?

5. Communicate Describe your soil sample. Tell about its color, the parts that make it up, and how well it holds water.

Materials

plastic cup with soil

plastic bin

forceps

spoon

glove

plastic cup with water

hand lens

Be careful! **Wear a glove. Wash hands when finished.**

316

myscienceonline.com | **Explore It!** Animation

Words to Know

soil	humus
weathering	inorganic
organic matter	matter

Soil Formation

Most of Earth's land is covered by soil. **Soil** is a mixture
of nonliving materials and decayed materials from
organisms. Plants need soil to live. Many animals such
as earthworms and chipmunks make their homes in soil.

Soil takes many years to form. The natural process of
weathering helps make soil. **Weathering** is a slow process
that breaks rocks into smaller pieces called sediments.
Freezing and melting water, plant roots, and chemicals
in rain and snow are causes of weathering. For example,
water that drips into cracks in a rock can freeze and
thaw over and over. When water freezes, it gets larger. Ice
pushing against the sides of the cracks widens the cracks.
The rock breaks apart and eventually becomes sediment.

1. **Hypothesize** How might the tree roots growing into the
   rock in this picture cause weathering? Explain.

....

....

....

....

Parts of Soil

Pieces of different kinds of weathered rock are a major part of soil. Soil is full of other things too.

Organic Matter

Soil contains organic matter. **Organic matter** includes living materials and materials that were once alive. The living material contains tiny organisms such as bacteria, fungi, worms, and insects. They break down plant and animal remains into the substances that plants can use as food.

Soil contains decaying plant and animal remains. This decaying material is called **humus.** Humus is a rich, dark brown color. Humus helps make spaces in soil for the air and water that plants need. Humus also contains nutrients that plants need to grow.

Inorganic Matter

Soil also contains inorganic matter. **Inorganic matter** includes all the nonliving materials in soil. Water, air, and pieces of rock and minerals are inorganic materials in soil. Small spaces in soil hold the water and air.

Layers of Soil

Over time, soil develops layers. Most soil has three basic layers. These layers are topsoil, subsoil, and bedrock.

2. **Compute** The circle graph shows a good soil make-up for growing plants. What percentage of soil is organic matter?

25% air

45% mineral matter

25% water

organic matter

myscienceonline.com THE BIG I Will Know...

Topsoil
Topsoil is the top layer of soil. It is crumbly and dark brown because it is made mostly of humus. It is the layer with the most organic matter.

Subsoil
The second layer of soil is called subsoil. It is often a different color than topsoil. Subsoil contains many minerals and small rocks. It has less organic matter than topsoil.

Bedrock
Bedrock is mostly solid rock. It is deeper in some places than in others. Water may seep into cracks in bedrock and slowly weather it. Eventually, bedrock may become sediments in soil.

3. ⊙ **Compare and Contrast** How are subsoil and bedrock alike? How are they different?

....

....

....

....

....

4. **Hypothesize** Read the descriptions of soil layers. Where might burrowing animals such as moles live? Explain.

....

....

....

Soil Survey

With an adult, take a walk. Look closely at the soil. Use a hand lens. Identify organic and inorganic parts of the soil. Do you see more than one type? Create a chart in which you describe the soils you saw.

clay

silt

sand

Kinds of Soil

There are many kinds of soil. The size of the sediments in the soil determines the soil's texture and its ability to hold water. The color of the soil depends on what materials are in the soil.

Clay is smooth and has fine, tightly packed rock particles. Clay can hold a lot of water. Clay may be different colors because of the materials in it. For example, clay with iron particles looks red.

Silt particles are slightly larger than clay particles. Silt particles feel smooth. Silt feels slippery but not sticky when it is wet.

Larger particles are called sand. Water quickly passes through sand particles. Sandy soil contains particles from different materials. The most common mineral in sand is quartz. The color of sand depends upon the materials in it. Some sand is very light colored. Sand that forms from mostly volcanic rock can be black.

5. CHALLENGE In which kind of soil might plants grow best? Explain.

....

....

6. **Compare** Use the sizes given in the chart below to draw each type of soil particle. Then label each soil particle.

The chart gives the relative sizes of sand particles, silt particles, and clay particles.

Relative Sizes of Soil Particles		
Less Than $\frac{1}{256}$ mm	Less Than $\frac{1}{16}$ mm	Less Than 2 mm

Factors That Affect Soil

Certain factors affect how different soils form. Two of these factors are climate and the type of rock. The temperature and weather in a climate can affect how fast or slow soil forms. For example, rock might break down faster in a hot, humid climate than in a cold, dry climate. Some types of rock break down and become soil faster than others. For example, basalt contains the mineral feldspar, which easily weathers to form clay minerals. So basalt quickly weathers to form clay-rich soil.

7. Infer What kind of soil would you expect to find in this bayou?

....

....

....

....

Bayous are slow-moving streams.

Got it?

8. Summarize What are the parts of soil?

....

....

....

9. UNLOCK THE BIG ? How does weathering change Earth's surface?

....

....

....

....

◻ **Stop!** I need help with ....

⏸ **Wait!** I have a question about ....

▶ **Go!** Now I know ....

What are erosion and deposition?

Envision It!

Tell what you think caused this arch to form.

Inquiry **Explore It!**

How does melting ice cause erosion?

Materials

2 containers

2 plastic cups with sand

2 ice cubes

☐ **1.** Put 1 cup of sand on each container.
Make a model of 2 landforms.
Make a hill on one container.
Make a flat plain on the other container.

☐ **2.** Place 1 ice cube in the middle of each pile of sand.
Observe.

Explain Your Results

3. Which landform **model** eroded more?

....

....

4. Draw a Conclusion How does the shape of the land affect erosion?

....

....

....

myscienceonline.com | **Explore It!** Animation

I will know how erosion
and deposition can change
Earth's surface.

Words to Know

erosion

deposition

Erosion and Deposition

Materials such as rock particles on Earth move.
Water, wind, and ice can carry particles from one
place to another place. The movement of materials
away from a place is called **erosion.** Gravity is the
main force causing erosion. In a landslide, gravity
quickly pulls rocks and soil downhill. Landslides
often occur during earthquakes and after heavy
rains. Landslides are more likely to happen on steep
slopes with no trees.

Materials moved by erosion end up in other
places. **Deposition** is the process of laying down
materials, such as rocks and soil. These sediments
can be deposited in different places by wind or
flowing water. This process may happen quickly, or
it may take a long time.

1. **Infer** How might trees on steep slopes help prevent
landslides?

....

....

....

2. Conclude What conclusion can you draw about the speed of moving water on flatter land and its ability to cause erosion?

....

....

....

....

3. ⊙ **Cause and Effect** Reread the paragraph on rain. **Underline** the effect of rainwater flowing over bare farm fields.

As the brownish water of the Mississippi River flows along, it can carry sediment thousands of miles to the Gulf of Mexico.

Water Erosion and Deposition

Moving water causes much of the erosion that shapes Earth's surface. Water can also deposit materials in other places to create new landforms. Rivers, rain, waves, ocean currents, and glaciers are all forms of moving water.

Rivers

Gravity causes rivers to flow. As rivers flow downhill, they pick up and carry sediments, such as rock, soil, and sand. The sediments can erode the riverbeds by grinding against the riverbeds again and again. The faster a river flows, the more sediments it can carry and the heavier those sediments can be. Rivers also erode the land around them. A fast-flowing river can form V-shaped valleys. Slow rivers form looping bends, which erode the sides of the valley and make it wider. The deposited material from rivers forms areas called deltas.

Rain

Rain can loosen sediments from the soil and carry them away. Rain can cause flooding in low, flat areas. Flooding damages soil, roads, and buildings. Rainwater flowing over bare farm fields on slopes can erode tons of soil and deposit it downhill. To prevent soil erosion, farmers plow furrows perpendicular to the field's slope. The furrows catch rainwater, keeping the rain from carrying soil away.

Waves

Waves cause erosion along coastlines. As waves hit against rocks, the rocks can break. Sand and gravel in the waves act like sandpaper, weathering the rocks over time. Waves that erode one shoreline may drop sand somewhere else to form other beaches. Storms, tides, and currents can erode beaches. Grasses and plants can help hold soil in place to prevent beach erosion.

myscienceonline.com | THE BIG ? | I Will Know...

Glaciers

Water frozen in glaciers can cause erosion. Gravity pulls glaciers down along a valley. As this movement happens, glaciers grind rocks beneath them into sediments. The glaciers deposit sediments downhill. Over a long time, the action of glaciers wears away the bottom of a valley, which becomes U-shaped.

4. Infer Why might it have taken many years for a glacier to form this U-shaped valley?

....

....

....

....

Do the math!

Calculate Rates

Because of water erosion, a sandy coast can erode about 5 meters every 5 years.

1 Suppose that the coast continues to erode at the same rate. How much will the coast erode in 50 years? Show your work.

....

....

....

2 Suppose that during each severe storm the coast erodes an additional 4 meters. If there were 15 severe storms in one year, how much did the coast erode because of the storms?

....

Wind Erosion and Deposition

Wind erosion is caused by wind blowing dust, soil, or sand from one place to another. When sand and dust blow against a rock, tiny bits of the rock might break off. These bits are immediately blown away. Wind erosion also changes sand dunes and fields.

Sand Dunes

Sand dunes are large, loose deposits of sand. The size and shape of a sand dune depend on the speed and direction that the winds are blowing, the amount of sand available, and the number of plants that live in the area. The stronger the wind, the farther sand particles can move. Winds that move in a steady direction can move a dune. This kind of wind will consistently pick up sand from one side and deposit it on the other side. This process causes the entire dune to move slowly in the same direction the wind moves.

5. [CHALLENGE] Why is wind erosion more likely to happen in dry areas than moist areas?

....

....

6. **Hypothesize** How could sand dunes be held in place to keep them from drifting onto a road?

....

....

....

Fields

Wind erosion can be a serious problem on farms. Bare, plowed fields can become very dry. Winds can blow topsoil off the fields. This topsoil is the best kind of soil for growing crops. It cannot be quickly replaced. Farmers often plant rows of tall trees along the edges of fields to prevent wind erosion of topsoil. The trees prevent some of the wind from blowing on the field. Some farmers are able to grow their crops with less plowing. In this way, the soil stays in larger clumps that do not get blown away.

7. **Explain** How is wind erosion being prevented in the photo?

....

....

....

Got it?

8. **Identify** What is one cause of erosion? How can it be prevented?

....

....

....

9. **UNLOCK THE BIG ?** How does deposition change Earth's surface?

....

....

☐ **Stop!** I need help with ....

❚❚ **Wait!** I have a question about ....

▶ **Go!** Now I know ....

Lesson 5

How does Earth's surface change?

Envision It!

Describe what you think caused this part of Earth's surface to change.

Inquiry Explore It!

How do forces affect Earth's surface?

☐ **1.** Cut an index card to the size of a sponge. Tape it to the sponge. On the other side of the sponge, put a second sponge. Connect them with a rubber band.

☐ **2.** Join 2 other sponges with a rubber band.

☐ **3.** Place 2 desks about 10 cm apart. Put a pair of sponges on each side of the gap.

☐ **4.** Slowly move the sponges together. **Record** your **observations.**

 Be careful! Be careful with scissors

....

....

....

Materials

scissors

4 soft sponges

index card

2 rubber bands

2 strips of masking tape

Be sure to place the cardboard side down. Let the sponges hang over the edges of the desk.

Explain Your Results

5. Communicate How does this activity **model** how mountains form?

....

....

....

mysCienceonLine.com ◄ **Explore It!** Animation

I will know how forces change Earth's surface.

Words to Know

plate
constructive
force

destructive
force

Earth's Plates

The solid, rocky outer-most layer of Earth is called the lithosphere. The lithosphere covers all of Earth, but it is not a solid sheet of material. It is broken into several large sections and many smaller ones. A section of the lithosphere is called a **plate.** Several plates are larger than continents. A plate may include continents, parts of the ocean floor, or both. Earth's plates move slowly. They might move into each other, pull apart, or grind past each other.

1. Locate This map shows Earth's plates. **Circle** the plate that you live on.

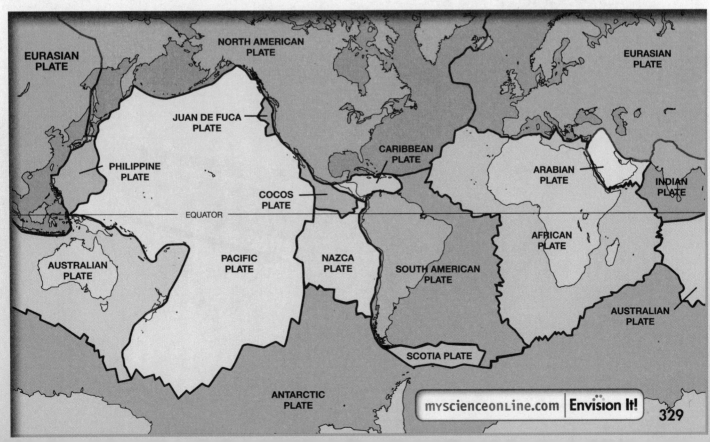

EURASIAN PLATE

NORTH AMERICAN PLATE

EURASIAN PLATE

JUAN DE FUCA PLATE

CARIBBEAN PLATE

ARABIAN PLATE

INDIAN PLATE

PHILIPPINE PLATE

COCOS PLATE

EQUATOR

AFRICAN PLATE

AUSTRALIAN PLATE

PACIFIC PLATE

NAZCA PLATE

SOUTH AMERICAN PLATE

AUSTRALIAN PLATE

SCOTIA PLATE

ANTARCTIC PLATE

Changes over Time

Plate movements are small. Some plates move less than one centimeter per year. Some plates move as much as ten centimeters per year. Even so, these movements can cause big changes to Earth's surface. Some changes occur slowly over thousands or millions of years. These changes include mountains being built and valleys being formed. Some changes happen quickly in days or even minutes.

Generally, mountains form, earthquakes occur, and volcanoes erupt in certain places. These places are where plates meet. The edges where Earth's plates meet are called plate boundaries. A converging boundary occurs when two plates move into each other. A spreading plate boundary may form when plates move apart from each other. At a sliding plate boundary, two plates move past each other in opposite directions. You can see a crack in the land in some places where two plates meet. This crack is called a fault.

2. Infer What might cause a rapid change in Earth's surface?

3. Classify Read about the land features in the diagram. Then write the type of plate boundary that forms each feature.

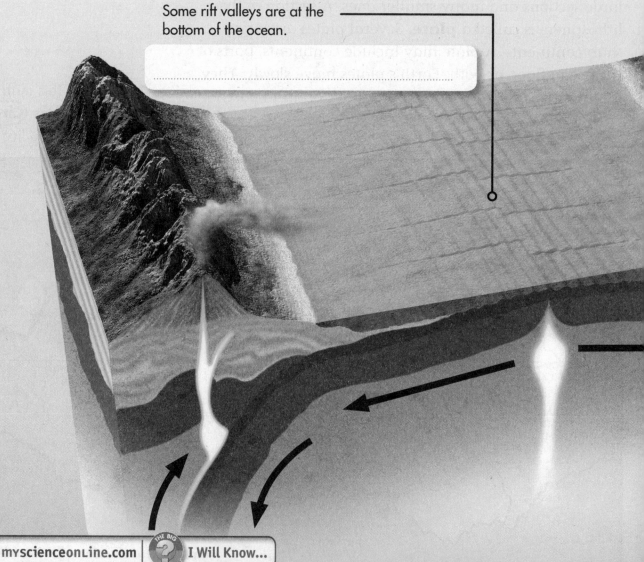

Some rift valleys are at the bottom of the ocean.

myscienceonline.com | THE BIG ? | I Will Know...

Constructive and Destructive Forces

Many forces change Earth's surface. These changes mostly occur at plate boundaries. **Constructive forces** build new features on Earth's surface. Forces that wear away or tear down features are **destructive forces.**

Mountains and Valleys

Constructive forces form new mountains and valleys. Mountains form when Earth's crust folds, tilts, and lifts as plates collide. New valleys can form at spreading plate boundaries, such as the one under the Atlantic Ocean. At this boundary, the ocean floor looks like a mountain range. It is called the mid-Atlantic ridge. The low area between the plates is a rift valley. It is slowly becoming wider.

4. **Demonstrate** Use the illustration on these pages and tell about the results of constructive and destructive forces.

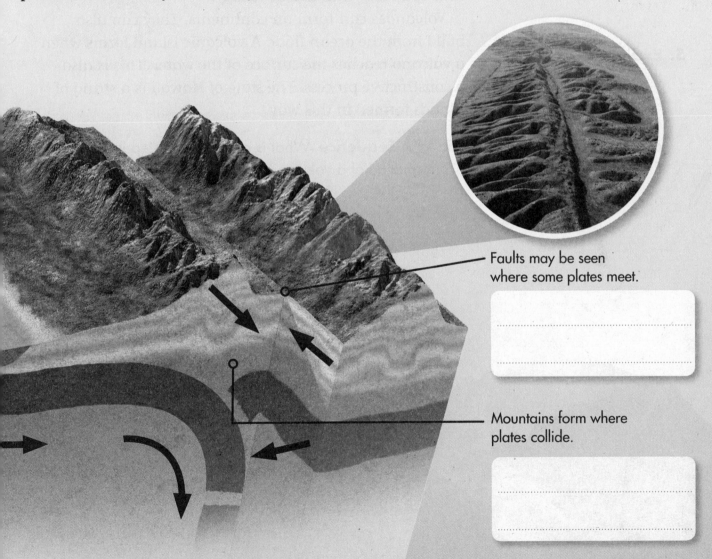

Faults may be seen where some plates meet.

Mountains form where plates collide.

331

Volcanoes

Most volcanoes on land form near converging plate boundaries. As one plate moves below another plate, rock partially melts into magma. Magma is a hot liquid material inside Earth. Sometimes the magma is forced to the surface through a weak spot in the lithosphere. This action is called an eruption. The magma that reaches Earth's surface is called lava. Volcanoes can do more than ooze fountains of lava. Gases such as water vapor and carbon dioxide are often mixed with the lava. Trapped gases can have enough pressure to blow apart the side of a volcano during an eruption. These trapped gases can push lava high into the air. While it is still in the air, this lava may cool into ash or rocks.

Volcanoes can form on continents. They can also build from the ocean floor. A volcanic island forms when a volcano reaches the surface of the water. This is also a constructive process. The state of Hawaii is a string of islands formed in this way.

5. **Explain** Do you think the volcano in this picture is an example of a constructive or deconstructive force? Explain.

6. ◉ **Sequence** What is often the first step in the formation of a volcano?

Earthquakes

Earthquakes happen along faults. Faults are cracks in Earth's lithosphere where the surrounding rock has shifted. Faults can form anywhere. Earthquakes most often occur at faults along plate boundaries. The plates get "hung up" and lock in place. Eventually the plates jerk into a new position. This sudden movement and the resulting vibrations cause an earthquake. Plate movements often happen far below ground.

Energy released in an earthquake can destroy things quickly. It can cause landslides, which are downhill movements of large amounts of rock. Earthquakes under the ocean can cause tsunamis. Tsunamis are large waves of water that can crash into a coastline, destroy things, and wash away soil.

7. CHALLENGE Is a landslide a constructive or destructive force? Explain.

....

....

....

An earthquake can cause sections of road to be cracked, twisted, or completely destroyed.

Got it?

8. **Compare** How are volcanic eruptions, earthquakes, landslides, and Earth's plates related?

....

....

....

9. **Exemplify** What are some possible results of constructive forces on Earth's surface?

....

....

◻ **Stop!** I need help with ....

❚❚ **Wait!** I have a question about ....

▶ **Go!** Now I know ....

What are some energy resources?

Envision It!

Explain how wind turbines might use the energy in wind.

my planet diary

Science Stats

Did you know that the sun's energy can be used to make electricity? Solar power stations are being built around the world to do just that. In Spain, the power station PS10 is already in use. The station consists of 624 reflectors with surfaces that are 120 square meters each. That's the size of about half of a tennis-court surface! These reflectors direct the sun's rays onto a central tower. In the tower, solar energy is converted into electricity in a two-step process. PS10 is an 11-Megawatt station. It produces enough electricity to supply about 6,000 homes!

Where in the United States might be a good place to put a solar power station? Explain.

....

....

myscienceonline.com | my planet diary

I will know renewable, nonrenewable, and inexhaustible energy resources.

Words to Know
....
renewable resource
inexhaustible resource
nonrenewable resource

Energy Resources

A resource is something that will meet a need. An energy resource is something that will meet energy needs. The sun is an energy resource. It gives off energy in the forms of light and heat. People can use this light to make electricity. Trees are also an energy resource. Trees provide wood. Wood produces heat when it burns, so people can use it to heat their homes. There are different kinds of energy resources. Renewable, nonrenewable, and inexhaustible resources are three major types of natural resources.

1. ◎ **Sequence** Complete the graphic organizer below. Write what happens when people burn wood in their homes.

First

Next

Last

2. **Classify** What is the energy resource in this photo?

Go Green

Compost It!
Make your own compost pile. Ask an adult to cut off the top of a plastic gallon jug. Fill it with leaves, grass clippings, and fruit and vegetable wastes. Cover your jug with plastic wrap. Then wait for your biomass to become soil!

Renewable and Inexhaustible Resources

Resources that can be replaced are **renewable resources.** Renewable energy resources include the wood from trees, leaves, food wastes, and even manure. These resources belong to a group of fuels called biomass fuels, which are made by living things or from recently living things. Some biomass, such as corn, is turned into fuels that can run cars and trucks. People will never run out of biomass because garbage is always being made. By using biomass as a resource, less garbage will be taken to landfills. One disadvantage is that burning biomass causes air pollution.

Sun, wind, moving water, and energy from inside Earth are inexhaustible resources. **Inexhaustible resources** will not run out.

3. ◉ **Cause and Effect** **Underline** two effects of using biomass for energy.

Do the math!

Read a Circle Graph

The circle graph shows the percentage of energy from inexhaustible and renewable resources used in 2007 in the United States.

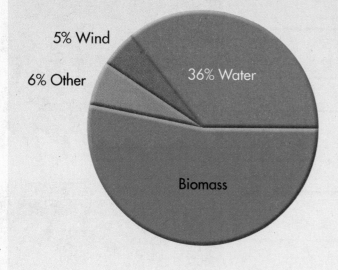

5% Wind

6% Other

36% Water

Biomass

Use the graph to answer these questions.

1. What percentage of energy use from these resources came from biomass fuels?

2. The energy from these resources is measured in energy units. In 2007, energy use from these resources was 6.8 energy units. Estimate how many energy units came from biomass fuels. Explain how you got your answer.

Biomass

Trees provide wood. Wood is probably the first fuel that people ever used for both heat and light. Although wood is a renewable fuel, it takes time for new trees to grow that will replace those that have been cut down. Also, burning wood increases the amount of carbon dioxide in the air, which may contribute to global warming.

Wind

Wind is the motion of air. People have used the wind for energy for thousands of years. For example, the blades of windmills were connected to machines that ground grain and pumped water. Today, a wind turbine uses the wind's energy to spin a generator that makes electricity. Wind is an inexhaustible resource.

Solar Energy

Solar energy is energy from sunlight. A device called a solar cell changes solar energy into electrical energy. When light hits the cell, an electric current is produced. Groups of solar cells form solar panels. Some homes, buildings, and cars have solar panels to provide energy. Solar energy is also used to heat things, such as the air in greenhouses.

Geothermal Energy

The rock material deep inside Earth is very hot. Energy from the high temperature inside Earth is called geothermal energy. One way to get geothermal energy is to pump water down deep holes into hot rock. The hot rock heats the water or turns the water into steam. The steam rushes back to Earth's surface and can be used to make electricity.

4. [CHALLENGE] Tell where the energy in wood originally comes from.

Nonrenewable Resources

Energy resources that either cannot be replaced at all or cannot be replaced as fast as people use them are **nonrenewable resources.** Nuclear energy and fossil fuels are nonrenewable energy sources.

Nuclear Energy

Nuclear power plants often use a metal called uranium to heat water into steam. This steam is used to power generators that produce electricity. Nuclear power plants do not release pollution into the air. But their wastes are dangerous and must be stored in special places.

Fossil Fuels

Coal, oil, and natural gas are also nonrenewable energy sources. They are called fossil fuels because they are made from the remains of organisms that lived long ago.

Coal forms from plants. Under certain conditions, layers of dead plants build up and form a material called peat. Peat gets buried and slowly changes into soft coal and then into hard coal. Today, coal fuels many electric power plants. Burning coal turns water into steam. Steam causes generators to spin and make electricity.

5. **Estimate** Does the process of coal formation take tens, hundreds, or millions of years? Explain.

....

....

....

Coal Formation

plant life

peat

coal

Nuclear power plant

Most scientists think that oil forms the same way that coal forms. However, oil forms from the remains of tiny sea organisms, not dead plants. Oil may be found beneath land or beneath the ocean floor. Drills make deep holes in Earth's surface to reach the oil. Millions of cars, trucks, trains, and ships use the fuels made from oil. Oil is also used to heat homes.

Natural gas is often found where oil is found. The gas is usually pumped into pipelines. Pipelines carry the gas to storage tanks until it is needed. Natural gas is a common fuel used for heating homes and household appliances such as grills, stoves, and water heaters.

Oil is pumped out of the ground and then heated and separated to make different products. In addition to fuel, oil is made into products such as asphalt, plastic, grease, and wax.

6. **Explain** Read the caption for the picture to the right. Explain how people use one of the products mentioned.

....

....

Got it?

7. **Classify** Give an example of a renewable, nonrenewable, and inexhaustible energy resource.

....

....

....

8. **Differentiate** Why is coal not considered biomass?

....

....

....

⬜ **Stop!** I need help with ....

⏸ **Wait!** I have a question about ....

▶ **Go!** Now I know ....

What is pollution?

Circle the items that may harm this environment.

Inquiry Explore It!

How can pollution affect water?

People and other living things affect the environment. In this activity, you observe "water pollution" and infer how it could affect water plants.

☐ **1.** Shine a flashlight through a cup of water.
Observe how clear the water is.
Observe how much light shines out the other side.

☐ **2.** Add 10 drops of milk. Stir with a spoon.
Repeat Step 1.

Explain Your Results

3. Draw a Conclusion How did the milk affect the amount of light that traveled all the way through the water and out the side of the cup?

....

4. Infer How might cloudy water caused by pollution affect plants that grow in lakes or rivers?

....

....

....

Materials

plastic cup of water

milk

dropper

spoon

flashlight

Word to Know

pollutant

Pollutants

When you ride in a car or brush your teeth, you are
using natural resources. People must use natural resources
to live. However, sometimes pollutants harm these
resources. A **pollutant** is an unwanted substance added
to the water, air, or soil. Pollutants result in pollution.
Sources of pollutants may be natural. A volcanic eruption
can throw dust, ash, and other particles into the air. The
particles can block sunlight for a long period of time.
Without this sunlight, temperatures may drop or plants
might die. People may also be sources of pollutants.
Chemicals that people use to kill insects and weeds may
harm other organisms.

1. ◎ **Cause and Effect** What are the effects of a
volcanic eruption?

....

....

....

....

....

2. CHALLENGE A sandstorm
can send dust and sand
hundreds of miles away.
Give one way that the
dust and sand might
harm a natural resource.

....

....

....

sandstorm

3. **Infer** Air pollution can get into rain as it falls to the ground. This kind of pollution is called acid rain. How might acid rain harm the environment?

....

....

....

Pollutants in Air

Some air pollution is caused by volcanoes and forest fires, which add ash and dust to the air. But more and more often, air pollution results from the actions of people. Automobiles and coal-burning power plants release harmful chemicals into the air. These chemicals can be unhealthy to breathe. Chemicals in the air can also harm plants. Animals that depend on the plants may lose their source of food or shelter.

Pollutants in Water

Water is sometimes polluted by factories that dump harmful chemicals into rivers, lakes, and oceans. Some of these chemicals can harm or kill fish and other plants and animals that live in the water.

Oil is often moved from one place to another in large ships called tankers. If a tanker leaks, oil gets into the water and can wash up onto shore. Oil spills can harm or kill animals and plants that live in the water and on the coast.

4. **Identify** What is one way future oil spills might be prevented?

....

....

Smog is a kind of air pollution that results from the burning of coal and oil.

myscienceonline.com | Got it? 🕐 60-Second Video

Pollutants in Soil

Soil becomes polluted by garbage, litter, and other solid waste. Garbage used to be put into open dumps. Dumps created many problems. Rain that fell on a dump washed harmful chemicals into the soil. Today, most garbage is buried under the ground in landfills. Trees and grass can then be planted on top of the ground, and people can use the land again.

Sometimes people throw bottles, cans, wrappers, and other garbage onto the ground. This kind of pollution is called litter. Litter can be harmful to many animals. Litter can also spread germs.

garbage in a dump

5. Explain How might you reduce the amount of trash you throw away?

....

....

Got it?

6. Identify What are some problems polluted air can cause?

....

....

7. UNLOCK THE BIG ? What is an example of a pollutant in air? in water? in soil?

....

....

⬜ **Stop!** I need help with ....

⏸ **Wait!** I have a question about ....

▶ **Go!** Now I know ....

What are some properties of minerals?

Materials

6 minerals

streak plate   hand lens

Follow a Procedure

☐ **1.** Use a hand lens. **Observe** the properties of each mineral.

☐ **2.** **Record** their color and luster in the Table of Observed Properties on the next page.

☐ **3.** Rub each mineral across a streak plate. Record the color of its streak.

Inquiry Skill

You can use a hand lens to help you **observe.** If it has more than one power, try looking through each.

Be careful! Put the streak plate flat on the table during testing. If you hold it in your hand, it could break.

☐ **4.** Scratch Mineral A against Mineral F. Check if Mineral A is harder than Mineral F in the Table of Observed Properties.

☐ **5.** Compare the properties you observed with the Table of Diagnostic Properties shown below. Identify each mineral.

Table of Diagnostic Properties

Mineral	Properties			
	Color	Luster (glassy or metallic)	Streak	Hardness
Rose quartz	pink	glassy	white	7
Calcite	white/clear	glassy	white	3
Feldspar	varied	glassy	white	6
Mica (muscovite)	varied	glassy	white	2.5
Hornblende	dark green to black	glassy	pale gray	5.5
Pyrite	gold	metallic	green to brown to black	6.5

Table of Observed Properties

Mineral	Observed Properties				Identity of Mineral
	Color	Luster (glassy or metallic)	Streak	Hardness	
Mineral A				6	
Mineral B				not measured	
Mineral C				not measured	
Mineral D				not measured	
Mineral E				not measured	
Mineral F				2.5	

Analyze and Conclude

6. What is Mineral E? Which of its properties did you **observe**?

....

....

....

7. What properties did you use to describe and identify the minerals?

....

....

....

8. **UNLOCK THE BIG ?** Minerals are one of Earth's important resources. What are some properties of Earth's minerals?

....

....

....

Florence Bascom

(1862–1945)

Dr. Bascom was the second woman in the United States to receive a doctorate degree in geology. A doctorate degree is the highest academic degree a person can receive. She is considered by many to be "the first female geologist in this country." A geologist studies the history and structure of Earth, including rocks.

Dr. Bascom attended the University of Wisconsin, where she received two degrees. Then she studied at and earned her doctorate degree from Johns Hopkins University in 1893. Dr. Bascom soon became an expert in crystals, minerals, and rocks. She spent much of her time studying metamorphic rocks of the Piedmont Plateau. The Piedmont Plateau is the strip of land between the Appalachian Mountains and the Atlantic coast that stretches from New Jersey to Alabama. Dr. Bascom is known today for her contributions to the current understanding of mountain-building processes.

UNLOCK THE BIG ?

How did Florence Bascom's work help us understand how Earth's surface changes?

Vocabulary Smart Cards

mineral
igneous
sedimentary
metamorphic
rock cycle
soil
weathering
organic matter
humus
inorganic matter
erosion
deposition
plate
constructive force
destructive force
renewable resource
inexhaustible
   resource
nonrenewable
   resource
pollutant

Play a Game!

Cut out the Vocabulary Smart Cards. Work with a partner. One person puts the cards picture-side up. The other puts the cards picture-side down. Take turns matching each word with its definition.

metamorphic

metamórfica

mineral

mineral

rock cycle

ciclo de las rocas

igneous

ígnea

soil

suelo

sedimentary

sedimentaria

a nonliving, naturally occurring solid that has its own regular arrangement of particles in it

Write three examples of this word.

....

....

sólido natural, sin vida, cuyas partículas están regularmente organizadas

---

rocks formed inside Earth from other rocks under heat and pressure

Write an example of this word.

....

....

rocas que se forman dentro de la Tierra a partir de otras rocas, bajo calor y presión

---

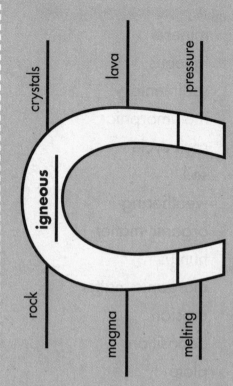

Make a Word Magnet!

Choose a vocabulary word and write it in the Word Magnet. Write words that are related to it on the lines.

---

rocks that form when melted rock cools and hardens

Write an example of this word.

....

....

....

rocas que se forman cuando la roca derretida se enfría y se endurece

---

a process in which rocks are constantly being formed and destroyed

Draw an example.

proceso en el cual las rocas se forman y se destruyen constantemente

---

rocks that form when layers of materials and rock particles settle on top of each other and then harden

Write an example of this word.

....

....

rocas que se forman cuando materiales y partículas de roca se asientan unos sobre los otros y se endurecen

---

a mixture of nonliving materials and decayed materials from organisms

Write three examples of this word.

....

....

mezcla de materiales sin vida y de materiales descompuestos procedentes de organismos

plate  **placa**	**inorganic matter** 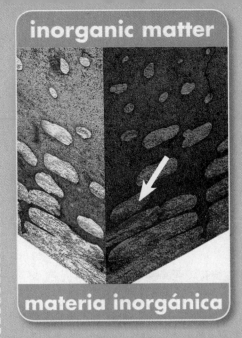 **materia inorgánica**	**weathering**  **meteorización**
constructive forces  **fuerzas constructivas**	**erosion**  **erosión**	**organic matter**  **materia orgánica**
destructive forces  **fuerzas destructivas**	**deposition**  **sedimentación**	**humus** 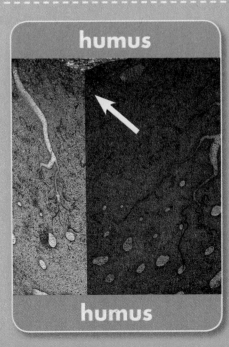 **humus**

a slow process that breaks rocks into sediments

Write a sentence using this word.

....

....

....

proceso lento que descompone las rocas en sedimento

---

all the nonliving materials in the soil

Write an example of this word.

....

....

....

todos los materiales sin vida que se hallan en el suelo

---

a section of the lithosphere

Write a different meaning of this word.

....

....

....

....

sección de la litosfera

---

all living materials and materials that were once alive

Write an example of this word.

....

....

....

todo material vivo o que alguna vez tuvo vida

---

the movement of materials away from a place

Write a sentence using the verb form of this word.

....

....

....

....

movimiento de materiales que se alejan de un lugar

---

forces that build new features on Earth's surface

Write an example of this word.

....

....

....

fuerzas que generan nuevas formaciones en la superficie de la Tierra

---

the decaying material in soil

Write a sentence using this word.

....

....

....

materia en descomposición que se halla en el suelo

---

process of laying down materials, such as rocks and soil

Draw an example.

proceso por el cual materiales como rocas y partículas de suelo se asientan

---

forces that wear away or tear down features on Earth's surface

Write an example of this word.

....

....

....

fuerzas que desgastan o destruyen las formaciones de la superficie terrestre

pollutant

contaminante

renewable resource

recurso renovable

inexhaustible resource

recurso inagotable

nonrenewable resource

recurso no renovable

a type of energy resource that can be replaced

Write a sentence using this word.

....

....

....

....

tipo de recurso energético que puede reemplazarse

---

an unwanted substance added to the land, water, or air

Write three examples of this word.

....

....

....

sustancia indeseable que se añade a la tierra, al agua o al aire

---

a type of energy resource that will not run out

Write three examples of this word.

....

....

....

....

tipo de recurso energético que nunca se agota

---

a type of energy resource that cannot be replaced at all or cannot be replaced as fast as people use it

What is the prefix of resource?

....

tipo de recurso energético que no se puede reemplazar o que no se puede reemplazar con la misma rapidez con que se lo usa

Lesson 1

What are minerals?

- A mineral is a nonliving, naturally occurring solid that has its own arrangement of particles.
- Mineral properties include hardness, luster, shape, streak, and color.

Lesson 2

What are rocks?

- The three kinds of rocks are igneous, sedimentary, and metamorphic.
- Rocks are constantly being formed and destroyed in the rock cycle.

Lesson 3

What makes up soil?

- Soil contains organic matter such as humus and organisms and inorganic matter such as rock, air, and water.
- Three kinds of soil are clay, silt, and sand.

Lesson 4

What are erosion and deposition?

- Wind, water, ice, changes in temperature, and chemical changes can weather, or break down, rock.
- Erosion moves rock away. Deposition places rock in other areas.

Lesson 5

How does Earth's surface change?

- Earth's surface is divided into slow-moving sections called plates.
- Movement of Earth's plates can cause earthquakes, volcanic eruptions, and landslides.

Lesson 6

What are some energy resources?

- Biomass and solar energy are renewable resources.
- Nuclear energy and fossil fuels cannot be replaced at all or cannot be replaced as fast as people use them.

Lesson 7

What is pollution?

- Some sources of pollutants are natural. Some are made by people.
- Air, water, or soil can become polluted.

Chapter Review

Lesson 1

What are minerals?

1. Identify Suppose you find an interesting mineral but you do not know what it is. What properties could help you identify the mineral?

....

....

2. Write About It Explain the uses of a diamond.

....

....

Lesson 2

What are rocks?

3. Identify Is the rock shown an igneous, sedimentary, or metamorphic rock? Explain.

....

....

....

Lesson 3

What makes up soil?

4. Identify What are the organic parts of soil? What are the inorganic parts?

....

....

....

5. Name What are the three kinds of rock particles in soil?

....

....

....

Lesson 4

What are erosion and deposition?

6. Explain How can water cause the loss of soil from bare farm fields on slopes? How can this erosion be prevented?

....

....

....

....

Lesson 5

How does Earth's surface change?

7. ⊙ **Sequence** **Underline** and number the steps in an earthquake's formation.

Earthquakes happen at faults along plate boundaries. The plates lock in place. Then the plates jerk into a new position. These movements usually happen far below ground but can be so strong that people feel them as earthquakes.

Lesson 6

What are some energy resources?

Do the math!

8. In 2007, energy use from some inexhaustible and renewable resources was 6.8 energy units. In 2008, energy use from the same resources was 7.3 energy units. By how many energy units did energy use increase in 2008?

....

....

Lesson 7

What is pollution?

9. **Summarize** Is the steam that a nuclear power plant releases into the air a pollutant? Explain.

....

....

....

....

10. **APPLY THE BIG ?** **What kinds of processes change Earth's surface?**

....

How is Earth's surface changed by both slow and fast changes? Give examples.

....

....

....

....

....

Fill in the bubble next to the answer choice you think is correct
for each multiple-choice question.

1 Which energy resource takes the shortest time to form?

Ⓐ natural gas
Ⓑ biomass
Ⓒ coal
Ⓓ oil

2 Which is most likely to cause erosion to a beach?

Ⓐ wind
Ⓑ gravity
Ⓒ rain
Ⓓ waves

3 What is a common use of the rock granite?

Ⓐ as kitchen counters
Ⓑ as cement
Ⓒ as a polisher
Ⓓ as a cleaner

4 Which part of soil is inorganic?

Ⓐ humus
Ⓑ water
Ⓒ bacteria
Ⓓ earthworm

5 What landform is a result of the movement of these two plates?

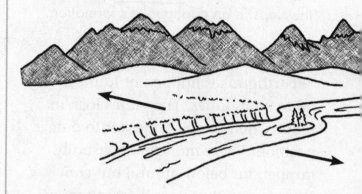

Ⓐ mountain
Ⓑ volcano
Ⓒ rift valley
Ⓓ fault

6 Suppose you are walking in a park near a river. The sun is shining and a strong wind blows. Identify three energy resources around you. Then explain how they might be used to power lights for the park.

....

....

....

....

....

....

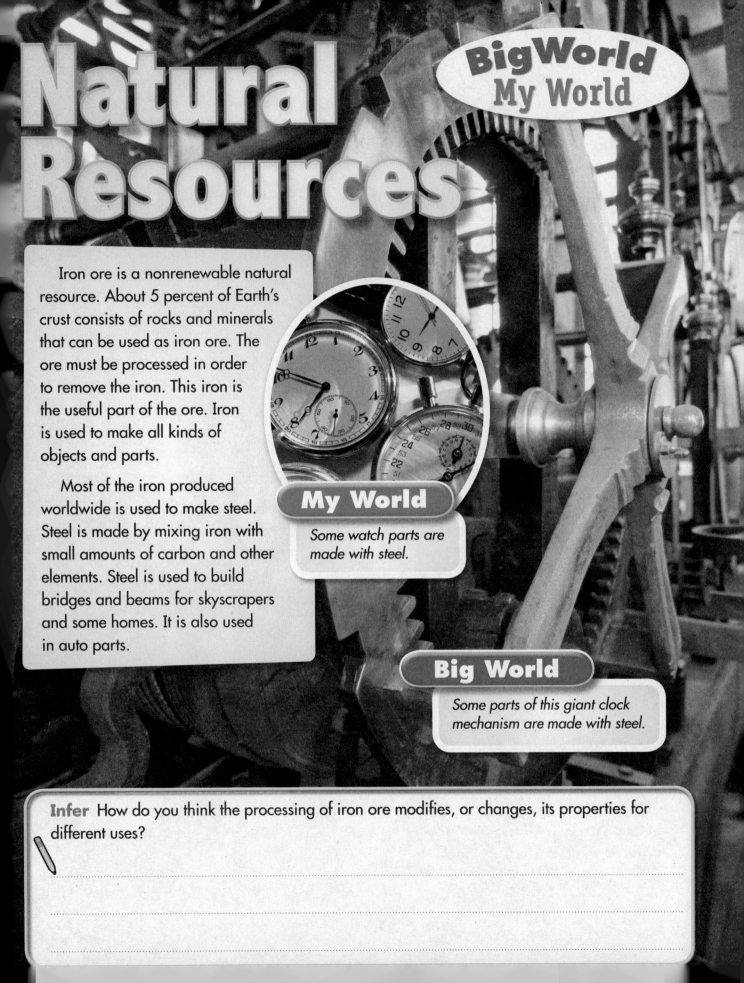

Natural Resources

Iron ore is a nonrenewable natural resource. About 5 percent of Earth's crust consists of rocks and minerals that can be used as iron ore. The ore must be processed in order to remove the iron. This iron is the useful part of the ore. Iron is used to make all kinds of objects and parts.

Most of the iron produced worldwide is used to make steel. Steel is made by mixing iron with small amounts of carbon and other elements. Steel is used to build bridges and beams for skyscrapers and some homes. It is also used in auto parts.

My World

Some watch parts are made with steel.

Big World

Some parts of this giant clock mechanism are made with steel.

Infer How do you think the processing of iron ore modifies, or changes, its properties for different uses?

What is happening in the SKY?

Earth and Space

Chapter 9

Try It! What does a spiral galaxy look like from different angles?

Lesson 1 How does Earth move?

Lesson 2 What is a star?

Lesson 3 What are the inner planets?

Lesson 4 What are the outer planets?

Lesson 5 What are asteroids, meteors, comets, and moons?

Investigate It! How can spinning affect a planet's shape?

You may have seen the moon when it looks like a crescent, a shape that looks like a circle with a bite taken out of it. This happens when we can see only part of the moon's sunlit side. The sun usually looks like a full circle, but sometimes the sun can look like a crescent too.

Predict When do you think the sun might look like a crescent?

....

....

THE BIG ? How do objects move in space?

What does a spiral galaxy look like from different angles?

Materials

25 cups

☐ **1.** Use cups to make this spiral galaxy.

These cups represent a spiral galaxy. The sun is a star near the edge of the Milky Way, a spiral galaxy.

☐ **2. Observe** the cups from directly above. The Milky Way Galaxy looks like this from outside the galaxy. Draw a diagram from this angle.

☐ **3.** Kneel to observe the cups at eye level from the edge. The Milky Way Galaxy looks like this from Earth, which is near the edge of the galaxy. Draw a diagram from this angle.

Inquiry Skill
You can use a physical **model** to help see things from different angles.

Explain Your Results

4. UNLOCK THE BIG ? Describe the differences in **observations** from different angles.

....

....

....

5. How is your **model** like a spiral galaxy? How is it different?

....

....

....

Drawings of Spiral Galaxy Model

Viewed from Above

Viewed from the Edge

Compare and Contrast

- When you **compare** things, you tell how they are alike.
- When you **contrast** things, you tell how they are different.

Deciding About Distance

Mercury takes 88 days to travel around the sun. Neptune takes about 164.5 years. Each planet travels in its own path and is a different distance from the sun. Mercury is closer to the sun, so its path is shorter. Neptune is farther from the sun, so its path is longer.

Practice It!

Use the graphic organizer to show how Mercury and Neptune are alike and how they are different.

The sizes and distances in this diagram are not true to scale. Also, the planets rarely line up.

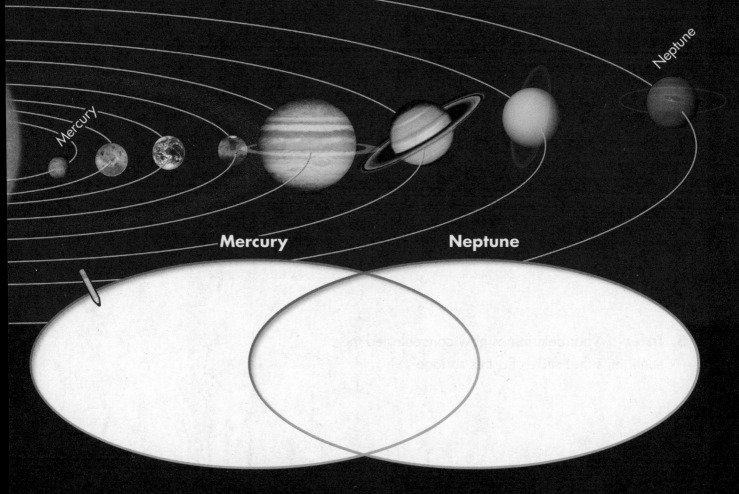

Mercury

Neptune

How does Earth move?

Envision It!

The sun is rising in the eastern sky. Describe the path you think the sun will take across the sky during the day.

Inquiry Explore It!

How does sunlight strike Earth's surface?

☐ **1.** Hold a flashlight about 15 cm directly above a piece of cardboard. Turn the flashlight on.

☐ **2. Observe** the light on the cardboard. Trace the shape the light makes.

☐ **3.** Repeat Step 1 slowly tilting the flashlight to the side. Repeat Step 2.

Explain Your Results

4. How did the light change?

....

....

5. Infer What determines how concentrated the sunlight is that strikes Earth's surface?

....

....

Materials

flashlight

white cardboard

marker

myscienceonline.com | **Explore It!** Animation

I will know how Earth rotates and revolves. I will know why the sun, the moon, and stars appear to move across the sky.

Words to Know

axis	orbit
rotation	revolution

Earth and the Sun

Think about a time thousands of years ago, before telescopes had been invented and before astronauts had ever traveled into space. If you look at the daytime sky, the sun rises in the east and sets in the west. People naturally thought the sun was moving around Earth.

We now know that the sun is the center of our solar system. Earth and the other planets move around the sun. Earth spins, causing the sun and other objects, such as other stars, to appear to move across the sky.

1. ◉ **Compare and Contrast** Use the graphic organizer below to list what is alike about and different between the way people used to think about Earth and the sun and what we know now.

Before telescopes and space exploration, some people thought Earth was the center of the universe.

Then   **Now**

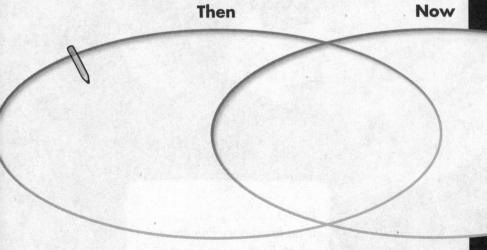

Earth's Rotation

Earth and the other planets of the solar system rotate, or spin, much like a top spins. They each rotate around an imaginary line called an **axis.** The northern end of Earth's axis is the North Pole. The southern end of Earth's axis is the South Pole. One whole spin of an object on its axis is called a **rotation.** One full rotation is what we call a *day.*

Earth rotates around its imaginary axis from west to east. As Earth spins, the sun, moon, stars, and planets only seem to rise in the east and set in the west. When you watch the sun set, remember that it is you who are moving. You are riding on the rotating Earth.

2. Explain Why does the sun appear to move from east to west across the sky?

....

....

3. Fill in the Blank In the illustration below, fill in the missing words in the labels.

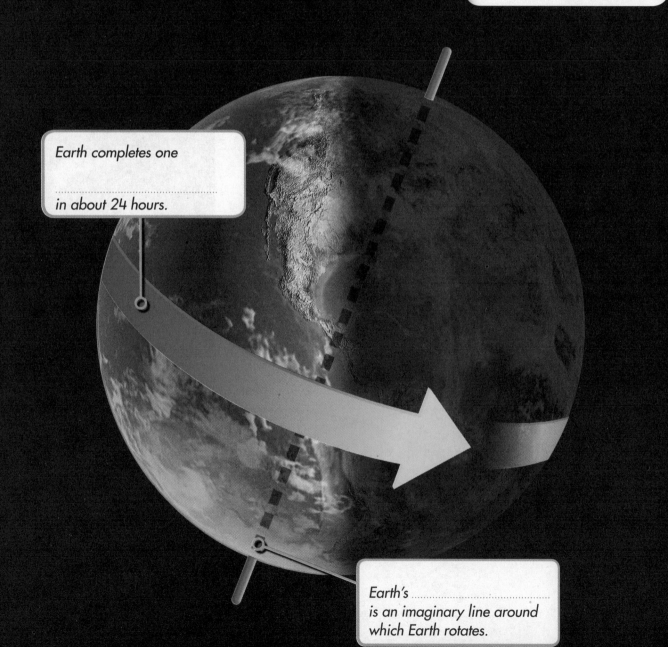

Earth completes one

....

in about 24 hours.

Earth's ....
is an imaginary line around
which Earth rotates.

Earth's Revolution

Earth also moves in an orbit. An **orbit** is the path an object takes as it revolves around a star, planet, or moon. Earth's orbit is elliptical—it has an oval shape. The moon's orbit around Earth is also elliptical. One full orbit of an object around another object is called a **revolution.** Earth's revolution around the sun lasts for just a few hours longer than 365 days. This period may sound familiar to you. It is one year. The moon's revolution around Earth takes 27.3 days, or about a month.

Just as gravity keeps you on Earth, gravity keeps Earth in its orbit around the sun. Because the sun is so massive, its gravity pulls all the planets toward it. This pull keeps the planets from moving in straight lines into space.

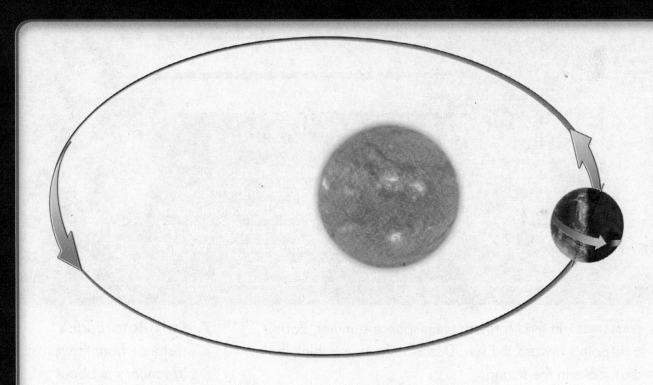

4. **Infer** Draw a representation of the moon's orbit in the diagram above.

5. ⊙ **Compare and Contrast** How are the orbits of Earth and the moon alike? How are they different?

....

....

Seasons

Earth always tilts the same way during its revolution around the sun. Earth's tilt affects how much sunlight parts of Earth receive. The amount of sunlight an area receives affects its climate and seasons. Seasons change as Earth's axis tilts either toward or away from the sun at different times during its revolution. When the North Pole is tilted away from the sun, sunlight is less concentrated in the Northern Hemisphere. Temperatures drop, and winter sets in. At the same time, the South Pole is tilted toward the sun. The Southern Hemisphere receives concentrated sunlight and has the warm temperatures of summer.

axis

In this diagram, look at how the sun's rays strike Earth. During the Southern Hemisphere summer, the Sun's rays strike Earth more directly south of the equator. The rays are concentrated, not spread out. Concentrated energy gives this region warm summer weather.

equator

6. CHALLENGE In the Northern Hemisphere summer, Earth's axis points toward the sun. Describe how you think the axis looks in the spring.

....

....

....

....

....

....

7. **Calculate** Earth's distance from the sun in January is about 147,000,000 km. In July its distance from the sun is about 152,100,000 km. About how much closer is Earth to the sun in January than in July?

The number of daylight hours also changes as the seasons change. On the first day of its summer, a hemisphere has more hours of daylight than at any other time of the year. The least number of daylight hours occurs on the first day of winter. Twice a year the hours of day and night are equal. At this time, Earth's axis points neither toward nor away from the sun.

8. Identify In the diagram, label each part of Earth's orbit with the Northern Hemisphere season that it represents.

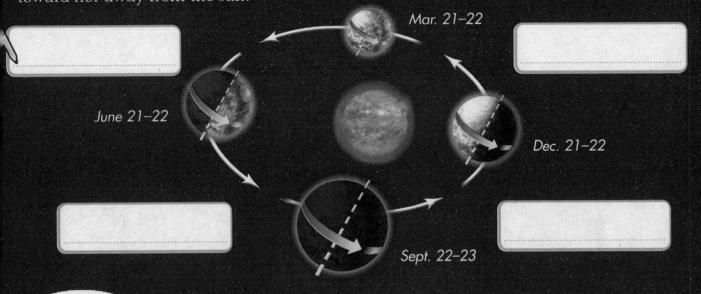

Mar. 21–22

June 21–22

Dec. 21–22

Sept. 22–23

Got it?

9. Describe What is a rotation? What is a revolution?

....

....

....

10. Explain In what direction do stars, the moon, and the sun seem to move across the sky? Why?

....

....

....

⬜ **Stop!** I need help with ....

⏸ **Wait!** I have a question about ....

▶ **Go!** Now I know ....

What is a star?

Envision It!

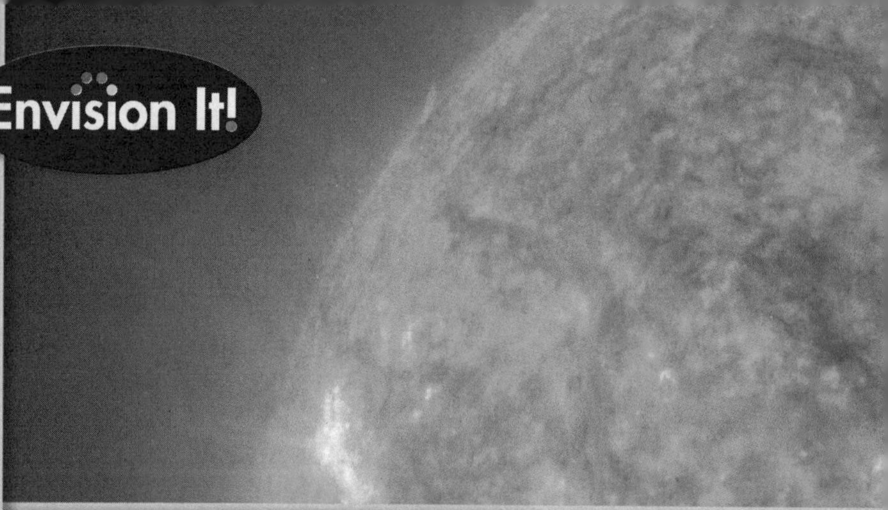

Discuss whether or not you think the sun has a hard surface like Earth.

my planeT DiARY

//// **MISCONCEPTION** ////

What happens to the stars during the day? You might think they disappear, but they do not. The stars are always in the sky during the day just as they are at night. However, the sun's light is so much brighter than the faint light coming from the stars that the stars cannot be seen. On a dark clear night, without the aid of a telescope, you might see over a thousand stars in the sky.

Do all stars look the same? Explain.

....

....

....

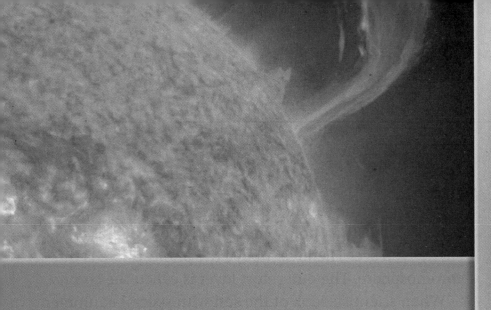

I will know the physical characteristics of the sun. I will know why the star Polaris is important.

Words to Know

solar flare   constellation

Stars

Stars are gigantic balls of very hot gases that give off radiation. The sun is a medium-sized star. Stars known as giants may be eight to 100 times as large as the sun. Supergiants are even larger. They may be up to 300 times as large as the sun. A star at the end of its life can collapse and become very small—only about the size of Earth.

Even though the sun is only a medium-sized star, it is the largest object in our solar system. Scientists have been able to calculate the sun's mass from the speeds of the planets and the shapes of their orbits around the sun. The sun's mass is nearly two million trillion trillion kilograms — you can write that as a two followed by 30 zeros! The sun has almost 100 percent of the mass in the solar system. The sun is huge when compared to Earth. In fact, the sun has more than one million times the volume of Earth. If you think of the sun as a gumball machine, it would take over one million Earth gumballs to fill the sun gumball machine!

1. **Summarize** Compare the size of the sun to the size of other stars. Compare its size to Earth.

2. **Recognize** How can scientists determine the mass of the sun?

sun

Earth

Lightning Lab

Measuring Shadows
Have a partner measure your shadow at different times during the day. Write down what you find. Describe how your shadow changes as the sun moves.

4. **Apply** Why might space agencies not want to send astronauts into space during solar flares?

....

....

....

....

Characteristics of the Sun

The sun is a fiery ball of hot gases and has no hard surfaces. It gives off enormous amounts of light and heat. The outer part of the sun is about 5,500°C. The inner core could be as hot as 15,000,000°C.

The Sun's Atmosphere

Like Earth, the sun has an atmosphere. The innermost layer is called the photosphere. It gives off the light energy you see. The layer above the photosphere is the chromosphere. The outermost layer is called the corona.

When scientists look at the sun with special equipment, they see dark spots, called sunspots, moving on the face of the sun. Sunspots are part of the photosphere. They may be the size of Earth or larger. They look dark because they are not as hot as the rest of the photosphere. The number of sunspots increases and decreases in cycles of about eleven years.

Solar Eruptions

Two types of eruptions that take place on the sun are prominences and solar flares. A prominence looks like a ribbon of glowing gases that leaps out of the chromosphere into the corona. Prominences may appear and then disappear in a few days or months.

A **solar flare** is an explosive eruption of waves and particles into space. Solar flares are similar to volcanoes here on Earth. A solar flare causes a bright spot in the chromosphere that may last for minutes or hours. Along with extra-bright light, solar flares also give off other forms of energy. This energy is powerful enough to interrupt radio and satellite communication on Earth.

3. **Identify** What are the physical characteristics of the sun?

....

....

....

....

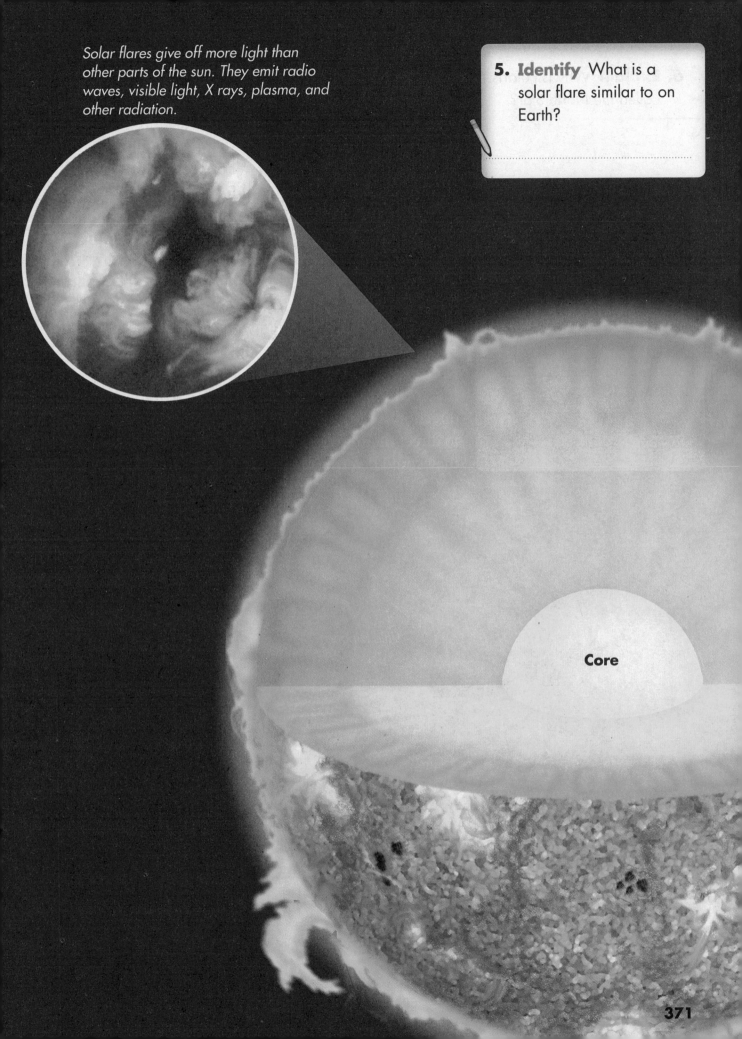

Solar flares give off more light than other parts of the sun. They emit radio waves, visible light, X rays, plasma, and other radiation.

5. Identify What is a solar flare similar to on Earth?

Core

Constellations

In the past, people looked up at the night sky and "connected the dots" formed by the stars. They saw patterns that reminded them of bears, dogs, and even a sea monster! Today, scientists divide the night sky into eighty eight constellations. A **constellation** is a group of stars that forms a pattern. Many constellation names are the names of the star patterns that people used long ago.

The star pattern called the Little Dipper contains a star called Polaris. Polaris, or the North Star, is a very hot and very large yellow-white star. It is almost 2,500 times brighter than the sun. It does not look larger than the sun because it is much farther away. Polaris is an important star in navigation. Because it is almost directly above the North Pole, Polaris doesn't seem to move as Earth rotates. If you can find Polaris in the sky, you can tell which direction is north. Early explorers used Polaris as a guide to direct them in their travels. If they located Polaris, then they could determine in which direction they were headed.

Little Dipper

Polaris

Big Dipper

myscienceonline.com | Got it? | 60-Second Video

Stars on the Move

Stars are not always in the same place in the sky. They move in predictable ways. Suppose you looked at the sky early one evening and found the Big Dipper. When you looked two hours later, the Big Dipper seemed to have moved toward the west. Actually, the Big Dipper did not move, but you moved. The spinning of Earth makes the stars appear to move from east to west across the sky.

8. **Infer** This time-lapse photo shows how stars seem to move as Earth rotates. Why are the stars in a circular pattern?

....

....

....

Stars appear to spin around Polaris in this time-lapse photo.

Got it?

9. **Summarize** If other stars are brighter and larger than the sun, why does the sun appear so large?

....

....

10. **Describe** What is the significance of Polaris, the North Star?

....

....

....

⬛ **Stop!** I need help with ....

⏸ **Wait!** I have a question about ....

▶ **Go!** Now I know ....

What are the inner planets?

Envision It!

What planet do you think this picture shows?

Inquiry Explore It!

How does distance affect orbiting time?

Materials

clay

meterstick

ruler

- [ ] **1.** Make 2 clay balls the size of golf balls.

- [ ] **2.** Push one ball onto the end of a meterstick. Push the other ball onto the end of a ruler.

- [ ] **3.** Hold up each stick. Set the empty ends on the floor.

- [ ] **4.** Let go of both sticks at the same time. **Observe** closely.

Explain Your Results

5. Which ball hit the ground first?

....

6. Infer How might a planet's distance from the sun affect the time it takes to make one orbit?

....

....

myscienceonline.com | **Explore It!** Animation

UNLOCK THE BIG ?

I will know the inner and outer planets and Earth's position in the solar system. I will know how technology has helped people explore space.

Words to Know

planet   space probe
inner planet   moon

Planets

There are eight known planets that revolve around the sun. A **planet** is a large, round object that revolves around a star and has cleared the region around its orbit. The four closest planets to the sun are called **inner planets.** Inner planets have rocky surfaces. Mercury, Venus, Earth, and Mars are the inner planets.

Because all the planets revolve around the sun and the stars that we see in the sky are much further away, we can see the planets change positions relative to the stars from one night to the next.

Even though some planets seem to shine, they do not give off their own light like stars do. A planet shines because light from a nearby star reflects off the planet's surface.

1. **Locate** The illustrations show what the night sky might look like three weeks apart. **Circle** the object in the sky that might be a planet.

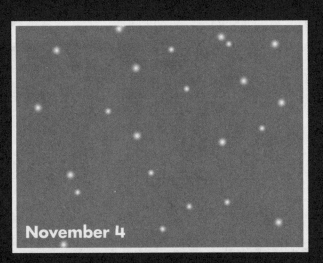

November 4

November 25

Orbiting Objects

Every planet in the solar system revolves around the sun. The orbits of the planets have a slightly elliptical shape.

Objects in the solar system stay in their orbits because of gravity. Gravity is the force of attraction between objects. The force of the sun's gravity is large enough to keep planets around the sun. Without this force, the planets would not stay in their orbits.

2. Infer Planets have years of different lengths because of the lengths of their orbits. Draw an ✗ on the planet with the longest year.

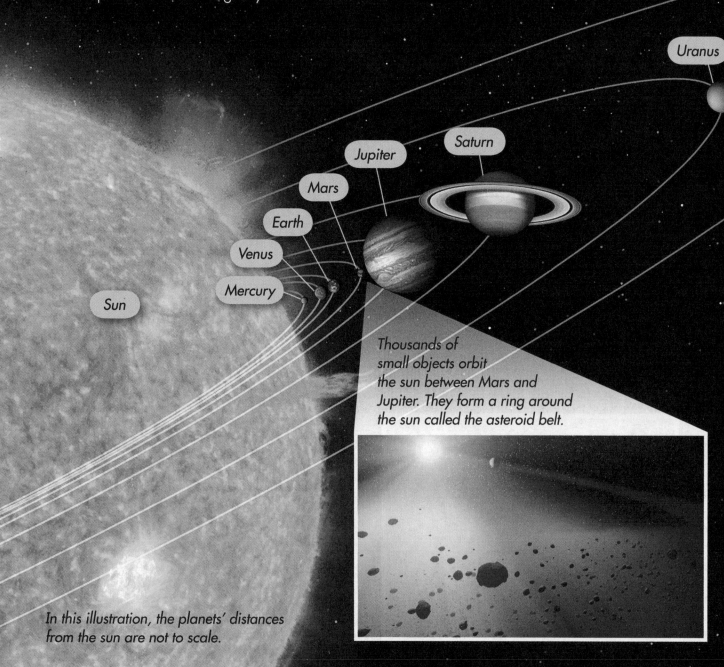

Sun

Mercury

Venus

Earth

Mars

Jupiter

Saturn

Uranus

Thousands of small objects orbit the sun between Mars and Jupiter. They form a ring around the sun called the asteroid belt.

In this illustration, the planets' distances from the sun are not to scale.

376

Mercury

Mercury is the closest planet to the sun. It is a small planet, slightly bigger than Earth's moon. Mercury is covered with thousands of low spots called craters. Craters are made when meteorites, or rocks that fall from space, crash into the surface.

The *Mariner 10* was the first spacecraft to visit Mercury. Scientists sent the *Mariner 10* space probe in 1973, and it reached the planet in 1974. A **space probe** is a spacecraft that gathers data without a crew. It carries cameras and other tools for studying different objects in space.

Mercury has almost no atmosphere. Because it is so close to the sun, Mercury is scorching hot during the day. Daytime temperatures are much higher than those in the hottest place on Earth. But with no atmosphere to hold in the heat, Mercury is very cold at night.

3. Predict How might Mercury be different if it had a thicker atmosphere?

Neptune

Without an atmosphere to protect it, Mercury is struck by many objects that leave craters on its surface.

Venus

Venus is the second planet from the sun. It is about the same size as Earth, but Venus rotates in the opposite direction. Like Mercury, Venus is very hot and dry. Unlike Mercury, Venus has an atmosphere made of thick, swirling clouds. There are strong winds and lightning.

The clouds of Venus are very hot and toxic. They reflect the sun's light very well. This makes Venus one of the brightest objects in Earth's night sky. The clouds also hide the surface of Venus, but scientists have mapped the surface in spite of the clouds. The image on the right was made using radar data from a space probe. The colors were added by computer for better viewing.

Venus with clouds

This image shows what Venus would look like without clouds.

4. ◎ **Cause and Effect** What makes Venus so bright?

Do the math!

Analyze a Bar Graph

How much does an astronaut weigh? That depends. Weight is the measure of the pull of gravity on an object. Different planets have different amounts of gravitational pull.

When an astronaut wears a complete space suit, he or she might weigh about 480 pounds on Earth! The astronaut would weigh less on Mars. The graph shows how much the astronaut would weigh on different planets.

1. The astronaut's weight on Venus would be about $\frac{9}{10}$ of his or her weight on Earth. How much would the astronaut weigh on Venus? Fill in the bar graph to show your answer.

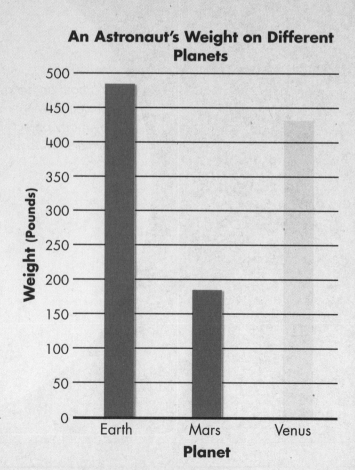

An Astronaut's Weight on Different Planets

Weight (Pounds) / Planet

Earth and the Moon

Earth, our home, is the third planet from the sun. It is also the solar system's largest rocky planet. Earth is the only planet that has liquid water on its surface. In fact, about $\frac{3}{4}$ of Earth's surface is covered with water.

Earth is wrapped in a layer of gas that is about 150 kilometers thick. This layer of gas, or atmosphere, makes life possible on Earth. It filters out some of the sun's harmful rays. It also contains nitrogen, oxygen, carbon dioxide, and water vapor. Plants and animals use these gases. Earth is the only planet in the solar system known to support life.

Earth has one large moon, which is about $\frac{1}{4}$ as wide as Earth. A **moon** is a natural object that revolves around a planet. Our moon has almost no atmosphere. It has many craters that formed when meteorites crashed into its surface. The moon is Earth's natural satellite. A satellite is an object that orbits another object in space. Gravity keeps the moon revolving around Earth, just as it keeps Earth revolving around the sun.

It takes the moon 27 days to revolve around Earth.

Earth spins, or rotates, once every 24 hours.

5. [CHALLENGE] The circles below represent Earth and the moon. Measure the diameter of the large circle, and multiply it by 30. That would be the correct distance from Earth to the moon at this scale. Draw the two circles in the space provided. Use the correct distance you found.

● = Earth   • = moon

Mars

Mars is the fourth planet from the sun. The soil that covers most of this rocky planet contains iron oxide. This is a reddish-brown material that makes up rust. This material is why Mars is sometimes called the "Red Planet." Mars has two very small and deeply-cratered moons.

The atmosphere of Mars does not have enough oxygen for plants or animals to live. Winds on Mars cause dust storms. These storms are sometimes large enough to cover the whole planet.

Mars has seasons. It also has polar ice caps that grow in the winter and shrink in the summer. Mars has a canyon that is nearly 10 times longer than the Grand Canyon in Arizona.

A Martian day is called a sol and lasts just 40 minutes longer than an Earth day. However, the day sky on Mars looks pink instead of blue!

Lightning Lab

Model Planets
Work in small groups. Make models of the inner planets to scale. The diameter of Mercury is 0.4 that of Earth. The diameter of Venus is 0.9 that of Earth. The diameter of Mars is 0.5 that of Earth.

6. **Infer** Mars is the coldest of the inner planets. What could be a reason?

....

....

A Mars rover with instruments and solar panels extended

Several probes have landed on Mars. The first, *Viking I,* landed on Mars in 1976. In 1997, a robot named *Sojourner* explored part of Mars. In 2004, two robot rovers, *Spirit* and *Opportunity,* landed. These rovers gathered information and sent it back to Earth. Scientists have used the data to learn about the rocks and soil on Mars. The scientists also found evidence that Mars has frozen water and that it once had liquid water.

7. ◎ **Sequence** Number the sentences to show the sequence of events described above.

◯ *Viking I* landed on Mars.

◯ *Spirit* and *Opportunity* landed on Mars.

◯ *Sojourner* explored parts of Mars.

Got it?

8. **Describe** What are the characteristics of the inner planets?

....

....

9. **Explain** How has technology allowed people to explore space?

....

....

....

⬛ **Stop!** I need help with ....

⏸ **Wait!** I have a question about ....

▶ **Go!** Now I know ....

Lesson 4

What are the outer planets?

The surface of Jupiter changes every day. What do you think causes these changes?

Inquiry Explore It!

How are the sizes of the inner and outer planets different?

☐ 1. **Measure** the diameter of each paper planet. Use your measurements and the chart to identify and label the planets. Cut out each planet.

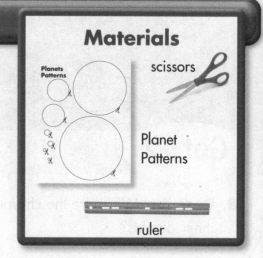

Materials

Planets Patterns

scissors

Planet Patterns

ruler

☐ 2. Put the **models** of the planets in order by size. Compare the sizes of the inner and outer planets.

Explain Your Results

3. After **observing** your models, compare the sizes of the inner and outer planets.

	Comparing Planetary Diameters		
	Planet	Diameter of Planet (rounded to the nearest 100 km)	Diameter of Model* (mm)
Inner Planets	Mercury	4,900	5
	Venus	12,100	12
	Earth	12,800	13
	Mars	6,800	7
Outer Planets	Jupiter	143,000	143
	Saturn	120,500	121
	Uranus	51,000	51
	Neptune	49,500	50

*1mm = 1000km

I will know that the outer planets are Jupiter, Saturn, Uranus, and Neptune and that they have common characteristics.

Words to Know

outer planet

Gas Giants

There are still four more planets in our solar system beyond Mars—Jupiter, Saturn, Uranus, and Neptune. They are known as the **outer planets.**

The outer planets are much larger than the inner planets. They do not have clearly defined surfaces, like those of the inner planets. We only see the atmospheres of the outer planets. For these reasons these planets are often called gas giants. However, they have liquid inner layers and solid cores.

Each of the outer planets has rings of particles and many moons orbiting it.

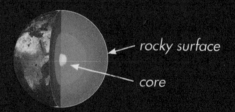

Inner planets have solid crusts.

rocky surface

core

1. **Compare and Contrast** Write some similarities and differences between the inner planets and the outer planets.

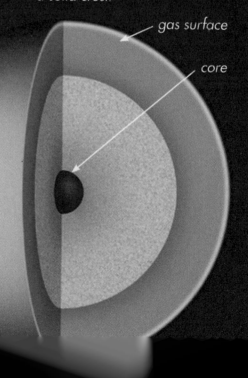

Outer planets do not have a solid crust.

gas surface

core

Jupiter

Jupiter, the fifth planet from the sun, is the largest planet in the solar system. It is a gas giant. Jupiter's atmosphere is mostly hydrogen and helium. The atmosphere of Jupiter shows many bands of color. The planet rotates much faster than Earth. In the time it takes Earth to complete one rotation, Jupiter completes more than two.

Jupiter has many moons. A moon is a natural object that orbits a planet. Some planets, especially the outer planets, have several moons. In 1610, Galileo was the first person to see the four largest moons of Jupiter through his telescope. They are shown to the right.

2. Contrast How are Jupiter and Earth different?

Ganymede

Io

Europa

Great Red Spot

Callisto

Saturn

The sixth planet from the sun is Saturn. Like Jupiter, Saturn has an atmosphere that contains mostly hydrogen and helium. Saturn is very large, but its density is low.

When Galileo looked at Saturn through his telescope, he saw what looked like a planet with handles! The "handles" were really the brilliant rings that orbit Saturn. The particles making up the rings vary in size from tiny grains to boulders, and they are made of ice, dust, and rock. The inner rings of Saturn revolve faster around the planet than the outer rings.

In 2009 a giant new ring was discovered. The ring is invisible, but its infrared glow was detected by the Spitzer Space Telescope. This ring is tilted relative to the other rings, and rotates in the opposite direction.

3. CHALLENGE Two rocks on the rings of Saturn start orbiting at points 1 and 2. After a while, the rock that started at point 1 has moved to point 3. Fill in the number that shows where rock 2 is likely to be, considering its speed.

Lightning Lab

Reading in the Dark
Make a night vision flashlight for reading star charts in the dark. Fold a sheet of red cellophane in half and then into quarters. Use a rubber band or tape to attach it to the end of a flashlight. Test the light. If necessary, add more layers to make the light as red as possible.

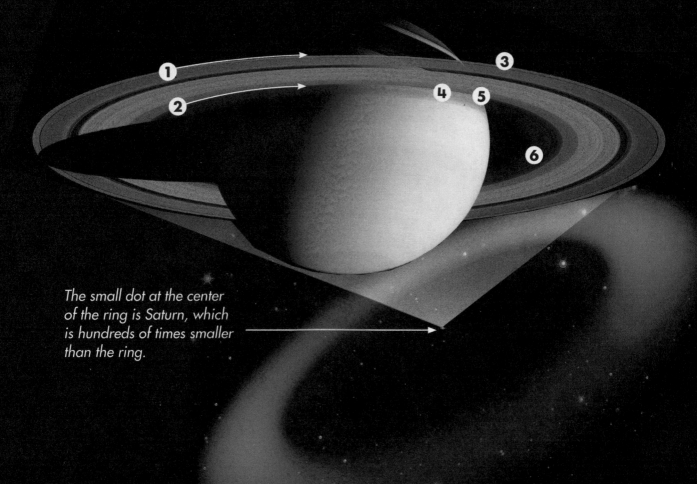

The small dot at the center of the ring is Saturn, which is hundreds of times smaller than the ring.

Uranus

Uranus is the seventh planet from the sun and the most distant planet you can see without a telescope. Uranus is a gas giant with an atmosphere of hydrogen, helium, and methane. The planet is so cold that the methane can condense into a liquid. Tiny drops of this liquid methane form a thin cloud that covers the planet, giving it a fuzzy, blue-green look.

Like other gas giants, Uranus has rings and many moons. Unlike the rings of Saturn, the rings of Uranus are dark and hard to see with Earth-based telescopes.

Uranus rotates on its side. No one knows why Uranus has this odd tilt. Scientists think a large object may have hit the planet when the solar system was still forming. This bump may have knocked Uranus onto its side.

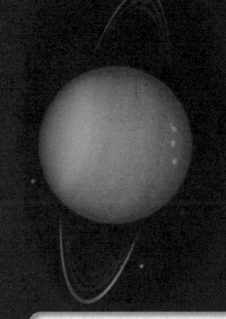

4. Infer How might Uranus's odd tilt affect its seasons?

....

....

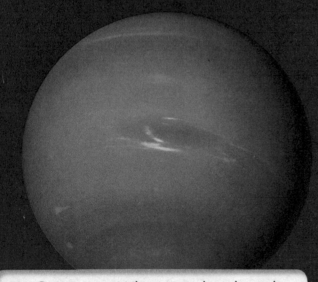

Neptune

Neptune is too far away to see without a telescope. It is the eighth planet from the sun. Astronomers discovered Neptune in 1846. It takes more than one hundred Earth years for Neptune to orbit the sun. Neptune is the smallest of the gas giants. Even so, if Neptune were hollow, it could hold about 60 Earths.

Neptune's atmosphere is like that of Uranus. Like Uranus, Neptune has a bluish color because of the methane in its atmosphere. Neptune also has storms and bands of clouds like Jupiter.

Neptune has at least 13 moons. The largest one is Triton, which may be the coldest object in the solar system.

5. Compare What is similar about the atmospheres of Uranus and Neptune?

....

....

mysɪᴄɪᴇɴᴄᴇᴏɴʟɪɴᴇ.com | Got it? 60-Second Video

Exploring the Giants

Several probes have been sent to explore the outer planets. They were launched from Florida. *Pioneer 10* and *Pioneer 11* were launched in the 1970s, followed by *Voyager 1* and *2*. The *Galileo* probe explored Jupiter in great detail, and the *Cassini* mission has sent back a huge amount of information on Saturn. A smaller probe, named *Huygens*, was launched from *Cassini* and was able to land on Saturn's largest moon, Titan.

6. **Write About It** What information might you like to have sent to you from a space probe?

_____

_____

_____

Got it?

7. **Group** Think of three terms to describe some characteristics of the inner planets and the outer planets. Use the terms to contrast the inner and outer planets.

_____

_____

8. **UNLOCK THE BIG ?** What are some common characteristics of all planets?

_____

_____

▢ **Stop!** I need help with ....

❚❚ **Wait!** I have a question about ....

▶ **Go!** Now I know ....

What are asteroids, meteors, comets, and moons?

Write an ✗ on the rock that might have started out as an asteroid. Tell why you made that choice.

Inquiry Explore It!

How does a meteoroid fall through Earth's atmosphere?

☑ **1.** Lightly place a chunk of a fizzy antacid tablet into a bottle of water.

☑ **2.** Describe what you **observed.**

....

....

....

Explain Your Results

3. After completing this lesson, compare the process of a meteoroid entering Earth's atmosphere with what you **observed** in this **model.**

....

....

....

....

....

Materials

chunk of fizzy antacid tablet

2 L plastic bottle with water
(filled to the bottom of the neck)

chunk of tablet = meteoroid

water = Earth's atmosphere

bottom of bottle = Earth's surface

  myscienceonline.com | **Explore It!** Animation

I will know the difference between moons, asteroids, comets, meteoroids, meteors, and meteorites.

Words to Know

asteroid   dwarf planet
comet

Asteroids

A rocky mass up to several hundred kilometers wide that revolves around the sun is an **asteroid.** In our solar system, most asteroids orbit in the region between Mars and Jupiter called the asteroid belt.

Most asteroids have uneven shapes. Some have smaller asteroids orbiting them. The smallest asteroids are pebble-sized. Most asteroids complete a revolution in three to six years.

Can Earth be hit by asteroids? It has happened, and you can see the huge craters that have been the result. Such collisions are very rare. Fortunately, Jupiter's gravity holds most asteroids in the area beyond Mars.

1. **Explain** Why is the gravitational force of Jupiter important to Earth?

....

....

....

....

....

Asteroid Ida has a smaller asteroid orbiting around it. The smaller asteroid is named Dactyl.

Dactyl

Ida

Meteor Shower
Work with an adult. Go online to find information about meteor showers that are visible from where you live. Note the date, the time, and the area of the sky in which they will occur.

Meteors

Have you ever seen a shooting star? Shooting stars look like bright lines of fast-moving light that form in the night sky. They last a very short time. Shooting stars are not really stars but meteors.

A meteor forms when a meteoroid hits Earth's atmosphere. A meteoroid is a small piece of rock moving in space. Meteoroids are boulder-sized or smaller. Most are the size of pebbles or grains of sand. When a meteoroid shoots through the air, it heats up quickly. It gets so hot that it glows as a streak of light. Very bright meteors are called fireballs.

Most meteors burn up before they hit Earth's surface. If a meteor does not burn up completely, it may fall to Earth. A piece of a meteor that lands on Earth is called a meteorite. Most meteorites are quite small. The biggest known meteorite is in Namibia, Africa, and weighs 60 tons.

2. **Calculate** The diameter of this crater may be 24 times larger than the diameter of the meteor that formed it. Measure the crater from point A to point B. Then, measure the circles and draw an ✕ on the circle that best represents the probable size of the meteor.

....

....

Meteor Crater, in Arizona, was formed by a meteorite impact.

390

Comet Lulin

Comets

A frozen mass of different types of ice and dust orbiting the sun is a **comet.** Rocky matter may be frozen in the ice. Comets come from areas of the solar system beyond Neptune. Most pass through the solar system in very stretched out and elliptical paths. Several comets a year may travel into the solar system and orbit the sun. You may not see them, though. Only the largest comets can be seen without a telescope.

At certain times each year, meteor showers take place. These occur when Earth passes through the orbit of a comet. A comet heats up and loses dust and rocky matter each time it orbits the sun. These loose pieces remain in the comet's orbit. When these pieces collide with Earth's atmosphere, they become meteors.

Discovering a comet is exciting. How can you discover one? Most comets today are found by people who use telescopes to photograph the sky each night. The photos may show a fuzzy object. Another clue is that stars stay in the same relative position with other stars, but comets do not. If an unknown object keeps changing position compared with stars over a few hours or days, it might be a comet. If you are the first person to discover a comet, it could be named after you.

3. ⊚ **Cause and Effect** What causes a meteor shower?

Some objects in the solar system have been classified as dwarf planets. A **dwarf planet** is a large, round object that revolves around the sun but has not cleared the region around its orbit.

In 1930, Clyde Tombaugh discovered Pluto. Pluto has an icy solid surface. Astronomers thought for a long time that Pluto was the ninth planet—the only outer planet that is not a gas giant.

Today, astronomers do not consider Pluto a planet. Pluto is a dwarf planet. It is even smaller than Earth's moon. Pluto has an odd orbit. The other planets travel around the sun at the same angle, while Pluto's orbit is tilted. During parts of the orbit, it is closer to the sun than Neptune. This occurred from 1979 to 1999. The next time this will occur is in the year 2227.

Clyde Tombaugh with a telescope

4. Calculate In how many more years will Pluto be closer to the sun than Neptune?

....

....

The orbit of Pluto is not aligned with the orbits of the other planets.

Charon was the first moon of Pluto to be discovered. Since then, other moons have been found orbiting Pluto.

myscienceonline.com | Got it? | 60-Second Video

Moons

The solar system contains many moons. You may remember that a moon is a natural object that orbits a body bigger than itself. Like planets, moons often have a spherical shape. Earth and Mars are the only inner planets that have moons. The outer planets have many moons.

The moons in the solar system are very different from one another. Earth's moon has no atmosphere. Saturn's largest moon, Titan, has an atmosphere so thick that it lets little light pass through. Jupiter's moon Io has volcanoes on its surface that release sulfur. Sulfur gives Io a colorful appearance.

Moon craters like these form when a moon is struck by another object.

5. ⊙ **Compare and Contrast** How are moons and asteroids alike? How are they different?

Got it?

6. **Explain** How can you tell the difference between a comet and a star?

7. **UNLOCK THE BIG ?** How are comets and asteroids alike and different?

☐ **Stop!** I need help with

⏸ **Wait!** I have a question about

▶ **Go!** Now I know

Inquiry ▸ Investigate It!

How can spinning affect a planet's shape?

Follow a Procedure

☐ **1.** Cut 2 strips of construction paper, each 2 cm × 45 cm. Cross them at the center and staple them to make an X.

☐ **2.** Bring the 4 ends together and overlap them. Staple them to form a sphere.

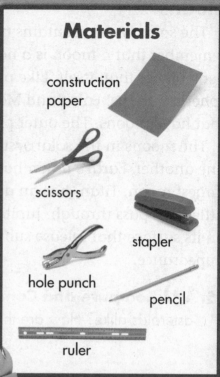

Materials

construction paper

scissors

stapler

hole punch

pencil

ruler

Inquiry Skill Scientists **use a model** when the real object is hard to study.

☐ **3.** Punch a hole through the center of the overlapped ends.

☐ **4.** Push a dull pencil through the hole. Only about 5 cm of the pencil should go in.

about 5 cm

5. Hold the pencil between your palms. Move your hands back and forth to make your **model** spin.

6. What shape do you **observe** when it spins?

....

7. Record your observations.

| Effect of Spinning on a Planet's Shape ||
Shape When Not Spinning	Shape When Spinning
⬭	

Analyze and Conclude

8. How did the sphere change shape when you spun it? Make an **inference** about what happened.

....

....

9. How is your **model** similar to a spinning planet? How is it different?

....

....

....

....

Planet Hunting

You may think you need a telescope to view planets from your backyard. This is not necessarily true! Planets look like bright stars in the night sky. If you view the sky for several nights, the stars will appear to stay in the same place relative to the other stars, but a planet's position will change. This is how you can tell a planet from a star. Two of the planets that appear the brightest are Venus and Jupiter.

Ask an adult to help. Go outside at night to view the sky. The sky should be relatively clear, with few or no clouds. Do you see any planets? Record your observations. Repeat your sky watching on another night. What do your observations tell you about the objects you see?

Vocabulary Smart Cards

axis
rotation
orbit
revolution
solar flare
constellation
planet
inner planet
space probe
moon
outer planet
asteroid
comet
dwarf planet

Play a Game!

Work with a partner. Choose a Vocabulary Smart Card. Do not let your partner see your card.

Play Password. Try to get your partner to say the word or phrase by giving only one-word clues, one at a time. Take turns giving clues and guessing.

revolution

traslación

axis

eje

solar flare

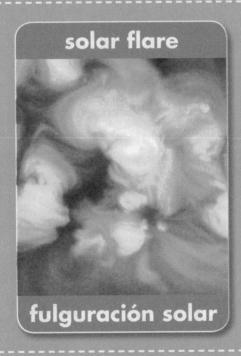

fulguración solar

rotation

rotación

constellation

constelación

orbit

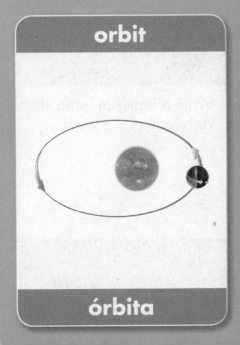

órbita

an imaginary line around which an object spins

Draw an example.

línea imaginaria en torno a la cual gira un objeto

---

one full orbit around the sun

Write a sentence using this word.

una órbita completa alrededor del Sol

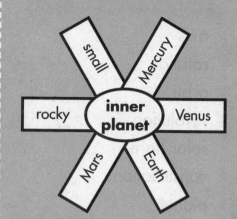

small · Mercury · rocky · inner planet · Venus · Mars · Earth

Make a Word Wheel!

Choose a vocabulary word and write it in the center of the Word Wheel graphic organizer. Write examples or related words on the wheel spokes.

---

one whole spin of an object on its axis

Write a sentence using this term.

una vuelta completa de un objeto en torno a su eje

---

an explosive eruption of waves and particles into space

Write one fact about this word.

erupción explosiva de ondas y partículas emitidas hacia el espacio

---

the path an object takes as it revolves around a star, planet, or moon

Write a sentence using the verb form of this word.

el camino que sigue un objeto al girar alrededor de una estrella, un planeta o una luna

---

a group of stars that forms a pattern

Write a fact about this word.

grupo de estrellas que forma una figura

comet

cometa

moon

luna

planet

planeta

dwarf planet

planeta enano

outer planet

planeta exterior

inner planet
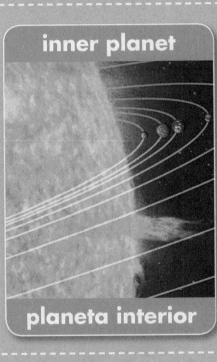
planeta interior

asteroid

asteroide

space probe

sonda espacial

a large, round object that revolves around a star and has cleared the region around its orbit

Write two related words.

....

....

cuerpo grande y redondo que orbita una estrella y que ha despejado la zona que rodea su órbita

---

a natural object that revolves around a planet

Draw an example.

satélite natural que orbita un planeta

---

a frozen mass of different types of ice and dust orbiting the sun

Draw an example.

masa helada de distintos tipos de hielo y polvo que orbita el Sol

---

any of the four closest planets to the sun

Write three examples.

....

....

....

cualquiera de los cuatro planetas más cercanos al Sol

---

any of the four planets in our solar system beyond Mars

Write a sentence using this term.

....

....

cualquiera de los cuatro planetas de nuestro sistema solar que quedan más allá de Marte

---

a large, round object that revolves around the sun but has not cleared the region around its orbit

Write one example.

....

....

cuerpo grande y redondo que orbita el Sol, pero que no ha despejado la zona que rodea su órbita

---

a spacecraft that gathers data without a crew

Write a sentence using this term.

....

....

....

nave espacial sin tripulantes que recoge datos

---

a rocky mass up to several hundred kilometers wide that revolves around the sun

Write one fact about this word.

....

....

masa rocosa de hasta varios cientos de kilómetros de ancho que gira alrededor del Sol

---

....

....

....

Lesson 1

How does Earth move?

- Earth rotates around an imaginary line called an axis.
- Earth revolves around the sun in an elliptical orbit. Earth's tilt and revolution cause seasonal differences in parts of Earth.

Lesson 2

What is a star?

- The sun is a medium-sized star.
- A constellation is a group of stars that forms a pattern.
- Stars appear to move across the sky because Earth rotates.

Lesson 3

What are the inner planets?

- Mercury, Venus, Earth, and Mars are the inner planets.
- The inner planets have solid surfaces and are relatively small.
- Objects in the solar system stay in their orbits because of gravity.

Lesson 4

What are the outer planets?

- Jupiter, Saturn, Uranus, and Neptune are the outer planets.
- The outer planets have gaseous surfaces and are relatively large.
- Space probes have been sent to study the outer planets.

Lesson 5

What are asteroids, meteors, comets, and moons?

- An asteroid is a rocky mass that revolves around the sun.
- A comet is a frozen mass that orbits the sun.
- A piece of a meteor that lands on Earth is called a meteorite.

Lesson 1

How does Earth move?

1. **Vocabulary** Earth's _____ takes 365 days.
   A. rotation
   B. revolution
   C. orbit
   D. axis

2. **Explain** The picture below shows how the moon moves in the sky. Why does the moon appear to move from east to west?

3. **Predict** What would happen to the seasons of the world if Earth's axis tilted in the opposite direction?

Lesson 2

What is a star?

4. **Vocabulary** What is a constellation?

....

....

....

5. **Identify** Which layer of the sun gives off the light energy we see?

....

6. ◉ **Compare and Contrast** Read the passage below and then answer the question.

> Prominences and solar flares are eruptions on the surface of the sun. A prominence looks like a ribbon of glowing gases that leaps into the corona. Prominences may appear for days or even months. Solar flares appear as bright spots on the chromosphere. They may last for minutes or hours.

What do prominences and solar flares have in common? How are they different?

....

....

....

Lesson 3

What are the inner planets?

7. 🎯 **Sequence** List the inner planets in order of distance from the sun.

....

....

....

....

....

....

Lesson 4

What are the outer planets?

Do the math!

8. Venus orbits the sun at an average distance of 108 million km. Uranus orbits the sun at an average distance of 2.8 billion km. How many times farther from the sun is Uranus than Venus?

....

....

....

....

Lesson 5

What are asteroids, meteors, comets, and moons?

9. **Summarize** Explain the difference between asteroids, meteors, comets, and moons.

....

....

....

....

10. **APPLY THE BIG ?** **How do objects move in space?**

··

Think about what you have learned about the solar system. Why would it be difficult for humans to travel to visit the planets that you have learned about? Name specific planets and moons in your answer.

....

....

....

....

Fill in the bubble next to the answer choice you think is correct
for each multiple-choice question.

1 Earth and the other planets closest to
the sun are made mostly of

Ⓐ gas.

Ⓑ metal.

Ⓒ water.

Ⓓ rock.

2 What kind of technology has allowed
people to explore the outer planets?

Ⓐ robot rover

Ⓑ space probe

Ⓒ space shuttle

Ⓓ robot

3 Which shows the inner planets
correctly ordered from farthest to
closest from the sun?

Ⓐ Mars, Earth, Venus, Mercury

Ⓑ Mars, Venus, Mercury, Earth

Ⓒ Venus, Mercury, Earth, Mars

Ⓓ Earth, Mercury, Mars, Venus

4 What type of object is abundant
between the orbits of Mars and Jupiter?

Ⓐ planet

Ⓑ star

Ⓒ comet

Ⓓ asteroid

5 What kind of movement does this
diagram show?

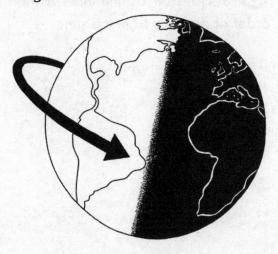

Ⓐ Earth' orbit

Ⓑ Earth's revolution

Ⓒ Earth's rotation

Ⓓ Earth's axis

6 Suppose you are an astronaut taking
a trip to the moon. Write about what
you see when you arrive. Include what
you see on the surface of the moon
and what you see in the sky.

Green Bank Observatory

Do you like learning more about the universe? The National Radio Astronomy Observatory in Green Bank, West Virginia, is just the place for young scientists like you to come and explore space.

Green Bank is located in the Allegheny Mountain Range. The telescope there, the Green Bank Telescope, is the world's largest fully movable radio telescope. A radio telescope works by receiving information in the form of radio waves. These waves come from all over the universe. The telescope at Green Bank can be turned so that it can get data from all angles.

APPLY THE BIG ? How might a trip to the Green Bank Telescope help you know more about the solar system and other objects in space?

....

....

....

....

If you take a trip to Green Bank, you can take a guided tour of the telescope. You can also stop at the science center and view and interact with exhibits about space.

Materials

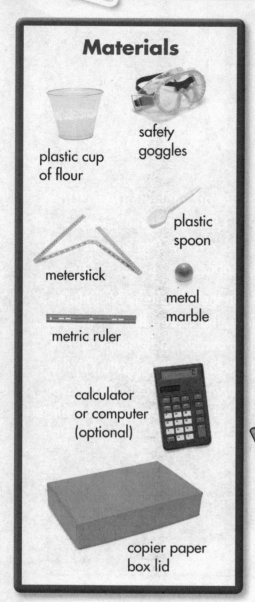

plastic cup of flour

safety goggles

meterstick

plastic spoon

metal marble

metric ruler

calculator or computer (optional)

copier paper box lid

 Be careful! Wear safety goggles.

Inquiry Skill

When scientists conduct an experiment, they identify the **independent variable,** the **dependent variable,** and the **controlled variables.**

How does the speed of a meteorite affect the crater it makes?

In this **experiment** you will create a model to find out how a meteorite's speed affects the size of the impact crater.

Ask a question.

Will meteorites that move faster make a smaller or larger crater than meteorites that move more slowly?

State a hypothesis.

1. Write a **hypothesis** by circling one choice and finishing the sentence. If a meteorite is moving faster, then it will make a crater with a width that is

a) *larger than*

b) *smaller than*

c) *about the same size as*

a crater made by a slower-moving meteorite because

....

Identify and control variables.

2. The marble is a **model** of a meteorite. The flour is a model of the surface the meteorite hits. **Controlled variables** are things you must keep the same in an experiment if you want a fair test. What will you keep the same?

....

3. The **independent variable** is the variable you change in an experiment. What will you change in this experiment?

....

....

4. The **dependent variable** is the variable you **measure** in an experiment. What will you measure in this experiment?

....

Design your test.

☐ **5.** Draw how you will set up your **model.**

☐ **6.** List your steps in the order in which you will do them.

Do your test.

☐ **7.** Follow the steps you wrote.

☐ **8.** Select a tool to **measure** the width of the crater in millimeters. **Record** your results in a table.

☐ **9.** Scientists repeat their tests to improve their accuracy. Repeat your test if time allows.

Collect and record your data.

☐ **10.** Fill in the chart.

Interpret your data.

☐ **11.** Use your data to make a bar graph.

Work Like a Scientist
Scientists work with other scientists. They compare their methods and results. Talk with your classmates. Compare your methods and results.

12. Study your chart and graph. What patterns do you see in your data?

....

....

....

13. Infer Describe your results. What can you infer from your results?

....

....

....

....

....

....

Technology Tools
Your teacher may want you to use a computer (with the right software) or a graphing calculator to help collect, organize, analyze, and present your data. These tools can help you make tables, charts, and graphs.

State your conclusion.

14. Communicate your conclusion. Compare your **hypothesis** with your results. Share your results with others.

....

....

....

....

....

....

APPLY
THE BIG
?
Unit C Earth Science
Performance-Based Assessment

Earth
Science

Crater Formation

The surfaces of Earth's moon and of the planet Mercury are covered with craters. Craters are bowl-shaped low spots that form when meteorites crash into the surface of a moon or planet.

Write a hypothesis about how the mass of a meteorite affects the size of the crater it makes. Then design and carry out an experiment to test your hypothesis.

Rain Gauge

A rain gauge is an instrument used to measure how much rain falls at a given place. Rain gauges may be of different sizes or shapes. What effect do you think changing the size of the opening of the rain gauge has on the amount of rain the gauge collects?

Write a hypothesis to answer the question. Then design and carry out an experiment to test your hypothesis.

Model a Planet's Orbit

What is the shape of a planet's orbit? Position two pushpins near the center of a square of cardboard. The pins should be about 5 cm (2 in.) apart. Tie the ends of a piece of string together to form a loop. Place the loop around the pins. Place the point of a pencil against the inside of the loop and stretch the string tight. Move the pencil around inside the loop unit it is back at the starting point. What shape can you draw using only one pin?

Using Scientific Methods

1. Ask a question.
2. State a hypothesis.
3. Identify and control variables.
4. Test your hypothesis.
5. Collect and record your data.
6. Explain your data.
7. State your conclusion.
8. Go further.

Physical Science

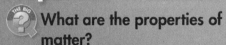

What makes up these GIANT crystals?

Properties of Matter

Try It! How are weight and volume affected when objects are combined?

Lesson 1 What makes up matter?

Lesson 2 How can matter be described?

Lesson 3 What are solids, liquids, and gases?

Lesson 4 What are mixtures and solutions?

Lesson 5 How does matter change?

Investigate It! What are some ways to separate a mixture?

You see small crystals, such as sugar or salt, every day. But have you ever seen crystals like these? These giant crystals are in a cave in the Chihuahuan Desert.

Predict This cave was once filled with water that had minerals dissolved in it. How do you think the crystals formed?

....

....

THE BIG ? What are the properties of matter?

How are weight and volume affected when objects are combined?

Materials

graduated cylinder

beads

plastic cup

plastic spoon

spring scale with bag

sand

☐ **1.** Fill a graduated cylinder with 25 mL of beads. **Record** the volume on the chart.

☐ **2.** Hold up the spring scale with the bag. Set the scale to zero. Now the spring scale will only show the weight of what is in the bag.

☐ **3.** Put the beads in the bag and weigh them. Record. Pour the beads into a cup.

☐ **4.** Repeat Step 1 and Step 3 with sand. Pour the sand into the cup with the beads.

☐ **5.** Mix the beads and sand with a spoon. Repeat Step 1 and Step 3 with the mixture of beads and sand.

Inquiry Skill
When you interpret data, you can make an **inference.**

Measurements of Matter

Objects	Volume (mL)	Weight (g)
beads		
sand		
beads and sand		

Explain Your Results

6. Interpret Data Did the total volume or weight change after mixing? Explain.

....

....

7. **UNLOCK THE BIG ?** **Infer** What did you learn about volume?

....

....

....

⊙ Compare and Contrast

- You **compare** when you tell how things are alike.
- You **contrast** when you tell how things are different.

Copper and Malachite

Copper is a very useful metal. It has a reddish color. It can be formed into sheets and wires without breaking. Malachite is a green mineral. It breaks if you try to change its shape. Malachite and copper are solid and durable. They are often used for decoration.

This jewelry box is carved from malachite. The legs are made from copper.

Practice It!

Complete the graphic organizer below to compare and contrast copper and malachite.

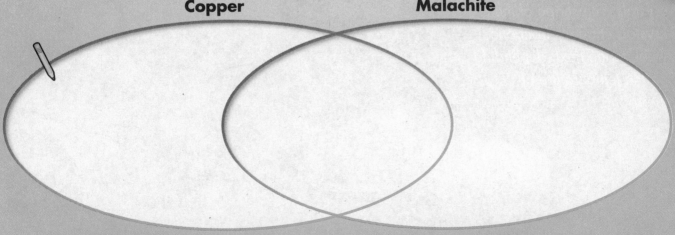

Copper   Malachite

Lesson 1

What makes up matter?

Stand back and look at this picture from a distance. **Tell** what colors you see.

my planet diary

FunFact

Have you ever noticed how nice it smells when you walk into some buildings? There is a type of air freshener that comes in solid lumps, about the size of a soap bar. These scented lumps do not melt at room temperature, but microscopic particles of them become loose and are released into the air, where we can enjoy their fragrance. If you keep these particles in a closed container, they will slowly collect on the sides, forming beautiful crystals. The shape of the crystals changes from one week to the next, depending on the temperature of the room.

Describe what you think would happen over time to this air freshener if you left the container open.

....

....

....

....

Now look at the dots closely. **Tell** what colors you see.

UNLOCK THE BIG ?

I will know that all things are made of very small particles called atoms and molecules, which cannot be seen without magnifying instruments.

Words to Know

atom	compound
atomic theory	molecule

Matter

Like ice, water, and air, you are made of matter. All living and nonliving things are made of matter. Matter is anything that has mass and takes up space. Mass is the amount of matter in an object. Matter includes the food we eat, our homes, our furniture, the sun, the moon, and this book.

A large sand sculpture is made of matter. It takes up a lot of space. It has a large mass. But if you look at it closely, you will see that it is made of tiny sand grains. A sand grain is also made of matter. It is gritty and tan colored, like the sculpture. But unlike the sculpture, a sand grain has a small mass and it does not take up a lot of space. All matter is made of tiny parts.

1. ◉ **Compare and Contrast** Use the graphic organizer below to describe how a sand sculpture and a grain of sand are alike and different.

Sand Sculpture   Grain of Sand

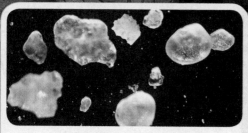

These sand grains are small particles. They are easy to see under a microscope. They are made of even smaller particles, too small to see with a regular microscope.

Elements

You can probably think of many kinds of food, many different medicines, or several types of fabric. Have you ever wondered how many different kinds of matter exist?

The world around you is made of thousands of materials, but all these materials are made of the same basic kinds of matter, called elements. Elements are the ingredients that make up all the other substances. Elements cannot be broken down into other substances with ordinary physical or chemical processes.

There are over 100 elements. Each element has specific characteristics. Each element will react in its own way with other elements.

Metals

Most elements are metals. Metals are good conductors of electricity and heat. They can be shaped into sheets or wires that can bend without breaking. Most metals, such as iron, are solids and have a gray color. Smooth metal surfaces can reflect light, which makes them appear shiny.

Aluminum *is light and strong. It is used to make ladders, airplane parts, and other items that need to be strong without being heavy.*

3. Identify What metal properties can you see in this ladder?

....

....

Calcium *is important for strong bones. You get calcium from food, but pure calcium is a metal! The calcium in food is combined with other elements. Dairy products can be good sources of calcium.*

2. List Write one food that is probably rich in calcium.

....

Mercury *is a liquid metal. It has many uses. For example, it can be used in thermometers and in energy-saving light bulbs. Mercury is toxic and must be handled with care.*

Nonmetals and Semimetals

Elements that do not conduct heat or electricity very well are called nonmetals. Some nonmetals are gases. One example is the oxygen you breathe. Other nonmetals, such as carbon, are solid.

Semimetals are elements that are sometimes like metals and sometimes like nonmetals. For example, they may conduct electricity, but only when light is shining on them. One of the most useful semimetals is silicon.

Silicon can be obtained from sand. The rod on the right is made of purified silicon. It will be used to make chips for electronic devices such as pocket calculators and computers.

4. Give an Example What other electronic devices might have silicon chips inside?

_____

_____

_____

Sulfur is a solid nonmetal. It can be found in nature as a mineral. Sulfur is brittle and burns easily. Sulfur compounds are used to make matches.

5. Interpret What would happen if you tried to break down a sample of sulfur?

_____

_____

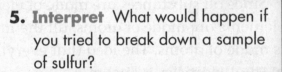

Neon belongs to a group of elements called the noble gases. These gases usually do not combine with other elements. Neon is used in neon signs.

Atoms

The smallest part of an element that still has the properties of the element is called an **atom**. Atoms are too small to be seen with a regular microscope, but special instruments can show how atoms are arranged.

The atoms of each element are different from the atoms of other elements. However, the atoms of all elements have something in common. They are made of the same three types of particles—protons, neutrons, and electrons.

The number of protons determines what element an atom will be. For example, an atom of carbon always has six protons. No other element has atoms with six protons. Carbon atoms usually have six neutrons and six electrons as well, but some atoms of carbon may have different numbers of electrons and neutrons. As long as an atom has exactly six protons, it will be an atom of carbon.

Since all substances are made of elements and all elements are made of atoms, all the matter around you is made of atoms. The idea that everything is made of small particles is known as the **atomic theory.**

6. List What types of particles make up a carbon atom?

7. CHALLENGE Draw what you think a carbon atom might look like. Use the gold atom below as a model.

Gold is a pure element. All gold is made of the same type of atoms. Every atom of gold has exactly 79 protons.

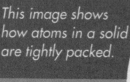
This image shows how atoms in a solid are tightly packed.

Protons and neutrons cluster at the center of the atom. This cluster is called the nucleus. Electrons move around the nucleus.

mysscienceonline.com | THE BIG ? | I Will Know...

Atomic Arrangement

Atoms are often connected to other atoms in specific ways. The way atoms are connected affects the properties of an element. For example, when carbon atoms are connected as flat sheets, the carbon is soft and black. This form of carbon is called graphite. If the same carbon atoms are connected as pyramids, they form diamonds. Unlike graphite, diamonds are transparent and very hard. However, diamonds and graphite are both made of carbon atoms.

8. ⊙ **Compare and Contrast** Tell how a diamond and a piece of graphite are alike and different.

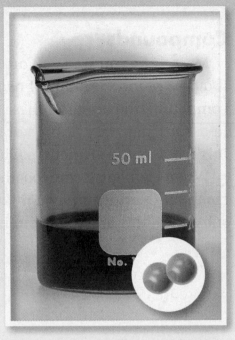

Bromine is an orange-red liquid. It evaporates easily. Its atoms are connected in pairs.

9. **Infer** In the picture above, do you think there are more atoms of bromine in liquid or gas form?

Diamonds are used to make jewels. The model below shows how carbon atoms are connected in a diamond.

The "lead" of a pencil is made of graphite. The model on the left shows how carbon atoms are connected in graphite.

Lightning Lab

Letters and Atoms
There are more than 100 kinds of atoms. Most arrangements are not possible, but there still are millions of ways to combine atoms. Write the letters *A, B, C, D,* and cut them out. How many ways can you put them in order? (Examples: *DBCA, CADB*)

421

Compounds

Most things around you are compounds. A **compound** is a type of matter made of two or more elements. In a compound, the atoms of these elements are joined together in a particular way. Table salt is an example of a compound. It is made of the elements sodium and chlorine.

When elements come together to form a compound, the compound is not simply a mixture of elements. It is a new substance. It is different from its ingredients.

chlorine molecules

Chlorine *is a poisonous gas. It is greenish-yellow. Chlorine reacts strongly with sodium.*

Table salt *is white and solid. It is not poisonous. Chlorine and sodium combine to form ordinary table salt.*

sodium chloride

sodium atoms

Sodium *is a soft metal. It can be cut with a knife. It reacts strongly with chlorine.*

10. Contrast List two ways in which salt is different from chlorine.

....

....

....

myscienceonline.com | Got it? | 60-Second Video

The smallest particle of a compound that still has the properties of that compound is called a **molecule.** For example, the smallest particle of water is a water molecule. A water molecule only has three atoms, but other molecules, like those of sugar, may have many atoms.

Changing the number, kind, or position of the atoms in a molecule would result in a molecule of a different substance. For example, a water molecule always has one atom of oxygen and two atoms of hydrogen. Adding an extra oxygen atom would turn a water molecule into a molecule of a different substance.

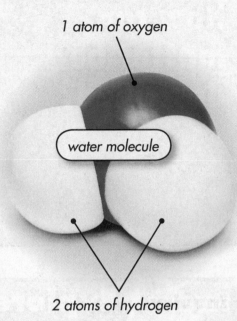

1 atom of oxygen

water molecule

2 atoms of hydrogen

11. **Calculate** Suppose you count all the hydrogen atoms in a group of water molecules. There are 8 hydrogen atoms in total. How many water molecules are in the group?

....

....

Got it?

12. **Explain** What makes up matter? Use the definition of atomic theory to answer.

....

13. **UNLOCK THE BIG ?** A scientist is combining two gray elements. He thinks he will get a gray compound. Use what you learned in this lesson to explain why this prediction may not be correct.

....

....

⬜ **Stop!** I need help with ....

⏸ **Wait!** I have a question about ....

▶ **Go!** Now I know ....

Lesson 2

How can matter be described?

☐ Colorful

☐ Lighter than air

☐ Pointed nose

☐ Smooth surface

Four properties are shown. **Check** the one that you think allows the blimp to float in air.

Inquiry **Explore It!**

What are some properties of solids?

☐ **1. Observe** the sand and salt. Use a hand lens.

☐ **2.** Put 1 spoonful of sand into both Cup A and Cup B. Put 1 spoonful of salt into both Cup C and Cup D.

☐ **3.** Fill each cup halfway with water. Stir only Cup A and Cup C. Observe.

Explain Your Results

4. What properties did you **observe**?

....

....

....

5. Identify the substance that dissolved. What helped it dissolve? Which substance did not dissolve?

....

....

....

....

....

....

Materials

goggles

hand lens

salt   sand

spoon

4 plastic cups

water

masking tape

Be careful! Wear safety goggles. Do not taste.

Cup A sand
Cup B sand
Cup C salt
Cup D salt

mYscienceonLine.com | **Explore It!** Animation

I will know how to compare and contrast solids, liquids, and gases by using their basic properties.

Words to Know

mass   temperature
volume

Color

Many solids and liquids have color. Some gases also have color. Color is a physical property of matter. Every solid, liquid, and gas has its own set of physical properties. The physical properties of a material can be observed, described, and measured without changing the material.

Some properties can be measured with tools such as rulers, thermometers, and balances. Color is very useful because you can determine the color of a piece of matter just by looking at it, and color often helps you determine the kind of matter you are looking at, or the state or condition of that piece of matter.

The liquids in this cylinder do not mix. They float on top of each other.

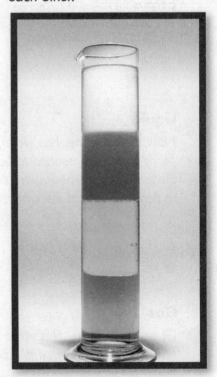

1. **Describe** The glass cylinder to the right contains a column of liquid. What can you learn from looking at the colors?

....

....

....

Solid iodine is dark purple, almost black. Heat turns it into a purple gas. Solid and gaseous iodine have different colors.

Mass

The amount of matter in a solid, liquid, or gas is called its **mass.** Mass is measured by using a balance, often using units of grams or kilograms.

We often weigh objects to get an idea of their mass, but mass and weight are not the same thing. The weight of an object on Earth is different from its weight on Mars, but the mass of the object is the same on both planets.

To find the mass of a solid, such as a toy car, you place the object on one side of a balance. On the other side, you place objects of known mass, such as gram cubes. When the two sides balance each other, the total mass of all the known masses equals the mass of the object.

2. Find Out Look at the balance that has water. Count the cubes. What is the mass of the water inside the container?

....

....

....

....

Solid

The empty container on the left has a mass of 8 g. We know this because it takes 8 cubes to balance it. Each cube has a mass of 1 g.

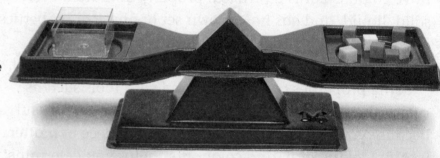

Liquid

Now the container has water. More cubes are needed to balance the extra mass. These extra cubes match the mass of the water.

Gas

Gases have mass. This inner tube has more mass when it is pumped full of air than when it is flat.

myscienceonline.com | ? THE BIG | I Will Know...

Volume

The amount of space an object takes up is its **volume.** Volume can be measured in milliliters (mL).

You can use a graduated cylinder to find the volume of a liquid. You just pour the liquid into the cylinder and read the volume off the scale, at the surface.

Solids also have volume. If you put liquid in a graduated cylinder and let a solid object sink in the liquid, the solid takes up some space. The liquid that was in that space is forced to go up. The change in the height of the liquid column tells you the volume of the solid.

Gases have volume. In fact, a small mass of gas can fill a large volume. You can measure the volume of a gas using an upside-down, partially submerged graduated cylinder filled with water. If you blow air into the cylinder with a straw, the bubbles will push some water out. The volume of water pushed out is the same as the volume of the gas.

3. ⊙ **Compare and Contrast** Look at the picture below. Explain how the mass and volume of the air in the tube and the water that was pushed down are alike and different.

....

....

....

....

....

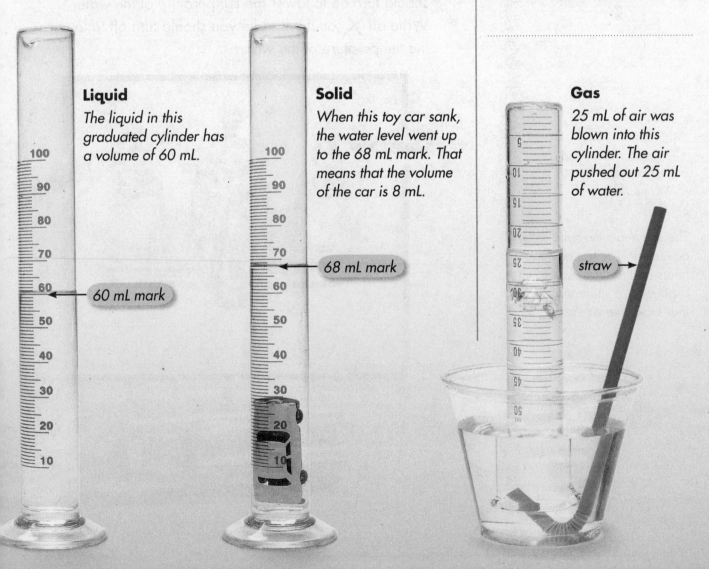

Liquid
The liquid in this graduated cylinder has a volume of 60 mL.

60 mL mark

Solid
When this toy car sank, the water level went up to the 68 mL mark. That means that the volume of the car is 8 mL.

68 mL mark

Gas
25 mL of air was blown into this cylinder. The air pushed out 25 mL of water.

straw

Temperature

The **temperature** of an object is a measure of how fast its particles are moving. The higher the temperature, the faster the particles move. We cannot see the particles that make up the object, but we can tell when they are moving faster because the object becomes hotter.

There are different scales for measuring temperature. In science books, you may find the melting point of a solid in degrees Celsius (°C). In a recipe, you may find a cooking temperature given in degrees Fahrenheit (°F).

Knowing the temperature of solids, liquids, and gases is very useful. For example, the water in a fish tank needs to be kept at the right temperature. A weather report gives us the temperature of the air. And the temperature of your body can help monitor a health problem.

4. **Infer** Look at the sink below. (Circle) the handle that you should turn on to lower the temperature of the water. Write an ✗ on the handle you should turn off to lower the temperature of the water.

The sun heats the solid pavement. The hot pavement heats up the air closest to it, producing a shimmering effect that looks like water.

mYscienceonLine.com | Got it? 60-Second Video

Texture

When you touch a solid object, you can feel if it is hard, smooth, lumpy, grooved, spongy, or rough. This surface structure that you can feel by touching a material is its texture.

You can also feel the texture of a liquid by rubbing a drop between two fingers. A drop of shampoo may feel soapy. A drop of oil will feel oily. Other liquids may feel slimy, sticky, or thick. For example, people who make soap may use the texture of the liquid mixture of ingredients to decide when it is ready for the next step in the process.

5. List Write two surfaces with a smooth texture and two surfaces with a rough texture.

....

....

....

....

The rough texture of sandpaper can scratch other materials.

Many stones can be polished to give them a very smooth texture.

Liquid soap feels slippery.

 Got it?

6. Analyze A heavy brick weighs more than a fluffy cushion, but the cushion takes up more space. Which object has more matter? How do you know?

....

....

7. UNLOCK THE BIG ? Which property might be more useful to tell two materials apart: their mass, their temperature, or their color?

....

....

◻ **Stop!** I need help with ....

⏸ **Wait!** I have a question about ....

▶ **Go!** Now I know ....

What are solids, liquids, and gases?

Envision It!

Where are some solids, liquids, and gases in the picture? **Tell** how you know.

Inquiry Explore It!

How can water change state?

- ☐ **1.** Stick a straw halfway inside a bag. Seal the bag up to the straw.

- ☐ **2.** Slowly exhale through the straw. Remove the straw and seal the bag shut.

- ☐ **3.** Lay the bag on dark paper under bright light. Use a hand lens to **observe.**

Materials

plastic bag

straw

dark paper

hand lens

Explain Your Results

4. Communicate What did you **observe**? Explain.

....

....

....

....

Be careful! Do not use a straw that someone else has used.

myscienceonline.com | **Explore It!** Animation

I will know some basic properties of solids, liquids, and gases.

Words to Know

solid   gas
liquid

States of Matter

Water has three forms. Water is a solid when it is frozen as ice. Water is a liquid in the ocean. In the air, water can be a gas. Solid, liquid, and gas are the most familiar states, or phases, of matter.

The phase of water, or of any material, is due to the motion and arrangement of its particles—its molecules or its atoms. The particles are always moving.

Most materials around you are solids, liquids, or gases. For example, cooking oil is a liquid. Butter is a solid when it is cold, but butter can turn into a liquid if it gets hot.

1. ⊚ **Compare and Contrast** Look at the picture. How are the solid butter and liquid oil alike and different?

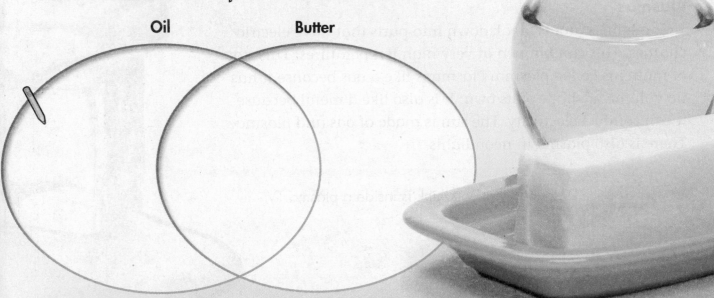

Oil   Butter

Solids

A **solid** is a substance that has a definite shape and volume. Volume is the amount of space an object takes up. The particles of a solid are very close together. For the most part they stay in the same place. They do not slide easily past each other. However, they vibrate in place.

Liquids

A **liquid** is a substance that has a definite volume but no definite shape. The particles of a liquid can move by gliding past each other. A liquid can take the shape of its container. Forces hold liquid particles together, so a liquid keeps a definite volume.

Gases

A **gas** is a substance without a definite volume or shape. The particles of a gas are far apart compared to the particles of solids and liquids. A gas can be squeezed into a smaller volume. Gas particles only affect one another when they collide as they move. If a gas is placed in an empty container, its particles will spread out evenly. The gas will fill all the space and take the shape of that container.

Plasmas

Sometimes atoms break down into parts that have electric charges. This can happen at very high temperatures. This state of matter is called plasma. Plasma is like a gas because it has no volume or shape of its own. It is also like a metal because it can conduct electricity. The sun is made of gas and plasma. There is also plasma in neon lights.

 2. CHALLENGE Describe what you think is inside a plasma TV.

_____

_____

_____

 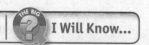 myscienceonline.com | THE BIG ? | I Will Know...

Freezing and Melting

As liquids get colder, their particles slow down. At some point they stop gliding past each other and can only vibrate in place. The liquid becomes a solid. The temperature at which a material changes between solid and liquid states has two names. It is called the freezing point when a liquid turns into a solid. It is called the melting point when a solid turns into a liquid. Therefore, the melting point and the freezing point are the same temperature. This temperature is often just referred to as the melting point.

Each material has its own melting point. Therefore, the melting point can be used to help identify a material.

Some materials are more useful in their solid state than in their liquid state. For example, lead is a metal that is dense. Solid lead is used to weigh down or sink fishing hooks.

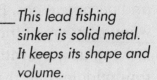

← *This lead fishing sinker is solid metal. It keeps its shape and volume.*

The melting point of lead is 327°C. At this temperature, solid lead becomes liquid and can be poured into molds to give it any shape we want.

3. **Compare** What is the difference between the melting point and freezing point of a substance?

....

....

4. **CHALLENGE** Why might you want to consider the melting point of a substance before choosing materials for frying pans or engine parts?

....

....

....

....

5. **Recognize** Water has a melting point of 0°C. What is its freezing point?

....

Lightning Lab

Wandering Ice
Place an ice cube on a dish and set it in a place where it will not be disturbed. Observe how long it takes for the ice cube to melt. Observe how long it takes for the water to evaporate.

Evaporation

Evaporation takes place when particles leave a liquid and become a gas. Particles evaporate from a liquid when they are at the surface of the liquid and are moving upward with enough speed. This is how rain puddles and the water in wet clothes evaporate.

If the temperature of a liquid is high enough, particles will change to a gas not only at the surface, but also throughout the liquid. As gas particles move quickly upward through a liquid, bubbles of gas form under the surface of the liquid. The boiling point of a liquid is the temperature at which this occurs.

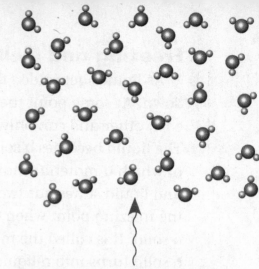

Molecules of water evaporate from the clothes as they dry. In water vapor, the molecules of water are far apart.

6. **Explain** How can clothes dry without heating them to the boiling point of water?

....

....

....

Do the math!

Ranges

The chart shows the temperatures at which 5 different substances change form.

Boiling Points (°C)	
Liquid	**Boiling Point**
Water	100°C
Acetic acid (found in vinegar)	118°C
Chlorine	–34°C
Propane	–42°C
Iodine	185°C

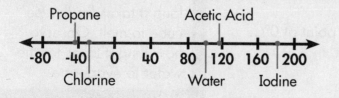

1. Which liquid has the highest boiling point?
   A. Water   C. Acetic acid
   B. Iodine   D. Propane

2. In which temperature range is the greatest gap between boiling points?
   F. 185°C to 100°C
   G. –34°C to –42°C
   H. 118°C to –42°C
   I. 100°C to –34°C

3. CHALLENGE Choose a common substance, such as ammonia or rubbing alcohol. Research its boiling point, and add this information to the chart. Plot the new data point on the number line.

myscienceonline.com | Got it? | 60-Second Video

Condensation

Condensation occurs when a gas turns into a liquid. This process often occurs when gas particles touch a cold surface and the temperature of the gas drops. Clouds in the sky and dew on the ground form through condensation of water vapor.

As air temperature decreases, the molecules of water vapor come together and condense, forming the liquid water droplets we call dew.

7. **Describe** What is one thing needed for condensation to occur?

8. **Infer** The dew on the spider's web formed before sunrise. What might this tell you about the air temperature before sunrise?

Got it?

9. **Interpret** A substance fills a 1-liter bottle. A scientist transfers the substance to a 2-liter bottle. The substance increases in volume and fills the new space. What is the state of matter of this substance?

10. **UNLOCK THE BIG ?** Why can you use the melting point to help identify a material?

⬛ **Stop!** I need help with ....

⏸ **Wait!** I have a question about ....

▶ **Go!** Now I know ....

Lesson 4

What are mixtures and solutions?

Once per year, the Chicago River in Illinois is dyed green. What are the parts of the mixture shown in the picture?

Inquiry **Explore It!**

How can a mixture be separated?

☐ **1.** Place the paper clips and fasteners in a cup. Move the magnet around in the cup slowly. Lift out the magnet. **Observe.**

☐ **2.** Fill the cup with water. Observe.

Explain Your Results

3. Infer What property made it possible to separate the mixture with a magnet?

....

....

4. What property made it possible to use water to separate the mixture?

....

....

Materials

5 brass fasteners

5 metal paper clips

5 plastic paper clips

magnet

water

plastic cup

436 mys<scienceonline.com | **Explore It!** Animation

UNLOCK
THE BIG

I will know properties of solutions and that mixtures can be separated based on properties of their parts.

Words to Know

mixture
solution

Mixtures

In a **mixture,** different materials are placed together but each material in the mixture keeps its own properties. If vegetables are cut and put together to make a mixture, different vegetables do not change their flavors or colors. Most foods that you eat are mixtures of different materials.

Different parts of a mixture can be separated from the rest of the mixture. Suppose your favorite breakfast is a mixture of cereal and raisins. You could easily separate out the raisins with a spoon to eat them first. The parts of a mixture may be combined in different amounts. The bowl of cereal you eat today could have more raisins than the one you ate yesterday.

The bowl of fruit is a mixture. It contains several different parts.

1. **Suggest** What mixture is your favorite to eat? List the parts.

....

....

....

2. **Support** Why is the bowl of beads to the right not a mixture?

....

....

At-Home Lab

Mixed-Up Foods

Find two different mixtures you eat at home. What are the parts of the mixtures? Tell whether you would ever eat any of the parts separately.

Separating Mixtures

You can use the physical properties of a substance to separate it from a mixture. The materials in a simple mixture can be separated because they have different physical properties. For example, a magnet can separate iron filings from sand. This separation happens because iron has the property of being attracted by magnets. Sand does not have that property. A screen filter can be used to separate a mixture of pebbles and sand. The smaller particles go through the screen but the pebbles do not. Sometimes you can sort the parts of a mixture by hand.

3. **Classify** Complete the chart below. Draw a mixture in the first row. Write how to separate the erasers and screws and the items in the new mixture.

Mixture			
How Can You Separate?	Pour through a strainer.		

4. CHALLENGE Suppose you had a mixture of sand and small, hollow beads. How might you separate the mixture?

....

....

....

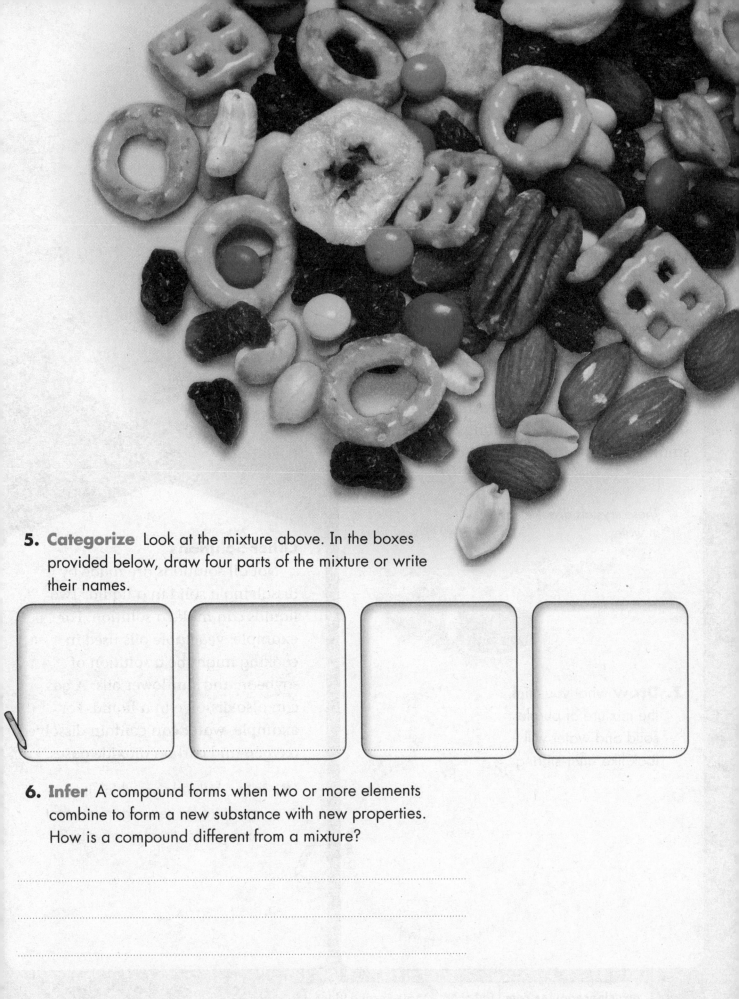

5. Categorize Look at the mixture above. In the boxes provided below, draw four parts of the mixture or write their names.

6. Infer A compound forms when two or more elements combine to form a new substance with new properties. How is a compound different from a mixture?

Solutions

A mixture in which substances are spread out evenly and will not settle is called a **solution.** In a solution, the substance that is dissolved is called the *solute*. The substance in which the solute is being dissolved is called the *solvent*. In a solution of sugar and water, the solute is sugar and the solvent is water. Water is sometimes called a "universal solvent" because it can dissolve many substances.

Solutions of a Solid in a Liquid

When a solid dissolves, individual particles separate from the solid and spread evenly throughout the liquid. You can make solids dissolve in a liquid faster by stirring or heating the solution. Grinding a solid into smaller pieces will also help it dissolve faster.

These crystals dissolve easily in water.

7. **Draw** what you think the mixture of purple solid and water will look like after stirring.

Other Solutions

Not all solutions are made by dissolving a solid in a liquid. Two liquids can make a solution. For example, vegetable oils used in cooking might be a solution of soybean and sunflower oils. A gas can also dissolve in a liquid. For example, water can contain dissolved oxygen and carbon dioxide gases.

8. **Infer** Why do you think it is important for sea organisms that some gases dissolve in water?

....

....

....

mYscienceonL

This toy has a colorless liquid floating on a blue-colored liquid. The colorless liquid and the plastic figures will not dissolve in the blue liquid. They are insoluble in it.

Solubility

Many materials can make solutions with water. You can dissolve more of some materials than others in the same amount of water. Some materials will not dissolve in water at all. This describes a material's solubility in water. Different substances can have different solubility in other solvents.

9. **CHALLENGE** The plastic figures in the picture are insoluble in the blue liquid. What else can you tell about their solubility?

....

....

....

Got it?

10. **Predict** To make a gelatin dessert, first you must boil water and then dissolve the gelatin powder in it. What do you think might happen if the water were not hot?

....

....

11. **UNLOCK THE BIG ?** Write one way you can use properties of matter to separate mixtures.

....

....

○ **Stop!** I need help with ....

❚❚ **Wait!** I have a question about ....

▶ **Go!** Now I know ....

Lesson 5
How does matter change?

The pictures above show a possible series of steps in the process of preparing to eat an orange. **Label** the steps.

Inquiry **Explore It!**

What happens when air heats up?

☐ **1.** Stretch a balloon over the top of each bottle.

☐ **2.** Set 1 bottle in each bowl. Wait 1 minute. **Observe.** Look closely.

Explain Your Results

3. Compare your **observations** of the balloons.

....

4. Infer How did temperature affect the air in the bottles?

....

....

....

5. Was the change you observed a physical or chemical change? Explain.

....

....

....

Materials

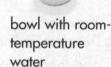

2 balloons

bowl with warm water

bowl with room-temperature water

2 plastic bottles

timer, stopwatch, or clock with second hand

warm water

room-temperature water

myscienceonline.com | **Explore It!** Animation

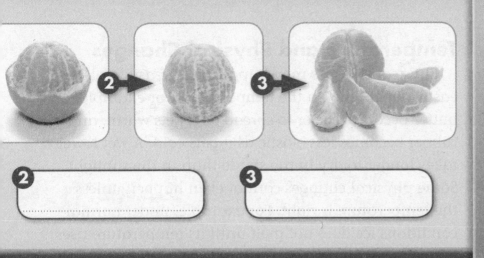

2 ....

3 ....

UNLOCK
THE BIG
?

I will know that many physical changes are affected by temperature. I will know that many chemical changes are affected by temperature.

Words to Know

physical change
chemical change

Physical Changes

Matter changes all the time. Some changes are physical changes. A **physical change** is a change in some properties of matter without forming a different kind of matter. There are many kinds of physical changes.

When you cut a piece of paper into smaller pieces, you do not produce a new material. You still have paper. The paper has undergone a physical change. Some of its properties have changed, but the properties that make it paper are still there. For example, the cut pieces are smaller than the original sheet and do not have the same shape. However, these pieces can burn or absorb water. They also keep their original color.

Breaking glass and stretching a rubber band are also physical changes. After breaking glass or stretching a rubber band, you still end up with glass or rubber.

1. ⊙ **Compare and Contrast** How are the physical properties of a small piece of paper similar to those of a large piece of the same paper? How are they different?

....

....

....

....

When this green slime stretches, it changes shape but does not turn into a new material. The slime keeps its color, its smell, and other properties.

Twin Balloons

Blow up two balloons to the same size. Put one of the balloons in the refrigerator. Leave the other at room temperature. After an hour, compare the sizes of the balloons. Share your findings with your class.

Temperature and Physical Changes

Physical changes may happen more easily or less easily depending on the temperature. For example, butter becomes easier to spread as it gets warm, and rubber becomes less elastic as it gets cold. A wet towel takes longer to dry in the shade than in the sunlight. Some physical changes cannot even happen unless the temperature is right. For example, under normal conditions ice does not melt until its temperature rises above its melting point, 0°C.

Melting, freezing, evaporation, and condensation are all physical changes. For example, water vapor still is water. We may call it water vapor, but it is just water that has gone through a physical change. In the same way, the melted wax of a candle still is wax. It hasn't turned into a new substance. It has just become liquid for a while. It becomes solid again as soon as it cools off.

2. **Infer** What physical change do you think is happening to this scented oil below? How does the candle help?

....

....

....

Heated milk dissolves cocoa powder. The cocoa does not stir easily into cold milk.

mYscienceonLine.com | THE BIG ? | I Will Know...

Chemical Changes

To form a new substance, a chemical change has to happen. In a **chemical change,** one or more types of matter change into other types of matter with different properties. When a chemical change occurs, atoms rearrange themselves to form new kinds of matter.

It is not always easy to tell if a substance has changed chemically. Evidence of chemical change may include the release of heat and light, a change in color, a new smell, gas bubbles, or the formation of a solid.

Chemical changes happen all the time around us. The rusting of iron is a familiar chemical change. When you leave an iron object outside, it slowly becomes rusty. Rust is red and brittle. It is a new substance. The process of photosynthesis, in which plants use water and carbon dioxide, is a chemical change because a new substance is made—sugar. When newspapers burn, they also go through a chemical change. They change into ash.

3. ⊙ **Compare and Contrast** How are physical and chemical changes alike? How are they different?

....

....

....

These two solutions have no color. A bright yellow substance forms when we mix them. This suggests that a chemical change has happened.

4. **Describe** Write whether each image below shows a physical change or chemical change.

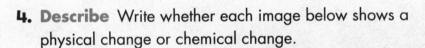

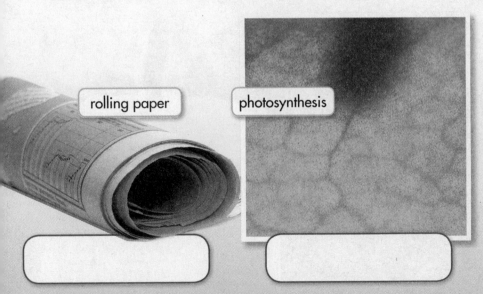

rolling paper

photosynthesis

rusting metal

445

A chemical reaction inside these glow sticks causes them to glow. The faster the reaction, the brighter the glow.

Temperature and Chemical Changes

When a candle burns, it goes through a chemical change that releases light and heat. But this chemical change cannot start on its own. You need to light the candle with a match. The flame of the match is hot enough to start the burning. After the burning starts, the reaction keeps itself going by the heat it releases.

Many chemical changes can happen without high temperatures, but they often happen faster if the temperature increases. Remember that particles move faster in a material when the temperature rises, so they may have more chances to rearrange themselves into new substances quickly. For example, if you put a fizzy antacid tablet in a glass of water at room temperature, the bubbles will form faster than if you used cold water.

5. **Conclude** The glow sticks to the left were started at the same time, but the one in water glows more brightly. What does this suggest about the water temperature?

....

....

6. CHALLENGE Look at the picture below. As a candle burns, it becomes shorter and shorter. Does it disappear? Explain.

....

....

The tip of this candle is still burning. When a candle burns, the wax and the wick combine with oxygen in the air to become smoke, soot, and hot gas.

Just as higher temperatures can speed up a chemical change, low temperatures can slow it down. When you buy fruit that is not ripe, you can often let it ripen in the kitchen at room temperature. Ripening involves chemical changes that slowly change the color and flavor of a fruit. If you place unripe fruit in a refrigerator, the fruit will often ripen more slowly than if you leave it on the kitchen counter.

after one week

One of these tomatoes was kept in a refrigerator. The other was kept at room temperature.

7. Look at the pictures to the right. (Circle) the tomato that was stored in the refrigerator. Tell how you know.

....

....

8. **Infer** Why do you think medicine labels usually say, "Store in a cool, dry place"?

....

....

Got it?

9. **Summarize** How can temperature affect many kinds of chemical changes?

....

....

10. **UNLOCK THE BIG ?** What properties might change during a chemical reaction?

....

....

▢ **Stop!** I need help with ....

❚❚ **Wait!** I have a question about ....

▶ **Go!** Now I know ....

Inquiry Investigate It!

What are some ways to separate a mixture?

Follow a Procedure

☐ **1.** Label the 4 cups *A*, *B*, *C*, and *D*. In Cup A place 1 spoonful of salt, 2 spoonfuls of sand, 3 marbles, and 100 mL of water.

☐ **2.** Carefully make 4 holes in the bottom of Cup B by pushing a pencil through the bottom of the cup from the inside.

☐ **3.** Hold Cup B over Cup C. All at once, pour the mixture from Cup A into Cup B. Move Cup B around to clean the marbles. **Record** the part of the mixture that was removed by straining.

Materials

safety goggles

spoon

4 plastic cups

warm water and graduated cylinder

salt

sand

3 metal marbles

coffee filter and a rubber band

pencil

foil

Be careful! Wear safety goggles.
Do not taste.
Be careful with sharp objects.

Inquiry Skill
Scientists record data on charts and use the data to help **make inferences.**

Results of Separation

Separating Method	Part Removed	Part Not Removed
Straining		
Filtering		
Evaporation		

4. Put a coffee filter in Cup D. Slowly pour the mixture from Cup C into Cup D. Record the part of the mixture that was removed by filtering.

5. Remove the filter. Use the spoon to drip 2 drops of the liquid onto the foil. Let the liquid evaporate. Record the results.

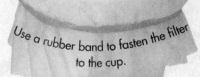

Use a rubber band to fasten the filter to the cup.

Analyze and Conclude

6. Communicate Name a property you used to separate parts of the mixture.

....

7. **Infer** Describe another mixture. How could the properties of matter help you separate it into its parts?

....

....

....

Sidewalks & Playgrounds

Concrete is everywhere in our world. Highways, skyscrapers, sidewalks, and skate parks are often made of concrete. Ancient Romans used materials similar to concrete to build structures. Some of those structures are still standing today.

Concrete is made of many different materials. The main ingredient is cement—a human-made material. Cement is a fine powder that includes several different minerals. To make concrete, cement is mixed with sand, gravel, crushed rock, and water. Once concrete is set, or hardened, it is very strong and long-lasting.

What makes concrete so strong? One of the materials that makes it so strong is water. Surprised? When workers pour concrete it is very wet, but days later it is dry. The water does not just evaporate—it changes chemically! The water and cement react to form a gel. As the water and cement continue to react, they harden into concrete.

REVIEW THE BIG ? How does mixing water and cement change their properties?

Vocabulary Smart Cards

atom
atomic theory
compound
molecule
mass
volume
temperature
solid
liquid
gas
mixture
solution
physical change
chemical change

Play a Game!

Cut out the Vocabulary Smart Cards.

Work with a partner.

Player 1 chooses a Vocabulary Smart Card.

Say as many words as you can think of that describe that vocabulary word to Player 2.

Player 2 guesses the word.

molecule

molécula

atom
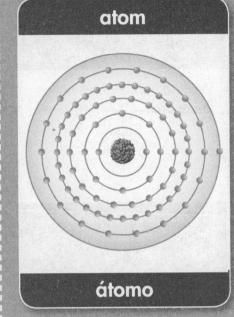
átomo

mass

masa

atomic theory

teoría atómica

volume
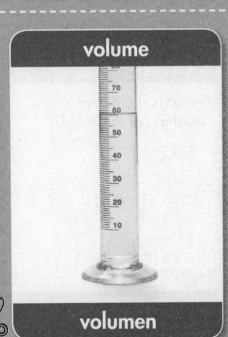
volumen

compound

compuesto

the smallest part of an element that still has the properties of the element

Write a sentence using this word.

....

....

la partícula más pequeña de un elemento, que todavía tiene las propiedades de ese elemento

the smallest particle of a compound that still has the properties of that compound

Draw an example of this word.

la partícula más pequeña de un compuesto, que todavía tiene las propiedades de ese compuesto

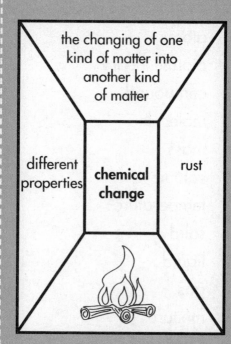

the changing of one kind of matter into another kind of matter

different properties

chemical change

rust

Make a Word Frame!

Choose a vocabulary word and write it in the center of the frame. Write or draw details about the vocabulary word in the spaces around it.

the idea that everything is made of small particles

Write a sentence using this term.

....

....

....

la idea de que la materia está formada por partículas pequeñas

the amount of matter in a solid, liquid, or gas

Write a sentence using this word.

....

....

....

cantidad de materia que tiene un sólido, líquido o gas

a type of matter made of two or more elements

Write a different meaning of this word.

....

....

....

tipo de materia formada por dos o más elementos

the amount of space an object takes up

What is a different meaning of this word?

....

....

....

el espacio que ocupa un objeto

physical change	gas	temperature
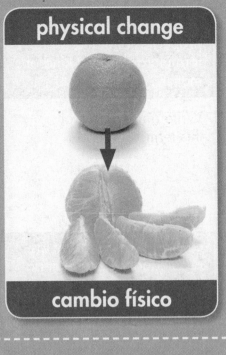	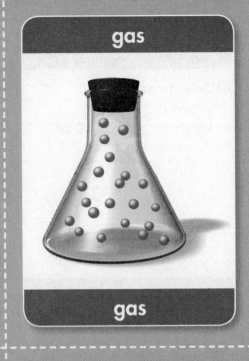	
cambio físico	gas	temperatura

chemical change	mixture	solid

cambio químico	mezcla	sólido

	solution	liquid

	solución	líquido

a measure of how fast the particles in an object are moving

Write a sentence using this word.

....

....

....

....

medida de la rapidez con que se mueven las partículas de un objeto

---

a substance without a definite volume or shape

Write an example of this word.

....

....

....

....

sustancia que no tiene ni volumen ni forma definidos

---

a change in some properties of matter without forming a different kind of matter

Write an example of this term.

....

....

cambio de algunas de las propiedades de la materia sin que se forme un nuevo tipo de materia

---

a substance that has a definite shape and volume

What are two other meanings of this word?

....

....

....

sustancia que tiene una forma y un volumen definidos

---

different materials placed together, but each material keeps its own properties

Write three other forms of this word.

....

....

....

unión de materiales diferentes en la cual cada material mantiene sus propiedades

---

a change of one or more types of matter into other types of matter with different properties

Write an example of this term.

....

....

cambio de uno o más tipos de materia a otros tipos de materia con propiedades diferentes

---

a substance that has a definite volume but no definite shape

Draw an example.

sustancia que tiene un volumen definido pero no una forma definida

---

a mixture in which substances are spread out evenly and will not settle

What is a different meaning of this word?

....

....

mezcla en la cual una sustancia se dispersa de manera uniforme en otra sustancia y no se asienta

REVIEW THE BIG ?

What are the properties of matter?

Lesson 1

What makes up matter?

- Matter is made of atoms. Atoms may combine to form molecules.
- Elements are basic kinds of matter. Each element has different atoms.
- Compounds are made up of two or more elements.

Lesson 2

How can matter be described?

- Mass is the amount of matter in an object.
- Volume is the amount of space an object takes up.
- Temperature is a measure of how fast the particles of an object move.

Lesson 3

What are solids, liquids, and gases?

- States of matter include solid, liquid, gas, and plasma.
- Changes in state are caused by changes in the motion of particles.
- Melting, freezing, evaporation, and condensation are state changes.

Lesson 4

What are mixtures and solutions?

- A mixture is made up of two or more materials.
- The parts of a mixture can be separated.
- A solution is a type of mixture. Parts do not settle out of a solution.

Lesson 5

How does matter change?

- Physical changes do not change materials into new materials.
- In a chemical change, one or more new substances form.
- Temperature can affect physical and chemical changes.

Chapter Review

REVIEW THE BIG ?

What are the properties of matter?

Lesson 1

What makes up matter?

1. **Summarize** Your classmate has a magnifying glass, and he is looking for atoms. What would you tell him?

2. **Predict** A scientist finds that a sample of matter contains three types of atoms. The sample can be any of the following except
   A. a compound.
   B. a molecule.
   C. an element.

Lesson 2

How can matter be described?

3. **Vocabulary** The amount of matter an object has is its
   A. weight.
   B. volume.
   C. size.
   D. mass.

4. **Describe** What does the property of volume tell you about an object?

Lesson 3

What are solids, liquids, and gases?

5. ◉ **Compare and Contrast** Write two ways water and ice are different and two ways they are the same.

6. **Infer** A substance has a melting point of 104°C. Its freezing point will be
   A. lower than 104°C.
   B. higher than 104°C.
   C. 104°C.

Do the math!

7. What is the range of temperature between the boiling points of −42°C to 118°C?
   A. 42°C
   B. 18°C
   C. 118°C
   D. 160°C

8. **Compare** How are liquids and solids alike? How are liquids and gases alike?

Lesson 4

What are mixtures and solutions?

9. Explain Sulfur burns easily. Iron is attracted by magnets. The mineral below is made of sulfur and iron, but it does not burn and it is not attracted by magnets. Is it a mixture? Why or why not?

....

....

....

Lesson 5

How does matter change?

10. Vocabulary In a chemical change
   A. materials retain their properties.
   B. the new material has different properties.
   C. materials always change states.

11. Classify List three examples of physical changes.

....

....

....

12. APPLY THE BIG ? **What are the properties of matter?**

....

Think about the materials used to make a car. Some materials are glass, steel, leather, and paint. Choose any three materials. For each one, describe one property that makes it useful in the car. For example, windshield glass is clear so that people can see through it.

....

....

....

....

....

....

....

....

....

....

....

....

....

....

Benchmark Practice

Fill in the bubble next to the answer choice you think is correct for each multiple-choice question.

1 A gas

Ⓐ does not have a definite volume.
Ⓑ does not have a definite shape.
Ⓒ fills its container.
Ⓓ all of the above.

2 Which of the following statements is true?

Ⓐ Atoms are made of molecules.
Ⓑ Atoms can join to form molecules.
Ⓒ Atoms contain more than one element.
Ⓓ Some atoms do not have protons.

3 Fill in the blank: When two materials mix evenly and do not settle, that mixture is called a _____.

Ⓐ solution
Ⓑ compound
Ⓒ sugar
Ⓓ solute

4 What can affect the rate of a chemical change?

Ⓐ color
Ⓑ texture
Ⓒ temperature
Ⓓ gas bubbles

5 Suppose you boil an egg. What kind of change is taking place?

Ⓐ physical and chemical
Ⓑ chemical
Ⓒ physical
Ⓓ No change is occurring.

6 Describe how you would separate a mixture of water, sand, pebbles, and paper clips.

....
....
....
....
....
....
....
....
....
....

Aerogels

When many people think of oil polluting the environment, they often think on a large scale, such as an oil tanker spilling millions of gallons of oil into the ocean. Small amounts of oil are deposited every day in sewers and streams and pose a threat to the environment.

One way to clean up oil contamination is with a substance called aerogels. Aerogels are strong solids made from gels. The liquid is removed from a gel and replaced with gas, which changes the properties of the substance. Aerogels are nicknamed "frozen smoke" because they are translucent and can take on either a blue or yellow color, depending on the amount of light present.

Aerogels made from silica gel are especially good at cleaning up spilled oil because they have a low density and are very absorbent. Scientists have been testing the ability of silica aerogel beads to clean up oil by mixing them with water and corn oil. In one investigation, the aerogel absorbed seven times its weight! Because they work so well at removing corn oil from water and are relatively cheap to produce, aerogels may become one of the best methods for removing oil pollution from the environment.

Underline one reason why using silica aerogels may be a good way to clean up oil in the environment.

aerogel

Which way
is he
MOVING?

Forces and Motion

 Try It! How can you make a paper helicopter drop slowly?

Lesson 1 What are forces?

Lesson 2 What are Newton's laws?

Lesson 3 What are machines?

Investigate It! What forces affect the motion of a rocket?

A surfer has to have perfect timing to ride an ocean wave. He has to balance the sideways motion of the water with the upward force of the wave on his board.

 Predict Where do you think the surfer will end up after the wave passes? Why?

....

....

....

THE BIG ? What affects the motion of objects?

How can you make a paper helicopter drop slowly?

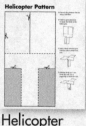

☐ **1.** Use the Helicopter Pattern to **make a model** of a helicopter. Add a paper clip to the bottom.

☐ **2.** Drop the helicopter. **Observe** its motion. Describe how it moves.

....

....

☐ **3.** Modify the design to make the helicopter stay in the air longer.

Materials

scissors

paper clip

heavy paper or card stock (optional)

Helicopter Pattern

additional small or large paper clips (optional)

Explain Your Results

4. What force pulls the helicopter down? What force slows its fall?

....

....

5. **UNLOCK THE BIG ?** **Interpret Data** How did your change affect the helicopter's motion?

....

....

....

....

Inquiry Skill

You can **make and use a model** to help explain an object or event.

◉ Main Idea and Details

- Learning to find **main ideas** and **details** can help you understand and remember what you read.

Small but Strong

Small animals can be very strong for their size. For example, tortoise beetles are the size of a ladybug, but it is very difficult to pull them off a leaf or a stem. These beetles have sticky feet and strong legs that allow them to hold on very tight. Leaf-cutting ants use their strength to carry heavy weights. A leaf-cutting ant can carry a leaf that is many times heavier than the ant itself! A flea is able to jump more than 100 times its own height. That would be like a human jumping from street level to the top of a 50-story building!

Practice It!

Use the graphic organizer below to list the main idea and details from the article shown above.

Detail	Detail	Detail

Main Idea

What are forces?

Tell why the metal ring on the string does not fall.

my planet diary

//// MISCONCEPTION ////

You may have seen video clips of astronauts floating around in a spacecraft. People often think astronauts have no weight at all in space. In fact, they do. Most astronauts work just 300 km above ground. This is relatively close to Earth. At that height, they are only a few pounds lighter. They seem to float because their spacecraft is moving along with them. However, the spacecraft and the astronauts are both in fact falling, just like a skydiver. They don't crash because they are also moving forward fast enough to follow the curvature of the Earth.

Which everyday activities do you think would be easier in orbit?

....

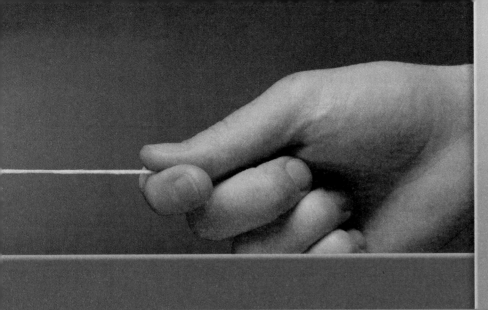

I will know some forces that cause objects to move.

Words to Know

force
contact force
friction
non-contact force
gravity

Forces

When one object pushes or pulls another object, the first object is exerting a force on the second one. A **force** is a push or pull that acts on an object.

Every force has a strength, or magnitude. This strength is measured in units called newtons (N). A force also has a direction. The direction of a force can be described by telling which way the force is acting. The dog is pushing the ball with a force of around 2 N.

Forces can change the way objects move. When an object begins to move, it is because a force has acted on it. When an object is already moving, forces can make it speed up, slow down, or change direction.

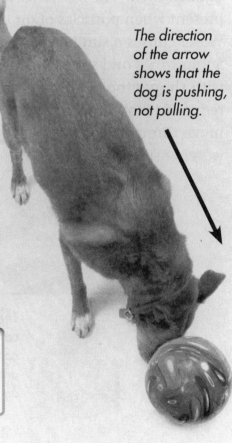

The direction of the arrow shows that the dog is pushing, not pulling.

1. ◉ **Main Idea and Details** Use the graphic organizer below to list two details and the main idea found in the last paragraph of the text.

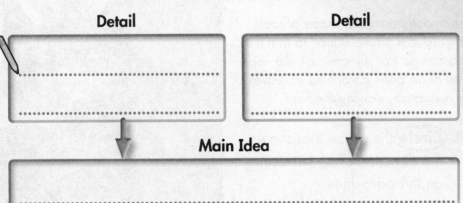

Detail	Detail

Main Idea

Contact Forces

Car mechanics use forces to lift tires and pull tool carts. These forces cannot act unless the mechanic touches the object to be moved. The object may be touched directly with a hand or using a handle or a rope, but there must be contact. A force that requires two pieces of matter to touch is called a **contact force.** You exert a contact force when you push or pull a piece of furniture.

One kind of contact force is friction. **Friction** is the force that results when two materials rub against each other or when their contact prevents sliding. Friction makes it harder for one surface to move past another. The amount of friction between two objects may depend on their texture, shape, speed, and weight. It may also depend on whether or not the surfaces are wet.

Solids are not the only materials that can cause friction. Air and water also resist motion when an object pushes against them. Air resistance is a type of friction that is present when particles of air contact a surface. Water causes a similar type of friction. Submarines and ships are designed with shapes that help them reduce friction and move through water easily.

3. [CHALLENGE] Why do you think mechanics need to change tires during races?

The smooth, compact shape of race cars reduces air resistance so that the cars can go fast. By contrast, the wide area of an open parachute increases air resistance, slowing the fall.

2. Circle the arrow that shows the direction of air resistance on the parachute.

The large amount of friction between the tires and the track makes it harder for cars to slide out of control. Friction also causes the brakes on the back of inline skates to slow or stop the skater.

4. **Explain** How do brakes help an inline skater stop?

....

....

....

....

This mechanic is pushing on a lever so she can lift one side of the car.

This member of the pit crew is pulling a worn-out tire off the car.

Many shoes have rough soles that increase friction with the ground and prevent slipping.

Non-Contact Forces

For friction to work, two things need to touch. There has to be contact between two surfaces, or contact with a gas or a liquid. But there are forces that can act at a distance. They work even if the object that is pushing or pulling is not touching the object being pushed or pulled! A force that acts at a distance is called a **non-contact force.** Three examples of non-contact forces are gravity, electric forces, and magnetic forces.

Gravity

Every object in the universe exerts a pull on every other object. This force of attraction between any two objects is called **gravity.** Only the gravity of a large object such as Earth is strong enough to cause effects that we can notice easily. Without gravity, things would not fall. Gravity pulls objects toward Earth's center without touching them.

The weight of an object is just the force of Earth's pull on that object. As an object moves away from Earth, the object weighs less and less because the pull of Earth's gravity becomes weaker and weaker with distance.

5. [CHALLENGE] Draw in the box at the right where you think the feather will be by the time the apple has hit the bottom of the box.

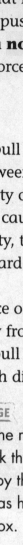

Gravity with no Air Resistance

Feathers normally fall slowly. You don't expect a feather to fall as fast as an apple. However, if you pump the air out of a box and drop a feather and an apple inside, they will fall at the same rate!

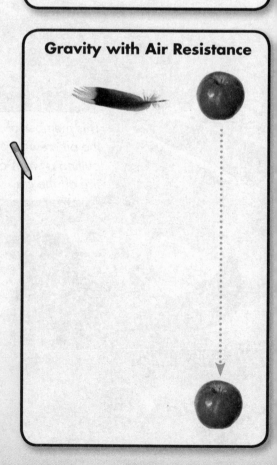

Gravity with Air Resistance

At-Home Lab

Does Gravity Affect You?

Stand. Stretch your left arm overhead. Leave your right arm at your side. Wait for 1 minute. Then compare the color of the palms of your hands. Share what you notice.

Electric and Magnetic Forces

Electric forces act between objects that are electrically charged. Oppositely charged objects are attracted to each other and tend to move toward each other. Objects with the same charge repel each other and tend to move away from each other.

Magnets will pull strongly on objects made of some metals, such as iron, cobalt, and nickel. Every magnet has a north pole and a south pole. Magnetic force is greatest at a magnet's poles. The north pole of one magnet will pull on the south pole of another magnet. The north poles of two magnets will push away from each other. The south poles of two magnets will act in the same way.

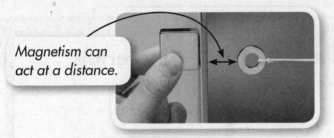

Magnetism can act at a distance.

6. Analyze What is happening to the cat's fur?

....

....

....

Got it?

7. Identify What are some forces that might affect a rock as it tumbles down a hill?

....

....

8. UNLOCK THE BIG ? **Conclude** If Earth is pulling down on you, are you pulling up on Earth? Explain.

....

....

Stop! I need help with ....

Wait! I have a question about ....

Go! Now I know ....

What are Newton's laws?

Envision It!

Draw the path you think the snowboarder will travel as she jumps off the slope.

Inquiry Explore It!

How can forces affect motion?

☑ **1.** Place the ruler on a flat, level surface.
Put Marble **A** in the groove of the ruler at the 10 cm mark.
Put Marble **B** in the groove at the 20 cm mark.

☑ **2. Predict** What will happen if you push **A** so that it hits **B**?

☑ **3.** Test your prediction. Repeat your test 4 times. Tell your results. Tell whether the results were the same each time.

Explain Your Results

4. Communicate Describe the forces that affected each marble.

....

....

5. Share your results. Discuss why tests should be repeated. Tell why an **investigation** should be repeatable by others.

Materials

2 metal marbles

metric ruler with groove

Marble **A**

Marble **B**

mYscienceonLine.com | **Explore it!** Animation

I will know that a given object will have more change of motion with a large force. I will know that a given force will cause more change of motion on small masses.

Words to Know

acceleration
inertia

Changes in Motion

Have you ever observed the motion of a car? When the car approaches a red light, the driver steps on the brake pedal. The speed of the car drops to zero. When the light turns green, the driver steps on the gas pedal. The speed climbs from zero. If the car has to turn a corner, the driver turns the steering wheel. The car changes direction.

When an object speeds up, slows down, or changes direction, its motion changes. The rate at which the speed or the direction of motion of an object changes over time is its **acceleration.**

When we speak of acceleration, we usually mean going faster and faster, but in science the word *acceleration* means *any* change in motion. For example, the circular motion of a Ferris wheel is accelerated. Even if the wheel turns with constant speed, the riders change direction all the time. They go up, then forward, then down, and then backward.

An object has no acceleration if it moves in a straight line without changing its speed or direction, or if it is not moving at all. Motion without acceleration is called uniform motion. The word *uniform* tells us that the motion does not change. A train traveling at a steady speed on a straight track has uniform motion. A book sitting on a table also has uniform motion. Its speed is zero.

1. **Explain** What kind of motion do the people on the escalator below have? Why?

....
....
....
....

Newton's First Law

Newton's first law of motion says that an object will stay in uniform motion unless a net force acts on the object. Without that force, an object at rest will stay at rest. An object in motion will keep the same speed and direction. For example, a marble will stay still on the floor unless you push it. If the marble is already moving, it will continue to move at a constant speed in a straight line until a force acts on it.

The tendency of an object to resist any change in motion is known as **inertia**. Objects with a lot of mass have more inertia than objects with less mass. Your body's inertia is what pushes you against the side of a car when the car turns. Your body tends to keep moving in a straight line when the car changes direction. The car must push you as it turns. Inertia is also what makes your body rise up from your seat when the car goes up and over a steep hill. At the top of the hill, your body tends to continue going forward as the car begins to move down the hill.

Things you push or throw eventually will stop. This is because there are other forces acting on these objects. For example, friction and air resistance will slow down a rolling marble until it stops. However, a space probe will keep moving through space because it has no friction to slow it down. Even without fuel, a space probe can travel a long distance by inertia. It only needs fuel to change direction or to slow down.

2. ⊙ **Main Idea and Details** Read the second paragraph again. (Circle) the main idea and **underline** two details.

3. **Infer** Why do standing passengers fall forward when a bus stops?

4. [CHALLENGE] Why is fuel needed to change the speed or direction of a probe in space?

A crash-test dummy has inertia. Even if a moving car is stopped in a crash, the inertia of the dummy will keep it moving forward.

The bowling ball has inertia. Inertia will keep it rolling for many meters, even after the player releases it.

5. Use blue to color the part of the arrow where a force is pushing the ball, and red to color the part of the arrow where the ball is moving only by inertia.

The ball is released here.

6. **Suggest** What could prevent the test dummy's inertia from carrying the dummy through the windshield?

....

....

473

Newton's Second Law

Newton's second law of motion describes how acceleration, mass, and force are related. Force is the product of mass and acceleration. The force acting on an object can cause the object to speed up, slow down, or change direction.

Same Force, Different Masses

Newton's second law says that the greater the mass of the object, the smaller its change in motion will be for a given force. This means that the same force will cause an object with small mass to accelerate more than an object with large mass. Large masses are harder to accelerate and harder to stop. For example, the engine and brakes of a truck provide the same forces whether the truck is empty or loaded. However, the loaded truck has more mass and will accelerate more slowly. It will also take longer to stop. Truck drivers must be aware of Newton's second law in order to drive safely.

7. **Compare** The boats below have no engines. The engine shown can push either boat with the same force. (Circle) the boat that is more likely to experience less acceleration with this engine. Tell why.

myscienceconline.com | I Will Know...

Same Mass, Different Forces

Newton's second law of motion also says that the greater the force applied, the greater the change in motion for a given mass. In other words, a large force will produce more acceleration than a small force acting on the same object.

You can see this law at work in the Olympic sport of archery. Archers shoot arrows at targets. The archer must be sure that the arrow starts moving with just the right speed and direction in order to reach the target. The arrow starts at rest. The archer bends the bow by pulling on the bow string. The amount of bending controls the force that will accelerate the arrow. This force changes the motion of the arrow. When the arrow leaves the bow, it is traveling very fast. The same arrow can experience different accelerations depending on the amount of stretching of the bow.

8. **Predict** If the archer pulls the string to B instead of to A, there will be less force on the arrow. How will this affect the acceleration of the arrow?

....

....

9. **Infer** Look at the shape of the bow and string to the right. How can you tell that a force will act on the arrow when the string is released?

....

....

Using Formulas

The formula that describes the relationship between force, mass, and acceleration is:

Force = Mass × Acceleration

This means that the stronger the force acting on an object, the more that object will accelerate. The formula is often written as follows:

F = m × a

The unit of force in the metric system is called a newton (N). The unit of mass in the metric system is the kilogram (kg).

The unit of acceleration is the meter per second squared ($\frac{m}{s^2}$).

$1 N = 1 kg \times \frac{m}{s^2}$

Example

A block with a mass of 12 kg is being pushed. Its acceleration is $5 \frac{m}{s^2}$. What force is acting on the block?

Solve for the force, F. Use $m = 12$ kg, $a = 5 \frac{m}{s^2}$

$F = m \times a$

$F = 12 \text{ kg} \times 5 \frac{m}{s^2}$

$F = 60 \text{ kg} \times \frac{m}{s^2}$

$F = 60 \text{ N}$

Think I know that $1 \text{ kg} \times \frac{m}{s^2} = 1 \text{ N}$, so $60 \text{ kg} \times \frac{m}{s^2} = 60 \text{ N}$

The force being applied to the block is 60 N.

---

1 A 25 kg block is being pushed and is accelerated at a rate of $6 \frac{m}{s^2}$. What force is being applied to the block? Show your work.

Work Area

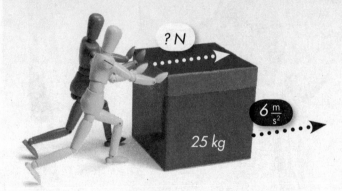

myscienceonline.com | Got it? | 60-Second Video

Newton's Third Law

Newton's third law of motion states that when one object exerts a force on a second object, the second object exerts a force on the first. These forces are equal in strength and opposite in direction.

It is impossible to have one force without an equal and opposite force. For example, if you have ever ridden bumper cars, you know that when a moving car collides with a stationary car, both drivers feel the force of the collision. The driver of the stationary car feels a force and starts to move. The driver of the moving car feels an opposite force that slows the moving car.

10. Choose Suppose the girl on the left bumps the car on the right. Which girl feels a bigger bump? Explain.

Got it?

11. Explain What is needed to give a large boulder a large acceleration?

12. UNLOCK THE BIG ? Suppose a train engine is pulling ten cars. The last car becomes separated from the train. What happens to the motion of the rest of the train?

⬛ **Stop!** I need help with

⏸ **Wait!** I have a question about

▶ **Go!** Now I know

What are machines?

Envision It!

Draw arrows to show which direction the fruit would move if the seesaw's fixed point were farther to the right.

Inquiry Explore It!

What can a wheel and axle do?

☐ **1.** Use the Make a Wheel and Axle activity sheet. Build the wheel and axle.

☐ **2.** Ask a partner to release Cup A. **Measure** its height. **Record** your data on the activity sheet.

☐ **3.** Gently add washers one at a time to Cup A until it moves to the floor. **Observe** what happens to Cup B. Measure and record its height.

Explain Your Results

4. Only .... washers in Cup A were needed to lift 10 washers in Cup B. However, Cup A had to move down .... cm to lift Cup B up only ....cm.

5. Infer How can a wheel and axle make work easier?

....

....

Materials

spool with pencil

2 paper cups

20 washers

masking tape

string

Make a Wheel and Axle

meterstick

The spool and pencil are a simple wheel and axle. The spool is the wheel. The pencil is the axle.

fixed point

Words to Know

simple machine	wheel and axle
lever	inclined plane
pulley	wedge
	screw

Simple Machines

Work is energy used when a force moves an object. A machine is a device that helps you do work. A **simple machine** is a machine made up of one or two parts. Machines can help you do work by changing the amount of force required. They may also change the distance or direction of the force. Machines do not reduce the amount of work.

When you do work, the force that you use is called the *input force*. A simple machine can increase or decrease your input force, change its direction, or cause it to move an object a longer or shorter distance. The force that the machine supplies is called the *output force*. A nutcracker is a simple machine. The nutcracker turns your small input force into a much larger output force that moves—or cracks—the nut.

There are six kinds of simple machines: the lever, the pulley, the wheel and axle, the inclined plane, the wedge, and the screw.

1. **Explain** How might a machine help you do work?

output force   input force

Levers

A nutcracker is a lever. A **lever** is a type of simple machine in which a bar moves around a fixed point or support called a *fulcrum*. Levers do work by using a bar, the fulcrum, and a force you apply to move a load. A lever like the nutcracker adds to your input force. The input force that you apply to crack a nut is also called *effort*. The object you want to move is called the *load*. Levers can also change the direction of the force.

A seesaw is a lever that changes the direction of a force. Look at the pictures at the right. When the person pushes down on one end of the seesaw, the box, or the load, goes up. The input force occurs when the person pushes down on the seesaw. The force, or effort, that the person must apply is less than the weight of the box. As the position of the fulcrum changes, the amount of input force needed to move the box will change. The farther the fulcrum is from the person using the lever, the easier the load is to lift.

2. Demonstrate Look at the size of the input force in the top illustration. Use a longer or a shorter arrow to show the input forces needed in the other two.

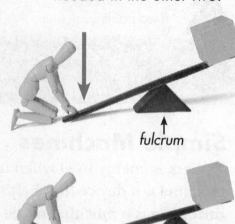

fulcrum

This wheelbarrow is a kind of lever. The load is located between the wheel, or the fulcrum, and the input force, or the effort.

effort

load

fulcrum

480

Pulleys

A **pulley** is a simple machine consisting of a rope or cable that runs around a grooved wheel. A simple pulley changes the direction of the force needed to do work. It does not change the amount of force needed. To lift a load, you must pull on the rope with a force equal to the force of the load that pulls down on the rope.

A system of two or more pulleys—known as a block and tackle—reduces the amount of input force needed to lift a load. A block and tackle has multiple lengths of rope. Each length of rope carries part of the weight of the load. Lifting the load thus requires less effort.

3. **Explain** How is the effect of a simple pulley different from that of a block and tackle?

....

....

....

pulley

The girls are using a simple pulley to lift the basket. Flagpoles and window blinds also use pulleys.

The steering wheel lets the boy turn the cart without using too much force.

Wheel and Axle

A **wheel and axle** is a simple machine made up of a circular object attached to a bar. You make the bar turn by turning the circular object. A wheel and axle reduces the amount of force needed to do work. Think how hard it is to tighten a screw with your fingers. The first few turns may be easy, but after that, the amount of force required would be too great. You need a screwdriver, which is a type of wheel and axle. The handle is the wheel. The metal rod that turns the screw is the axle. It takes less force to turn a screw with a screwdriver.

4. **Infer** A doorknob is another example of a wheel and axle. Tell how you think it makes work easier.

Inclined Planes

Have you ever tried carrying a heavy load up a flight of stairs? It is much easier to roll it up a ramp! A ramp is an inclined plane. An **inclined plane** is a simple machine that consists of a flat surface with one end higher than the other. The inclined plane can be a ramp large enough for a person or a vehicle to use, or it can be very small.

The input force on an inclined plane is the force that you use to push or pull an object along the plane. An inclined plane decreases the input force required to move an object but increases the distance the force is applied. Look at the picture below. The distance from the ground to the back of the truck is less than the distance along the ramp. But it takes more force to lift the box from the ground to the truck than to push the box up the ramp. Because the distance increases, the input force is spread over a larger distance when a ramp is used.

5. Show Look at the picture below. Label the load and the input force. Draw an arrow to show the direction of the input force.

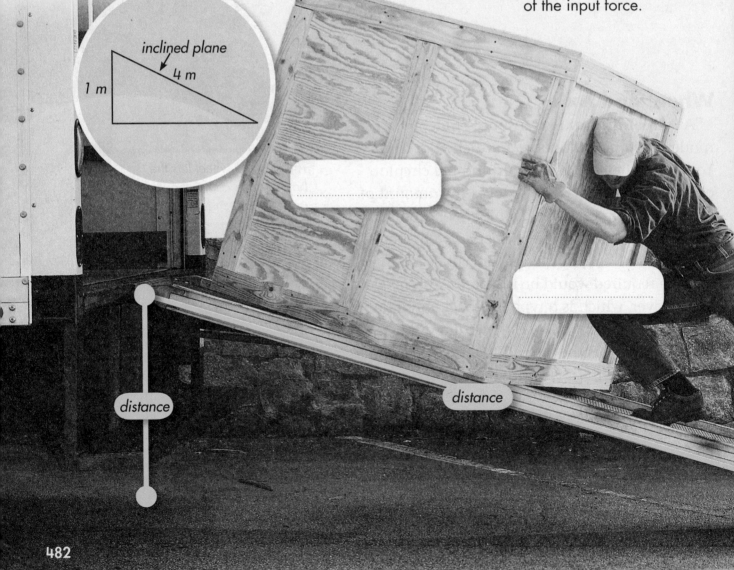

inclined plane

4 m

1 m

distance

distance

Several factors are related to the amount of force needed to move an object up an inclined plane. One factor is the steepness of the plane. Suppose you have two ramps that are the same height but different lengths. The shorter ramp will have a steeper incline. It will take more force to push an object up the shorter, steeper ramp than it will to push the same object up the longer ramp.

Another factor is the weight of the object being moved. It takes more force to move a heavier object than it takes to move a lighter object.

6. ◉ **Main Idea and Details** Underline two factors that are related to the force needed to move an object up an inclined plane.

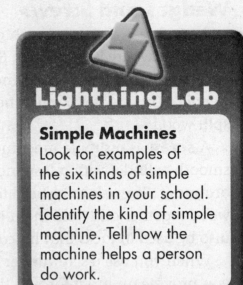

7. [CHALLENGE] This street is built in a zigzag pattern. Tell why this design makes it easier for cars to move up the hill.

The ramp reduces the input force. The person does the same amount of work.

Wedges and Screws

A **wedge** is a simple machine that can be made of one or two inclined planes. Some wedges, such as an axe, are made of two inclined planes placed back to back. This creates a machine that can be used to split wood.

A **screw** is a simple machine consisting of a smooth cylinder with a tiny inclined plane wrapped around it. Screws can be used to pull two pieces of wood together and hold them in place. Screws can also be used in jacks that lift cars.

When you use a screwdriver to turn a screw, you provide an input force to the screw. The input force turns the screw. The threads of the screw, or the inclined plane, increase the distance the screw travels. This reduces the input force.

8. **Interpret** When you screw a hinge onto a door, what are the directions of the input and output forces on the screw?

....

....

....

....

9. **Apply** Draw a simple machine that is a wedge.

An axe reduces the amount of force needed to split a log.

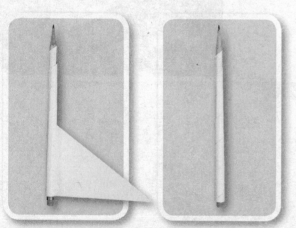

If you wrap a right triangle around a pencil, it forms a spiral. The right triangle is an inclined plane.

An inclined plane forms the spiral threads of a screw.

mYscienceonLine.com | Got it? 60-Second Video

Complex Machines

A machine that uses two or more simple machines is called a *complex machine*. Many complex machines use electricity, gravity, burning fuel, human force, or magnetism to operate each of the simple machines within it.

10. Demonstrate Label the simple machines that are part of the bicycle.

> A bicycle is a complex machine.

Got it?

11. Explain Name a simple machine and explain how it works.

....

....

12. UNLOCK THE BIG ? How can a simple machine help you do work?

....

....

⬛ **Stop!** I need help with ....

⏸ **Wait!** I have a question about ....

▶ **Go!** Now I know ....

What forces affect the motion of a rocket?

Follow a Procedure

☐ **1.** Tie one end of a 10-meter piece of string to a chair. Slide a straw onto the string. Tape a paper bag to the straw. Tie the other end of the string to another chair. Make the string tight by pulling the chairs apart. Slide the bag to the middle of the string.

☐ **2.** Blow up a long balloon. Hold the neck end closed. Put the other end in the bag.

☐ **3. Observe** Let go of the balloon. What happened?

....

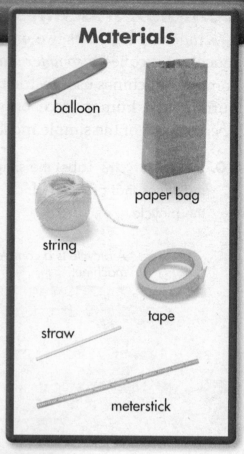

Materials

balloon

paper bag

string

tape

straw

meterstick

Do not blow up the balloon too much.

☐ **4.** Slide the bag to one end of the string. Blow up the balloon again. Place the balloon in the bag.

☐ **5. Predict** how far the rocket will move.

....

....

☐ **6.** Let go of the balloon. Use a meterstick to measure how far the rocket moved. Repeat 2 more times.

Inquiry Skill Before you **predict**, think about what you have already observed.

7. Record your data below. Find the average distance for the 3 trials. Add the 3 distances and divide by 3.

Rocket Data	
	Distance (m)
Trial 1	
Trial 2	
Trial 3	
Average	

Scientists often make observations again and again. Repeating trials helps them be sure what they have observed is accurate.

Analyze and Conclude

8. Observe   Compare how far the rocket moved in each trial.

....

....

9. Infer   What caused the rocket to move in the direction that it moved?

....

....

....

10. UNLOCK THE BIG ❓   What made the rocket move? How do you know?

....

....

....

....

Isaac Newton

Isaac Newton is considered one of history's greatest scientists. He had a deep curiosity about nature. He looked for logical ways to explain what he noticed. He put together ideas from different areas of science in creative ways. Among the results were his laws of motion. These laws and his definition of *force* made people think about science in a new way.

Newton graduated from Cambridge University in England in 1665. For more than 30 years, he was a teacher there. Later, he became the head of England's mint, which coined the nation's money. His scientific background helped him catch people making fake money and bring them to justice.

Newton's work gained him the respect of other scientists. His theories still form the basis of our understanding of the universe.

Newton (1642–1727) also studied the sky. He invented a telescope that worked with mirrors instead of lenses.

How do you think understanding Newton's laws of motion can help an engineer design a safer or faster car?

....

....

....

Vocabulary Smart Cards

force
contact force
friction
non-contact force
gravity
acceleration
inertia
simple machine
lever
pulley
wheel and axle
inclined plane
wedge
screw

Play a Game!

Cut out the Vocabulary Smart Cards.

Work with a partner.

Choose a Vocabulary Smart Card.

Say as many words as you can think of that describe that vocabulary word.

Have your partner try to guess the word.

non-contact force

fuerza sin contacto

force

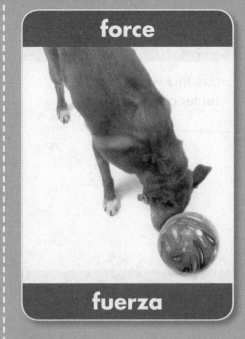

fuerza

gravity

gravedad

contact force

fuerza de contacto

acceleration

aceleración

friction

fricción

a push or pull that acts on an object

Use this word in a sentence.

....

....

....

....

empujón o jalón que se le da a un objeto

---

a force that acts at a distance

Use this word in a sentence.

....

....

....

....

fuerza que actúa a distancia

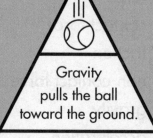

Gravity pulls the ball toward the ground.

Gravity is the force of attraction between any two objects.

---

a force that requires two pieces of matter to touch

Draw an example of this word.

fuerza que requiere que dos porciones de materia se toquen

---

the force of attraction between any two objects

Use this word in a sentence.

....

....

....

....

fuerza de atracción entre dos cuerpos cualesquiera

Make a Word Pyramid!

Choose a vocabulary word and write the definition in the base of the pyramid. Write a sentence in the middle of the pyramid. Draw a picture of an example, or of something related, at the top.

---

the force that results when two materials rub against each other or when their contact prevents sliding

Write an example of this word.

....

....

fuerza que resulta al frotar un material contra otro o cuando el contacto entre ambos impide el deslizamiento

---

the rate at which the speed or direction of motion of an object changes over time

Write three other forms of this word.

....

....

ritmo al cual cambia la rapidez o la dirección del movimiento de un objeto con el tiempo

wedge	**pulley**	**inertia**
		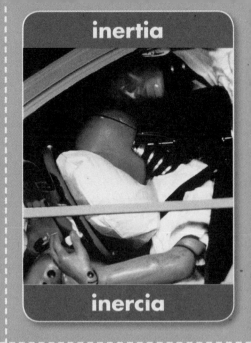
cuña	**polea**	**inercia**

screw	**wheel and axle**	**simple machine**
		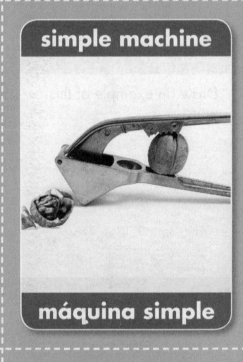
tornillo	**eje y rueda**	**máquina simple**

	inclined plane	**lever**

	plano inclinado	**palanca**

the tendency of an object to resist any change in motion

Write an example of this word.

....

....

....

tendencia de un cuerpo a resistirse a cualquier cambio de movimiento

---

simple machine consisting of a rope or cable that runs around a grooved wheel

What is the base word in this word?

....

....

....

máquina simple que consiste en una soga o cable que se hace pasar por la ranura de una rueda

---

simple machine made of one or two inclined planes

List three examples of this word.

....

....

....

máquina simple formada por uno o dos planos inclinados

---

a machine made up of one or two parts

Draw an example of this word.

máquina formada por una o dos partes

---

simple machine made up of a circular object attached to a bar

Draw and label a machine that has a wheel and axle.

máquina simple que consiste en un objeto circular unido a una barra

---

simple machine consisting of a smooth cylinder with a tiny inclined plane wrapped around it

Write a sentence using this word.

....

....

máquina simple que consiste en un cilindro liso con un pequeño plano inclinado enrollado a su alrededor

---

a simple machine in which a bar moves around a fixed point called a fulcrum

Write an example of this word.

....

....

....

máquina simple en la cual una barra se mueve alrededor de un punto fijo llamado fulcro

---

simple machine consisting of a flat surface with one end higher than the other

Write a synonym for this word.

....

....

....

máquina simple que consiste en una superficie plana con un extremo más elevado que el otro

---

....

....

....

....

Lesson 1

What are forces?

- A force is any push or pull.
- Contact forces, such as friction, only happen when objects touch.
- Non-contact forces, such as gravity, can act from a distance.

Lesson 2

What are Newton's laws?

- Due to inertia, objects tend to resist changes in motion.
- Acceleration depends on an object's mass and the force acting on it.
- Every force creates an equal and opposite force.

Lesson 3

What are machines?

- Simple machines include the inclined plane, the wedge, the screw, the pulley, the lever, and the wheel and axle.
- Complex machines use two or more simple machines.

Lesson 1

What are forces?

1. **Main Idea and Details** Underline the main idea and circle the details in the following paragraph.

> Forces that are applied on objects by other objects can be either contact or non-contact forces. Friction and air resistance are two types of contact forces. Electric forces, gravity, and magnetic forces are non-contact forces.

2. **Interpret** Write a *T* for true or an *F* for false in front of the following statements.

    _____ Magnetism is a contact force because magnets make contact.

    _____ Friction is a kind of force.

    _____ Gravity only acts on heavy objects.

3. **Explain** How can the shapes of a boat and an airplane help them move faster?

....

....

....

Lesson 2

What are Newton's laws?

4. **Synthesize** What laws of motion are demonstrated by a hammer pounding a nail into a board?

....

....

5. **Explain** A batter hits a baseball with a bat. The bat exerts a force on the ball. Does the ball exert a force on the bat?

....

....

6. **Vocabulary** In space, where there is no air and gravity is weak, space probes can travel millions of miles without using any fuel. What allows them to do this? Use the term *inertia* in your answer.

....

....

....

....

Lesson 3

What are machines?

7. Identify A ramp, a doorstop, and a car jack are made with at least one of which of the following simple machines?

  A. wheel and axle
  B. inclined plane
  C. lever
  D. pulley

8. Think About It You want to use a lever to lift a heavy box off the ground. Which placement of the fulcrum will make it easiest for you to lift the box? How do you know?

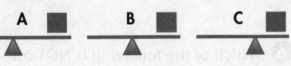

....

....

....

9. Analyze How does an inclined plane change the amount and distance of the input force a person must use to move an object?

....

....

....

....

10. **ANSWER THE BIG** **What affects the motion of objects?**

· ·

A student kicks a soccer ball by applying a force. Describe what happens to the soccer ball.

....

....

....

....

....

....

What other forces affect the soccer ball after the student's foot stops touching it?

....

....

....

....

....

Fill in the bubble next to the answer choice you think is correct for each multiple-choice question.

1 A car runs out of gas while moving forward on a flat, straight road. The car keeps rolling for a while because

Ⓐ gravity pulls it forward.
Ⓑ it still has force.
Ⓒ it has acceleration.
Ⓓ it has inertia.

2 A force of 20 N accelerates a 2 kg object. How much force is needed to give the same acceleration to a 20 kg object?

Ⓐ 10 N
Ⓑ 10 kg
Ⓒ 200 N
Ⓓ 400 kg

3 A drummer hits a drum with a drumstick. The drumstick exerts a force on the drum. The reaction

Ⓐ is stronger than the action.
Ⓑ changes the motion of the drumstick.
Ⓒ drives the drum forward.
Ⓓ creates inertia.

4 What kind of simple machine is a bottle opener?

Ⓐ lever
Ⓑ wheel and axle
Ⓒ pulley
Ⓓ inclined plane

5 Which of the following is a contact force?

Ⓐ friction
Ⓑ magnetism
Ⓒ gravity
Ⓓ electricity

6 Which of the following is NOT an example of accelerated motion?

Ⓐ an elevator going up at constant speed
Ⓑ an elevator slowing down
Ⓒ an elevator speeding up
Ⓓ a car taking a curve at constant speed

7 What is Newton's first law of motion? What term summarizes this law?

....

....

....

NASA's Space Centers

NASA researches airplane and rocket engines. Scientists at NASA have improved engine design. These engines produce thrust, which is a force that moves an airplane forward or a rocket upward.

The engines on jet airplanes produce more thrust than engines that use propellers. In a jet airplane, a huge fan brings cool air into the front of the engine and compresses it. Then fuel is mixed with the air. After the mixture of fuel and air is burned, the gases that are produced greatly expand. The gases rush out the back of the engine. The force of the gases moving backward pushes the plane forward.

Jet engines produce a great deal of thrust, but they also produce noise. Jet engines can be much more noisy than engines with propellers. NASA has a program that is trying to make jet engines quieter.

A jet airplane is still going very fast when it lands. How do you think the jet could use its engines to help the plane slow down?

....

....

Where is the ENERGY?

Changing Forms of Energy

Try It! How can the amount of stored energy affect motion?

Lesson 1 What is energy?

Lesson 2 What is sound energy?

Lesson 3 What is light energy?

Investigate It! How can electrical energy change forms?

These drummers are playing traditional music. The dancer's steps require strength and coordination.

Predict Where do you think the dancer gets his energy? How do you know he has energy?

....

....

....

THE BIG ? How is energy transferred and transformed?

How can the amount of stored energy affect motion?

☐ **1. Observe** Turn the winder on the toy 2 turns. Release. Time how long the toy stays in motion. Record.

☐ **2.** Repeat 3 times, but use a different number of turns each time.

Inquiry Skill
You **communicate** when you explain your observations.

Stored Energy and Motion	
Number of Turns	**Time Toy Stayed in Motion** (seconds)

Explain Your Results

3. Communicate Explain how the number of turns affected the time the toy stayed in motion.

....

....

4. How did you change stored energy into motion?

....

....

◉ Cause and Effect

- A **cause** is why something happens. An **effect** is what happens.
- When you read, sometimes clue words such as *because* and *since* indicate a cause-and-effect relationship.

Expansion Under Heat

Many materials expand when the temperature rises. On a hot day, a steel beam will be a little longer than it is on a cold day. Since this expansion is very small, you may not notice it. But people who design railroads must take it into account because an expanding beam will push against other beams next to it. The force of the push is so great that it can bend beams out of shape. This would create a hazard for trains. When beams are laid down, engineers leave small gaps between them. This allows the beams to expand without pushing against each other.

Practice It!

Use the graphic organizer below to list one cause and one effect found in the example paragraph.

rail gap

Cause

Effect

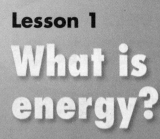

Envision It!

Circle the penguin you think has the most energy. Tell how you made your choice.

my planet diary

Let's Blog!

by Katieri
Spring Hill, Florida

There are different types of energy that I see at a construction site. I see the machine that has a ball tied to it that crashes into the side of the building to knock it down. I also see workers using their own energy to move tools and other equipment around the site. Some construction projects include buildings with lights, and the lights in the building use energy to shine brightly so the workers can see what they are trying to do. Those are some of the types of energy I see when I look at a construction site! What other types of energy have you seen being used at a construction site?

....

....

....

....

I will know what potential and kinetic energy are. I will know the different forms of energy into which energy can change.

Words to Know

energy
potential energy
kinetic energy

Energy

The word *energy* has different meanings. In science, **energy** is the ability to do work or cause a change. Energy can change an object's motion, color, shape, temperature, or other characteristics.

A jumping penguin has energy. Some of the energy is due to the penguin's motion, and some is due to its high position during the jump. The sum of the energy due to the motion of an object and the energy stored in the object due to the object's position is called mechanical energy.

Energy cannot be made or destroyed, but it can change form and it can move from one object to another. For example, the energy that a windup toy has when it begins to move does not disappear when the toy stops moving. The energy simply changes into other forms.

This windup toy uses energy to move. After its energy is used, more energy can be added to the toy by turning the key.

1. **⊙ Cause and Effect** Complete the graphic organizer below. List one cause and one effect found in the paragraphs above.

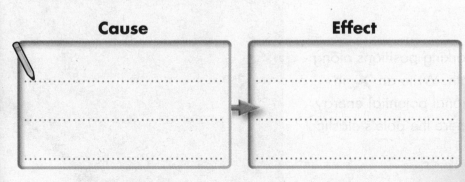

Cause	Effect

Potential Energy

An object does not need to be moving to have energy. **Potential energy** is energy that is not causing any changes now but could cause changes in the future. Potential energy, or stored energy, and kinetic energy make up mechanical energy.

Gravitational Potential Energy

One kind of potential energy depends on the position of an object relative to Earth. This kind is called gravitational potential energy. For example, as a pole-vaulter reaches the top of her jump, she gains potential energy relative to the ground. The higher she goes, the more potential energy she has. She loses potential energy as she falls. The potential energy does not disappear. It just changes form.

Elastic Potential Energy

Another type of potential energy is elastic potential energy. This is the energy of a stretched rubber band or a compressed spring. This type of potential energy is present when things are bent or stretched. It is present in the pole-vaulter's pole. When the pole bends, elastic potential energy increases. The more a rubber band is stretched, the more elastic potential energy it has. This energy can also cause the motion of objects to change.

2. **Infer** What clues from this picture tell you that the pole-vaulter has potential energy?

....

3. **Draw** Look at the circles marking positions along the pole-vaulter's possible path. Write an ✗ in the circle where her gravitational potential energy is highest. Fill in the circle where the pole's elastic potential energy is highest.

Kinetic Energy

Mechanical energy is the sum of the potential, or stored, and kinetic energies of an object. **Kinetic energy** is the energy due to motion. The amount of kinetic energy in a moving object depends on its speed and its mass.

The faster an object moves, the more kinetic energy it has. Think about a carpenter using a hammer to drive a nail into wood. When the carpenter swings the hammer slowly, the hammer has a small amount of kinetic energy. It does not have the energy to move a nail very much. When the carpenter swings the hammer quickly, it has more kinetic energy. It can push a nail farther into the wood with just one hit.

Similarly, the more mass a moving object has, the more kinetic energy it has. For example, a moving beach ball has kinetic energy. If the beach ball hits a sand castle, it might knock down a castle wall. A basketball has more mass than a beach ball. What would happen if a basketball, rolling at the same speed as the beach ball, hit the sand castle? Since the basketball has more mass, it has more energy. It might flatten the whole castle!

Potential energy can change into kinetic energy. As the pole-vaulter on the previous page falls, her potential energy becomes kinetic energy. She moves faster and faster.

Kinetic energy and potential energy can be present in the same object at the same time. For example, an airplane has potential energy because of its altitude and kinetic energy because it is moving forward.

4. **⊙ Draw Conclusions** **Underline** the facts in the third paragraph that support the conclusion that a basketball has more energy than a beach ball.

5. **⌈CHALLENGE⌉** If all the traffic is moving at the same speed, which vehicles do you think have the most kinetic energy?

Lightning Lab

Rubber-Band Release
Wear safety goggles. Stretch a rubber band as if to shoot it, but do not let it go. The energy in the stretched rubber band is potential energy. Aim the rubber band at a blank wall and let it go. How did the energy of the rubber band change?

Energy Everywhere

You can find energy in different forms everywhere you go. Anything in motion has kinetic energy. Objects raised above the ground have potential energy.

6. Label Look at the scene shown here and find as many examples of kinetic and potential energy as you can. Label the scene using the key below.

K = kinetic   **P** = potential

myscienceonline.com | THE BIG ? | I Will Know...

Energy Can Change Forms

Energy cannot be made or destroyed. However, it can move from one object to another. Energy can also change from one form to another. Electrical energy can be changed into many other forms of energy. Consider an electrical device, such as a photo copier. The electrical energy is changed to light energy and mechanical energy. The photo copier also changes electrical energy into sound energy when it beeps.

7. Apply Describe a machine and how it changes forms of energy.

....

....

....

Electrical Energy to Mechanical Energy

Mechanical energy is the energy an object has due to its position or motion. A bicycle in motion and a whirling blade of a fan have mechanical energy. Electrical energy can be changed into mechanical energy. One object this happens in is a washing machine.

8. Identify What other type of energy is electrical energy transformed into in a washing machine?

....

....

Chemical Energy to Light Energy

A lightning bug uses light to attract its mates or prey. The lightning bug has chemicals in its abdomen. These chemicals have stored potential energy. The chemical potential energy changes to light energy. Chemical energy is energy of the electrons that form bonds between atoms in molecules. Bonds form when electrons are shared by atoms or when electrons are transferred from one atom to another. When more electrons are involved in a bond, more chemical energy is in the bond. This insect produces a small amount of light energy.

9. Name What is a device that changes chemical energy into light energy?

....

myscienceonline.com | Got it? 60-Second Video

Magnetic Energy to Kinetic Energy

Magnetism is a force that pushes and pulls on other objects. The magnetic force is greatest at a magnet's poles. The poles of a magnet are at the two ends. Every magnet has a north pole and a south pole.

Magnets pull on objects made of iron, cobalt, nickel, and gadolinium. Magnets also exert forces on other magnets. An object being pulled by a magnet will gain more or less kinetic energy depending on how far it is from a magnet. The object has potential energy once it has been pulled towards or pushed away from the magnet.

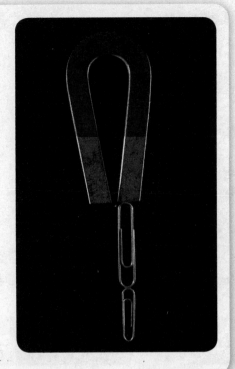

10. Infer In the picture to the right, the paperclips are pulled to the magnet. Which form of energy do they have?

....

....

Got it?

11. Recall Which has more kinetic energy, a 50 g basketball resting on a chair or a 75 g basketball resting on the floor?

....

....

12. Compare A squirrel drops an acorn from a tree. How does the potential energy of the acorn compare to its kinetic energy just before the acorn hits the ground?

....

....

....

○ **Stop!** I need help with ....

‖ **Wait!** I have a question about ....

▷ **Go!** Now I know ....

Lesson 2
What is sound energy?

Look at guitar strings 3 and 6. **Tell** what is happening and why you think they look different from each other.

Inquiry Explore It!

What can affect the sound made by a rubber band?

☐ 1. Stretch a thick rubber band and a thin rubber band around an open plastic tub.

2. **Observe** Pluck each band. Describe the sounds.

....

....

....

☐ 3. Slide a ruler under the rubber bands. Turn it edge up. Pluck each band. Describe the sounds.

....

....

Explain Your Results

4. **Draw a Conclusion** How does a rubber band's thickness affect the sound it makes?

....

....

....

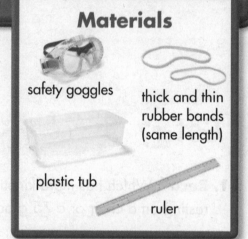

Materials

safety goggles

thick and thin rubber bands (same length)

plastic tub

ruler

Be careful! Wear safety goggles. Be careful not to snap the rubber bands.

myscienceonline.com | **Explore It!** Animation

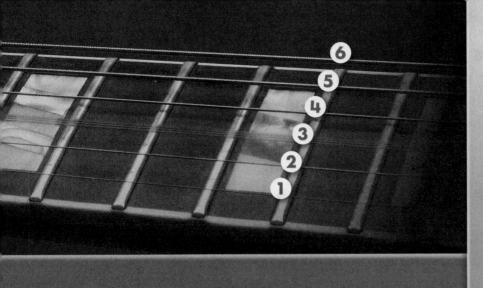

Word to Know

vibration

Sound

Sound is a wave of vibrations that spreads from its
source. A **vibration** is the back-and-forth motion of an
object. As sound waves travel through a material, such
as air, the molecules in the material vibrate in a regular
pattern. The molecules bump into each other, passing
this pattern on to other molecules. Sound is used by
many organisms to communicate.

Your vocal cords vibrate when you talk or sing.
Vocal cords make the particles in the air around them
vibrate. These vibrations travel outward through the air
as sound waves. The sound waves travel in all directions.
Even someone behind the girl can hear her singing.

1. ◉ **Compare and Contrast** How are your vocal cords
and the strings on a guitar alike and different?

....

....

2. **Infer** The girl is playing a guitar. How could she stop the
sound after she plucks the string?

....

....

mYscienceonLine.com | **Envision It!**   511

How Sound Behaves

Sound can travel through solids, liquids, and gases. Sound cannot travel through a vacuum, which is empty space with no particles. Without vibrating particles, sound cannot exist. When a sound wave reaches a border between different materials, it might bounce back to make an echo. Or, the sound wave might be absorbed or pass into the second material.

Sound waves travel through different materials at different speeds. In ocean water, sound travels at about 1,500 meters per second. In air at 0°C, sound travels at about 330 meters per second.

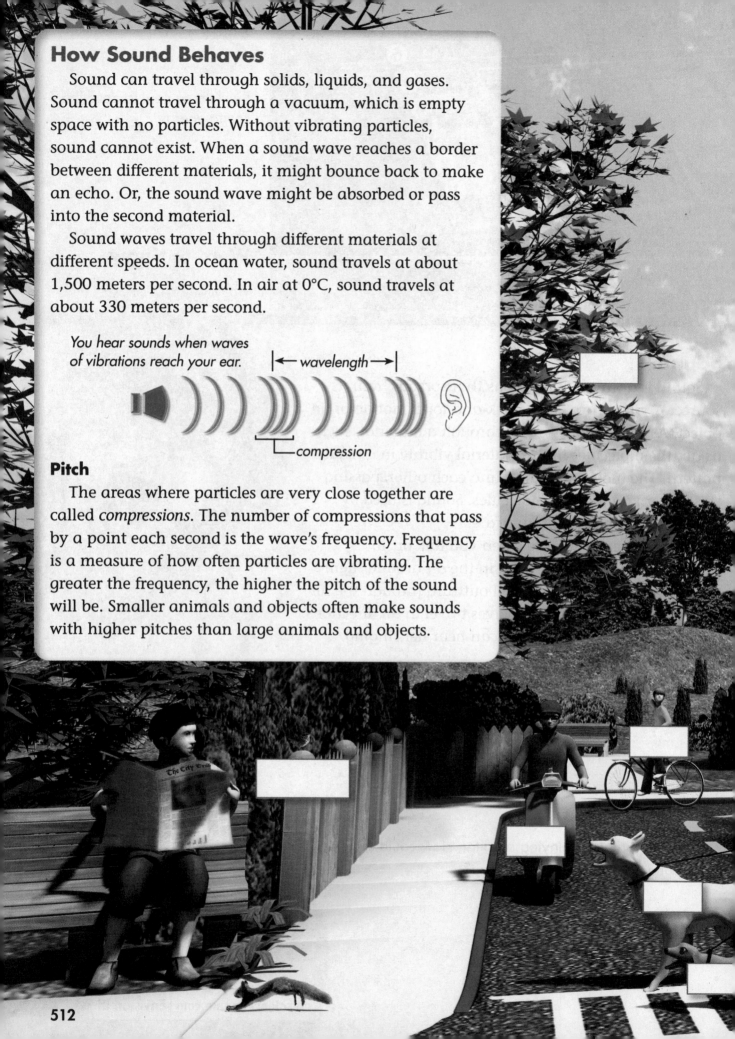

You hear sounds when waves of vibrations reach your ear.

|← wavelength →|

compression

Pitch

The areas where particles are very close together are called *compressions*. The number of compressions that pass by a point each second is the wave's frequency. Frequency is a measure of how often particles are vibrating. The greater the frequency, the higher the pitch of the sound will be. Smaller animals and objects often make sounds with higher pitches than large animals and objects.

Volume

Why are some sounds louder than others? The sound waves of a louder sound have more energy when they get to your ear. This could be because you are close to the source of the sound. It could also be because the source of the louder sound is vibrating more. When the higher energy gets to your ear, your eardrum will vibrate more than if the sound were softer.

3. **Decide** Use the key below to label the sounds in the picture as they would be heard by the man sitting on the bench. Explain your labels.

HP = high pitched **L** = loud
LP = low pitched **S** = soft

Sound and Energy Transfer

For a sound to be heard, energy must first cause an object to vibrate. Vibrating objects transmit, or send off, energy as sound waves in air. The energy is transferred through the air as the sound waves move. Eventually, some of the energy reaches your ear, and your eardrum absorbs some of the energy. Your eardrum will begin to vibrate, and vibrations are interpreted as sound in your brain. In this way, the energy of the original vibrations passes to you.

Energy from this vibrating tuning fork is being transferred to the liquid.

4. **Cause and Effect** Look at the picture to the left. What effects does this energy transfer have on the liquid and on the tuning fork?

....

....

....

Do the math!

Estimating Time

The speed of sound in air at 20°C is about 340 $\frac{m}{s}$. If you know how far away an object is, you can estimate the time it takes for its sound to reach your ear. Just divide the distance by the speed of sound.

Example

You are standing 705 m away from a soccer player when she kicks the ball. Estimate to the nearest second how long it will take for the sound of the kick to reach your ear.

Think 705 is close to 700.
340 is close to 350.

Since 700 ÷ 350 is 2, it will take about 2 s.

1 You watch the beginning of a volcanic eruption from 3,370 m away. Estimate to the nearest second how long it will take for the sound of the eruption to reach your ear.

Work area

myscienceonline.com | Got it? 60-Second Video

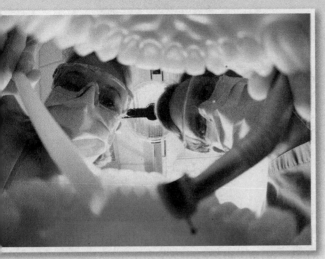

Sound can deliver energy for tooth cleaning. The sound vibrations of the instrument shake the dental plaque loose as a stream of water rinses it out.

Lightning Lab

The String Phone
Work with a partner. Punch a small hole in the bottom of each of two cups. Cut a piece of string about six meters long. Thread it through the cups. So the string cannot come out, knot it inside each cup. Hold the cups so the string is taut. Talk into one cup while a partner holds the other cup over one ear. Take turns talking and listening.

5. Infer Without a water stream in the picture above, the cleaning tip might overheat. Why do you think this happens?

Got it?

6. Explain Why is the pitch of a thick guitar string lower than the pitch of a thin string?

7. **UNLOCK THE BIG Q** How does an ear help you hear a sound?

⬜ **Stop!** I need help with

⏸ **Wait!** I have a question about

▶ **Go!** Now I know

What is light energy?

Envision It!

This picture was taken using a camera that senses infrared energy. **Tell** what you think the colors represent.

Inquiry **Explore It!**

What are some colors in white light?

☐ **1.** Fill a tub halfway with water. Place a mirror in the water at an angle.

☐ **2. Observe** Shine the flashlight on the mirror. Hold a piece of paper above the flashlight so that the reflected light bounces onto it.

☐ **3. Communicate** What colors do you see?

....

Explain Your Results

4. Infer What do you think causes the white light to spread into colors?

....

....

....

Materials

mirror

plastic tub
$\frac{1}{2}$ full of water

flashlight

white paper

metric ruler

Hold the paper about 30 to 60 c above the flashlight.

Set mirror at about this angle.

Shine flashlight here.

Put flashlight here.

Chemical energy in the battery changes to electric energy, which changes to light energy.

  myscienceonline.com | **Explore It!** Animation

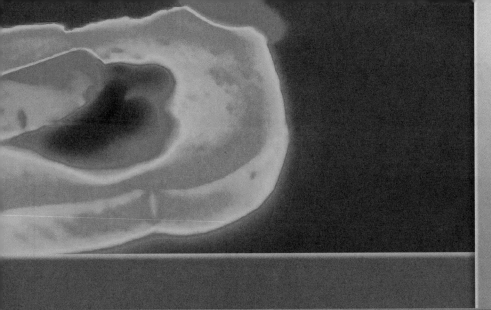

Words to Know

transparent   reflection
translucent   refraction
opaque

Light

Light is all around us. We can get it from the sun, from lamps, and from cell-phone screens. Light can travel in straight lines, reflect off objects, and bend as it passes around or through objects. There are several kinds of light. The kind we can see is called visible light.

You may know that light can pass through some materials and not others. **Transparent** materials let nearly all light pass through them. **Translucent** materials let some light pass through, but not all. Waxed paper and most lamp shades are translucent. A material is **opaque** if it does not let any light pass through it. Light hitting an opaque object is either reflected or absorbed.

1. **Find Out** Hold a page of your *Interactive Science* book up to a light. Is it translucent, transparent, or opaque?

2. **Classify** Write the name of one object you have seen or used today that is transparent, one that is translucent, and one that is opaque.

....

....

....

....

....

....

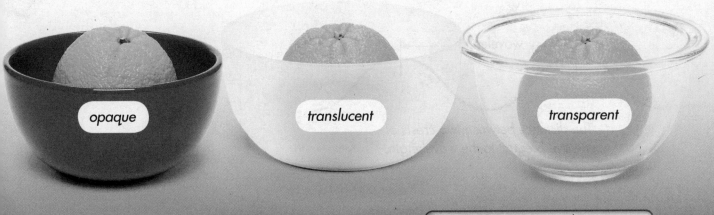

opaque   translucent   transparent

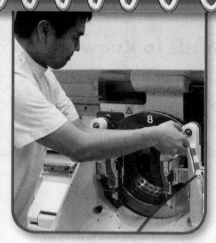
Gamma radiation can kill cancer cells.

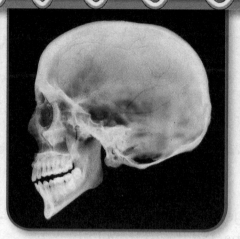
X rays show the shape of this skull.

Flowers look very different under ultraviolet light.

Light Waves and Color

Like sound, light travels in waves that have certain wavelengths. Also like sound, the speed of light is different in different materials. However, light is different from sound in many ways. For example, light can travel through empty space.

For you to see an object, the object must give off or reflect waves of visible light. The light must then enter your eyes. Different wavelengths of visible light are seen as different colors. When all the colors of visible light are mixed, the result is white light. If you shine white light on an object, some wavelengths bounce off the object and some are absorbed. The wavelengths that bounce off the object can enter your eyes, and they determine the color you see. The other wavelengths are absorbed by the object.

Visible light has wavelengths between violet and red. Our eyes cannot see wavelengths shorter than violet or longer than red.

3. [CHALLENGE] Why do you think an ultraviolet bulb is called a "black light"?

....

....

....

....

....

....

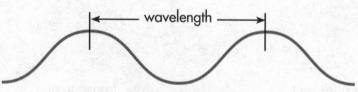

|← wavelength →|

The distance between two crests of a wave is equal to the wavelength.

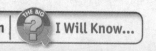
myscienceonline.com | THE BIG ? | I Will Know...

An infrared photograph shows that some parts of this house are hotter than others.

When food absorbs microwave radiation, its temperature rises.

Radio waves are used for radio, television, and astronomy.

Electromagnetic Spectrum

Unlike sound, light is not a vibration of particles. Light is an electromagnetic wave—that is, a combination of electrical and magnetic energy. Electromagnetic waves can have very long or very short wavelengths. The full range of electromagnetic wavelengths is called the electromagnetic spectrum. It includes visible light, but also short wavelengths such as those of X rays, and longer wavelengths such as those of radio waves.

Heat

When you feel the warmth of the sun or the heat of a light bulb shining a few centimeters from your hand, you are feeling electromagnetic waves. Infrared waves feel especially warm. Warm objects produce more infrared waves than cold objects.

4. **Compare and Contrast** Name one similarity and one difference between visible light and sound.

....

....

....

At-Home Lab

Shining Through
In a room that can be made very dark, turn off the lights and turn on a flashlight. Cover the bulb end with your hand. Does some light still shine through? Try blocking the light with other objects. Report what happens.

519

Light Changes Direction

Reflection

Light moves in straight lines. When light hits an object, some light is reflected. **Reflection** happens when light bounces off an object. The light still moves in a straight line but goes in a different direction. Mirrors reflect light very well.

Refraction

Light bends whenever it enters a new material at an angle different from 90°. For example, light bends when it goes from water to air. This bending is called **refraction.**

A lens is a polished piece of glass that makes things look larger or smaller when you look through the lens. Lenses do this by refracting the light. Microscopes, cameras, and prescription glasses have lenses.

5. **Identify** Which of the pictures below shows reflection? Which shows refraction? Label the pictures.

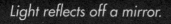

Light reflects off a mirror.

Light is refracted by a lens.

myscienceonLine.com | Got it? 60-Second Video

Dispersion

Different colors refract at different angles. Since white light is a mixture of colors, these colors separate, or disperse, when white light is refracted. Rainbows form because water droplets in the air disperse white light into its colors.

A prism can separate the colors that form white light.

6. Identify Look at the picture to the left. What colors refract more than green, and what colors refract less?

....

....

....

....

....

....

....

Got it?

7. Infer Things under a microscope often look like they have rainbow colors around. Why do you think this happens?

....

....

....

8. Explain Why do you think most lampshades are made of translucent materials instead of transparent materials?

....

....

⬜ **Stop!** I need help with ....

⏸ **Wait!** I have a question about ....

▶ **Go!** Now I know ....

How can electrical energy change forms?

Follow a Procedure

☐ **1.** Make a circuit. Use wires to connect each side of a battery holder to each side of a bulb holder.

Materials

safety goggles

2 pieces of insulated wire

flashlight bulb and holder

battery and battery holder

thermometer

Be careful! **Wear safety goggles.**

☐ **2. Observe** In which part of the circuit do you observe light?

....

....

Inquiry Skill Scientists make careful observations and record them. They use their observations to help make **inferences.**

522

3. Touch the bulb of the thermometer against the flashlight bulb for 1 minute. What do you observe?

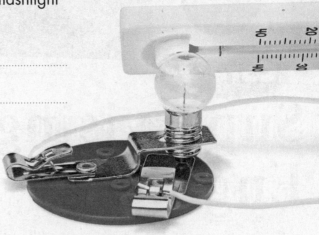

....

....

Analyze and Conclude

4. Make a diagram of your circuit. Show where you observed light energy and thermal energy. Identify the source of the electrical energy.

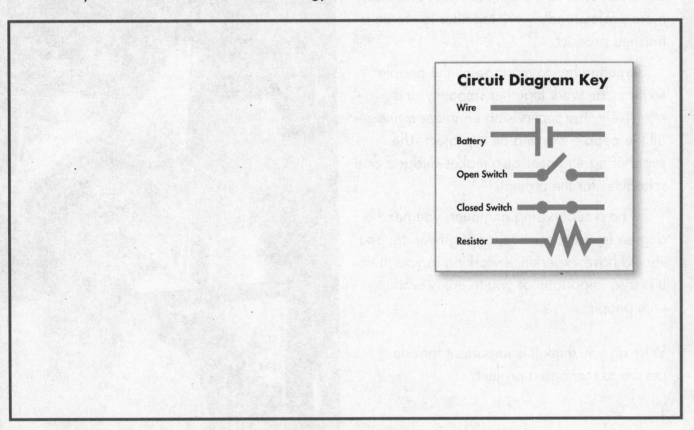

Circuit Diagram Key

Wire

Battery

Open Switch

Closed Switch

Resistor

5. **Infer** Tell how energy was transformed in your investigation.

....

....

....

Careers

Supervising Engineer

Scientists at NASA work on many different projects. These projects take many people with different skills to complete. Engineers, computer scientists, manufacturers, and many more professionals work together to create a finished product.

Someone has to manage all the people so they can work together smoothly and effectively. The supervising engineer manages all the people working on a project. The supervising engineer also makes budgets and schedules for the project.

To be a supervising engineer, you need a degree in math, science, or engineering. You should have experience working in your field. It is also important for you to enjoy working with people.

Why do you think it is important for one person to manage a project?

....

....

....

....

The supervising engineer oversees all aspects of a project.

Vocabulary Smart Cards

energy
potential energy
kinetic energy
vibration
transparent
translucent
opaque
reflection
refraction

Play a Game!

Cut out the Vocabulary Smart Cards.

Work with a partner. Choose a Vocabulary Smart Card. Do not let your partner see your card.

Draw a picture to show what the word means. Have your partner guess the word. Take turns drawing and guessing.

vibration

vibración

energy

energía

transparent

transparente

potential energy

energía potencial

translucent

translúcido

kinetic energy

energía cinética

ability to do work or cause change

Write three examples.

....

....

....

....

capacidad de hacer trabajo o causar cambios

---

the back-and-forth motion of an object

Write three other forms of this word.

....

....

....

movimiento de un objeto hacia adelante y hacia atrás

---

energy that is not causing any changes now but could cause changes in the future

Write one example.

....

....

energía que no está causando cambios actualmente pero que podría causarlos en el futuro

---

describes materials that let nearly all light pass through them

Use a dictionary. Find another meaning for this word.

....

....

describe materiales que dejan pasar a través de ellos casi toda la luz

---

energy due to motion

Write a sentence using this term.

....

....

....

energía que resulta del movimiento

---

describes materials that let some light pass through, but not all

Write three examples.

....

....

....

describe materiales que dejan pasar a través de ellos un poco de luz, pero no toda

---

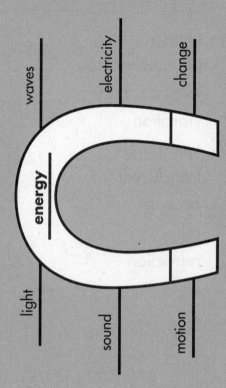

Make a Word Magnet!

Choose a vocabulary word and write it in the Word Magnet. Write words that are related to it on the lines.

opaque

opaco

reflection

reflexión

refraction

refracción

describes materials that do not let any light pass through them

Write a sentence using this word.

....

....

....

describe materiales que no dejan pasar a través de ellos la luz

---

light bouncing off an object

Use a dictionary. Find as many synonyms for this word as you can.

....

....

....

....

rebote de la luz contra un objeto

---

bending of light

Write a sentence using the verb form of this word.

....

....

....

....

desviación de la luz

Chapter 12
Study Guide
REVIEW THE BIG ? How is energy transferred and transformed?

Physical Science

Lesson 1

What is energy?

- Energy is the ability to do work or cause change.
- Kinetic energy involves motion. Potential energy is stored energy.
- Mechanical energy includes kinetic energy and potential energy.

Lesson 2

What is sound energy?

- Sound is a wave of vibrations that spreads from its source.
- Sound has pitch and volume.
- Sound waves transfer energy.

Lesson 3

What is light energy?

- Materials can be transparent, translucent, or opaque.
- Some electromagnetic waves are light, infrared, and radio waves.
- Light moves in straight lines, but it can be reflected or refracted.

Chapter Review

How is energy transferred and transformed?

Lesson 1

What is energy?

1. **Analyze** A book sits on a shelf high above the floor. What kind of energy does the book have?

2. **Think About It** A cat is chasing a mouse. Both are running at the same speed. Do they have the same amount of kinetic energy? Explain.

3. **Understand** When a student slides down from the top of a water slide,
   A. her kinetic energy becomes potential.
   B. her potential energy becomes kinetic.
   C. her total energy doubles.

4. **Summarize** What is mechanical energy?

Lesson 2

What is sound energy?

5. True or False:
   _____ When you speak, the sound of your voice only travels forward.
   _____ Sound cannot be heard underwater.
   _____ The pitch of a whistle is higher than the pitch of a drum.

6. **Cause and Effect** A soft sound suddenly becomes very loud. The cause of this could be that the instrument making the sound
   A. is vibrating less.
   B. is moving away from you.
   C. is moving closer to you.

7. **Explain** How does sound travel from its source to your ear?

Lesson 3

What is light energy?

8. Interpret This image shows
   A. refraction.
   B. reflection.
   C. conduction.

9. Describe Explain why a green computer looks green.

....

....

....

....

....

....

....

....

10. True or False:
   _____ Water is translucent.
   _____ Steel is opaque.
   _____ Light travels in straight lines.

11. Vocabulary When light bounces off Frederick's sunglasses, it is _____.
   A. absorbing
   B. reflecting
   C. refracting
   D. dispersing

12. APPLY THE BIG ? **How is energy transferred and transformed?**

....

A plant uses sunlight to make nectar. A moth drinks the nectar and flies to the top of a tall tree. What energy changes have happened here?

....

....

....

....

....

Fill in the bubble next to the answer choice you think is correct for each multiple-choice question.

1 When light bounces off the surface of a mirror, it is

Ⓐ conducted.
Ⓑ reflected.
Ⓒ refracted.
Ⓓ energized.

2 A brick is pushed across a smooth floor and slides until it stops. What happens to its kinetic energy?

Ⓐ It disappears completely.
Ⓑ It turns into potential energy.
Ⓒ It turns into other forms of energy.
Ⓓ It remains the same.

3 Magnetism is a force that

Ⓐ pulls all objects toward Earth's center.
Ⓑ pushes and pulls on other objects.
Ⓒ only pulls on other objects.
Ⓓ is always greatest between a magnet's two poles.

4 Materials that let nearly all light pass through them are

Ⓐ opaque.
Ⓑ interactive.
Ⓒ translucent.
Ⓓ transparent.

5 What can sound waves NOT travel through?

Ⓐ vacuum cleaners
Ⓑ empty spaces with no particles
Ⓒ liquids
Ⓓ rocks

6 What forms of energy can electrical energy change into? Tell how you know.

....

....

....

....

....

....

....

....

....

Cameras

Look! What is that? Have you ever seen that before? No one would believe us if we did not take a picture of it! Digital cameras help us capture special moments and scenes. Digital cameras use special technology to record images electronically. These images are patterns of light captured at one instant in time. Older cameras used chemical and mechanical processes to record the light as an image on paper. To record the information electronically, information is stored as a series of 1s and 0s electronically on a microchip. Each tiny colored dot, called a pixel, is a long string of 1s and 0s. All of the pixels together make up an image. There can be millions of pixels in one image.

```
101000111010100
101001010010101
101000111010100
101001010010101
101000111010100
101001010010101
```

Determine How have digital cameras changed how cameras take photos?

Materials

2 metric rulers

$\frac{1}{2}$ of a plastic cup and metal marble

2 books

tape and 4 pennies

balance and gram cubes

calculator or computer (optional)

Inquiry Skill

A **hypothesis** is a statement that explains an observation. It can be tested by an experiment.

How is motion affected by mass?

A force can cause an object to move. You will conduct an **experiment** to find out how the mass of an object affects the distance the object will move.

Ask a question.

What effect does the mass of a cup have on the distance a rolling marble will move the cup?

State a hypothesis.

1. Write a **hypothesis** by circling one choice and finishing the sentence.

If the mass of a cup is increased, then the distance the cup is moved by a rolling marble

(a) *increases*

(b) *decreases*

(c) *remains the same*

because

_____

_____

Identify and control variables.

2. In this experiment you will measure the distance the cup moves. You must change only one **variable.** Everything else must remain the same. What should stay the same? List two examples.

_____

_____

_____

3. Tell the one change you will make.

_____

_____

_____

Design your test.

☑ **4.** Draw how you will set up your test.

☑ **5.** List your steps in the order you will do them.

Do your test.

☐ **6.** Follow the steps you wrote.

*Use a balance and gram cubes
to find the mass of the cup.*

☐ **7.** Make sure to **measure** accurately. **Record** your results in a table.

☐ **8.** Scientists repeat their tests to improve their accuracy.
  Repeat your test if time allows.

Collect and record your data.

☐ **9.** Fill in the chart.

Work Like a Scientist
Clear and active communication is an essential part of doing science. Talk with your classmates. Compare your methods and results.

Interpret your data.

☑ **10.** Use your data to make a line graph.

☑ **11.** Look at your graph closely. Describe how the
distance the cup moved was affected by the mass
of the cup. Identify the evidence you used to answer
the question.

....

....

....

....

....

Technology Tools
Your teacher may wish to
have you use a computer
(with the right software)
or a graphing calculator
to help collect, organize,
analyze, and present your
data. These tools can help
you make tables, charts,
and graphs.

State your conclusion.

12. Communicate your conclusion. Compare your
hypothesis with your results. Compare your results with those
of others.

....

....

....

....

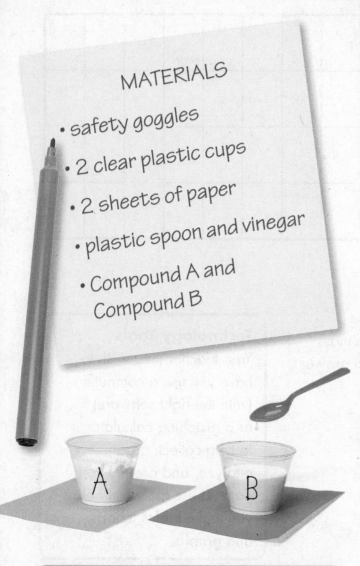

MATERIALS

• safety goggles

• 2 clear plastic cups

• 2 sheets of paper

• plastic spoon and vinegar

• Compound A and Compound B

Using Scientific Methods

1. Ask a question.
2. State a hypothesis.
3. Identify and control variables.
4. Test your hypothesis.
5. Collect and record your data.
6. Explain your data.
7. State your conclusion.
8. Go further.

Plan an Investigation

Solubility is one physical property of matter. Compare the solubility of materials to determine which material has the highest solubility in water. Choose several substances to compare. Predict which substance will have the highest solubility. Plan an investigation to test your prediction. Your investigation should include the following:

• A testable question

• Written instructions to measure solubility of a substance

• A list of materials and tools to carry out the investigation

Build a Better Door Opener

Use common objects to make a machine that will do a simple task such as close a door, water plants, crack an egg, or open a window. Name the machine and design a box or container to package it. Make a diagram with labels to show all the simple machines included in the new machine.

Take the Salt Out

Conduct research on ways to make fresh water from seawater. Try removing the salt from saltwater by evaporation and condensation or by freezing. Draw a diagram showing your equipment and your method.

Measurements

Metric and Customary Measurements

The metric system is the measurement system most commonly used in science. Metric units are sometimes called SI units. SI stands for International System. It is called that because these units are used around the world.

These prefixes are used in the metric system:

kilo- means *thousand*
1 kilometer = 1,000 meters

milli- means *one thousandth*
1,000 millimeters = 1 meter, or 1 millimeter = 0.001 meter

centi- means *one hundredth*
100 centimeters = 1 meter, or 1 centimeter = 0.01 meter

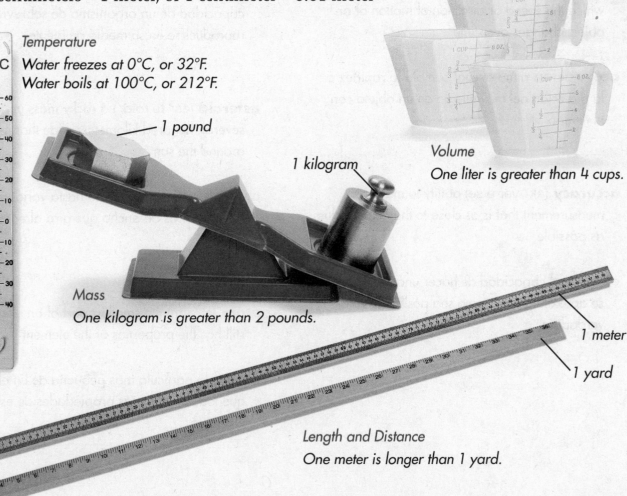

1 liter

1 cup

Temperature
Water freezes at 0°C, or 32°F.
Water boils at 100°C, or 212°F.

1 pound

1 kilogram

Mass
One kilogram is greater than 2 pounds.

Volume
One liter is greater than 4 cups.

1 meter

1 yard

Length and Distance
One meter is longer than 1 yard.

Glossary

The glossary uses letters and signs to show how words are pronounced. The mark ′ is placed after a syllable with a primary or heavy accent. The mark ′ is placed after a syllable with a secondary or lighter accent.

To hear these vocabulary words and definitions, you can refer to the AudioText CD, or log on to the digital path's Vocabulary Smart Cards.

Pronunciation Key

a	in hat	ō	in open	sh	in she
ā	in age	ò	in all	th	in thin
â	in care	ô	in order	ᴛʜ	in then
ä	in far	oi	in oil	zh	in measure
e	in let	ou	in out	ə	= a in about
ē	in equal	u	in cup	ə	= e in taken
ėr	in term	ů	in put	ə	= i in pencil
i	in it	ü	in rule	ə	= o in lemon
ī	in ice	ch	in child	ə	= u in circus
o	in hot	ng	in long		

A

acceleration (ak sel′ ə rā′ shən) the rate at which the speed or direction of motion of an object changes over time

aceleración ritmo al cual cambia la rapidez o la dirección del movimiento de un objeto con el tiempo

accuracy (ak′ yər ə sē) ability to make a measurement that is as close to the actual value as possible

exactitud capacidad de hacer una medición que se aproxime tanto como sea posible al valor verdadero

adaptation (ad′ ap tā′ shən) a characteristic that increases an organism's ability to survive and reproduce in its environment

adaptación característica que aumenta la capacidad de un organismo de sobrevivir y reproducirse en su medio ambiente

asteroid (as′ tə roid′) a rocky mass up to several hundred kilometers wide that revolves around the sun

asteroide masa rocosa de hasta varios cientos de kilómetros de ancho que gira alrededor del Sol

atom (at′ əm) the smallest part of an element that still has the properties of the element

átomo la partícula más pequeña de un elemento, que todavía tiene las propiedades de ese elemento

atomic theory (ə tom/ ik thē/ ər ē) the idea that everything is made of small particles

teoría atómica la idea de que la materia está formada por partículas pequeñas

axis (ak/ sis) an imaginary line around which an object spins

eje línea imaginaria en torno a la cual gira un objeto

B

barometric pressure (bar/ ə met/ rik presh/ ər) the pushing force of the atmosphere

presión atmosférica fuerza que ejerce la atmósfera

bladder (blad/ ər) a hollow organ that collects and stores urine formed by the kidneys

vejiga órgano hueco que acumula y almacena la orina que se forma en los riñones

brain (brān) the main organ, or control center, of the nervous system

cerebro órgano principal, o centro de control, del sistema nervioso

C

chemical change (kem/ ə kəl chānj) a change of one or more types of matter into other types of matter with different properties

cambio químico cambio de uno o más tipos de materia a otros tipos de materia con propiedades diferentes

circulation (sėr/ kyə lā/ shən) movement of air that redistributes heat on Earth

circulación movimiento del aire que redistribuye el calor en la Tierra

circulatory system (sėr/ kyə lə tôr/ ē sis/ təm) a body system that moves blood through the body and includes the heart, blood, and blood vessels

sistema circulatorio sistema del cuerpo que lleva la sangre por todo el cuerpo e incluye el corazón, la sangre y los vasos sanguíneos

classify (klas/ ə fī) to put similar things into a group

clasificar agrupar cosas similares

climate (klī′ mit) the average of weather conditions over a long time

clima promedio de las condiciones del tiempo durante un período largo

comet (kom′ it) a frozen mass of different types of ice and dust orbiting the sun

cometa masa helada de distintos tipos de hielo y polvo que orbita el Sol

community (kə myü′nə tē) the group of all populations in an area

comunidad grupo de todas las poblaciones de un área

competition (kom′ pə tish′ ən) the struggle among organisms for the same limited resources

competencia lucha entre organismos por los mismos recursos limitados

compound (kom′ pound) a type of matter made of two or more elements

compuesto tipo de materia formada por dos o más elementos

condensation (kon′ den sā′ shən) the process in which a gas turns into a liquid

condensación proceso en el que un gas se convierte en líquido

conservation (kon′ sər vā′ shən) an attempt to preserve or protect an environment from harmful changes

conservación intento de conservar o de proteger el medio ambiente de cambios dañinos

constellation (kon′ stə lā′ shən) a group of stars that forms a pattern

constelación grupo de estrellas que forma una figura

constructive forces (kən struk′ tiv fôrs ez) forces that build new features on Earth's surface

fuerzas constructivas fuerzas que generan nuevas formaciones en la superficie de la Tierra

consumer (kən sü′ mər) organism that cannot make its own food

consumidor organismo que no puede hacer su propio alimento

contact force (kon′ takt fôrs) a force that requires two pieces of matter to touch

fuerza de contacto fuerza que requiere que dos porciones de materia se toquen

control group (kən trōl′ grüp) a standard against which change is measured

grupo de control estándar que se usa para medir un cambio

data (dā′ tə) information from which a conclusion can be drawn or a prediction can be made

datos información de la cual se puede sacar una conclusión o hacer una predicción

decomposer (dē′ kəm pō′ zər) organism that gets its energy by breaking down wastes and dead organisms

descomponedor organismo que obtiene su energía descomponiendo desechos y organismos muertos

deposition (dep′ ə zish′ ən) process of laying down materials, such as rocks and soil

sedimentación proceso por el cual materiales como rocas y partículas de suelo se asientan

design process (di zīn′ pros′ es) a set of steps for developing products and processes that solve problems

proceso de diseño serie de pasos para desarrollar productos y procesos que resuelven problemas

destructive forces (di struk′ tiv fôrs ez) forces that wear away or tear down features on Earth's surface

fuerzas destructivas fuerzas que desgastan o destruyen las formaciones de la superficie terrestre

diaphragm (dī′ ə fram) a dome-shaped muscle that moves down to make more space in your chest for air

diafragma músculo en forma de cúpula que se mueve hacia abajo, haciendo más espacio en tu pecho para que entre el aire

dichotomous key (dī kot′ ə məs kē) a tool used to identify organisms

clave dicotómica método que se usa para identificar organismos

digestive system (də jes′ tiv sis′ təm) the body system that breaks down food into very small parts that the body can use

sistema digestivo sistema del cuerpo que descompone los alimentos en trozos pequeñitos que el cuerpo puede usar

dwarf planet (dwôrf plan′ it) a large, round object that revolves around the sun but has not cleared the region around its orbit

planeta enano cuerpo grande y redondo que orbita el Sol, pero que no ha despejado la zona que rodea su órbita

E

ecosystem (ē′ kō sis′ təm) all the living and nonliving things in an area and their interactions

ecosistema todos los seres vivos y las cosas sin vida que hay en un área y sus interacciones

elevation (el′ ə vā′ shən) height above sea level

elevación altura sobre el nivel del mar

energy (en′ ər jē) ability to do work or cause change

energía capacidad de hacer trabajo o causar cambios

environment (en vī′ rən mənt) all of the conditions surrounding an organism

medio ambiente todas las condiciones que rodean a un ser vivo

erosion (i rō′ zhən) the movement of materials away from a place

erosión movimiento de materiales que se alejan de un lugar

evaporation (i vap′ ə rā′ shən) the changing of a liquid to a gas

evaporación cambio de líquido a gas

evidence (ev′ ə dəns) observations that make you believe something is true

evidencia observaciones que te hacen creer que algo es cierto

excretory system (ek′ skrə tôr′ ē sis′ təm) a system of the body that removes waste from the blood

sistema excretor sistema del cuerpo que elimina los desechos de la sangre

exoskeleton (ek′ sō skel′ ə tən) a hard skeleton on the outside of the body of some animals

exoesqueleto esqueleto duro en el exterior del cuerpo de algunos animales

experiment (ek sper′ ə mənt) the use of scientific methods to test a hypothesis

experimento uso de métodos científicos para poner a prueba una hipótesis

extinct species (ek stingkt′ spē′ shēz) a species that has no more members of its kind alive

especie extinta especie de la que ya no queda vivo ningún miembro

F

food chain (füd chān) a series of steps by which energy moves from one type of living thing to another

cadena alimentaria serie de pasos mediante los cuales la energía pasa de un ser vivo a otro

food web (füd web) a diagram that combines many food chains into one picture

red alimentaria diagrama que combina varias redes alimentarias en una sola imagen

force (fôrs) a push or pull that acts on an object

fuerza empujón o jalón que se le da a un objeto

friction (frik′ shən) the force that results when two materials rub against each other or when their contact prevents sliding

fricción fuerza que resulta al frotar un material contra otro o cuando el contacto entre ambos impide el deslizamiento

gas (gas) a substance without a definite volume or shape

gas sustancia que no tiene ni volumen ni forma definidos

gravity (grav′ ə tē) the force of attraction between any two objects

gravedad fuerza de atracción entre dos cuerpos cualesquiera

habitat (hab′ ə tat) a place that provides all the things an organism needs to live

hábitat lugar que proporciona todas las cosas que necesita un organismo para vivir

hail (hāl) frozen precipitation that forms in layers

granizo precipitación congelada que se forma en capas

heart (härt) a muscular organ that pumps blood throughout your body

corazón órgano muscular que bombea sangre por todo el cuerpo

humidity (hyü mid′ ə tē) the amount of water vapor in the air

humedad cantidad de vapor de agua en el aire

humus (hyü′ məs) the decaying material in soil

humus materia en descomposición que se halla en el suelo

hydrosphere (hī′ drə sfir) all the waters of Earth

hidrosfera toda el agua de la Tierra

hypothesis (hī poth′ ə sis) statement of what you think will happen during an investigation

hipótesis enunciado de lo que crees que ocurrirá en una investigación

I

igneous (ig′ nē əs) rocks that form when melted rock cools and hardens

ignea rocas que se forman cuando la roca derretida se enfría y se endurece

inclined plane (in klīnd′ plān) simple machine consisting of a flat surface with one end higher than the other

plano inclinado máquina simple que consiste en una superficie plana con un extremo más elevado que el otro

inertia (in ėr′ shə) the tendency of an object to resist any change in motion

inercia tendencia de un cuerpo a resistirse a cualquier cambio de movimiento

inexhaustible resource (in′ ig zô′ stə bəl rē′ sôrs) a type of energy resource that will not run out

recurso inagotable tipo de recurso energético que nunca se agota

inference (in′ fər əns) a conclusion based on observations

inferencia conclusión basada en observaciones

inner planet (in′ ər plan′ it) any of the four closest planets to the sun

planeta interior cualquiera de los cuatro planetas más cercanos al Sol

inorganic matter (in′ ôr gan′ ik mat′ ər) all the nonliving materials in the soil

materia inorgánica todos los materiales sin vida que se hallan en el suelo

intestines (in tes′ təns) tube-shaped organs through which most nutrients and water are absorbed from food

intestinos órganos de forma tubular a través de los cuales se absorbe la mayoría de los nutrientes y el agua de los alimentos

invertebrate (in vėr′ tə brit) an animal without a backbone

invertebrado animal que no tiene columna vertebral

K

kidneys (kid′ nēs) a pair of organs that remove waste from the blood

riñones par de órganos que elimina desechos de la sangre

kinetic energy (ki net′ ik en′ ər jē) energy due to motion

energía cinética energía que resulta del movimiento

kingdom (king′ dəm) the level of classification of living things below domain

reino nivel de clasificación de los seres vivos que queda por debajo del dominio

L

latitude (lat′ ə tüd) a measure of how far a place is from the equator

latitud medida de la distancia entre un objeto y el ecuador

lever (lev′ ər) a simple machine in which a bar moves around a fixed point called a fulcrum

palanca máquina simple en la cual una barra se mueve alrededor de un punto fijo llamado fulcro

liquid (lik′ wid) a substance that has a definite volume but no definite shape

líquido sustancia que tiene un volumen definido pero no una forma definida

lungs (lungs) organs that help the body exchange oxygen and carbon dioxide with the air outside the body

pulmones órganos que ayudan a que el cuerpo intercambie oxígeno y dióxido de carbono con el aire fuera del cuerpo

M

mass (mas) the amount of matter in a solid, liquid, or gas

masa cantidad de materia que tiene un sólido, líquido o gas

metamorphic (met′ ə môr′ fik) rocks formed inside Earth from other rocks under heat and pressure

metamórfica rocas que se forman dentro de la Tierra a partir de otras rocas, bajo calor y presión

metamorphosis (met′ ə môr′ fə sis) the process of an animal changing form during its life cycle

metamorfosis proceso en el cual cambia la forma de un animal durante su ciclo de vida

microchip (mī′ krō chip) a small piece of a computer that contains microscopic circuits

microchip pequeña pieza de computadora que contiene circuitos microscópicos

mineral (min′ ər əl) a nonliving, naturally occurring solid that has its own regular arrangement of particles in it

mineral sólido natural, sin vida, cuyas partículas están regularmente organizadas

mixture (miks′ chər) different materials placed together, but each material keeps its own properties

mezcla unión de materiales diferentes en la cual cada material mantiene sus propiedades

molecule (mol′ ə kyül) the smallest particle of a compound that still has the properties of that compound

molécula la partícula más pequeña de un compuesto, que todavía tiene las propiedades de ese compuesto

moon (mün) a natural object that revolves around a planet

luna satélite natural que orbita un planeta

muscles (mus′ əls) organs that work together to move the body

músculos órganos que funcionan como una unidad para mover el cuerpo

muscular system (mus′ kyə lər sis′ təm) a system of the body that is made up of muscles and the tissues that attach them to bones

sistema muscular sistema del cuerpo formado por músculos y los tejidos que unen los músculos a los huesos

N

nervous system (nėr′ vəs sis′ təm) a system of the body that tells you what is going on in the world around you

sistema nervioso sistema del cuerpo que te dice qué está ocurriendo a tu alrededor

non-contact force (non kon′ takt fôrs) a force that acts at a distance

fuerza sin contacto fuerza que actúa a distancia

nonrenewable resource (non′ ri nü′ ə bəl rē′ sôrs) a type of energy resource that cannot be replaced at all or cannot be replaced as fast as people use it

recurso no renovable tipo de recurso energético que no se puede reemplazar o que no se puede reemplazar con la misma rapidez con que se lo usa

O

observation (əb′ zər vā′ shən) something you find out about objects, events, or living things using your senses

observación algo que descubres con tus sentidos sobre los objetos, sucesos o seres vivos

opaque (ō pāk′) describes materials that do not let any light pass through them

opaco describe materiales que no dejan pasar a través de ellos la luz

orbit (ôr′ bit) the path an object takes as it revolves around a star, planet, or moon

órbita el camino que sigue un objeto al girar alrededor de una estrella, un planeta o una luna

organ (ôr′ gən) a group of different tissues that join together into one structure

órgano grupo de diferentes tejidos que se unen en una estructura

organic matter (ôr gan′ ik mat′ ər) all living materials and materials that were once alive

materia orgánica todo material vivo o que alguna vez tuvo vida

outer planet (out′ ər plan′ it) any of the four planets in our solar system beyond Mars

planeta exterior cualquiera de los cuatro planetas de nuestro sistema solar que quedan más allá de Marte

phylum (fī′ ləm) the level of classification of living things below kingdom

filo nivel de clasificación de los seres vivos que queda por debajo del reino

physical change (fiz′ ə kəl chānj) a change in some properties of matter without forming a different kind of matter

cambio físico cambio en algunas de las propiedades de la materia sin que se forme un nuevo tipo de materia

planet (plan′ it) a large, round object that revolves around a star and has cleared the region around its orbit

planeta cuerpo grande y redondo que orbita una estrella y que ha despejado la zona que rodea su órbita

plate (plāt) a section of the lithosphere

placa sección de la litosfera

pollutant (pə lüt′ nt) an unwanted substance added to the land, water, or air

contaminante sustancia indeseable que se añade a la tierra, al agua o al aire

pollution (pə lü′ shen) any substance that damages the environment

contaminación cualquier sustancia que le hace daño al medio ambiente

population (pop′ yə lā′ shən) a group of organisms of one species that live in an area at the same time

población grupo de organismos de la misma especie que viven en un área al mismo tiempo

potential energy (pə ten′ shəl en′ ər jē) energy that is not causing any changes now but could cause changes in the future

energía potencial energía que no está causando cambios actualmente pero que podría causarlos en el futuro

precipitation (pri sip′ ə tā′ shən) water that falls from clouds as rain, snow, sleet, or hail

precipitación agua que cae de las nubes en forma de lluvia, nieve, aguanieve o granizo

precision (pri sizh′ ən) the ability to consistently repeat a measurement

precisión capacidad de repetir una medición de manera consistente

predator (pred′ ə tər) a consumer that hunts and eats another animal

predador consumidor que atrapa a otro animal y se lo come

prey (prā) any animal that is hunted by others for food

presa cualquier animal que es cazado por otros para alimentación

procedures (prə sē′ jərz) step-by-step instructions for completing a task

procedimientos instrucciones paso por paso para realizar una tarea

producer (prə dü′ sər) organism that makes its own food for energy

productor organismo que hace su propio alimento para obtener energía

prosthetic limb (pros the′ tik lim) an artificial arm, hand, leg, or foot that replaces a missing one

prótesis brazo, mano, pierna o pie artificial que reemplaza el miembro o la parte que falta

prototype (prō′ tə tīp) a version of a solution to a problem

prototipo versión de la solución de un problema

pulley (púl′ ē) simple machine consisting of a rope or cable that runs around a grooved wheel

polea máquina simple que consiste en una soga o cable que se hace pasar por la ranura de una rueda

R

reflection (ri flek′ shən) light bouncing off an object

reflexión rebote de la luz contra un objeto

refraction (ri frak′ shən) bending of light

refracción desviación de la luz

renewable resource (ri nü′ ə bəl rē′ sôrs) a type of energy resource that can be replaced

recurso renovable tipo de recurso energético que puede reemplazarse

reservoir (rez′ ər vwär) a storage area, usually for water

depósito lugar donde se almacena algo, como por ejemplo agua

respiratory system (res′ pər ə tôr′ ē sis′ təm) the system of the body that helps you breathe

sistema respiratorio sistema del cuerpo que te ayuda a respirar

revolution (rev′ ə lü′ shən) one full orbit around the sun

traslación una órbita completa alrededor del Sol

rock cycle (rok sī′ kəl) a process in which rocks are constantly being formed and destroyed

ciclo de las rocas proceso en el cual las rocas se forman y se destruyen constantemente

rotation (rō tā′ shən) one whole spin of an object on its axis

rotación una vuelta completa de un objeto en torno a su eje

S

---

screw (skrü) simple machine consisting of a smooth cylinder with a tiny inclined plane wrapped around it

tornillo máquina simple que consiste en un cilindro liso con un pequeño plano inclinado enrollado a su alrededor

sedimentary (sed′ ə men′ tər ē) rocks that form when layers of materials and rock particles settle on top of each other and then harden

sedimentaria rocas que se forman cuando materiales y partículas de roca se asientan unos sobre los otros y se endurecen

simple machine (sim′ pəl mə shēn′) a machine made up of one or two parts

máquina simple máquina formada por una o dos partes

skeletal system (skel′ ə təl sis′ təm) a body system made up of bones that support the body and help it move

sistema esquelético sistema del cuerpo formado por huesos que sostienen el cuerpo y lo ayudan a moverse

skeleton (skel′ ə tən) all the bones in the body

esqueleto todos los huesos del cuerpo

skin (skin) an organ that covers and protects the body and releases wastes from the blood through sweat glands

piel órgano que cubre y protege el cuerpo y elimina los desechos de la sangre a través de las glándulas sudoríparas

sleet (slēt) frozen raindrops

aguanieve gotas de lluvia congeladas

soil (soil) a mixture of nonliving materials and decayed materials from organisms

suelo mezcla de materiales sin vida y de materiales descompuestos procedentes de organismos

solar flare (sō′ lər flâr) an explosive eruption of waves and particles into space

fulguración solar erupción explosiva de ondas y partículas emitidas hacia el espacio

solid (sol′ id) a substance that has a definite shape and volume

sólido sustancia que tiene una forma y un volumen definidos

solution (sə lü′ shən) a mixture in which substances are spread out evenly and will not settle

solución mezcla en la cual una sustancia se dispersa de manera uniforme en otra sustancia y no se asienta

space probe (spās prōb) a spacecraft that gathers data without a crew

sonda espacial nave espacial sin tripulantes que recoge datos

species (spē′ shēz) a group of similar organisms that can mate and produce offspring that can also produce offspring

especie grupo de organismos parecidos que pueden aparearse y tener crías que a su vez pueden tener crías

stomach (stum′ ək) organ where food begins to break down after swallowing

estómago órgano donde los alimentos comienzan a descomponerse después de que los tragamos

system (sis′ təm) a set of things that work together as a whole

sistema conjunto de objetos que funcionan como una unidad

technology (tek nol′ ə jē) the knowledge, processes, and products that solve problems and make work easier

tecnología conocimiento, procesos y productos que se usan para resolver problemas y facilitar el trabajo

temperature (tem′ pər ə chər) a measure of how fast the particles in an object are moving

temperatura medida de la rapidez con que se mueven las partículas de un objeto

tissue (tish′ ü) a group of the same kind of cells that work together to do the same job

tejido grupo de células del mismo tipo que trabajan en conjunto para realizar una misma función

trachea (trā′ kē ə) a tube that carries air to the lungs

tráquea tubo que lleva aire hacia los pulmones

translucent (tran slü′ snt) describes materials that let some light pass through, but not all

translúcido describe materiales que dejan pasar a través de ellos un poco de luz, pero no toda

transparent (tran spâr′ ənt) describes materials that let nearly all light pass through them

transparente describe materiales que dejan pasar a través de ellos casi toda la luz

variable (vâr′ ē ə bəl) something that can change in a test

variable algo que puede cambiar durante una prueba

vascular (vas′ kyə lər) a type of plant with tubes that carry food and water to all parts of the plant

vascular tipo de planta que tiene tubos para llevar alimento y agua a todas las partes de la planta

vertebrate (vér′ tə brit) an animal with a backbone

vertebrado animal que tiene columna vertebral

vibration (vī brā′ shən) the back-and-forth motion of an object

vibración movimiento de un objeto hacia adelante y hacia atrás

volume (vol′ yəm) the amount of space an object takes up

volumen el espacio que ocupa un objeto

water cycle (wȯ′ tər sī′ kəl) repeated movement of water through the environment in different forms

ciclo del agua movimiento repetido del agua en formas distintas a través del medio ambiente

weather (weᴛʜ′ ər) the state of the atmosphere

tiempo atmosférico estado de la atmósfera

weathering (weᴛʜ′ r ing) a slow process that breaks rocks into sediments

meteorización proceso lento que descompone las rocas en sedimento

wedge (wej) simple machine made of one or two inclined planes

cuña máquina simple formada por uno o dos planos inclinados

wheel and axle (wēl and ak′ səl) simple machine consisting of a circular object (wheel) attached to a bar (axle)

eje y rueda máquina simple que consiste en un objeto circular (la rueda) conectado a una barra (el eje)

Index

transparent/translucent materials, 517

visible, 517

wavelength of, 518–519

Light bulb, 508

Lightning, 226

Lightning bug, 508

Lightning Lab

Blink of an Eye, 182

Breathe It In, 168

Climate Zones, 286

Coin Flip, 30

Comparing Apples and Lemons?, 446

Day and Night, 365

Develop a Dichotomous Key, 94

Do I Need a Thermometer?, 428

Estimate and Measure, 26

Letters and Atoms, 421

Measuring Shadows, 370

Model Forces, 332

Model Planets, 380

Reading in the Dark, 385

Rubber-Band Release, 505

Simple Machines, 483

String Phone, 515

Wandering Ice, 433

You in the Food Chain, 220

You Light Up My Leaf, 132

Limestone, 314, 315, 321

Limiting factors, 215

Lions, 138, 258–259

Liquid, 431–435, 451–454

immiscible, 425

properties, 425–429

and solutions, 440

List, 31, 179, 296, 418, 420, 429

Litter, 343

Little Dipper, 372

Liver, 186, 187

Living things, 122–127

Lizard, 211

Load, 480

Locate, 329, 375

Locusts, 227

Louisiana Museum of Natural Science, 108

Lulin, 391

Lungs, 126, 161, 167–169, 193–198

Luster, 306

Machines, 478–485

complex, 485

inclined planes, 482–483

levers, 480

pulleys, 481

screws, 484

simple, 479

wedges, 484

wheel and axle, 478, 481

Magma, 311, 332

Magnetic energy, 509

Magnetic forces, 469

Magnetic resonance imaging (MRI) scan, 48–49, 50

Magnetism, 509

minerals, 307

separating mixtures, 438

Magnetite, 307

Magnets, 469, 509

Main idea and details, 47, 49, 53, 74, 89, 91, 92, 98, 103, 115, 207, 209, 214, 221, 244, 262, 305, 463, 465, 472, 483, 494

Make and use models, 60, 68, 78, 134, 172, 256, 322, 328, 360, 382, 388, 394, 395, 406, 407, 462

Malachite, 307, 415

Mammals, 98–99

Manatees, 9, 117

Mangrove tree, 129

Maple tree, 123

Marble, 314, 315

Mariner 10, 377

Mars, 374–385

Marsh, 207

Mass, 23, 425, 426, 451–454

and acceleration, 474–476

and inertia, 472

and kinetic energy, 505

and motion, 534–537

See also Force

Matter, 416–443

atoms, 420–421

chemical changes, 445–447

elements, 418–423

evaporation and condensation, 434–435

freezing and melting, 262, 433

measuring, 414

physical changes, 442–445

properties of, 424–429

states of, 430–441

and volume, 23

Mean, 26

Measure, 20, 28, 190, 191, 382, 406, 408, 478, 536

Measurement, 26

angles, 176

force, 23, 476

length and distance, 23

mass, 23

temperature, 23

time, 23

volume, 23

Mechanical energy, 503–505, 508

Median, 26

Medical technology, 49–51

Melting, 256, 262, 433

Mercury (element), 418

Mercury (planet), 361, 377

Metals, 418

Metamorphic, 311, 312, 347–352

Metamorphosis, 141–145, 149–150

amphibian, 142–143

complete, 144

incomplete, 145

Meteor Crater, 390

Meteor showers, 390, 391

Meteorites, 377, 390, 406–409

Meteoroids, 388, 390

Meteorologists, 269

Meteors, 390

Meterstick, 23, 178

Mica, 314

Mice, 160, 214

Microchip, 49, 52, 71–72, 533

Microscope, 23

Microwave radiation, 519

Mid-Atlantic ridge, 331

Migration, 139, 238

Milk, 444

Millipedes, 225

Mineral, 173, 304–309, 347–352

comparing, 302

crystals, 304, 307

economic significance, 309

identifying, 308

properties of, 306–307, 344–345

in rock, 314

in soil, 320

Mississippi River, 324

Mixed forest, 212

Mixture, 436–439, 451–454

separating, 436, 438–439, 448–449

Mode, 26

Models, 14, 332

Credits

Staff Credits

The people who made up the *Interactive Science* team—representing core design digital and multimedia production services, digital product development, editorial, manufacturing, and production—are listed below.

Geri Amani, Alisa Anderson, Jose Arrendondo, Amy Austin, Lindsay Bellino, Charlie Bink, Bridget Binstock, Holly Blessen, Robin Bobo, Craig Bottomley, Jim Brady, Laura Brancky, Chris Budzisz, Mary Chingwa, Sitha Chhor, Caroline Chung, Margaret Clampitt, Karen Corliss, Brandon Cole, Mitch Coulter, AnnMarie Coyne, Fran Curran, Dana Damiano, Nancy Duffner, Amanda Ferguson, David Gall, Mark Geyer, Amy Goodwin, Gerardine Griffin, Chris Haggerty, Laura Hancko, Jericho Hernandez, Autumn Hickenlooper, Guy Huff, George Jacobson, Marian Jones, Kathi Kalina, Chris Kammer, Sheila Kanitsch, Alyse Kondrat, Mary Kramer, Thea Limpus, Dominique Mariano, Lori McGuire, Melinda Medina, Angelina Mendez, Claudi Mimo, John Moore, Phoebe Novak, Anthony Nuccio, Jeffrey Osier, Julianne Regnier, Charlene Rimsa, Rebecca Roberts, Camille Salerno, Manuel Sanchez, Carol Schmitz, Amanda Seldera, Sheetal Shah, Jeannine Shelton El, Geri Shulman, Greg Sorenson, Samantha Sparkman, Mindy Spelius, Karen Stockwell, Dee Sunday, Dennis Tarwood, Jennie Teece, Lois Teesdale, Michaela Tudela, Oscar Vera, Dave Wade, Tom Wickland, James Yagelski, Tim Yetzina, Diane Zimmermann

Illustrations

xiv, 283, 367, 368, 369, 399 Robert (Bob) Kayganich; **124, 171, 190** Big Sesh Studios; **125, 127, 191, 193** Jeff Mangiat; **134** Peter Bollinger; **160, 167, 168, 173, 183, 186, 197** Leonello Calvetti; **165, 172, 184, 199, 225, 232, 243, 245, 274, 278, 279, 285, 297, 370, 434, 455, 466, 470, 474, 489, 493** Precision Graphics; **228, 322, 334, 353** Adam Benton; **264, 266, 267, 270, 272, 295, 297** Studio Liddell; **465, 489** June Melber

Photographs

Photo locators denoted as follows: Top (T), Center (C), Bottom (B), Left (L), Right (R), Background (Bkgd)

COVER: ©Corbis/Superstock

iv Thinkstock Images/Stockbyte/Getty Images; **vi** Douglas Faulkner/Science Source; **vii** Oliver Leedham/Alamy; **viii** Formiktopus/Fotolia; **ix** George Bernard/Science Source; **x** DK Images; **xi** Wolfgang Pölzer/Alamy Images; **xii** les polders/Alamy Images; **xiii** Paul Springett 04/Alamy Images; **xv** MarcelClemens/Shutterstock; **xvi** Wrangler/Fotolia; **xvii** (CR) Jeff Hinds/Shutterstock; **1** (TL) niderlander/Shutterstock, (BC) Yuriko Nakao/Reuters/Landov LLC, (B) James Thew/Shutterstock, (C) Arthur Tilley/Getty Images; **2** (C) Arthur Tilley/Getty Images; **6** (T) Alexis Rosenfeld/Science Source, (CR) NOAA; **7** (CR) Niels Poulsen/Alamy Images, (B) Richard Carey/Fotolia; **8** Arctic Images/Alamy Images; **9** Douglas Faulkner/Science Source; **10** Stephen Frink Collection/Alamy Images; **11** Getty Images; **12** culture-images GmbH/Alamy Images; **13** Chris Ryan/Getty Images; **14** (BL) Jim West/Alamy Images, (BR) Hank Morgan/Science Source; **15** Masterfile; **18** Jaubert Bernard/Alamy Images; **20** Priit Vesilind/Getty Images; **21** David R. Frazier/Science Source; **25** Digital Vision/Getty Images; **26** Comstock/Getty Images; **27** Vicky Kasala/Getty Images; **28** (T) Elenarts/Fotolia, (TR) Getty Images; **29** (TC) Fedor Selivanov/Shutterstock, (B) ©James L. Amos/Science Source, (TL) ©Steve Byland/Shutterstock, (TR) Getty Images; **30** John Beatty/Science Source; **31** James Ingram/Alamy Images; **34** Image Source; **35** (BR) Chris Ryan/Getty Images, (TR) Douglas Faulkner/Science Source, (BL) Jaubert Bernard/Alamy Images, (CR) Stephen Frink Collection/Alamy Images; **37** (TR) David R. Frazier/Science Source, (CC) John Beatty/Science Source, (TC) Vicky Kasala/Getty Images; **39** (B) Arthur Tilley/Getty Images, (BCL) Elenarts/Fotolia, (TCL) culture-images GmbH/Alamy Images, (CL) Priit Vesilind/Getty Images, (TL) Alexis Rosenfeld/Science Source; **40** Martin Shields/Science Source; **43** (TL) geldi/Alamy Images, (TL) imagebroker/Alamy Images; **44** Yuriko Nakao/Reuters/Landov LLC; **47** (C) Bon Appetit/Alamy Images, (TR) Carl Keyes/Alamy Images; **48** Julia Hiebaum/Alamy Images; **49** Adam Gregor/Fotolia **50** (BC) AJPhoto/Hôpital Américain/Science Source, (BKGRD, CR) Karl Kost/Alamy Images, (BR) Mauro Fermariello/Science Source, (TL) Science Source; **51** (TL) Monkey Business/Fotolia, (CR) Mark Clarke/Science Source, (CL) TMI/Alamy Images, (TR) Steve Gorton/Old Operating Theatre Museum, London/DK Images; **52** (CL) ©Clive Streeter/Courtesy of The Science Museum, London/DK Images, (TL) ClassicStock/Alamy Images; **53** Yuji Sakai/Getty Images; **54** (T) Alex Segre/Alamy Images, (BR) Market Wire/NewsCom; **55** (R) Mikey Siegel/MIT Media Lab; **56** Erika Szostak/Alamy Images; **57** Touch Bionics; **58** (CL) Eric Maslowski, (BR) AP Images; **59** Andrea Danti/123RF; **60** Volker Steger/Science Source; **62** (TL) Gord Waldner/StarPhoenix, (B) Image Source; **63** Gresei/Fotolia; **64** Picture Partners/Alamy Images; **66** Bettmann/Corbis; **67** Oliver Leedham/Alamy Images; **70** Franck Camhi/Alamy Images; **71** (CR) Clive Streeter/Courtesy of The Science Museum, London/DK Images, (BR) Touch Bionics, (TR) Julia Hiebaum/Alamy Images; **73** (TL) Julia Hiebaum/Alamy Images, (CL) Alex Segre/Alamy Images, (BL) Volker Steger/Science Source, (BC) Yuriko Nakao/Reuters/Landov LLC; **77** (Inset) David J. Green-Technology/Alamy Images, (CR) JFK Space Center/NASA; **78** Linda Bucklin/Shutterstock; **83** Linda Bucklin/Shutterstock; **84** HomeStudio/Shutterstock; **85** (BKGRD) Flirt/SuperStock, (TC) Rolf Nussbaumer/Nature Picture Library, (C) Photoshot/Alamy Images, (CC) SPL/Science Source, (BC) John Cancalosi/Alamy Images; **86** Rolf Nussbaumer/Nature Picture Library; **89** (Inset) Terry Reimink/Shutterstock, (C) Photolocation Ltd./Alamy Images; **90** (TCR) Matt Jeppson/Shutterstock, (TR) Africa Studio/Shutterstock, (B) ermess/Fotolia, (CR) Heiko Kiera/Fotolia; **91** formiktopus/Fotolia; **92** (TR) Alexey Stiop/Fotolia, (CR) chamillew/Fotolia, (BR) Manamana/Shutterstock, (BCR) DK Images; **93** (TL) Dee Golden/Shutterstock, (TCL) Erni/Shutterstock, (TC) Manamana/Shutterstock, (T, TCR) DK Images, (TR) Jupiter Images/Getty Images, (TRR) Jerry Young/DK Images, (BL) Natural Visions/Alamy Images; **94** (CR) Emmanuel Lattes/Alamy Images, (BL, BCL, BC) DK Images, (BR) Getty Images; **95** Aina Jongman/ Shutterstock; **96** Getty Images; **97** (BR) Moremi/Shutterstock, (CR) Peter Cross/Courtesy of Richmond Park/DK Images; **98** (BC) Jason Patrick Ross/Shutterstock, (C) Torsten Dietrich/Shutterstock, (BKGRD) Manabu Ogasawara/Getty Images; **99** (C) blickwinkel/Alamy Images, (B) James De Boer/Shutterstock, (T) Linda Whitwam/DK Images; **100** (T) Dieter H/Shutterstock, (B) Jerry Schad/Science Source; **101** (TR, TL, BR) DK Images, (CL) Rod Planck/Science Source; **102** (TC) Jerry Young/DK Images, (TR) Royal Botanic Garen Edinburgh/Science Source, (BL, BC, BR) Getty Images, (BCR) Matthew Ward; **103** (TR) Cathy Keifer/ Shutterstock, (TL) Krzysztof Wiktor/Fotolia, (B) Biophoto Associates/Science Source; **104**, (CL) 977_ReX_977/ Shutterstock, (TL, BL) DK Images; **105** DK Images; **107** Getty Images; **108** (CR) Mark Bridger/Shutterstock, (BKGRD) David Kjaer/Nature Picture Library, (CL) Megan Lorenz/Fotolia; **109** (TL) Natural Visions/Alamy Images, (TR) Africa Studio/ Shutterstock, (TRR) Getty Images, (CR) Manamana/Shutterstock/ (BC) James De Boer/Shutterstock, (TCR, TCCR) DK Images, (BCCR) Jerry Young/DK Images; **111** (TR) Dieter H/Shutterstock, (CR) Biophoto Associates/Science Source; **113** (TL) reborn55/ Fotolia, (TCL) blickwinkel/Alamy, (BCL) DK Images, (B) Rolf Nussbaumer/Nature Picture Library; **115** Getty Images; **117** (BL) Comstock Images/Getty Images, (T) ©electrochris/Fotolia, (CR) Cyril Laubscher/©DK Images, (BKGRD) Gary Retherford/Science Source; **118** Photoshot/Alamy Images; **121** (B) Chip Porter/Getty Images; **122** (B) franzfoto/Alamy Images, (T) Gail Shumway/ Getty Images; **123** (CR) blickwinkel/Alamy Images, (BR) Cosmos Blank/Science Source; **124** (CR) Dole/Shutterstock, (TL) ImageDJ/ Getty Images; **125** (CR) Xavier Safont- V&W/Bruce Coleman Inc./Photoshot, (TR) Photographed by Ori Fragman-Sapir, Jerusalem Botanical Gardens; **126** (BR) Pascal Goetgheluck/ Science Source, (BR, BC) Stan Malcom; **128** Perov Stanislav/ Shutterstock; **129** Jon E. Oringer/Shutterstock; **130** (BKGRD) Gordon Galbraith/Shutterstock, (BR) Getty Images; **131** (TR) Tobias Bernhard/zefa/Corbis, (BL) Cathy Keifer/Shutterstock, (BC) underworld/Fotolia, (BR) Andrew McRobb/DK Images; **133** Ed Freeman/Getty Images; **134** (TR) Anthony Pierce/Alamy Images, (TC, CR) Getty Images; **135** (TL) McDonald Wildlife Photography/AGE Fotostock, (TC) Mint Images/SuperStock, (B) Roy Caldwell; **136** (BL) Audrey Snider-Bell/Shutterstock, (BC) Joze Maucec/Shutterstock, (BR) William Munoz/Science Source; **137** (TR) Ana de Sousa/Shutterstock, (CL) Raymond Kasprzak/ Shutterstock, (CR) Michael Sewell/Getty Images, (BR) Getty Images; **138** (TR, TCR) William Vann, (B) Siba/Fotolia; **139** Getty Images; **140** Millard H. Sharp/Science Source; **141** (TL, TC) Millard H. Sharp/Science Source, (BCR, BR) Scott Camazine; **142** (BKGRD) Dr. Keith Wheeler/Science Source, (C) Dan Suzio/ Science Source; **143** (TL) Dr. Keith Wheeler, (TR) Eric Isselee/ Shutterstock, (BL) Gary Meszaros/Science Source, (BR) George Bernard/Science Source; **144** (TL) John T. Fowler/Alamy, (TCL) Lori Skelton/ Shutterstock, (CL) claudiobphoto/Fotolia, (BCL) JPS/ Fotolia, (B) Donald Enright/Alamy; **145** (CL) The Natural History Museum/Alamy Images, (C) Marko König/ Alamy Images, (CR)

Imagebroker/Alamy Images; **146** (CL, BL) DK Images, (B) Donald Enright/Alamy Images; **148** (R) Seapics, (CR) Lisette Le Bon/SuperStock; **149** (TC) Millard H. Sharp/Science Source, (TR) Dole/Shutterstock, (CR) Jon E. Oringer/Shutterstock, (BR) Getty Images; **151** (TL) Gail Shumway/Getty Images, (TCL) Perov Stanislav/Shutterstock, (CL) McDonald Wildlife Photog/ AGE Fotostock, (BCL) Millard H. Sharp/Science Source, (B) Photoshot/Alamy Images; **152** (BC) Getty Images, (BR) Thinkstock/Getty Images; **153** (TL) Edward B/Fotolia, (TR) Thinkstock/Getty Images; **155** (L) Lebrecht Music and Arts Photo Library/Alamy, (BL) Thinkstock/Getty Images; **156** SPL/Science Source; **160** (T) JRC, Inc./Alamy Images, (CL) Arco Images GmbH/Alamy Images, (BCL) Francois Gohier/VWPics/Alamy Images; **161** (CR) Innerspace Imaging/Science Source, (BR) Sebastian Kaulitzki/Shutterstock; **163** (T) CNRI/Science Source, (B) SPL/Science Source; **164, 165** DK Images; **166** Corbis/Getty Images; **169** Susumu Nishinaga/Science Source; **172** Brownstock Inc./Alamy Images; **179** Fancy Collection/ SuperStock; **180** (C) DK Images, (L) Roger Harris/SPL/Science Source; **181** (T) Christian Darkin/Science Source, (C) Thinkstock/Getty Images; **182** Omikron/Science Source; **184** Bon Appetit/Alamy Images; **187** Eye of Science/Science Source; **188** (BL) BSIP/Science Source, (TR) tkachuk/Shutterstock; **192** (R) Sura Nualpradid/Fotolia, (TC) Massachusetts Hall of Black Achievement at Bridgewater State College; **193** (TR) Innerspace Imaging/Science Source, (CL) Sebastian Kaulitzki/ Shutterstock, (BL) Corbis/Getty Images, (BR) JRC, Inc./Alamy Images; **195** (CL) Roger Harris/SPL/Science Source, (BL) Christian Darkin/Science Source; **197** (TL) tkachuk/Shutterstock, (BC) BSIP/Science Source; **199** (TL) JRC, Inc./Alamy Images, (TCL) Corbis/Getty Images, (CL) Brownstock Inc./Alamy Images, (BL) Bon Appetit/Alamy Images, (B) SPL/Science Source; **201** Stockbyte/Getty Images; **203** (L) Masterfile, (TC) Don Hammond/Getty Images, (BC) Stockbyte/Getty Images; **204** John Cancalosi/Alamy Images; **207** (BKGRD) Robert Francis/ Alamy Images, (TR) Roger de Montfort/Shutterstock; **208** (T) Ray Copeland/Shutterstock, (B) Karl Ammann/Corbis; **209** Mark Conlin/Alamy Images; **210** (C) Martin Strmiska/Alamy Images, (B) J.W. Alker/Imagebroker/Alamy Images; **211** (TL) Michael Dwyer/Alamy Images, (TC) Buddy Mays/Alamy Images, (CR) Rick & Nora Bowers/Alamy Images, (TCR) Jerry L. Ferrara/ Science Source, (BL) Rod Planck/Science Source, (BC) blickwindel/Hecker/Alamy Images; **212** (TCL) James McLaughlin/Alamy, (CL) Marvin Dembinsky Photo Associates/ Alamy Images, (BL) Bob Blanchard/Shutterstock, (BC) Michael P. Gadomski/Science Source; **213** (TCL) David R. Frazier Photolibrary/Alamy Images, (CL) Corbis/Alamy Images, (BR) David Tipling/Nature Picture Library; **214** Anthony Mercieca/ Science Source; **215** K. Mantey/Shutterstock; **216** David Keith Jones/Alamy Images; **217** Catcher of Light, Inc./Shutterstock; **218** (TL) Michael P. Gadomski/Science Source, (CL) Rob Crandall/Alamy Images, (BL) Photoshot Holdings Ltd./Alamy Images; **219** (TR) Bill Coster/Alamy Images, (CR) Dabjola/ Fotolia, (BL) Eye of Science/Science Source, (B) Spring Images/ Alamy Images; **220** (BL) Jeff Greenberg/Alamy Images, (BC) pictureguy66/123RF, (BR) Jack Milchanowski/AGE Fotostock/Getty Images; **222** (TCL) Inga Spence/Science Source, (TL) Danny E. Hooks/Shutterstock; **223** Wolfgang Pölzer/Alamy Images; **224** (CR) Bettmann/Corbis, (B) Ragnar Th

Sigurdsson/Arctic Images/Alamy Images; **225** VR Photos/Shutterstock; **226** (B) Carsten Peter/Getty Images, (TL) Thinkstock/Getty Images; **227** (TR) Victor Ruiz/Reuters, (B) Maksymowicz/Fotolia, (T, TCR) DK Images; **230** Cordelia Molly/Science Source; **231** Kenneth B. Storey, F.R.S.C/Carleton University; **232** Ablestock/Getty Images; **234** (T) Maximilian Weinzeirl/Alamy Images, (B) Jason Patrick Ross/Shutterstock; **235** Steve Shepard/Getty Images; **238** (BKGRD) Mike Briner/Alamy Images, (BR) Arco Images GmbH/Alamy Images; **239** (TL, BR) Martin Strmiska/Alamy Images, (TCL) J.W. Alker/Imagebroker/Alamy Images, (TR) Ray Copeland/Shutterstock, (CL, BL) Catcher of Light, Inc./Shutterstock; **241** (TCL) Jeff Greenberg/Alamy Images, (TC) pictureguy66/123RF, (TR, CR) Bill Coster/Alamy Images, (TCR) Jack Milchanowski/AGE Fotostock/Getty Images, (BR) Dabjola/Fotolia, (BL) Steve Shepard/Getty Images, (CL) Ablestock/Getty Images, (BC) VR Photos/Shutterstock; **243** (TL) Ray Copeland/Shutterstock, (TCL) David Keith Jones/Alamy Images, (BCL) Dabjola/Fotolia, (BL) Ablestock/Getty Images, (B) John Cancalosi/Alamy Images; **245** Thinkstock/Getty Images; **247** (BKGRD) Peter Anderson/DK Images, (CL) Stuart Kelly/Alamy Images; **252** Getty Images, **253** (BKGRD) Morgan Lane Photography/Shutterstock, (TC) Martin Amm, (C) Imagebroker/Alamy Images, (BC) AP Images; **254** Martin Amm; **257** (BKGRD) John R. McNair, (BR) John R. Foster/Science Source; **258** (T) infocusphotos/Alamy Images, (B) Stockbyte/Getty Images; **259** Mike Timo/Getty Images; **264** NOAA; **265** Digital Wisdom/Getty Images; **269** Lisa Lehmann Photo Art & Design; **270** Paul Seheult/Corbis; **271** Steven May/Alamy Images; **272** (TL) Stephen Oliver/DK Images, (CL) David Philips/Shutterstock; **273** (BC) Col/Shutterstock, (BR) David J. Green/Alamy Images; **277** Minerva Studio/Fotolia; **278** (BL) University Corporation for Atmospheric Research/Science Source, (BC) SpxChrome/E+/Getty Images; **279** (BL) Alexey Klementiev/Fotolia, (BC) Dmitry Sharanutsa/Fotolia, (BR) Jim W. Grace/Science Source; **280** (TL) Lorraine Crawley/Fotolia, (TCL) orleijunior.com/Flickr Open/Getty Images, (CL) fovito/Fotolia, (BCL) Brian Cosgrove/DK Images, (BL) James A. Sugar/Corbis; **282** Steve Bly/Getty Images; **283** Jim Lopes/Shutterstock; **285** (TL) Yadid Levy/Alamy Images, (CL) les polders/Alamy Images, (BL) Antonio Jorges Nunes/Shutterstock; **286, 287** NASA; **290** NOAA; **291** (CL) NOAA, (BL) Digital Wisdom/Getty Images; **293** (TL) Steve Bly/Getty Images, (CR) Paul Seheult/Corbis, (BR) David J. Green/Alamy Images, (BC) SpxChrome/E+/Getty Images, (C) Dmitry Sharanutsa/Fotolia, (BL) NASA; **295** (TL) infocusphotos/Alamy Images, (CL) NOAA, (BL) Steve Bly/Getty Images, (B) Martin Amm; **296** Clint Farlinger/Alamy Images; **299** Thinkstock/Getty Images; **300** Imagebroker/Alamy Images; **303** psamtik/Shutterstock; **304** Dirk Wiersma/Science Source; **305** (TL) everythingpossible/Fotolia, (TR) Sellingpix/Fotolia, (BR) Petur Asgeirsson/Shutterstock; **306** (BR) Jiri Vaclavek/Shutterstock, (ALL) DK Images; **307, 308** DK Images; **309** Volker Steger/Science Source; **310** Bauman/Shutterstock; **311** (CR) Mark A. Schneider/Science Source, (BR) Biophoto Associates/Science Source; **312** (CR) Joel Arem/Science Source, (ALL) DK Images; **313** (CL) J.B. Judd/U.S. Geological Survey, (ALL) DK Images; **314** (TL) NeonLight/Shutterstock, (BL) Mark A. Schneider/Science Source, (BC) Andrew J. Martinez/Science Source, (BR) Mark A. Schneider/Science Source; **315** David R. Frazier Photolibrary/Alamy; **316** Fcarucci/Shutterstock; **317**

Dennis Flaherty/Science Source; **320** DK Images; **321** Doug Webb/Alamy Images; **322** Robert E. Barber/Alamy Images; **323** John E. Marriott/Alamy Images; **324** Sframe/Fotolia; **325** apply pictures/Alamy Images; **326** frans lemmens/Alamy Images; **327** Ian Bracegirdle/Shutterstock; **328** Imagebroker/Alamy Images; **329** U.S. Geological Survey; **331** Stocktrek/Brand X Pictures/Getty Images; **332** Beboy/Shutterstock; **333** Jim Sugar/Corbis; **334** (T) Danita Delimont/Alamy Images, (B) Kevin Foy/Alamy Images; **335** Corbis/Getty Images; **337** (TL) Szfei/Shutterstock, (TCL) Thinkstock/Getty Images, (CL) John Dickey/Alamy Images, (BL) Theodore Clutter/Science Source; **338** (B) Getty Images, (ALL) DK Images; **339** Getty Images; **340** Robert Brook/Alamy Images; **341** Andrew McConnell/Alamy; **342** (BL) dmac/Alamy, (BR) AP Images; **343** Robert Brook/Alamy Images; **346** (BKGRD) Raymond Gehman/National Geographic Image Collection/Getty Images, (C) Science Source; **347** (TR) Petur Asgeirsson/Shutterstock, (TCL) Biophoto Associates/Science Source, (TL) Andrew Martinez/Science Source, (BR) Joel Arem/Science Source, (BL) Fcarucci/Shutterstock, (ALL) DK Images; **349** (TL) U.S. Geological Survey, (TR) Dennis Flaherty/Science Source, (C) Robert E. Barber/Alamy Images, (BL) Stocktrek/Brand X Pictures/Getty Images, (BC) Powered by Light/Alan Spencer/Alamy Images; **351** (TC) Robert Brook/Alamy Images, (TR) Szfei/Shutterstock, (CR) Thinkstock/Getty Images, (BCR, BR) DK Images; **353** (BKGRD) Imagebroker/Alamy Images, (TL) Jiri Vaclavek/Shutterstock, (TCL) DK Images, (CCL) Robert E. Barber/Alamy Images, (CL) Beboy/Shutterstock, (BCL) Danita Delimont/Alamy Images, (BL) Robert Brook/Alamy Images; **354** Joel Arem/Science Source; **357** (BKGRD) Anne-Marie Palmer/Alamy Images, (C) Amazing Images/Alamy Images; **358** AP Images; **361** (CL) Corbis, (CCL, C) Getty Images, (CR, R) NASA; **362** Olivier Blondeau/Getty Images; **363, 364, 365** NASA; **368** (T) NASA, (B) Babak Tafreshi/Science Source; **369** (CL) Corbis, (CCL, C) Getty Images, (CR, R) NASA; **371** NASA; **372** Gerard Lodriguss/Science Source; **373** Babk Tafreshi/Science Source; **374** Frank Krahmer/Masterfile; **375** Andre Nantel/Shutterstock; **376, 377, 378, 379** NASA; **380** (C) NASA, (TR) U. S. Geological Survey; **381, 382, 383, 384, 385, 386, 387** NASA; **388** I. Pilon/Shutterstock; **389** (T) Joel Arem/Science Source; (B) NASA; **390** Charles & Josette Lenars/Corbis; **391** Johannes Schedler/Panther Observatory; **392** Bettman/Corbis; **393** Jim Mills/Fotolia; **396** Amana Images/SuperStock; **397** (TL, CL) NASA, (BL) Gerard Lodriguss/Science Source; **399** (TL) Johannes Schedler/Panther Observatory, (ALL) NASA; **401** (TL, BCL) NASA, (CL) Frank Krahmer/Masterfile, (BL) I. Pilon/Shutterstock, (B) AP Images; **402** Stocktrek/Getty Images; **405** National Science Foundation; **411** (TR) Carsten Peter/Speleoresearch & Films/National Geographic Image Collection, (CR) Sean Davey/Aurora Photos/Corbis, (BR) Bruno De Hogues/Getty Images, (BKGRD) Taro Yamada/Corbis; **412** Carsten Peter/Speleoresearch & Films/National Geographic Image Collection; **415** Judith Miller/333 Auctions LLC/DK Images; **416** Bill Kennedy/Shutterstock; **417** Stuart Hannagan/Getty Images; **418** (B) Andraz Cerar/Shutterstock, (BL) iofoto/Shutterstock, (TR) vnlit/Shutterstock, (BR) Comstock/Getty Images; **419** (BL) Smart7/Shutterstock, (BR) Sonya Etchison/Shutterstock, (TR) AnutkaT/Shutterstock, (CR, C) DK Images; **420** Marcel Clemens/Shutterstock; **421** (TR) Richard Megna/Fundamental

This is your book.
You can write in it.

Take Note

This space is yours. It is great for drawing diagrams and making notes.

This is your book.

You can write in it.

This is your book.

You can write in it.

This is your book.
You can write in it.

This is your book.

You can write in it.